Twenty years of my life

Douglas Brooke Wheelton Sladen, Yoshio Markino

TWENTY YEARS OF MY LIFE

THE ROOF GARDEN AND POMPEIAN FOUNTAIN AT 32 ADDISON MANSIONS.
(From the Painting by Yoshio Markino.)

TWENTY YEARS OF MY LIFE

BY

DOUGLAS SLADEN

AUTHOR OF "WHO'S WHO"

WITH FOUR COLOURED ILLUSTRATIONS AND TWELVE PORTRAITS

BY

YOSHIO MARKINO

NEW YORK
E·P·DUTTON & COMPANY
PUBLISHERS

Printed in Great Britain by
Richard Clay & Sons, Limited,
Brunswick St., Stamford St., S E.,
and Bungay Suffolk.

AFFECTIONATELY DEDICATED

TO

JEROME K. JEROME

ONE OF THE EARLIEST AND DEAREST OF MY

LITERARY FRIENDS

INTRODUCTION

When I wrote *Who's Who*, sixteen or seventeen years ago, I used to receive shoals of funny letters from people who wanted, or did not want, to be included, and now, when I have not edited the book for more than a dozen years, I still receive letters of criticism on the way in which I conduct it, and usually consign them to limbo. A few months ago, however, I received the subjoined letter, which is so out of the ordinary that I quote it to show what illustrious correspondents I have. I must not attach the author's name, though every grown-up man in the civilised world would be interested to know it.

" Dear Sir,

" Kindly cease to omit my name from your ever-increasing list of persons as annually placed before the public for sale at any price it is worth. Just put me down in place of Victoria Alice, who is an American pure and simple, while I am left out in the cold. I am the daughter of King Edward VII . . . .[1] I am the legal spouse of Nicholas II, Czar of Russia, being legally married to him in 1890, Aug. 14, a ratification of which occurrence was held by me in hallway of British Embassy, Paris, France, 1900, same date. Just give me a notice, will you, instead of harping on the sisterhood of King George V, who form among themselves a similar affair to that held by female contingent of Synagogue, doing more damage in the community, and eventually in the world, than any one set of people anywhere, with method so secret that even Rabbi is unable to uncover the original design known as main point in England.

" Sincerely,

" Etc., etc.

" *October 23, 1913.*"

If I could tell all I know about the interesting people I have met, the book would read like my own *Who's Who* re-written by Walter Emanuel for publication in *Punch*. As it is, the book contains a great deal of information about

---

[1] This portion of the letter could not be printed.

celebrities which could never appear in *Who's Who*, and all the best anecdotes which I remember about my friends, except those which would turn my friends into enemies, and even some of those I mean to give in this preface, minus the names, to prevent their being lost to posterity.

The twenty years of my life which I here present to readers are the twenty years which I spent at 32, Addison Mansions, Kensington, during which I was in constant intercourse with most of the best-known writers of the generation. The book is therefore largely taken up with personal reminiscences and impressions of them—indeed, not a few of them, such as Conan Doyle, J. K. Jerome, I. Zangwill, H. A. Vachell, Charles Garvice, Eden Phillpotts, Mr. and Mrs. C. N. Williamson, Mrs. Croker, Mrs. Perrin, Madame Albanesi, Compton Mackenzie, and Jeffery Farnol's mentor, wrote specially for this book an account of the circumstances which led to their being authors. For it must be remembered that the majority of authors start life in some other profession, and drift into authorship as they discover their aptitude for it. Conan Doyle was a doctor, in busy practice when he wrote *The White Company*; Jerome was a lawyer's clerk when he wrote *Three Men in a Boat*; both Hardy and Hall Caine began as architects; Zangwill was a teacher, and W. W. Jacobs was a clerk in the General Post Office.

An index of the authors of whom personal reminiscences are told in this book will be found at the end.

Its earlier chapters deal with my life prior to our going to Addison Mansions, giving details of my parentage and bringing-up, of the seven years I spent in Australia and the United States, and my long visits to Canada and Japan. From that point forward, except for the four chapters which deal with the writing of my books, the present volume is occupied chiefly with London literary society from 1891 to 1911.

It was in the 'nineties that the late Sir Walter Besant's efforts to bring authors together by the creation of the Authors' Club, and their trade union, the Authors' Society, bore fruit. English writers, who had hitherto been the reverse of gregarious, began to meet each other very often at receptions and clubs.

In those days one made new friends among well-known authors, artists, and theatrical people every day, at places like the Authors', Arts, Vagabonds, Savage, Hogarth and Argonauts' Clubs, the Idler teas, and women's teas at the Pioneer Club, the Writers' Club, and the Women Journalists', and various receptions in Bohemia. It was almost an offence to spend an entire afternoon, or an entire evening, in any other way, and though it made inroads on one's time for work, and time for exercise, it gave one an intimacy, which has lasted, with men and women who have since risen to the head of their professions. That intimacy is reflected in these pages, which show a good deal of the personal side of the literary movement of the 'nineties and the literary club life of the period.

I have endeavoured in this book to interest my readers in two ways—by telling them the circumstances in my bringing-up, and my subsequent life, which made me a busy man of letters instead of a lawyer, and by giving them my reminiscences of friends who have won the affection of the public in literature, in art, and on the stage.

As I feel that a great many of my readers will be much more interested in my reminiscences than in my life, I advise them to begin at Chapter VI—or, better still, Chapter VIII—from which point forward, with the exceptions of Chapters XVI–XIX, the book is taken up more with the friends I have had the good fortune to know than with myself.

Before concluding, I will give three or four stories too personal to have names attached to them.

I once heard a Bishop, who in those days was a smug and an Oxford Don, remark to a circle of delighted undergraduates, "My brother Edward thinks I'm an awful fool." As his brother Edward was Captain of the Eton Eleven, and amateur champion of something or other, there is no doubt that his brother Edward did think him an awful fool.

I once heard an author, at the very moment that Robert Louis Stevenson, as we had learnt by telegram that afternoon, was lying in state under the sky at Samoa, awaiting burial, say, replying to the toast of his health at a public dinner, that he had been led to write his most popular book by the perusal of Stevenson's *Treasure Island*.

"I said to myself," he naïvely remarked, "that if I could not write a better book than that in six weeks, I would shoot myself."

The same man, when another of his books had been dramatised, and he was called before the curtain on the first night of its production, informed the audience that it was a very good play, and that it would be a great success when it was decently acted. So complacent was he about it that the friend who tried to pull him back behind the curtain by the tails of his dress-coat failed until he had split the coat up to the collar.

This man has the very best instincts, but he has a genius for poking his finger into people's eyes.

I once knew the brother of a Bishop, who left the Church of England, and went to America to be a Unitarian clergyman, because he wished to marry a pretty American heiress, and he had a wife already in England. By and by his new sect heard of it, and expelled him with conscious or unconscious humour for " conduct incompatible with membership in the Unitarian Church." He hired a hall from the piano company opposite, and nearly the whole congregation moved across the street with him. Except in the matter of monogamy, he was a most Christian man, and his congregation had the highest respect and affection for him and his bigamous wife; and this in spite of the fact that he constantly alluded to the Trinity as he warmed to his subject in sermons for the edification of Unitarians. If he noticed it, he corrected himself and said Triad. He was one of the most delightful men I ever met, and his influence on his congregation was of the very best.

In the days when I saw so much of actors at our own flat, and went every Sunday night to the O.P., I was once asked to arbitrate in a dispute between an actor-manager and the critic of a great daily, who had exchanged " words " in the theatre. The critic either dreaded the expense of a lawsuit, or had no desire to make money if he could obtain the *amende honorable.* I heard all they had to say, and then I turned round and said to the great actor, " Did you say that about Mr. ——? " and he replied with an Irishism which I got accepted as an apology: " I really couldn't say; I'm such a liar that I never know what I have said and what I haven't said."

These are stories to which I could not append the names, but the reader will find as good and better if he turns up the names of S. H. Jeyes, Oscar Wilde and Phil May in the index.

CONTENTS

LIST OF ILLUSTRATIONS

COLOURED PICTURES BY YOSHIO MARKINO

PORTRAITS BY YOSHIO MARKINO

INDEX OF REMINISCENCES

At the end of the book will be found an index of the well-known people about whom personal reminiscences or new facts are told—such as Prince Alamayu of Abyssinia, Mme. Albanesi, Sir Edwin Arnold, Lena Ashwell, Sarah Bernhardt, Sir Walter Besant, Rolf Boldrewood, Hall Caine, Dion Clayton Calthrop, Mrs. Clifford, Bishop Creighton, Mrs. Croker, Sir A. Conan Doyle, Lord Dundonald, Sir J. Forbes-Robertson, Charles Garvice, Bishop Gore, Sarah Grand, George Grossmith, Thomas Hardy, Bret Harte, W. E. Henley, Robert Hichens, John Oliver Hobbes, Oliver Wendell Holmes, Anthony Hope, J. K. Jerome, S. H. Jeyes, C. Kernahan, A. H. Savage Landor, Maarten Maartens, Compton MacKenzie, Yoshio Markino, "Bob" Martin, George Meredith, Frankfort Moore, Dr. G. E. Morrison of Peking, F. W. H. Myers, Nansen, Cardinal Newman, Mrs. Perrin, Eden Phillpotts, Rt. Hon. Sir Geo. Reid, Whitelaw Reid, Lord Roberts, the late Lord Salisbury, F. Hopkinson Smith, Father Stanton, Mrs. Flora Annie Steel, August Strindberg, Mark Twain, H. A. Vachell, J. M. Whistler, Percy White, Oscar Wilde, Mr. and Mrs. C. N. Williamson, Lord Willoughby de Broke, Margaret Woods, Sir Charles Wyndham and Israel Zangwill.

D. S.

TWENTY YEARS OF MY LIFE

CHAPTER I

MY LIFE (1856–1886)

I WAS born on February 5, 1856, in the town-house of my maternal grandfather. My father, a solicitor by profession, who died in the last days of 1910, at the age of eighty-six, was almost the youngest of the sixteen children of my paternal grandparents, John Baker Sladen, D.L., J.P., of Ripple Court, near Dover, and Etheldred St. Barbe. The name St. Barbe has been freely bestowed on their descendants because the first St. Barbe in this country has the honour of appearing on the Roll of Battle Abbey.

My maternal grandparents were John Wheelton and Mary Wynfield. Mr. Wheelton (I was never able to discover any other person named Wheelton, till I found, among the survivors of the loss of the *Titanic*, a steward called Wheelton; truly the name has narrowly escaped extinction), from whom I get my third Christian name, was in business as a shipper on the site of the General Post Office, and was Master of the Cordwainers' Company. He was Sheriff of London in the year of Queen Victoria's marriage. Though he lived at Meopham near Tonbridge, he came from Manchester, and I am, therefore, a Lancashire man on one side of the house. But oddly enough I have never been to Manchester.

Charles Dickens, when he first became a writer, was a frequent guest at his hospitable table, and has immortalised him in one of his books. He was in a way immortalised by taking a leading part in one of the most famous law cases in our history, Stockdale *versus* Hansard. As Sheriff he had to levy an execution on Hansard, the printer to the House of Commons, who had published in the reports of the debates

B

a libel on Mr. Stockdale. The House declared it a breach of privilege, and sentenced the Sheriff to be imprisoned in the Speaker's house, from which he was shortly afterwards released on the plea of ill-health. But with the City of London as well as the Law Courts against them, the members of the House of Commons determined to avoid future collisions by bringing in a bill to make the reports of the proceedings of Parliament privileged and this duly became law.

I have in my possession an enormous silver epergne, supported by allegorical figures of Justice and others, which the City of London presented to my grandfather in honour of this occasion, with a few survivors of a set of leather fire-buckets, embellished with the City arms, which now do duty as waste-paper baskets.

I was baptised in Trinity Church, Paddington, and shortly afterwards my parents went to live at 22, Westbourne Park Terrace, Paddington, continuing there till 1862.

It was in this year that my last sister, Mrs. Young, was born, just before we changed houses. My eldest sister, who married the late Rev. Frederick Robert Ellis, only son of Robert Ridge Ellis, of the Court Lodge, Yalding, Kent, and for many years Rector of Much Wenlock, was born in 1850. My second sister, who married Robert Arundel Watkins, eldest surviving son of the Rev. Bernard Watkins, of Treeton, and afterwards of Lawkland Hall, Yorkshire, was born in 1851; and my brother, the Rev. St. Barbe Sydenham Sladen, who holds one of the City livings, St. Margaret Patten, was born in 1858.

My father, having become better off by the death of my two grandfathers in 1860 and 1861, bought a ninety-six years' lease of Phillimore Lodge, Campden Hill, which I sold in 1911.

I believe that I never left London till I was four years old, when we all went to stay with my uncle, the Rev. William Springett, who still survives, at Dunkirk Vicarage, near Canterbury. While we were there I first saw and dipped my hands in the sea, which I was destined to traverse so often, at a place called Seasalter, to which we drove from Dunkirk.

From 1862 to 1868, when my mother died, we children generally spent the summer at Brighton, from which my father went away to a moor in Yorkshire for the grouse-shooting. As a child, I soon grew tired of Brighton, which seemed so like a seaside suburb of London. I used to think that the sea itself, which had no proper ships on it, was like a very large canal. I longed for real sea, like we had seen at Deal, where we went to stay in my grandmother Sladen's dower-house, shortly after our visit to Dunkirk. There we had seen a full-rigged ship driven on to the beach in front of our house in a gale, and had seen the lifeboat and the Deal luggers putting out to wrecks on the Goodwin Sands, and had seen the largest ships of the day in the Downs. I loved the woods we had rambled in, between Dunkirk and Canterbury, even better still. I never found the ordinary seaside place tolerable till I became enamoured of golf. Without golf these places are marine deserts.

I never tasted the real delights of the country till we went in the later 'sixties to a farmhouse on the edge of the Duke of Rutland's moors above Baslow, in Derbyshire. With that holiday I was simply enchanted. For rocks meant fairyland, as they still do, to me. And there I had, besides rocks, like the Cakes of Bread, the clear, trout-haunted mountain-river Derwent, and romantic mediæval architecture like Haddon Hall. Besides, we were allowed to run wild on the farm, to sail about the shallow pond in a cattle-trough, to help to make Wensleydale cheeses (this part of Derbyshire arrogates the right to use the name), and to hack the garden about as much as we liked. It was there that I had my first real games of Red Indians and Robinson Crusoe, and there that I had the seeds of my passion for architecture implanted in me.

We drove about a great deal—to the Peak, with its caverns and its queer villages, to the glorious Derbyshire Dales, and to great houses like Chatsworth. Certainly Baslow was my fairy-godmother in authorship, and my literary aspirations were cradled in Derbyshire. My father gave me a good schooling in the beauties of England. We were always taken to see every place of any interest for its scenery, its buildings, or its history, which could be reached in a day by a pair of horses from the house, where we were spending our summer holidays. He had the same *flair* for guide-books as I have, and taught me how to use them intelligently.

Up till 1864 I was taught by governesses with my elder sisters. There were three of them, Miss Morrison, Miss Bray, and Miss Rose Sara Paley, an American Southerner, whose parents had been ruined by the Civil War. She was a very charming and intelligent woman, and taught my eldest sister to compose in prose and verse. For a long time this sister was the author of our home circle. I was too young to try composition in those days, but seeing my eldest sister do it familiarised me with the idea of it. I also had a music mistress, because it was hoped that playing the piano would restore my left hand to its proper shape, after the extraordinary accident which I had when I was only two years old. She was Miss Rosa Brinsmead, a daughter of the John Brinsmead who founded the famous piano-making firm. The point which I remember best about her was that she had fair ringlets like Princess (now Queen) Alexandra, who had just come over from Denmark and won all hearts.

The accident happened by my falling into the fireplace, when my nurse left me for a minute. To raise myself up I caught hold of the bar of the grate with my left hand, and scorched the inside out. It is still shrivelled, though fifty-five years have passed since that awful day for my mother, when she found her only son, as she thought, crippled for life.

But though it chapped terribly every winter, and would not open properly for the next three or four years, I soon got back the use of my hand, and no one now suspects it of being the least disfigured till I hold it open to show them. The back was uninjured, and it looks a very nice hand by X-rays, when only the bones are visible.

The doctor recommended that, being a child of a very active brain (I asked quite awkward questions about the birth of my brother shortly afterwards), I should be taught to read while I was kept in bed, as the only means of keeping my hand out of danger, and I was given a box of letters which

I always arranged upon the splint of my wounded hand. By the time that it was well I could read, and on my fifth birthday I was given the leather-bound Prayer-book which I had been promised whenever I could read every word in it. I have the Prayer-book still, half a century later.

Poor Miss Brinsmead had a hopeless task, for though I could learn to read so easily, I never could learn to play on the piano with both hands at the same time, except in the very baldest melodies, like " God Save the Queen," and the " Sultan's Polka." These I did achieve.

In 1864 I was sent to a dame's school in Kensington Square, kept by the Misses Newman, from which I was shortly afterwards transferred to another kept by Miss Daymond, an excellent teacher, where I had Johnny and Everett Millais, and sons of other great artists, for my schoolfellows.

In 1866, though it nearly broke my mother's heart, I was sent to my first boarding-school, Temple Grove, East Sheen—in the old house where Dorothy Temple had lived, and Henry John Temple, Viscount Palmerston, the greatest of that illustrious race, was born—the school, moreover, which had numbered Benjamin Disraeli among its pupils. How many people are there who know that Dizzy was schooled in the house in which Palmerston was born—those two great apostles of British prestige?

Here I stayed for three years before I won the first junior scholarship at Cheltenham College, and here, from my house-master, I had a fresh and wonderful department of knowledge opened to me, for he used to take me natural-ising (both by day and by night, when the other boys were in bed) on Sheen Common, then wild enough to have snakes and glow-worms and lizards, as well as newts and leeches, and rich in insect prizes. I won this favour because he accidentally discovered that I knew " Mangnall's Questions " and " Common Subjects " by heart. But though he was Divinity Master, he never discovered that I knew my Bible quite as well.

He also taught me to lie. I had never told a lie till I went to Temple Grove. But as he prided himself on his acuteness, he was constitutionally unable to believe the truth. It was too obvious for him. When I found that he invariably thought I was lying while I still obeyed my mother's teaching, and was too afraid of God to tell a lie, I suddenly made up my mind that I would humour him, and tell whatever lie was necessary to this transparent Sherlock Holmes. After this he always believed me, unless I accidentally forgot and told him the truth. And I liked him so much that I wished him to believe me.

He did not injure my character as much as he might have done, because I was born with a loathing for insincerity. The difficulty came when he and Waterfield, the head master, questioned me about the same thing, for Waterfield mesmerised one into telling the truth, and he tempted one to tell a lie. It reminds me now of Titian's "Sacred and Profane Love."

At Temple Grove I acquired my taste for games and taste for natural history.

In 1868, my mother, to whom I was passionately attached, died. I used to dream that she was alive for months afterwards. And the great theosophist to whom I mentioned this sees in it an astral communication. To divert my thoughts from this, the greatest grief I had ever had, I was sent to stay with my cousin, Colonel Joseph Sladen, who had already succeeded to Ripple Court, and was then a Gunner Captain, stationed at Sheerness. He belonged to the Royal Yacht Squadron, and had a schooner yacht in which we used to go away for cruises up the Channel. I was a little boy of twelve, and his two eldest sons, Arthur Sladen, now H.R.H. the Duke of Connaught's Private Secretary in Canada, and Sampson Sladen, now the Chief of the London Fire Brigade, were hardly more than babies, but I enjoyed it very much, because I was interested in the yachting and in the firing of the hundred-pounder Armstrongs, which were the monster guns of those days. We went in my cousin's yacht to see the new ironclad fleets of Great Britain and France, and we went over the *Black Prince* and the *Minotaur*, the crack ships of the time.

A year after that, exactly on the first anniversary of my

mother's death, I went to Cheltenham College, where I had
taken a scholarship. I was at Cheltenham College six years,
and took four scholarships and many prizes at the school,
the most interesting of which, in view of my after life, was
the prize for the English Poem. I was also Senior Prefect,
Editor of the school magazine, Captain of Football, and
Captain of the Rifle Corps. I shot for the school four times
in the Public School competitions at Wimbledon, and in 1874
won the Spencer Cup, which was open to the best shot from
each of the Public Schools. I was the school representative
for it also in 1873.

At Cheltenham, I suppose, I laid the foundations of my
literary career, because, besides editing the school magazine
for a couple of years, and writing the Prize Poem, I read
every book in the College library. It was such a delight to
me to have the run of a well-stocked library. The books at
home were nearly all religious books. I was brought up on
the sternest low-Church lines; we went to church twice a day
on Sunday, besides having prayers read twice at home, and
hymns sung in the afternoon. The church we attended was
St. Paul's, Onslow Square, where I had to listen to hour-long
sermons from Capel Molyneux and Prebendary Webb-
Peploe. The dull and long services were almost intolerable,
except when Millais, the great painter, who had the next
pew, asked me into his pew to relieve the crush in ours.
Millais sat so upright and so forward when he was listening
that my father could not see me, and I used to bury my
face in the beautiful Mrs. Millais' sealskin jacket; I had
such an admiration for her that I did not go to sleep. Millais
—he was not Sir John in those days—did not make his children
go to church; I suppose he went because he was fascinated
by the eloquence of the sermons. Molyneux, Marston and
Peploe were all great preachers, though they bored an unfortunate small boy to the verge of nervous prostration.
We were only allowed to read Sunday books on Sunday, and
the newspapers were put away, as they were to the day of
my father's death in 1910.

After my mother's death I always longed to get back to
school, because, though we had to go to chapel every day,

and twice on Sunday, there was not that atmosphere of
religion which made me, as a small boy, begin to feel unhappy
about lunch-time on Saturday, and not thoroughly relieved
till after breakfast on Monday. I hated Sunday at home;
the two-mile walk to and from church was the best part
of it.

I have forgotten two other preparations for a literary
career which I perpetrated at Cheltenham. I and my
greatest friend, a boy called Walter Roper Lawrence (now
Sir W. R. Lawrence, Bart., G.C.I.E.), who afterwards rose
to a position of the highest eminence in India, wrote verses
for the school magazine, and I published a pamphlet to
avenge a contemptuous reference, in the Shotover Papers,
and was duly summoned for libel. The late Frederick
Stroud, the Recorder of Tewkesbury, who was at that time a
solicitor, got me off. I never saw him in after life, which
I much regretted, because he was, like myself, a great student
of everything connected with Adam Lindsay Gordon, the
Australian poet. He died while I was writing our life of
Gordon.

At the beginning of 1875 I won an open classical scholarship at Trinity College, Oxford, where I commenced residence
in the following October. At Oxford again I read voraciously
in the splendid library of the Union.

There my love of games continued unabated. I shot
against Cambridge four years, and won all the shooting
challenge-cups. I also played in the 'Varsity Rugby Union
Football XV when I first went up.

I had delightful old panelled rooms on Number 7 staircase
—a chance fact, which won me a great honour and pleasure.
One afternoon, when I came in from playing football, the
College messenger met me, saying, " Grand company in your
rooms this afternoon, Mr. Sladen—the President, and all the
Fellows, and Cardinal Nooman," and he added, " When the
President looked at your mantelpiece, sir, he *corfed*." My
mantelpiece was strewn with portraits of Maud Branscombe,
Eveleen Rayne, Mrs. Rousby, and other theatrical stars of
that day—about a couple of dozen of them.

Shortly afterwards the President's butler arrived with a

note, which I supposed was to reproach me with the racy appearance of my mantelpiece, but it was to ask me to spend the evening with the President, because Cardinal Newman had expressed a desire to meet the present occupant of his rooms.

The Cardinal, a wan little man with a shrivelled face and a large nose, and one of the most beautiful expressions which ever appeared on a human being, talked to me for a couple of hours, prostrating me with his exquisite modesty. He wanted to know if the snapdragons, to which he had written a poem, still grew on the wall between Trinity and Balliol; he wanted to compare undergraduate life of his day with the undergraduate life of mine; he asked me about a number of Gothic fragments in Oxford which might have perished between his day and mine, and fortunately, I had already conceived the passion for Gothic architecture which pervades my books, and was able to tell him about every one. He told me the marks by which he knew that those were his rooms; he asked me about my studies, and hobbies, and aims in life; I don't think that I have ever felt any honour of the kind so much.

At Oxford I spent every penny I could afford, and more, on collecting a library of standard works, and I have many of them still. I remember that the literary Oxonians of that day discussed poetry much more than prose, and could mostly be classified into admirers of William Morris and admirers of Swinburne, and I think the Morrisians were more numerous. All of them had an academic admiration for Matthew Arnold's poems, and could spout from " Thyrsis " and the " Scholar Gipsy," which was compared with Keat's " Ode to a Nightingale."

Thackeray's daughter (Lady Ritchie) was at that time the latest star in fiction, as I occasionally remind her.

I had the good fortune to know some of the greatest of the authors who lived at Oxford when I was an undergraduate— Max Müller, Bishop Stubbs the historian, Edward Augustus Freeman, Lewis Carroll, Dean Kitchin, Canon Bright and W. L. Courtney.

Oxford in those days (as I suppose it does still) revolved

largely round "Bobby Raper," then Dean of Trinity, a
man of infinite tact and kindness, swift to discern ability
and character in an undergraduate, and to make a friend
of their owner, and blessed with a most saving sense of
humour. When they had finished at Oxford, a word from
him found them coveted masterships, or secretaryships to
Public Men. He was the link between Oxford and Public
life, as much as Jowett—the "Jowler" himself—who sat
in John Wycliffe's seat at Balliol. Lord Milner, St. John
Brodrick and George Curzon have gone farthest of the
Balliol men of my time. Asquith was before me, Edward
Grey after. Trinity ran to Bishops. Most of the men
who sat at the scholars' table at Trinity in my time who
went into Holy Orders are Bishops now, Archie Robertson,
now Bishop of Exeter, being the senior of them, Bishop
Gore of Oxford, who had rooms on the same floor as I had,
and was one of my greatest friends in my first year, was the
Junior Fellow. He was a very well-off young man, and used
to spend huge sums on buying folios of the Latin Fathers,
and then learn them by heart. There is no one who knows
so much about the Fathers as the Bishop of Oxford. The
present Archbishop of Canterbury was at Trinity, but before
my time, and so was Father Stanton, who went there because
he came of a hunting family, and it was a hunting College,
and he was a Rugby man. Bishop Stubbs and Freeman were
also Trinity men, and generally at the College Gaudies, where
the Scholars used to dine at the same table as the Dons and
their guests. Sir Richard Burton came once to a Gaudy
when I was there, and told me that he was very surprised
that they had asked him, because he had been sent down.

I said, " You are in very good company. The great Lord
Chatham and Walter Savage Landor were sent down from
Trinity as well as you."

But one well-known literary man of the present day holds
the record over them all, because he was sent down from
Trinity twice.

Although I was a classical scholar, I refused to go in for
Classics in the Final Schools. " Greats," otherwise *Literæ
Humaniores*, as this school is called at Oxford, embraces the

study of Philosophy in the original Greek and Latin of Plato, Aristotle and Cicero, and Philosophy and Logic generally. I was sick of the Classics, and I never could take the smallest interest in Philosophy, so I knew that I should do no good in this school, and announced my intention of going in for the School of Modern History. This was too revolutionary for my tutor. He said—

" Classical scholars are expected to go in for Greats, and if you fail to do so, we shall have to consider the taking away of your scholarship."

I was astute in my generation; I went to Gore (the Bishop), who was my friend, and always met undergraduates as if he were one of themselves, and said to him, " Will you do something for me, Gore ? "

" It depends on what it is," he replied, with his curious smile.

" Tell the Common-room (*i. e.* the Dons, who used to meet in the Common-room every night after dinner) that I really mean to go in for History whether they take away my scholarship or not, but that if they do take it away, I shall take my name off the books of Trinity and go and ask Jowett if he will admit me at Balliol. You were a Balliol undergrad; you know the kind of answer that Jowett would make to a man who was willing to give up an eighty pounds a year scholarship in order to go in for the School which interested him."

" Jowett will take you," he said, " but I will see what can be done here."

That night I received the most unpleasant note an undergraduate can receive—a command to meet the Common-room at ten o'clock the next morning. They were all present when I went in. The President invited me to take a seat, and my tutor (the Rev. H. G. Woods, now Master of the Temple, of whom I still see something) said—

" Are you quite determined to go in for the School of History, Mr. Sladen ? "

" Quite," I replied.

" Then we hope that the degree you take will justify us in assenting to such a very unusual procedure."

Then they all smiled very pleasantly, and I thanked them and went out.

They must have felt quite justified when, two years afterwards, I took my First in History with congratulatory letters from all my examiners, while all the scholars of Trinity who went in for the *School of Literæ Humaniores* took Seconds and Thirds. I should have got a Fourth, I am convinced.

Again I read voraciously. For the first year I hardly bothered about my text-books at all. I read biographies, books about architecture and art and literature, historical novels, the writings of historical personages, everything which threw brilliant sidelights on my subject. And in the second year I learnt my text-books almost by heart, except Stubbs's *Constitutional History* and *Selected Charters*. I simply could not memorise them—they were so dry, and I hated the dry bones of *Constitutional History* almost as badly as philosophy. I learned digests of them, which took less time, and were no dryer, and proved equally efficacious in answering the papers.

In after years, when I was entertaining Bishop Stubbs at a reception, which Montague Fowler and I gave in honour of Mark Twain at the Authors' Club, he roared with laughter when I told him that I got a First in History without reading his books, by learning the Digests of them by heart.

He said, "I know they are dreadfully dull. Did you find my lectures very dull when you came to them?" He had not forgotten that I had attended his lectures for a couple of years.

I said, "No, not at all."

"Honestly, did you get any good from them?"

"Quite honestly?"

He nodded.

I said, "Not in the usual way."

"Well," he asked, "how did you get any good from them?"

"You must forgive me if I tell you."

"Tell me; it cannot be worse than what you said about my books."

"Well," I confessed, "the reason why I attended your

lectures was that you never bothered as to whether I was there or not, and I hardly ever was there.   I did not think any lectures were any good, but my tutor made me attend sixteen a week, and the time which I was supposed to spend at your lectures, I used to spend in my rooms reading.   You were the only gentleman among my lecturers—all the rest used to call the names, and report me to my tutor if I was absent."

He was immensely tickled, and said, " You deserved to get a First, if you took things as seriously as that."

But Bishop Stubbs was very human.   He always read the lightest novel he could lay hands on before he went to bed, to relieve his mind after working, and save him from insomnia.

" They are so light," he said, " that I keep other books in front of them in my book-case."

As an author, I have found the education I was given and gave myself a very useful foundation.   Those ten years I gave to the study of Latin and Greek and classical history and mythology were not thrown away, because I have written so many books about Italy and Sicily and Egypt, in which having the classics at my fingers' ends made me understand the history, and the allusions in the materials I had to digest.   It is impossible to write freely about Italy and Greece unless you know your classics.

The two years of incessant study which I gave to taking my degree in Modern History at Oxford have been equally useful, because it is impossible to write guide-books and books of travel unless you have a sound knowledge of history.

For a brief while my degree in history had a most practical and technical value, for it won me the Chair of Modern History in the University of Sydney, New South Wales.

Beyond a week or two in Paris, I had never left England before I went to Australia in the end of 1879, a few months after I left Oxford, but I knew my England pretty well, because my father had always encouraged me to see the parts of England which contained the finest scenery and the architectural *chefs d'œuvres*, like cathedrals.   Ireland I had never visited, and of Scotland I only knew Dumfriesshire, where my father rented a shooting-box and a moor for four years; and where I had enjoyed splendid rough shooting when

I was a boy, in the very heart of the land of Burns. "The Grey Mare's Tail" was on one shooting which we had, and the Carlyle cottage was right under our Craigenputtock shooting.

When I left Oxford my father gave me three hundred pounds to spend on a year of travel, and I chose to go to Australia to stay with his eldest brother, Sir Charles Sladen, K.C.M.G., who had been Prime Minister of the Colony of Victoria, and was at that time leader of the Upper House, and of the Constitutional Party in Victoria. I wanted to see if I should like to settle in the Colonies, and go to the Bar with a view to a political career. We were not rich enough for me to think of the House of Commons seriously, and I have always taken a very keen interest in politics.

Further, I wanted to go and stay on my uncle's station to get some riding and shooting, and to see something of the outdoor life of Australia, of which I had heard so much. And I wanted desperately to try living in a hot country. I knew by intuition that I should like heat.

I had not been staying with my uncle for a year before I had made up my mind to live in Australia, a conclusion to which I was assisted by my marriage with Miss Margaret Isabel Muirhead, the daughter of a Scotsman from Stirling, who had owned a fine station called the Grampians in the Western District of Victoria, and had been killed in a horse accident. As I had not been called to the Bar before I left home, I found that I had to go through a two years' course, and take a law degree at the Melbourne University. This I did, though the position was sufficiently anomalous. For instance, I had to attend lectures by a Member of the Government, the Solicitor-General. I knew him intimately at the Melbourne Club and in private life, and we generally used to walk down to the Club after the lecture. Sometimes we went into a pub, to have a drink together, and we discussed anything from the forthcoming Government Bills to Club stories. He told me one day, before the public knew anything about it, of the intention of the Government to bring in a Bill to make sweeps on racing illegal. As much as forty-five thousand pounds had been subscribed for the Melbourne Cup Sweep the year before.

I said, " It is no good making them illegal; it only means that they will be carried on under the rose, and that a whole lot of the sweeps will be bogus. You can't stop sweeps; all you can do is to put the bogus sweep on a level with Jimmy Miller's."

" What would you do, then ? " he asked.

" Well, if you really want to stop them, you should legalise them, and put a twenty-five per cent., or fifty per cent. for the matter of that, tax upon them. You'd spoil the odds so that sweeps would die a natural death; and if they didn't, you'd get a nice lot of money to save the taxpayer's pocket. You would be like the Prince of Monaco, who lives by the gambling at Monte Carlo."

He duly put the suggestion before the Government, but they thought that this would be paltering with eternal sin, and passed their Bill to help the bogus-sweep promoter.

This same man and I were asked one night to take part in a Shakespeare reading at the Prime Minister's. My friend was late, and the Prime Minister, who was not a discreet man, began talking about him. Somebody remarked what a wonderfully well-informed man he was.

" Yes," said the Prime Minister, " my Solicitor-General is one of those people who know nothing about everything. And the way he does it is that he never opens a book; he just reads what the magazines and papers have to say about books."

Suddenly the Premier felt that his remarks were no longer being received with enthusiasm, and looking up, saw his Solicitor-General waiting to shake hands with him.

At the Melbourne University I formed one intimate friendship, which has lasted ever since. Among my fellow-students was Dr. George Ernest Morrison, the famous *Times* correspondent of Peking. He was famous in those days as the finest football player in the Colony, and he began his adventures while he was at the University. For months we missed him; nobody knew where he was—or if his father, who was head master of Geelong College, did know, he never told. Then suddenly he turned up again, and said that he had been walking from Cape York, which was the northern-most point of Australia, to Melbourne. He had undertaken

—and I don't think he had any bet on it—to make his way from Cape York to Melbourne, alone, unarmed and without a penny in his pocket. In the northernmost part of his journey, at any rate, there were a great many wild blacks, and many rivers full of crocodiles to swim. But there are, of course, no large carnivora in Australia, and a snake can be killed with a stick. When he was swimming a river he used to construct a raft, and put his clothes and his pack on it; he carried a pack like any other sun-downer, and when he got to a station, did his bit of work to pay for his bed and supper, and when he left it, if the next station south was more than a day's journey, he was given enough food to carry him through. This is, of course, the universal custom in Australia when a man is going from station to station in search of work, such as shearing.

He had not a single misadventure. The reason why he took so long was that his way from station to station naturally took him out of the direct line to the south, and he made a stay at some of them. The newspapers were so impressed with his feat that, shortly afterwards, when the *Age* organised an expedition to explore New Guinea, he was given command of it. That was the last I saw of Morrison till we met a few years afterwards at my house in London.

I never practised for the Melbourne Bar, for no sooner had I taken my law degree than I was appointed to the vacant chair of Modern History in the University of Sydney.

I had, since I landed in Australia, made my debut as an author, and had already published two volumes of verse, *Frithjof and Ingebjorg* and *Australian Lyrics*. During the year that I held my chair, we had apartments in the Old Government House, Parramatta, which had become a boarding-house, and spent our vacations on the Hawkesbury and in the Blue Mountains.

While I was at Parramatta I published a third volume of verse, *A Poetry of Exiles*.

Then occurred an event which deprived me of one of my principal reasons for remaining in Australia, the premature death of my uncle. This closed my short cut to a political career; and I had long since come to the conclusion that

Australia was not the place for a literary career, because there was no real publishing in Australia. Publishers were merely booksellers, who acted as intermediaries between authors and printers; they took no risks of publication; the author paid, and they received one commission as publishers and another as booksellers. This did not signify much for verse; the printing bill for books of verse is not large, and poets are accustomed to bringing out their works at their own risk in other countries besides Australia. But a large prose work of a hundred or a hundred and fifty thousand words is, at Australian prices, extremely expensive to produce, and when it is produced, has only a small sale because it does not bear the name of any well-known English publishing house.

So I suddenly made up my mind to return to England.

The five years I spent in Australia were fruitful for my career as an author, though I have never published anything about Australia, except my own verses, and anthologies of Australian verse, and a life, and an edition of the poems, of Adam Lindsay Gordon. The last was phenomenally successful; I am sure that no volume of Browning has ever sold so well. And one of the anthologies had a sale of twenty thousand copies in the first ten years of its existence.

Australia supplied exactly the right element for my development. At Cheltenham I was the most prominent boy of my time, and the prestige with which I came up from school gave me a certain momentum at Oxford. So I went out to Australia with a very good opinion of Public Schools, and Oxford, and myself.

I soon discovered that nothing was of any importance in Australia except sport and money. If Tennyson or Walter Scott had gone to a bush-township, he would have been judged merely by his proficiency or absence of proficiency as a groom. Horsemanship is the one test of the inhabitants of a bush-township.

In Melbourne and Sydney and on "stations" it was different. Hospitality was prodigal, and there was a disposition to regard with charity one's shortcomings from the Colonial point of view, and to accept with sympathy the fact

c

that one had distinguished oneself elsewhere.   The Australian man is very manly, and very hearty; the Australian woman is apt to be very pretty, and to have a strong personality—to be full of character as a lover.

The climate of Australia I found absolutely delightful. It is a land of eternal summer : its winters are only cooler summers.   The unchanging blue of its skies is appalling to those whose prosperity depends on the rainfall.

When I went out to Australia, just after leaving Oxford, I was enough of a prig to profit very greatly by being suddenly thrown into an absolutely democratic community.   I was saved from finding things difficult by the fact that I was born a Bohemian, in spite of my very conventional parentage, and really did delight in roughing it.   The free and easy Colonial life was a great relief to me after the prim life in my English home; and staying about on the great stations in the western district of Victoria, which belonged to various connections of my family, furnished the finest experience of my early life.   I spent most of my first year in Australia in that way, returning, in between, to pay visits to my uncle at Geelong.   Being in the saddle every day never lost its thrill for me, because I had hardly ever been on a horse before I went to Australia; and wandering about the big paddocks and the adjoining stretches of forest, gun in hand—I hardly ever went out without a gun—had something of the excitement of the books about the American backwoods which I read in my boyhood.   It is true that I would rather have shot grizzly bears than the native bears of Australia, mere sloths, and lions and tigers than kangaroos, but a big " forester " is not to be sneezed at, and Australia has an extraordinary wealth of strange birds—the cockatoos and parrots and parakeets alone give a sort of tropical aspect to the forest, and the snakes give an unpleasantly tropical aspect, though, fortunately, in Australia, they shrink from human habitations.   .

When I married I went to live in Melbourne, close to public gardens of extraordinary beauty and almost tropical luxuriance, and soon became absorbed in the maelstrom of dancing and playing tennis, and watching first-class cricket and racing.

When we went to Parramatta it was easy to make excursions to the marvellous gorges of the Blue Mountains, which are among the grandest valley scenery in the world.

Everything was large, and free, and sparsely inhabited—most expanding to the mind, and the glimpse of the tropical glories of Oriental Ceylon, which I enjoyed for four days on my voyage home, made me hear the " East a callin' " for ever afterwards.

I found London desperately dull when we returned to it in 1884. I had no literary friends, except at Oxford, where we took a house for three months to get some colour into life again. It was on the banks of the Cherwell, facing the most beautiful buildings of Magdalen, and the Gothic glories of Oxford were manna to my hungry soul.

The summer, spent in Devonshire and Cornwall and Scotland, was well enough, and in the winter, which we spent at Torquay, we had grand scenery and beautiful ancient buildings, but the climate seemed treacherous and cold after the fierce bright summers of Australia.

I must not forget that I came very near not going to Australia at all. I felt the parting with my father extremely, and he was quite prostrated by it. I had, a few days before starting, been introduced to the captain of the old Orient liner *Lusitania*, in which I made the voyage—a hard, reckless sea-dog—and he did me good service on that occasion. Two letters came on board for me when we put in at Plymouth to pick up the last mails and passengers. One of these letters contained a letter from my father to the effect that if I wished to give up the passage and return home I might do so. The captain, for some reason or other, whether from having had a conversation with my father, or what, suspected that the letter might have some message of that kind—he may have had the same thing occurring in his experience before—so he did not give me the letter till the next day, when I had no possible chance of communicating with England until I got to the Cape de Verde Islands. By that time, of course, I had thoroughly settled down to the enjoyments of the voyage, and looked at the matter in a different light.

CHAPTER II

MY LIFE (1886–1888)

ABOUT this time I was struck with the idea that for a person who intended to make his living by writing books, Travel was a necessity, and while one had no ties, it cost no more to live in various parts of the Continent than to live in London.

The desire materialised sooner than it might have done, because Arthur Chamberlain, whom we had met when we were sharing a house in Scotland with the Wilkies (wife and daughters of the famous Melbourne doctor), wrote letters, which would brook no refusal, for us to come and join him at Heidelberg, where he was now a student, for the Quincentenary of the Heidelberg University.

Before we went abroad we had a foretaste of the many pilgrimages to archæological paradises which we were to make. We spent six weeks at Canterbury, peculiarly delightful to me, because my family have been landowners in East Kent from time immemorial, which made the neighbourhood of Canterbury full of landmarks for me, and Canterbury is, after Oxford, fuller of the Middle Ages than any town in England. Here, having the run of the Cathedral library given me by its curator, Dr. Shepherd (I hope I have spelt his name right), I commenced my studies of Edward, the Black Prince—the local hero, who lies buried in the Cathedral. This led to my writing the most ambitious of my poems, "Edward, the Black Prince." I wrote it among the ruins of the old Cathedral Monastery at Canterbury, and the first edition was printed in the Piazza of Santa Croce at Florence.

At Heidelberg, living for economy in a delightful pension kept by Miss Abraham, who had been the Kaiser's English governess, we met the set who pass their years in wandering from one pension to another on the Continent. Our immediate future was marked out for us. One family booked us for a favourite pension at Zurich, another for Lucerne, another for Lugano, another for Florence, another for Rome, another for Castellamare di-Stabia below Pompeii.

And so we began the great trek. We summered at Heidelberg. Autumn in Switzerland was perfectly beautiful, but the two or three months which we spent in Florence formed one of the turning-points of my life. It was there that we found a pension, which called itself an hotel, replete with the atmosphere and charm and the little luxuries which Italy knows so well how to give for seven francs a day. There we met people who came to Florence year after year, and knew every picture, almost every stone, in it—almost every ounce of pleasure which was to be got out of it. They initiated us, in fact, into Florence, which was more of an education than anything in the world.

Florence is Renaissance in architecture, Gothic in feeling. Its inhabitants, native and foreign, live in the past. It was here that I, born with a passion for realising the Middle Ages, acquired the undying desires which have taken me back so often and for such long periods, and have inspired me to write so many books about Italy and Sicily. From the very beginning I plunged into the life of Florence and the study of things Italian with extraordinary zest.

Going on to Rome for a month or two inspired me with the same feeling for the classics as Florence had inspired in me for the Middle Ages.

I own that, when I was persuaded to go on from Rome to Castellamare, I did so with certain misgivings. There did not seem to be the same chances in it. We were going to a villa outside the town, whose sole attraction seemed to be that it was six miles from Pompeii.

But when we got there, it had a profound influence on our lives. It proved to be the villa where the Countess of Blessington had entertained Byron and others of the immortals, a beautiful southern house, standing on the green hill which buries in its bosom the ashes of Vesuvius, and the ruins of Stabiæ, a city which shared the fate of Pompeii. It had a vineyard round it; its quaint garden was overrun with sleepy lizards, which you never catch asleep—the lizards in which the genius of Italy seems to live.

We saw the sunset every night on the Bay of Naples and Ischia, which all the world was talking about then because of the earthquake which had lately ravished it. Every night we saw a tree of fire rising from Vesuvius.

We used to spend our days in the orange groves of Sorrento, or driving in donkey-carts to Pompeii, that city of the resurrection of the ancient world. The weather was somnolently mild; for the first time we were eating of the fruit of the lotus, which we have eaten so often since, and which has pervaded my writings.

If Castellamare had only done that for us, it would be a milestone in my life, but it also planted the seeds of unrest— *die Wanderlust*—in my veins. Some one we met there—I don't remember who it was now—had a craze for Greek ruins; Roman ruins meant nothing to him, he said; there were only two places for him, Athens and Sicily.

In Sicily it was Girgenti which won his heart, not Syracuse or Taormina, and he almost persuaded us to go there. He obviously preferred it, even to Athens. But the name meant nothing to me; I had read of Agrigentum in the classics, and he showed me photographs of the glorious Greek temples, which are still preserved in the environs of modern Girgenti. Athens, on the contrary, had been before my mind ever since I was a boy. The literature of Greece is, with the exception of Homer and Theocritus, roughly speaking, the literature of Athens. I knew most of its principal buildings almost as well as if I had seen them. I heard the call of Athens, and to Athens we went from Castellamare.

Going there showed how comparatively cheap and easy it is to get to distant places. We went through Taranto— Tarentum—to Brindisi; from Brindisi to Corfu, in the Ionian Islands, the earthly paradise of the fair Nausicaa, and the empresses of to-day; from Corfu to Patras and Corinth; from Corinth to Athens.

The moral effect began before ever we reached Athens; it was so vivifying to a student of the classics to pass Tarentum, and Cæsar's Brundusium, the Lesbos of Sappho, the Ithaca of Ulysses, Corinth and the Piræus.

Lesbos! Corinth! Athens! Sappho! Ulysses! there was romance and undying poetry in the very names.

The Greece of those days really was something out of the beaten track. There were only two little railways of a few miles each, and there was not an hotel worthy of the name anywhere outside of Athens. Even in Athens, if you were not at a first-class hotel, kid's flesh, and sheep's-milk butter, black bread and honey of Hymettus, and wine which was full of resin, were the staples of diet. But what did it matter? We lived in a house and a street with beautiful classical names—we lived in the house of Hermes. And when we climbed up to the Acropolis at sunset, we were in an enchanted land midway between earth and heaven, for we were in the very heart of history surrounded by milk-white columns of the marble of Pentelicus, and facing a rich curtain of sunset, which hung over Ægina, and trailed into the waters of the Bay of Salamis. Athens is gloriously romantic and beautiful, and Time has laid its lightest fingers on her rocks and ruins, whose names are the commonplaces of Greek history.

We spent some glorious weeks at Athens, made interesting by the acquaintance of Tricoupis, the famous Prime Minister, and the presence of the President of my college at Oxford— now Bishop of Hereford, from whom I heard only the other day. From Athens Miss Lorimer's unappeasable hunger to see the world swept us on, after several happy weeks, to Constantinople—the outpost of the East in Europe. Constantinople was one of the most delightful experiences of my life. There is no call which I hear like the call of the East, and in Constantinople you have the noblest mosques west of India, and bazaars almost as barbarous as the bazaars of North Africa, thronged, like the broad bridge of boats which crosses the Golden Horn, with the mixed races of the Levant, in their gay, uncouth costumes. The scene, too, is one of rare beauty, for the great mosques are rooted in dark cypress-groves, and rear their domes and minarets on the horizon, and the calm waters of the Golden Horn and the Sea of Marmora are dotted with fantastic *caiques.*

We spent all too short a time there, dipping into the bowl of Oriental mystery, in perfect April weather, when we were called home to meet a sister-in-law coming from Australia.

I had, in the interval, published two more volumes of verse, *A Summer Christmas* and *In Cornwall and Across the Sea*, and I had printed at Florence *Edward, the Black Prince*, begun during that long visit to Canterbury in the spring of 1886, during which I steeped myself deeper and deeper in the study of Gothic architecture, not yet realising what an important part it was to play in my writing.

When we returned from Constantinople I had *The Black Prince* properly published in England, and though its sales were trifling, like those of *A Summer Christmas*, it met with warm commendation from the critics.

Shortly after this we were inspired with the desire to visit the United States in the autumn of 1888, and as we were going so far, we determined so stay in one place while we were in England.

The place we chose was Richmond. I had always loved it since I was a little boy at Temple Grove School in the neighbouring village of East Sheen. It was sufficiently in the country for us to pass a spring and summer there without irksomeness, and sufficiently beautiful and old-fashioned to satisfy my cravings.

At Richmond we took a house in the Queen's Road, and but for the very large sum demanded for fixtures, we should have abandoned our American trip, and taken the part of the Old Palace which has now been restored at great expense by Mr. J. L. Middleton, for which I had a great inclination. Mr. Middleton is a friend of mine and I have been over it many times with him. It stands right opposite my study window. We liked Richmond as much then as we do now, except for the long trail up from the railway station to the Queen's Road when we went to the theatre. We were in the Park or on the adjoining commons every day, watching the operations of Nature from the growth to the fall.

It was a busy time, for I wrote *The Spanish Armada* on the occasion of the Tercentenary of the immortal sea-fight, and I edited two anthologies of Australian verse, *Australian Ballads* and *A Century of Australian Song*, for Walter Scott, Ltd. The pleasure of compiling these two anthologies, the first books by which I ever made any money, was enhanced because I did them at the unsolicited invitation of the late William Sharp, the poet and author of the rhapsodies of " Fiona Macleod," who afterwards became a dear and intimate friend. He introduced me to Charles Mackay, the editor of the famous *Thousand and One Gems of English Poetry*, who adopted Marie Corelli as his daughter, and was father of Eric Mackay. It was through him that I received the invitation to do the Australian part of the *Slang Dictionary*, edited by M. Barrére, the French Ambassador's brother, for which also I received some money.

These encouragements made me ask my friend, the late S. H. Jeyes, who went to Trinity, Oxford, on the same day as I did, and was at the time one of the editors of the *St. James's Gazette*, from which he afterwards changed to the *Standard*, whether he thought that I ought to go to America, or stay and pursue my chances in England.

He said, " Go; in America they will take you at your own valuation, and when you get back, it will *be* your valuation."

And so it came that we took our passages in the old Cunarder *Catalonia* from Liverpool to Boston.

CHAPTER III

I GO TO THE UNITED STATES AND CANADA

THE only literary at homes I had been to before I went to America were Edmund Gosse's in Delamere Terrace, Louise Chandler Moulton's in Weymouth Street, and W. E. Henley's in an old house in which he resided at Chiswick.

I have written elsewhere how the Gosses used to receive their friends on Sunday afternoons. Not many came, but those who did come were generally famous in the world of letters.

Mrs. Moulton, on the other hand, often had a crowd at her receptions. It was in her drawing-room that I first met Sir Frederick Wedmore, Mrs. Alexander the novelist, and Coulson Kernahan, and Theodore Watts. She herself was a charming poet, and liked entertaining poets. I met her first at Sir Bruce and Lady Seton's, at Durham House, which at that time contained the finest collection of modern paintings in London.

It was fortunate that Henley's friends were devoted to him, because he was an invalid and could not get about. He was already a great power in journalism. His paper, called at first *The Scots Observer*, and later on *The National Observer*, had taken the place of the *Saturday Review*, which was not at that time conducted with the ability of the old *Saturday*. The men who gathered round him were very brilliant. I forget what evening of the week it was that he was at home, but whatever evening it was he kept it up very late, with much smoke and consumption of whiskey; and the conversation was always worth listening to. Henley was a magnificent talker, with a fund of curious knowledge, and he had a knack of turning the conversation on to some strange kind of sin or some strange kind of occultism, which was thoroughly

26

THE AUTHOR
Drawn by Yoshio Markino

threshed out by the clever people present. He rather liked morbid subjects.

Edmund Gosse gave me introductions to II. O. Houghton, head of the publishing firm of Houghton, Mifflin & Co., and he and Henley and Katherine Tynan gave me introductions to various authors. But my most useful introduction I had through my chief American friend of that time, Ada Loftus, who made the London correspondents of the *New York Herald* and the *Boston Globe* give full-length announcements of my approaching visit to America—as long as they would give to William Watson now. They labelled me in those announcements the "Australian Poet," and that label stuck to me during the whole of that visit to the United States. They asked Mrs. Loftus, I suppose, what I had done, and she told them that I had written several volumes of verse about Australia. Be that as it may, those friendly announcements resulted in so many hospitalities being offered to us by American authors and literary clubs that we really did not need our introductions, especially in Boston, where Mrs. Moulton was waiting to welcome us, and where I had old schoolfellows—the Peabodys—connected with most of the leading families.

But I did present the introduction to Mr. Houghton—when does an author neglect an introduction to a publisher?—and he showed us innumerable kindnesses all the time we remained in Boston. It was to him that I owed the invitations from Oliver Wendell Holmes and Whittier, and Longfellow's family to visit them in their homes—inestimable opportunities. We spent three months in Boston, seeing all the best of Boston literary society and the University bigwigs at Harvard, and then we went for a month to New York until it was time for the ice-carnival season at Montreal. At New York, with Edmund Clarence Stedman, the first of American critics, as a godfather, the hospitalities of Boston were repeated to us. But this was not our principal visit to New York.

Our first trip to Canada was intensely interesting to us, because there we were in a new world, where the temperature was below zero, and the snow several feet high in the streets, and the ice several feet thick on the great river, up which

ocean liners come from spring to autumn. The ice-palace
was already built, and rose like a mediæval castle of alabaster;
in the centre of the city the habitants were selling their milk
in frozen lumps in the market; all the world wore furs, for
the poorest could buy a skin of some sort made up somehow.
There were still buffalo-skin coats in those days in plenty,
at three pounds apiece, and those who could not afford a fur
cap to their liking, wore a woollen tobogganing tuque, which
could be drawn down over the forehead and the ears, just
as some of the younger women and the children wore their
blanket tobogganing coats.

It was a new world, where nobody skated in the open,
because of the impossibility of keeping the ice free from snow,
and where skating was so universal an accomplishment
that in the rinks people danced on skates as naturally as on
their feet in a ballroom.

One soon took for granted the monstrous cold, learned to
swathe in furs every time one left the house, even if it was
only to go to the post, to wear thin boots, because they were
always covered with " arctics " when one went out, and thin
underclothing because one's furs were so thick out of doors,
and the houses so furiously hot indoors; to have double
windows always closed, and hot air flowing into the room
till the temperature reached 70° and over.

It is no wonder that ice-cream, as they call it, is a feature
at dinner in winter in a Canadian hotel.

Outside, all the land was white, and all the sky was blue.
Wrapped up in furs, people so despised the intense cold that
there was not one closed sleigh—at Montreal in winter all
the cabs were sleighs. By day we sleighed up the mountain
for tobogganing and came back in time for tea-parties; by
night we sleighed to dances or picnics. The merry jingle of
sleigh-bells was never out of one's ears; and everything was
so delightfully simple—it was always beer and not champagne
—and every one took an interest in Australia and Colonial
poetry. The tea-parties were generally impromptus got up
on the telephone. Every one in Montreal had a telephone,
though it was only the beginning of 1889.

Lighthall, the Canadian littérateur, came to call upon us

the very first afternoon that we were in Montreal, and he introduced us to our life-long friends, the Robert Reids, and the George Washington Stephens's. Mrs. Reid and Mrs. Stephens were sisters. Mr. Stephens, the Astor of Montreal, shortly afterwards became Treasurer of the Colony. Lighthall introduced us also to Sir William Van Horne, the President of the great Canadian Pacific Railway, which led to important results. We only stayed in Canada a month then, but that was sufficient to convince me that I did not want to live in a climate where the cold was as dangerous as a tiger. It was brought home to me in an extraordinary way. I was out walking with Mrs. Reid's daughter, coming back from a tea-party one evening. We saw a drunken man lying in the gutter. She said, " We must get a sleigh and take that drunk to the police-station. He will be dead in an hour if he lies there."

When roused, he was sufficiently coherent to tell us where he lived, and we took him home. The cold was so intense that she found one of her ears frost-bitten before she got home; she had gone out in an ordinary hat instead of a fur cap, because it was a tea-party and near home. The unexpected delay in the open air to rouse the man, and driving him home, made her pay the penalty of risking a frost-bite. We knew that it was frost-bitten, because it had turned as white as if it had been powdered. The policeman took up a handful of snow, and rubbed it for her—another act of ordinary good Samaritanism in Canada.

We went straight down from Canada to Washington to see the change of Administration from President Cleveland's regime to President Harrison's. The climatic contrast was strong; Washington was as warm as Rome. Our arctics and furs looked simply idiotic when we arrived in the station.

The change of Administration in the United States is invested with a good deal of magnificence. All the important people in America, who can spare the time, go to Washington for it. There were many functions during our visit. We were President Cleveland's guests at his farewell-party, and went to all the Harrison functions. Mrs. Cleveland had a delightful personality; she was very pretty, very elegant, very gracious, a tall woman, rather suggestive of the beautiful Dowager Lady Dudley, with brilliant dark eyes and a brilliant smile. Cleveland was not a pleasant man to meet. When I knew him he was a very strong man who had become very stout. Everything about him suggested power. His face, in spite of its fleshiness, was very powerful. He had a deliberate, rather ungracious way of speaking, and his silences, accentuated by rather resentful eyes, were worse. But a man who starts to sweep the Augean stable for America needs these qualities; and he undoubtedly improved the tone of the party opposed to him in the State by giving them an opposition which they had to respect. But he had no conscience in foreign politics.

The most interesting house we went to was Colonel John Hay's. Hay was a millionaire twice over, and had been Abraham Lincoln's private secretary. He was one of America's best poets, and no man in the country was more renowned for his personal charm or his lofty character. He was afterwards Secretary of State, and Ambassador to Great Britain, and could have been either then, if President Harrison had been able to overcome Hay's rooted objection to office. And Adalbert Hay, the American Consul-general, who did so much for captive Britons in the Boer War, was his son.

At Hay's house you met alike the most famous politicians, the most famous members of the Diplomatic Corps, and the most famous authors and artists in America. There we met all the most distinguished members, perhaps I might say the leaders, of the Republican Party.

Washington will always be a bright spot in my memory for another thing. Henry Savage Landor, the explorer, was turned out of his room because the whole hotel was wanted for President Harrison's party, and as there was not a room to be had in Washington, he slept for the remainder of the time on a shakedown in my room. Both he and I used to spend a great deal of our time with our next-door neighbour in K Street, General William Tecumseh Sherman, the hero of the famous march through Georgia in the Civil War—a grand old man, with a hard-bitten face, but very human.

I was present at his funeral in New York; thirty thousand veterans—"the Grand Army of the Republic"—marched behind the riderless horse, which bore his jack-boots and his sword.

From Washington we went to New York, and stayed there till the heat drove us back to Canada, where we had an extraordinarily delightful holiday in store for us. Sir William Van Horne had invited us to go as the guests of the Canadian Pacific Railway right over their line from Montreal to Vancouver and back, and as we had a month or more to spare before the time we settled for our journey, we went first of all to the land of Evangeline—Nova Scotia—and afterwards across the Bay of Fundy to the valley of the St. John river in New Brunswick, and thence to Quebec and Montreal, where we were the guests of the Reids, and for a fortnight of the Stephens's, in their summer home on the shores of Lac Eau Clair in the Maskinonge forest, and of Agnes Maule Machar at Gananoque on the Thousand Islands of the St. Lawrence.

This experience of Canadian summer life was an extraordinary education in beauty. A more perfect summer could not be imagined; the sky was always blue, the sun was always vigorous, and there was generally a light breeze. We half lived on the water, since all Canadians near a river or lake have canoes and can manage them with the skill of an Indian. The bathing was enchanting : we could catch a hundredweight of fish sometimes, in that land of many waters. The wild flowers and wild fruits of the meadows and woods were as plentiful as buttercups and daisies in England; it was a land of many forests, many lakes, many rivers; mountains near or distant were always in sight.

Nor was this all. On the lofty shores of the Bay of Fundy and the rock of Quebec, and under the " Royal Mountain " at Montreal there were dear old French houses, built in the days of the Thirteenth or Fourteenth Louis, and most of them intertwined in the romance of Canadian history.

What a lovely and romantic land it was ! And we saw it to perfection, for Bliss Carman and Roberts, two Canadian poets, were our guides everywhere. In all my years in Australia I never had half the enjoyment out of the country-life that I derived from those two or three months of a Canadian summer.

The wonders of our journey had hardly begun, though the first sight of the old fortress of Quebec towering over the St. Lawrence, and of the historic Fields of Abraham, are events never to be forgotten.

Still, we felt that a new era in our lives was beginning on that night in early autumn when we steamed out of the chief station of the world's greatest railway westwards on a journey which would not terminate till we stood on the shores of English Bay, and looked out on to the Pacific Ocean.

We were so anxious to hurry out west to the new land that we only spared ourselves a few days at Toronto to cross Lake Ontario to Niagara, and spend an afternoon and evening with Goldwin Smith and George Taylor Denison. They presented such a contrast—Goldwin Smith, the Cassandra whose voice was always lifted against his country, except when he was among her enemies, and Denison, a descendant of the famous Loyalist, and the leader of Canadian loyalty to England. Denison was the winner of the Emperor of Germany's prize for the best book on Cavalry Tactics.

From Toronto we had not far to go by train before we found ourselves at Lake Huron, and took a steamer of the company, built like a sea-going vessel, to cross those two vast lakes, Huron and Superior, to Port Arthur. They look like seas, and have storms as violent, though they are fresh water, and in Lake Superior, at any rate, you could immerse the whole of the British Islands. From Port Arthur we trained to Winnipeg, the city of the plains, where we only stayed a few days before flying across the prairie—a limitless plain as broken as the Weald of Kent, jewelled with flowers in spring, and with game fleeing to the horizon when cover is short.

After three days of eye-roaming, we woke to find our view barred by the long wall of the Rocky Mountains, like castles of the gods.

At Banff, in the Rocky Mountains, we were to stay to contemplate the finest open mountain scenery conceivable, and at the Glacier House to contemplate a glacier, a forest and a stupendous peak threatening to overwhelm a mountain inn. The scenery between the two was finer than anything in the Apennines, with its torrents dashing between mighty precipices, and its pine forests sweeping like a prairie fire over mountain and valley, and its background of heaven-piercing Alps.

We entered the Glacier House at a dramatic moment, for Jim, the sports' guide from Missouri, had just finished pegging out on the floor of one of the sitting-rooms a trophy of his rifle that took me straight back to the happy hours of my boyhood which I spent with Captain Mayne Reid—the rust-coloured skin of a mighty grizzly bear which had turned the scale at twelve hundredweight. Jim the guide had on a buckskin coat and breeches, much stained with killing or skinning the bear : the spectacle was a most impressive one.

From the glacier we tore down the valleys of the Thompson and the Fraser to Vancouver, then a new wooden town perched on a forest clearing with the tree stumps still scattered about its roads, but one of the great seaports of the world in embryo —Canada's Western Gate, the realisation of the dream of La Salle.

We loved Vancouver, because here we were in a town and country in the making, with a glorious piece of the forest primeval preserved for ever as a national park. For a month we lived there, going every day to see the sun set over the ocean which divided us from the mysterious Orient— thinking over all that we had seen of a country which is like a continent, in that three or four thousand miles' journey on the newly-opened line.

Then one day a little old bull-dog of a Cunarder, in the service of the great railway, ran up the harbour, and moored herself to the wharf beside the railway station. A tall dark officer, whose voice I heard across the telephone a few hours before writing these lines, was leaning over the gunwale. He and our party smiled pleasantly at each other, and he invited us to go on board. The litter of the Orient was about the decks. Chinese seamen and Japanese passengers were talking the pigeon-English of the East to each other. And we felt that here was the opportunity for stretching our hands

D

across to the East.   I accepted the omen, and we booked our passages to Japan—drifting on as we had drifted ever since we landed at Boston a year before.

The stout old *Parthia* was going to lie a week or two in port before she turned her head round for Yokohama and Hong Kong, and we spent most of this time in an excursion across the strait to Victoria, the capital of Vancouver's Island, a little bit of England in the West, with a dockyard still in Imperial hands.

As we returned from Victoria early in November, we met, on the steamer, Admiral Sir Michael Culme-Seymour, who was about to be Commander-in-Chief in the Mediterranean, on his way back from a Big-horn expedition in the North.

" Where are you on your way to ? " he asked me.

" Japan," I replied.

" What now ? " he said; " you must be fond of bad weather."

CHAPTER IV

I GO TO JAPAN

THE Admiral's prognostications were correct. We met such heavy seas passing Cape Flattery that the ship seemed to be trying to turn turtle. We were unable to sit on deck from that day until the day that we sighted Japan, and once we had to heave-to for eighteen hours. The worst of the weather being so terrible was that the Captain was unable to execute the Company's instructions to take us to see the Aleutian Islands, which only whalers know, and drop some stores there for shipwrecked mariners.

But on that December morning, when we found ourselves in smooth water and soft, summery temperature off the flat-topped hills of Japan, surrounded by the billowing sails of countless junks, the very first vessels we had seen since Cape Flattery faded out of sight, we felt rewarded.

The East, the Far East, which I had heard " a-calling " all my life, was right within my grasp. In a few hours' time I should be standing on the shores of fanciful and mysterious Japan, able to remain there as long as I chose, for we had no fixed plans. We were just drifting on—drifting through our lives—drifting across the world. My heart beat high; I might have written nothing but a few books of verse which hardly anybody read, but, at any rate, I had gone half round the world, and if I wished to stay and dream for the rest of my life in the East, who was to say me nay?

Whatever the causes, the effect was to give me the subject for which I had been waiting to make my position as an author. From the day that I published *The Japs at Home*, I shed my label of the " Australian Poet," and became known as the author who has been to Japan.

35

I even enriched the English language with a word—*Japs*. It had long been in use in America, but no one had ventured to put it into a book in England. Some thought it was undignified; some thought that it would incense the Japanese. I not only put it into a book, but on the cover of a book, which has sold a hundred and fifty thousand copies. Only to-day I discovered that Japan's great poet, Yone Noguchi, and the Japanese publicist, T. G. Komai, use it in their books, which are written in English.

I had, in Montreal, bought a No. 1 Kodak—a novelty in those days—and with it I took several hundred photographs in Japan—it was from these that Fenn, the artist, of McClure's Syndicate, afterwards drew his illustrations for my articles, which were reproduced in the earlier editions of the book. The " Kodaks " not only served as the basis of the illustrations, they made a most admirable journal for me to write from.

I commenced Kodaking and taking notes from the hour that we entered the harbour of Yokohama, and kept it up without flagging till the day that we left Yokohama for San Francisco. It was to those snapshots with camera and pencil that my books on Japan owed the lively touches which gave them their popularity.

We were a winter and a spring and a summer in Japan—for all except six weeks which we spent in China. I paid most of my hotel bills in Japan by writing my *Handbook to Japan* for the Club Hotel Company.

In Japan we spent our entire days in sight-seeing. If we were not going over interesting buildings (and I over Yoshi-waras), temples, castles, baths or tea-houses in marvellous gardens—we were wandering about the streets or the country in our *rikishas*, dismounting when there was anything to photograph or examine or purchase. The *rikisha* is a most convenient way of getting about for a person who is making notes, because he can write as he goes along, and pull up as often as he likes when there is anything which needs his attention. Also, your *Jinrikisha* boy, if you choose carefully, speaks enough English to act as an interpreter, and, from having taken foreigners to the sights so often, is usually a tolerably efficient guide. Besides which, it is a novel, pleasant and exciting method of locomotion.

We hired the best two *rikisha* men we could hear of by the week, and never regretted the extravagance. They were always there when we wanted them, and in a very few days grasped exactly what we wished to do and see. One was called Sada and the other Taro.

It was in this way that I acquired my knowledge of the Japan which can be seen on the surface, and which is all that the average foreigner wishes to see, and gave myself one of the three or four subjects with which my name is identified.

We spent the first month in Yokohama, a much-maligned place, for it had in those days an unspoiled native town at the back of the settlement, and its environs were charming, whether one went towards Negishi or towards Ikegami: I found enough to keep me hard at work for a month.

On the last day of the year we went to Tokyo. We had a reason for that; we wished to see the great fair in the Ginza, which is one of the most typical sights of Japan. Savage Landor, who had been in Tokyo for some time, wrote that we must on no account miss it, and he took rooms for us in the Tokyo hotel—which the Japanese called *Yadoya*, " the hotel."

The Tokyo hotel was an experience : it had originally been the *Yashiki* or town-house of a feudal prince, in the days when the Shogun reigned at Tokyo. It had a moat (into which Miss Lorimer, who accompanied us on all our travels, fell on the first night we were there, but which fortunately contained more mud than water), and stood in an angle of the outer works of the castle.

Just below it, small craft made a port of the outer moat of the castle : in its courtyard carpenters were using up the large amount of waste space which there is in a *Yashiki* by nailing fresh rooms on to the Daimio's house, to make the hotel larger. It could not be called anything but nailing on, because it was made of wood and paper, and was not properly dovetailed into the existing building, but simply tacked on. We learnt many upside-down notions by watch-

ing the builders and carpenters, who did most things inside-
out or upside-down, according to our notions. Also the
Japanese manager, the Abè San who was murdered a few
months ago, borrowed my clothes to have them copied by
a Japanese tailor, and the waiters wore their European
clothes over their native dress, and wriggled out of them
behind a screen as soon as a meal was over. If you called
them at such a moment, whatever your sex, they might come
forward with their trousers half on and half off. The Japanese
have their own ideas of conventions between the sexes.

Wandering through that fair at the Ginza took one into
the very heart of Japan : it is held to enable people to
settle their debts before New Year's Day.

Apart from the obituary parks of Shiba and Ueno, Tokyo
is not reckoned rich in temples, though it has a few very
famous temples in the suburbs, and more than a few within
a short excursionary distance. But Shiba and Ueno—and
especially the former—present an epitome of Japanese life,
art, scenery and history.

It is difficult to imagine anything more beautiful than
Shiba, though the Japanese have a proverb that you must
not call anything beautiful till you have seen Nikko. The
fir woods in which it stands are on a low ridge commanding
an exquisitive view of the Gulf of Tokyo, and in this wood
are embosomed the mausolea of most of the earlier Shoguns
of the Tokugawa House, which came to an end this winter
with the death of the abdicated Shogun. Each mausoleum
has a beautiful temple beside the tomb. The presence of so
many temples has led the Japanese to exhaust their landscape art on Shiba with lake and cherry-grove and crypto-
meria. Such natives as do not go there for religion are
attracted by the pleasure city, with its famous tea-houses,
like the Maple Club, its shows, and, above all, by its dancing.
Here you may see the *No*-dance, the *Kagura*-dance, and some
of the best Geishas.

But the chief charm of Shiba to me was its absolute
Orientalness compared to the rest of Tokyo.

No sooner are you inside the great red gateway of the
temples than you are in the world of fairy-tales. For temple

after temple opens up before you, low fantastic structures, on which Oriental imagination has run riot in colour and form. You are bewildered by the innumerable courtyards of stone lanterns, the paraphernalia of drum-tower and bell-tower, fountain and dancing-stage, which surround them. You are sobered by the dark groves between the temples, which contain the tombs.

Temple and tomb are thronged by streams of dignified natives, some come to worship and some to see the sights. Here you will find a service going on, with white-robed priests kneeling on the mirrored floor of black lacquer, for which you have to remove your boots. Outside the actual temples the shows are in full blast, and picnicking proceeds everywhere. All the Japanese are in their native dress. Gay little musumes and gorgeous geishas flutter before you. The grand tea-houses offer fresh visions of the Orient with their Geisha dances and their fantastic gardens.

Ueno has the added charm of a large lake, covered with lotus-blossoms in summer.

At no great distance from Shiba is the Shinagawa Yoshiwara, which, for fantastic beauty, surpasses anything in Japan. With these and the water life of the Nihombashi, and the life of the poor going on all day in the streets—for the poor Japanese takes the front off his house all through the day to air it—I should have found good occupation for my notebook and camera for years.

If we had not been urged by other foreigners, I do not know when we should have left Tokyo. And we saw little enough of them except at meal-times, or when we went to the Frasers (Hugh Fraser was British Minister of Tokyo, and husband of the well-known author, Mrs. Hugh Fraser, Marion Crawford's sister), or the Napiers. The Master of Napier, the Lord Napier and Ettrick, just dead, was his First Secretary. But at meal-times they talked so much of Easter at Miyanoshita, and the cherry-blossom festival at Kyoto, and the annual festival at Nikko, and the Great Buddha at Kamakura, and the sacred shrines of Ise, that we fortunately felt obliged to visit them.

Miyanoshita, the favourite holiday-resort of the Europeans

in Japan, is high up in the mountains. The valley on the right of the long ridge which leads up to it in spring is ablaze with azaleas and flowering trees. It, itself, is perched on a mountain-side, above a densely-wooded valley. Exquisite walks can be taken from it, such as the trip to Hakone, the beautiful village which stands on the blue lake at the foot of Fujiyama, in which the immortal grace of the great mountain is reflected whenever the sun or moon is above the horizon. Miyanoshita is equally famous for its mountain air and its mountain baths. The boiling water, highly impregnated with sulphur, is brought down in bamboo pipes from the bosom of the mountain to deep wooden baths sunk in the floor of the hotel bathing-house. Life here is one long picnic : the energetic take walks, the lazy are carried in chairs over the hills : people fly here for week-ends in spring, and from the heat and damp of the summer.

Its great rival is Nikko, another mountain village, embosomed in shady groves, with woods full of wild hydrangeas. In June Nikko is crowded for the festival of Toshogu, the deified founder of the dynasty of Shoguns, which was ended by the revolution of 1868—the principal festival of Japan, inaugurated with the grandest procession to be seen nowadays, in which all who take part in it wear the ceremonial dresses of three hundred years ago.

Nikko has the two most beautiful temples in the magic land—those of Iyeyasu, the founder of the Tokugawa dynasty, and his grandson, Iyemitsu. Here you see the most perfect lacquer and carving in all Japan. And their courtyards are exquisitely terraced on the mountain-side. Here, too, besides these and other glorious temples, there are the added charms of scenery, a foaming sky-blue river, running beneath the sacred scarlet bridge, and between the avenue of Buddhas, commons of scarlet azalea, and thickets of wild wistaria.

Having seen Nikko, the sacred city of the Shoguns, one must needs see Kyoto, the city of the Mikados, and Nara.

For seven centuries prior to the revolution in our own day, Kyoto was the capital of the Mikados. Here they lived like gods behind a veil, only penetrated by the hierarchy :

they never left the palace gates except in a closed palanquin :
they added little but tombs to the city, and their tombs
were never shown. But the Shoguns, who ruled in their
name, and others great in the land, adorned Kyoto with some
of the greatest and most interesting temples in Japan,
such as the temples of the Gold and Silver Pavilions, the
two Hongwanji temples, the temple of the Thirty-Three
Thousand Images, and the chief temple of Inari the Goddess
of Rice. And it being the ancient capital, we found the city
full of old prints and curios, and the old-fashioned pleasure
resorts of Japan.

Kyoto was a city of the pleasure-seeker of old time, as
capitals are wont to be. It has wonderful tea-houses in the
city; its temple grounds are like permanent fairs; and within
a *rikisha* drive is Lake Biwa, one of the most exquisite lakes
in the world, whose shores exhibit the *chefs d'œuvres* of
the Japanese landscape-creator. Nothing could be more
exquisite than the temple grounds on the shores of Lake
Biwa.

Of the many old-time festivals of Kyoto, the most famous
survival is the Miyako-odori, or cherry-blossom festival,
held every year, when visitors flock to Kyoto to see the
cherry-groves in full blossom. The feature of the festival
is a wonderful ballet, for which the best dancers in Japan
gather in Kyoto. Even the Duke and Duchess of Connaught
came to Kyoto for it, when they were in Japan. We stayed
for a long time at Yaami's when they were there, and when
the Duke learned from Colonel Cavaye, his private secretary,
that I was a journalist, he gave me permission to accompany
his party to any function or expedition which I wished to
describe. The most interesting of them was the shooting
of the rapids of the Katsuragawa, some miles from Kyoto,
where thirteen miles of cataracts are negotiated in huge
punts, built of springy boards. As we were buffeting down
the rapids, the Duke told me that our present King, then
Prince George of Wales, had said that shooting those rapids,
and the baths of Miyanoshita, where you have natural hot
water in wooden boxes sunk in the floor, were the two best
things in the world.

In Kyoto, an antique city on a broad plain, embosomed in hills, capped by temples, one has the very essence of old Japan. We stayed there a long time, absorbing an atmosphere which may soon pass away, never to return.

Within a day's *rikisha* drive of Kyoto is Nara, with its thousand-year-old treasury of the most notable possessions of the Mikados, and its glorious temples, and its sacred deer-park, and its acres of scarlet azalea thickets.

We visited all; we visited the two great cities of Osaka and Nagoya, with their magnificent castles, and Kamakura, with its gigantic Buddha and its ancient monasteries. We visited all the most famous cities and points of scenery in Japan; and the pleasure of our visit was heightened by our going away to China for six weeks in the middle of it, because when we came back our eyes were far keener to observe and to appreciate, while we had the knowledge acquired in our former visit to guide us.

We were truly sorry to leave Japan. I should be quite content to be living there still; but if we had remained there, Japan would not have taken its part in my development as a writer, for though I should doubtless have compiled a book or books about Japan, they would have been sent home as the productions of an amateur, and very likely have had such difficulty in finding a publisher that they would have been brought out in some hole-and-corner way, instead of my selling *The Japs at Home* in the open market, and thereby laying the foundation of my career as a travel-book writer.

Japan supplied me with the material for several books, not counting the handbook which I wrote for the Club Hotel—*A Japanese Marriage*, next in point of sales to *The Japs at Home*; *Queer Things About Japan*, which sold best of all my books in guinea form; *More Queer Things About Japan*, which I wrote with Norma Lorimer; *When We Were Lovers in Japan*, a novel which was originally published under the title of *Playing the Game*; and *Pictures of Japan*; while I have written countless articles and short stories about the country.

I had almost forgotten that I had a book—my *Lester the Loyalist*—published in Japan. Though it only contained about twenty pages, it took two months to print. How the result gratified me, I wrote in *The Japs at Home*.

" I forgot all the delays when I saw the printed pages, they were so beautiful, and really, considering that Mr. Mayeda was the only man in the establishment who could read a word of English, the printing was exceedingly correct. The blocks had turned out a complete success, though, of course, the proofs of the covers did not look as well as they would when mounted and crêped.

" The Japanese have a process by which they can make paper crêpe book-covers as stiff as buckram.

" ' Well, Mr. Mayeda, how did your little boy like the stamp-book you mended up for him so beautifully? ' I asked one day.

" ' Ah ! it is very sad; he has gone to hell. But the little boy, he has loved the stamp-book so that he has taken it to hell with him. It is on his *grave*, do you call it? '

" Mr. Mayeda was thinking of what the missionaries had told him when he was learning English.

" A few weeks more passed. Mr. Mayeda brought us the perfect book. He was so flushed and tearful that I poured him a couple of bumpers of vermouth, which he drank off with the excitement of an unemployed workman in England when he makes a trifle by chance, and spends it right off on his beloved gin.

" ' Is anything the matter, Mr. Mayeda? ' I asked.

" ' It is so sad. My other little boy has gone to hell, too. And I am so poor, and I have to keep my wife's uncle, and my father is very silly, and so I get drunk every night.'

" The books he had brought were exquisite. The printing was really very correct, and the effect of the long hexameter lines, in the handsome small pica type, on the oblong Japanese double leaf of silky ivory-tinted paper, every page flowered with maple-leaves in delicate pearl-grey under the type, was as lovely as it was unique.

" The block printings on every single leaf were done by hand—the leaf being laid over the block, and rubbed into it by a queer palm-leaf-pad burnisher.

" The covers were marvels of beauty, made of steel-grey

paper crêpe, ornamented, the back one with three little
sere and curled-up maple leaves drifting before the wind,
and the front one with a spray of maple leaves in all their
autumn glory and variety of tints, reproduced to the life.

" Across the right-hand end of the sprig was pasted a long
white silk label in the Japanese style. The good taste, the
elegance, the colours of this cover, fairly amazed me."

Our visit to China was taken at the instigation of friends
in Japan, who made an annual trip to the Hong Kong races.
I cannot say that it interested me as much as Japan ; but
we only had time to visit Hong Kong, Shanghai, Canton and
Macao, and of these, Canton alone was absolutely Chinese.
Canton is as typical a Chinese city as one could desire—
supreme in commerce, a hot-bed of Chinese aspirations.
But it is very poorly off for fine old buildings ; it is more
interesting for its huge water population, living in long
streets of boats, and for the wonderful gardens of some of
its merchants.

Macao is chiefly interesting as a very ancient outpost of
Europe in the East, old enough for Camoens to have lived
and written his immortal Lusiad there in the sixteenth
century. It has little to call for the attention of the stranger,
except nice old gardens with huge banyan-trees, and gambling
hells, where you learn to play *Fan-tan*. It only flourishes
as an Alsatia for rogues outside of British and Chinese
jurisdiction.

Shanghai is a fine European town, with luxuries and
conveniences, for which Hong-Kongers sigh, and a most
picturesque walled native town, which contains one of the
most beautiful tea-houses in the East.

Hong Kong is a gay city, because it is so full of British
naval and military officers. It is also rather a beautiful
place, having a mountain right over the town, which is the
sanatorium and summer-resort. I met many old schoolfellows there, who took care that invitations should be sent
to us for all the Service festivities, which are so thick at
Race-time. And they also told me what to see in Hong
Kong and Canton and Macao.

But, knowing that I was only to be in China for a month

and a half, I made no effort to ground myself in knowledge of everyday China, but gave myself up to enjoying the gaieties and tropical luxuries.

China thus had no effect on my literary development. Our stay there was a mere holiday, at which I had a fresh and exhaustive round of military and naval festivities.

The island of Hong Kong is not a good place for studying the Chinaman, except as an employé of the Englishman.

On our return from China to Japan we were fascinated by the almost tropical beauty of the Japanese summer. There was also a good deal of British gaiety, for the Fleet had moved just before us from China to Japan.

CHAPTER V

BACK TO CANADA AND THE UNITED STATES

THE Pacific as we crossed it on our return from Japan to America was very different to the Pacific of our outward journey. Instead of being on a small ship, so buffeted by the seas that we could not remain on deck, with hardly another white passenger on board except missionaries, we were on a large ship—the finest which crossed the Pacific in those days—full of " Society " people returning from the East, and the sea was like the traditional mill-pond.

We landed at San Francisco and stayed a week at the Palace to see something of life in the Californian capital. It struck me as very like life in Australia, especially in the character of the buildings and the appearance of the people. But the cold winds of the San Francisco summer have no parallel in Australia.

The chief effect of my visit to California in the development of my writing was that, receiving a contract to write a number of articles for the *San Francisco Chronicle*, my first prose writing had to be lively enough to satisfy the lively Californian audience. This was a good training.

From San Francisco we went up the Pacific coast to Vancouver, with good opportunities for learning the humours and vulgarities of Western America.

The tail-end of summer and the autumn we spent in working our way back from Vancouver to Montreal, breaking our journey wherever we felt inclined to try the joys of wild life in Canada—at the head waters of the Fraser, the Sicamous lakes in the Kootenay country, various spots on Lake Nepigon and the wild North shore of Lake Superior, Lake Nipissing, the Lake of the Woods, Trout Lake, and so on, besides the chief towns like Winnipeg, and the regular tourist stopping-places at Banff and the Glacier House. At some places we had the opportunity of watching the life of the Siwashes, or Coast Indians, of Esquimaux blood, who live chiefly by catching and drying the salmon which we saw coming up the Fraser like a river of fish in a river of water. At others we saw the lordly Red Indian—Stony or Blood or Blackfoot—and on the Rainy Lake we saw two thousand Ojibways on the war-path—all cartridge-belts and feathers—camped on the outskirts of a Canadian town (without inflicting the smallest scare on the inhabitants), while they were waiting to see if they should have to go and support the Ojibways across the border in their war upon a Baltimore Company, which had infringed their rights.

The Indians, in their shrewd way, first tried their luck in the United States Courts, who decided in their favour, so war was not declared.

At Sicamous we saw eighty fresh skins of black bears, who had been slaughtered while they were feeding on the salmon stranded in shallow water, owing to the failure of the berry crop. In their anxiety to spawn in shallow water, the salmon crush their way up into tiny brooks and ponds where the bears can catch them easily, and the farmers sweep them out of the water with branches.

At the Glacier House, Jim the guide's slaying of the great grizzly bear, when we were there before, inflamed my imagination. I cultivated Jim. I climbed the great Assulkan Glacier with him after the first fall of autumn snow, and made a vow about glaciers which I have religiously kept; and having a Winchester sporting rifle with me, I went out with him to try and get a shot at a grizzly, whose track he had seen. But we saw no more of that bear, which was, perhaps, fortunate for me, for though I had won many prizes at rifle-shooting, I had not been brought face to face with any dangerous game, and a grizzly decidedly falls into that category.

We had splendid fishing all the way across, and delightful camping out; and altogether had an experience of outdoor life in Western Canada, which is very unspoiled and wild—

a snakeless Eden, that certainly told in my development as a writer.

At last the autumn came to an end. We felt the first breath of winter standing by the river side, where Tom Moore wrote his famous *Canadian Boat Song*—the woods were a glory of crimson and gold.

We said good-bye to Canada and turned our footsteps to New York. There we met a warm-hearted American welcome. Our numerous friends seemed to find an almost personal gratification in the fact that we had been to the Far North West and to the Far East, to the Pacific Coast and to Japan and China.

I was now no longer exclusively the " Australian Poet," I was a sort of mild explorer, and people talked Japan to me whenever they were not talking about themselves. There was a good deal of this to do, because I had a commission from Griffith, Farran & Co. to compile a book on the younger American Poets, and nearly every one I met seemed to be a poet.

I was sitting next to H. M. Alden, the editor of *Harper's Magazine*, one night at dinner. Suddenly he pulled out his watch. " It is now nine o'clock," he said; " at this moment there are a hundred thousand people in America writing poetry, and most of them will send it to me."

One of them was the English curate of the most fashionable church in New York, and he was in a quandary. He wished to be in the book, but he had heard that there was to be a biography of each poet, giving his date of birth, parentage, career, etc. He did not wish his date of birth to be known— he thought that it would interfere with his prospects as a lady-killer. " Was it compulsory for him to say how old he was? " he whined.

" You need not tell the truth about it," I suggested.

In the compilation of that book I saw a great deal of human nature, because I met the poets, whereas in *Australian Poets*, which I edited simultaneously, I had to do my work entirely by correspondence.

We spent a delightful winter and spring in New York, because we had Miss Lorimer's beautiful sister, Mrs. Hay-

Chapman, one of the finest amateur pianists I ever heard, staying with us all the time, so that we had a feast of music, and as I was doing literary and dramatic criticisms for the *Dominion Illustrated*, the leading weekly of Canada, we had plenty of new books and theatre tickets. This, and the articles on Japan I was writing for the American Press and McClure's Syndicate, kept me quite busy.

My sojourn in America had a most important influence on my literary career, because it taught me my trade as a journalist. Needing money, and having no connections, I had to make my way as a journalistic free lance in the open market, and I succeeded in making a fair income out of it.

But I never tried to get a publisher (though one came to me), for the simple reason that I never contemplated entering the lists as a prose-writer. A large and well-known firm bought editions in sheets of my various volumes of verse, which surprised me very much, till they went bankrupt shortly afterwards without paying for them. The purchase was not of sufficient magnitude to be the cause of the bankruptcy, as the ill-natured might suggest.

I have often regretted that I did not form a close personal connection with a single publishing house over there, instead of having each individual book, as it was ready, sold to whichever publisher the agent happens to do business with.

Also I blame myself for not learning the art of pleasing the American novel-reader. Their book market is a much more valuable one than ours, and unfortunately the worst fault a novel can have in their eyes is its being " too British." A book like *The Tragedy of the Pyramids* is anathema to them.

The only prose book I published during my sojourn in America was *The Art of Travel*, for which the publisher, a Greek, forgot to pay me a single penny of what he contracted. I afterwards turned into it an advertisement for the North German Lloyd, and got something, about fifty pounds, I think, out of them.

I must not take leave of America without recording my impressions of the other American cities which I visited besides New York and Boston.

E

San Francisco, Seattle, Tacoma and other western towns were spoiled for me, because the working-classes in them were so " swollen-headed " and rude that any educated or gently-born person felt like a victim of the French Revolution as he was making his way to the scaffold, surrounded by wild mobs thirsting for his blood. The lower classes in the cities of the Pacific Coast insult you to show that they are your equals. And except as manual labourers, they never could be anybody's equals, because God created them so common. It is these people and the unscrupulous speculators who make money. The decent people get ground between the upper and lower grindstone in a land where living costs out of all proportion to the rewards of education.

We spent some time also in Washington, which is their exact converse. Washington has its vulgar rich, who go there to make a " season " of it, and its venal and lobbying politicians who make the vast temple, which acts as the American Capitol, a den of thieves, but they do not take the first place in the public eye. The really fine elements in the American nation are well represented at Washington, and form a natural Court, in which the President may or may not be prominent. That depends on whether he is fit to be their leader. It is they, and not the President, who keep up the traditions of their country before the eyes of the various Embassies. Such a man was Colonel John Hay. Their presence helps to make Washington a delightful city.

The American Government is extremely polite and hospitable to visiting authors. I was such a small author in those days that I felt positively embarrassed when, a few hours after our arrival in Washington, President Cleveland's private secretary, Colonel Dan Lamont, called with an invitation for us to go to supper with the President and Mrs. Cleveland and be present at the last reception they gave before they left the White House.

And when President Harrison came into office, Mr. Blaine, the new Secretary of State, invited us to share his private box to witness the inaugural procession.

These were civilities beyond one's dreams, and added to them were the never-ceasing hospitalities at houses like John

ISRAEL ZANGWILL
Drawn by Yoshio Markino

Hay's, and the Judges', and the delightful receptions at which one met the great scientists connected with the Smithsonian Institute, and the chief authors and editors congregated at Washington.

To witness a change of Administration at Washington and partake in its hospitalities is extraordinarily stimulating and interesting. It was a privilege far beyond my deserts to meet the great public men of America.

CHAPTER VI

LITERARY AT-HOMES AND LITERARY CLUBS

THE literary at-home is an American institution. It may not have been invented there, but it has certainly flowered there. I did not visualise the literary at-home at all until I attended the Sunday evenings of my dear old friend, Louise Chandler Moulton, the author of *Swallow Flights*, at Boston. Her house was the centre of literary society there. She knew every one who was worth knowing in literary circles in England and America, and she had a passion for collecting them on Sunday nights.

There I learnt the essential simplicity and common-sensibleness of American entertainments. No one went for the refreshments; there were none except coffee and various kinds of cakes. It was, in fact, afternoon tea, with coffee instead of the drink which cheers without inebriating, held at 9 p.m. instead of 5. Her evenings were crowded.

When I went to New York I found the New York people collected every Sunday night in the hospitable home of Edmund Clarence Stedman, the chief literary biographer of his day. Laurence Hutton, too, the author of *Literary Landmarks in London*, and editor of certain pages of *Harper's Magazine*, had a few people on Sunday nights. There was always the same simplicity about eating and drinking, and the same absence of any entertainment, except being introduced to American celebrities, or occasionally listening spellbound while one of them told a humorous story in the inimitable American way.

Charles de Kay, the chief art critic in New York of that day, was one of the few people who gave big afternoon teas in the English style. De Kay belonged to one of the oldest literary families in New York, for he was the grandson of Joseph Rodman Drake.

These were the private literary at-homes. They yielded in importance to the storytellers' nights of the various clubs, generally Saturday nights. Sometimes there was a large house dinner at the Club, sometimes nothing happened until the reception began, about nine, but in any case, the procedure was the same. First of all, the most brilliant men of the day told anecdotes, and then the assemblage broke up into small groups, when the introduction of strangers to each other was the feature of the evening. It was in this way that I came to know nearly every important American writer of that day. Sometimes two good anecdote-tellers would be put up to banter each other, and the encounters would be very witty. I remember one encounter in particular between a Bostonian and a professor of the University of Chicago. The professor alluded most feelingly to the departed glories of Boston—Boston which considered itself the hub of the universe—and dilated upon the new era which was dawning for Chicago. The Bostonian got up and agreed with every word he said.

" I am surprised at my friend's agreeing with this," said the professor.

" Not at all," said the Bostonian. " I speak as one of the owners of Chicago."

The audience rocked with laughter, recalling the fact that this Bostonian had turned a respectable fortune into millions by buying up a large area in Chicago when it was ruined by the great fire.

At another such evening Mark Twain said the circumstance which gave him the greatest satisfaction in his life was the fact that Darwin, for a year before his death, read nothing but his works. Darwin's doctors, he added, had warned him that he would get softening of the brain if he read anything but absolute drivel.

Sometimes there were discussions at these evenings, and one of them was about the merits of a certain Society poetess, whose poems enjoyed an unbounded sale without meeting with the approbation of the critics. " Do you not admit," asked one of the lady's admirers of the editor of the *Century Magazine,* " that Miss Van —— is the poetess of passion ? "

" Yes," said the editor, " Miss Van —— is the poetess of passion—of boarding-house passion."

I never came away from one of these evenings without feeling that I had been partaking of intellectual champagne.

When I was in America Eugene Field edited one of the great Chicago dailies, and was the principal author of the West. My first meeting with him was a characteristic one. I was at an at-home in New York, talking to the editress of a fashion paper, who had also written books of twaddly gush about travel. The hostess brought up Field, and introduced him to the editress.

" Very glad to meet you, ma'am," he said. " I think I may say that I have read all your books with the greatest interest."

" Are you a writer, Mr. Field ? " she asked. " I am sorry to say that I have never heard of you."

" Nor I you, ma'am; but you might have pretended, same as I did."

There used to be very large at-homes every Sunday night at the flat of a wealthy old lady who owned an important newspaper. Her guests were mostly authors and artists, and she hardly knew any of them by sight, and never gave any of them commissions to work for her paper. Sometimes she did not even put in an appearance at her at-homes, which went on just the same, as if she had been there. Her guests came to meet each other, not her. She was not at all literary; her only ambition was like Queen Elizabeth's—to be taken for a young and beautiful woman. She was no longer either, but she dressed the part. Young America used openly to make fun of her weakness on these occasions, and I well remember the editor of *Puck* (a New York comic paper), to whom she was showing a beautiful copy of Canova's nude statue of Napoleon's sister, Pauline Borghese, gravely pretending that he thought it was a statue of herself, and complimenting her on the likeness which the sculptor had achieved. His impudence carried him through; his delighted hostess believed that he believed it, and explained, with genuine colour coming into her rouged cheeks, that in spite of the likeness, it was not her, but " Princess Pauline."

As the refreshments at this house were on a very liberal scale, it was a good place to meet the section of the Press which is not satisfied with a mere feast of reason and flow of soul.   One also met fame-hunters, like the sculptor whom I will call Vermont, who came to cultivate the Press.   I was introduced to him at this house, and I hoped that I should never see him again, because he was such a colossal egotist. One day, a few years afterwards, to my dismay, I met him in Fleet Street.   I said, " How do you do, Mr. Vermont ? "

He said at once, " Can you do something for me ? " which was his invariable habit.

I said " yes " cheerfully, meaning to wriggle out of it, for I did not want to do it.   I was under no obligation to him, because I had been careful not to give him the opportunity of offering me any hospitalities while I was over there.   He said, " I have never been in England before.   Can you tell me if I ought to use a letter-writer ? "

I said, " I think so ; what is it—a new kind of type-writer ? "

He said, " No, it is a book which tells you the proper ways for writing letters."

Remembering that the last letter I had received from him began, " Mr. Douglas Sladen, Esq., Dear Sir," I said I thought he ought, and as we were in Fleet Street, recommended him to go to Hatchard's in Piccadilly.   I was interested to know the kind of impression he would make on Arthur Humphreys, to whom I sent him with my card.   I carefully gave him a card without an address in the hope that I should not see him any more.   But he got my address from Humphreys, and came to see me the next day.   It appeared that he had brought a large group of statuary with him, which he wished to present to the City of London.   Could I help him in this? he wished to know.   I said yes.   I gave him an introduction to the Lord Mayor, and to the editor of the *Illustrated London News,* to both of whom I was a total stranger.   He went away very pleased with himself.   The next time I met him

was at the Lord Mayor's Day banquet at the Mansion House.
I asked him how he had got on, and he said that he owed
more to me than any one he had ever met.   The Lord Mayor
had accepted the sculpture, and given orders for it to be
erected somewhere in the Guildhall Library until its final
position could be decided on, and the editor of the *Illustrated
London News* was going to give the front page of his next
number to a reproduction of the immortal work.   After this
I met him at every important function to which I received
an invitation.

CHAPTER VII

WE START OUR LITERARY AT-HOMES IN LONDON

I was well known at authors' clubs and authors' receptions long before I was known as an author. In fact, I doubt if many of those who swarmed to our at-homes ever thought of me seriously as an author, or even realised that I wrote. They knew of me as the friend of authors, artists, and actors, and people who were merely charming, and well enough off to entertain, and enjoyed meeting the celebrities of Bohemia. They credited me with a certain capacity as a host, who always introduced the right people to each other.

I had graduated in a good school for entertaining at Boston and New York, where the hostess takes care that each of her guests before they leave shall have been introduced to the persons most worth meeting. If Oliver Wendell Holmes was in the room at Boston or the American Cambridge, every guest was presented to him. At a large literary at-home in New York you were sure to have been introduced to a Mark Twain, or a Howells, or a Stockton before you left. Americans make a point of having a guest of honour at an at-home, and I tried to keep this up as a feature of our at-homes at Addison Mansions.

It was some time before we were able to start our Bohemian at-homes in London, because when we arrived we had hardly a single acquaintance in Bohemia, except Gleeson White, and *his* author, artist and actor friends, like ours, were all in America. Like ourselves, he had been three years absent from England.

The hundreds of English and American authors, artists and actors who knew us at 32, Addison Mansions will recollect chiefly a very narrow hall hung with autographed portraits of celebrities, 'a room whose woodwork and draperies suggested one of the old Mameluke houses at Cairo, a room whose walls were covered with Japanese curios, and two other rooms, one of which was lined to the height of several feet from the ground with ingeniously-fitted-in book-cases, and the other was a bedroom in disguise. These and a ten by seven telephone room, likewise lined with book-shelves, which only had enough chairs for a *tête-à-tête*, formed the suite in which we held the weekly receptions in the American style at which so many people, now famous, used to meet every Friday night, regaled only with cigarettes, whiskeys-and-sodas, claret cup, bottled ale and sandwiches.

There must have been some attractions about them when actors like the Grossmiths, and authors like Anthony Hope, and half-a-dozen R.A.s used to find their way out to these wilds of West Kensington Friday after Friday towards midnight. Perhaps it was that we never had any entertainment when we could help it, and friends were able to make our flat a rendezvous where they could be secure of having conversations uninterrupted by music, and to which they could bring a stranger whom they wished to introduce into Bohemia.

Occasionally a stranger so introduced, who happened to be a famous reciter, felt constrained, as a matter of returning hospitality, to insist on reciting for us. But in the main, as a large number of our guests were performers, they were glad that no performances were allowed, for if they had had to listen to other people, they would have felt bound, as a matter of professional etiquette, to perform themselves. If there are performances and you are a performer, it is a reproach not to be asked to perform.

It was Kernahan who first took us to the Idler Teas.

With Sir Walter Besant I had been in correspondence before I left England, and on my return he wrote asking me to join the Authors' Club, with which my name was so intimately associated for many years. But I did not meet so many Bohemians there as I did at the Idler Teas and the dinners of the Vagabonds Club, of which I became a member because the circle of brilliant young authors whom Jerome and Barr had enlisted for the *Idler Magazine* were many of them " Vagabonds."

At the Idlers and Vagabonds I met most of the rising authors, and when the American rush to London commenced, I took many distinguished Americans to the Idler Teas, and to the receptions of people whom we met there. In this way we soon had a very large acquaintance in Bohemia, eager to meet our American friends, when we commenced our at-homes on a modest scale to give our literary acquaintances from the opposite sides of the Atlantic the opportunity of meeting each other.

I met many authors as well as actors at the Garrick and the Savage—in addition to the authors I met at the Authors' Club and the Savile, and as I was at that time a member of the Arts, and the Hogarth, a very lively place, I met a great many artists. Of black-and-white artists, at any rate, who patronised the latter, I soon knew quite a number—Phil May, Bernard Partridge, Dudley Hardy, Reginald Cleaver, Ralph Cleaver, Hal Hurst, Melton Prior, Seppings Wright, Holland Tringham, Paxton, James Greig, John Gulich, Louis Baumer, F. H. Townsend, Fred Pegram, Chantrey Corbould, Frank Richards, Bernard Gribble, Will Rothenstein, Aubrey Beardsley, Willson, Starr Wood and Linley Samborne.

At the same time we saw a good deal of such well-known painters as David Murray, R.A.; Solomon J. Solomon, R.A.; Arthur Hacker, R.A.; J. J. Shannon, R.A.; Walter Crane; Llewellyn, the P.R.I.; Sir James Linton, P.R.I.; G. A. Storey, A.R.A.; Sir Alfred East, R.A.; R. W. Allan; J. H. Lorimer, R.S.A.; J. Lavery; Herbert Schmalz; Hugh de Trafford Glazebrook; Yeend King; William Yeames, R.A., who married my cousin, Annie Wynfield; and Alfred Parsons, A.R.A.

Various ladies' clubs, and clubs to which both sexes were admitted, contributed not a little to the extraordinary amount of social intercourse which then was a feature of Bohemia. The Pioneer Club, the Writers' Club, and the Women Journalists' were, frankly, associations of working women. And there were many members interested in literature in the Albemarle and the Sesame, ladies' clubs which admitted men as guests. Once a week at the Writers' Club, and very often at the Pioneer, they had large gatherings at which literary " shop " filled the air.

Thus in a short time we came to know hundreds of authors and artists (male and female), actors and actresses, and kept open house for them every Friday night.

The Pioneer, the forerunner of the Lyceum, was a great institution in those days. Rich women, interested in woman's work, established it and bore some of its expense for the benefit of women workers. It had a fair sprinkling of well-known authoresses, and the prominent women in all sorts of movements. Its afternoon and evening receptions—the latter generally for lectures—were most interesting affairs. There was no suffragist movement in those days to over-shadow everything else. Women's Rights were a joke like " bloomers," which are now suggestive of something very different.

The Writers' Club was more frankly literary, more frankly " shop." You met non-writing workers too in those base-ment premises in Norfolk Street, which have seen the birth of so many reputations. I remember meeting there a suffragist whose name is known all over the world now, but when I was introduced to her it was only known to her fellow-workers. She asked me what I thought of the suffragists. Not knowing who she was, and not having thought anything about them, I replied, " Oh, I've nothing against them except their portraits in the halfpenny papers ! " It made her my friend, for she had suffered from rapid newspaper reproduction that very morning.

I always enjoyed those gatherings of women workers very much, though many of them had ideas for the betterment of England which involved the destruction of all I cherished most, and some were terrifying in their earnestness like the she-Apostle of antivivisection, who had a hydrophobic glitter in her eye, which reminded me of a blue-eyed collie I once had, but had to give away because it bit.

This lady was the cause of my gradually dropping away from those pleasant receptions. It was no good going to them because no sooner had I been introduced to anybody interesting, than she came up and wanted me to start enlisting them for the cause, though I knew that I should never employ an antivivisectionist doctor in the case of a serious illness

any more than I should employ a homœopathist. She afterwards became an *advocatus diaboli*—an apologist for the
outrages of the Militants, which she said were necessary to
draw attention to the wrongs of women.

In after days, when I had written a novel which became
very popular (*A Japanese Marriage*), I was asked to lecture
before the Pioneer Club on some subject connected with the
book. Noticing that their lectures were generally rather of
an abstract nature, and not having at all an abstract mind
myself, I chose for my subject, " The Immorality of Self-
Sacrifice." The book was largely taken up with the un-
happiness inflicted on the hero and the heroine because she
was a good churchwoman, and his deceased wife's sister,
and would not marry him, though she was desperately in
love with him, until long afterwards she was disgusted with
the narrow-mindedness of a clergyman cousin.

I gave that lecture in the innocence of my heart. I
imagined that the Club would be so anxious to pioneer for
the Deceased Wife's Sister Bill, that I should carry the
audience with me. I made the mistake of being too abstract.
If I had contented myself with being "agin' the Government " and delivered a technical diatribe in favour of the
Bill, ladies with a mission on this particular subject would
have started up on every side.

As it was, speaker after speaker found my idea immoral.
Self-sacrifice was the order of the day; they preached self-
sacrifice; they plumed themselves upon self-sacrifice. They
did not approve of me at all. But what I objected to because
it was self-sacrifice, they objected to because they were
rebels, so the evening went off very well.

Bohemian Club evenings in those days differed from those
of the present day because most of them were confined to
men. The Playgoers' Club was almost the only one which
admitted ladies; and at that time it confined them mostly
to lectures. The ladies' Clubs certainly welcomed men, but
the serious element was more conspicuous there. The idea
of having a literary club at which ladies and gentlemen
constantly dined together for pleasure had not been born.

The actors and actresses and well-known speakers of our

acquaintance we met mostly at the old Playgoers' Club, or at Phil May's Sunday nights in the stable which had become his studio.

The old Playgoers' was a most breezy place, where no one was allowed to speak for more than a few minutes, unless he could bring down the house with his wit. The ordinary person making a good sound speech was howled down. The chairman sometimes interfered to save a more distinguished orator. I remember the chairman of the club saying at one of the Christmas dinners to the section in the audience who were far enough away from the speaker to be talking quite as loud as he was, " Will those bounders at the back of the room shut up? "

The women writers very appropriately established themselves as a Writers' Club in the area flat underneath A. P. Watt's literary agency. There was no connection, but I suppose it resulted in an illustrious man author occasionally coming on from Watt's to have a cup of tea at the Writers' Club. They had an at-home every Friday afternoon, which was always extremely well supported.

I enjoyed going to these Writers' Club teas very much, and went often, and on one or other occasion met most of the leading women workers of the day.

The Writers' Clubbists did not take women's theories so seriously as the Pioneers, perhaps because they were not subsidised, and had no fierce patron to keep them at concert pitch, but they were more literary, and, until the rise of the Women Journalists', had almost the monopoly of working women writers. The Sesame had some, and when it was founded later on, the Lyceum became a regular haunt of them.

It was only in our last days at Addison Mansions that we joined the Dilettanti, a dining club of authors and artists, run by Paternoster and his charming wife. It has only a few score members, who once a month eat an Italian dinner together, washed down by old Chianti, at the Florence Restaurant in Soho, and listen to a brilliant paper by one of their members, which they afterwards discuss, with a great deal of wit and freedom. Henry Baerlein, Mrs. George

Cran, and Herbert Alexander, are among its wittiest members, and Mrs. Adam, daughter of Mrs. C. E. Humphry, the ever-popular " Madge," is quite the best serious speaker.   The speaking is more really impromptu than at the Omar Khayyam, for the papers generally have titles which do not convey the least inkling of what they are to be about, and it is therefore impossible for people to prepare their speeches beforehand.

Literary at-homes were a great feature of that day.   There was a large set of Literary, Art and Theatrical people who used to meet constantly at the houses of Phil May, A. L. Baldry, A. S. Boyd, Moncure D. Conway, Gleeson White, Dr. Todhunter, William Sharp, Zangwill, Rudolph Lehmann, E. J. Horniman, Joseph Hatton, Max O'Rell, John Strange Winter, George and Weedon Grossmith, Mrs. Alec Tweedie, J. J. Shannon, Mrs. Jopling, and Jerome K. Jerome.   And the more eminent authors and artists, at any rate, used to meet a great deal at Lady St. Helier's, Lady Lindsay's, Lady Dorothy Nevill's, the Tennants' and the H. D. Traills'.

Sometimes they met in the afternoon, and sometimes in the evening—more often the latter, because the artists came in greater numbers, and the actors, when the Theatres were closed.   As I have said, there were very seldom performances at any of them, because the people met to talk, and be introduced to fresh celebrities, and whether the reception was in the afternoon or the evening, the hospitalities were of the simple American kind.   They were *bona fide* meetings of clever people who wished to make each other's acquaintance. Our friends came to us on Friday nights.   At first, like Phil May, we kept open house every week, but as the number of our friends increased, we gradually tailed off to once a fortnight and once a month, because we had almost to empty the house out of the windows to make room for all who came.

When we ceased to receive every week, we sent out notices to the friends we wanted to see most that we were going to be at home on such an evening, and from this we passed to giving each at-home in honour of some special person, whom our friends were invited to meet.   I cannot remember half the special guests they were invited to meet, but among them were Conan Doyle, Anthony Hope, Mark Twain, Mrs. Flora Annie Steel, Mrs. Frances Hodgson Burnett, Maarten Maartens, Hall Caine, H. G. Wells, W. W. Jacobs, Sir Frederick Lugard (then Captain Lugard) when he came back from his great work in Uganda, F. C. Selous when he came back from his mighty hunting in South Africa, Zangwill, J. J. Shannon, Frankfort Moore, Savage Landor and Dr. George Ernest Morrison.

In a very short time, Bohemian at-homes, at which author and artist and actor met, became the rage in the Bohemian quarters of London—West Kensington, Chelsea, Chiswick, and the North-west. There were many people who were never so happy as when they went to an at-home every afternoon and evening of the week. They were all workers, and most of them too poor to use cabs much, so one wondered when they found time to do their work. That they did it was obvious, for most of them were producing a good deal of work, and many of them were laying the foundations of not inconsiderable fame.

At some of these receptions they had a little music, but at most of them they had no entertainment. For the clever people who went to these receptions did not go long distances to sit like mutes while some third- or fourth- or fortieth-rate artist played or sang; they went to meet other well-known Bohemians—well-known men and charming women. The most successful hosts were those who asked celebrities and pretty people in equal quantities: the celebrities liked meeting pretty people, and the pretty people liked meeting the celebrities.

Some celebrities were quite annoyed if there were only celebrities to meet them; they wanted an audience.

I remember Whistler the painter and Oscar Wilde being the first two people to arrive at a reception at Mrs. Jopling's house in Beaufort Street, where I had been lunching. They were intensely annoyed at having only the Joplings and myself as audience; it was no good showing off before us, since we knew all about them. They were quite distant to each other, and more distant to us. But as the time wore on, and nobody

came, Wilde had time to think of something effective to say—
he never spoke, if he could help it, unless he thought he could
be effective.

"I hear that you went over to the Salon by Dieppe,
Jimmy," he sneered, "were you economising?"

"Don't be foolish," said Whistler.   "I went to paint."

"How many pictures did you paint?" asked the æsthete,
with crushing superiority.

Whistler did not appear to hear his question.   "How many
hours did it take?" he asked.

"You went, not I," said Oscar.   "No gentleman ever goes
by the Dieppe route."

"I do, often," said our charming hostess, who had this
great house in Chelsea, with an acre or two of garden: "it
takes five hours."

"How many minutes are there in an hour, Oscar?"
drawled Whistler.

"I am not quite sure, but I think it's about sixty.   I am
not a mathematician."

"Then I must have painted three hundred," said the
unabashed Whistler.

It was at this at-home later on that Whistler made his
often-quoted mot—not for the first time, I believe.   A pretty
woman said something clever, and Wilde, who could be a
courtier, gallantly remarked that he wished he had said it.

"Never mind, Oscar," said Whistler, who owed him one
for the gibe about the Dieppe route; "you will have said it."

They were really very fine that afternoon, because they
were so thoroughly disgusted at not having more people to
show off before; showing off is a weakness of many authors
and artists and actors, though Bernard Shaw is the only one
that I remember who has had the frankness to admit it in
Who's Who.

We used to begin receiving at nine for the sake of people
who had trains to catch to distant suburbs—as Jerome
K. Jerome remarked, "other people always live in such
out-of-the-way places"—and kept the house open till the
last person condescended to go away, which was generally
about three.   Any one who had been introduced to us was

F

welcome to come, and to bring any of his friends with him, and in this way we met some of the most interesting people who came to the flat during our twenty years of tenancy. For instance, Herbert Bunning, the composer, whose opera *La Princesse Osra*, presented at Covent Garden, was drawn from Anthony Hope's novel by a permission which I obtained for him, brought with him one night M. Feuillerat, who married Paul Bourget's delightful sister, and Madame Feuillerat. M. Feuillerat in his turn brought with him Emile Verhaeren, one of the greatest living Belgian poets. M. Feuillerat himself was at the time professor of English literature in the university at Rennes, and both he and Madame Feuillerat spoke admirable English. On another Friday they were going to bring Paul Bourget himself, but he did not fulfil his intention of coming to England at the time.

Another distinguished foreigner who came about the same time was Maarten Maartens, a Dutch country gentleman whose real name is Joost Marius Maarten Willem van der Poorten-Schwartz. Hearing so much of his beautiful chateau in Holland, I asked him how he could tear himself away so much as he did. His reply was that for nine months in the year the weather in Holland was awful, and for the other three generally awful. This great writer had an epigrammatic way of expressing himself. He said that an eminent critic, who constituted himself his patron when he was in England, had warned him not to go to the Authors' Club (of which I was the Honorary Secretary), because most of the people who went there were very small fry. He said that he had taken no notice of the warning because he had observed that his informant wore a piece of pink sarcenet ribbon for a tie, and that he, Maarten Maartens, knew enough of the Englishman's idea of dress to be aware that the critic could not be a judge of ties, and wear pink sarcenet ribbon; and he argued that a man so self-satisfied and so ignorant about ties might be equally self-satisfied and ignorant about Authors' clubs. I asked him if he had written any books in Dutch. He said, " No, what is the good, when there are so few people to write for ? Only Dutchmen speak

Dutch. It was a choice of writing in English or German, if I was to have an audience, and I chose English."

Georg Brandes, the great Danish critic, who had so much to do with the recognition of Ibsen, told me when he came to our flat and I asked him a similar question, that in his later books he had taken to writing in other languages for the same reason. He was extremely interested, I remember, in Sergius Stepniak, the exiled Russian revolutionary, as was the then permanent head of the Foreign Office, whom I approached with some diffidence on the subject when they were both dining at a Club dinner of which I had the arrangements. Stepniak, whom I always found, in my intercourse with him, a very amiable man, had all the stage appearance of a villain, with his coal-black hair, his knotty, bulbous forehead, his black Tartar eyes, black beard and sombre complexion.

Of Zola, a studious-looking man with a brown beard, a rather tilted nose, and pince-nez, I have spoken in another chapter.

Anatole France I never met till quite recently, at a little party at John Lane's. He was as abounding in *simpatica* as Zola was wanting in it. He was rather short, and held his head sideways like the late Conte de Paris, with his closely-cropped beard buried in his chest. But he had unmistakably the air of a great man, and extraordinarily bright and sympathetic eyes—a captivating personality.

As I began with foreigners I will deal with them before passing on to the many interesting Anglo-Saxons who assembled in those rooms during those twenty years.

August Strindberg, the Scandinavian novelist and dramatist, was to have come to see us when he was in England in the 'nineties. He forwarded an introduction, but did not follow it up owing to the distance of his sojourning place. Before he left Scandinavia, he had asked a friend who was supposed to know all about England for a nice healthy suburb of London, far enough out for the air to be pure. The friend suggested (without, I think, any idea of practical joking) that Gravesend should be the place, and at Gravesend Strindberg remained during the whole of his stay in London, doubtless composing novels or dramas upon London society.

Many well-known Frenchmen naturally came to see us, like Gabriel Nicolet, the artist, and Eustache de Lorey, who had been an attaché of the French Legation in Teheran, and who afterwards collaborated with me in *Queer Things about Persia* and *The Moon of the Fourteenth Night*. Since his return from Persia he had become eminent as a composer. He wrote the music of one of the most popular songs in *Les Merveilleuses*, in addition to being the composer of the opera *Betty*, which was produced in Brussels, with Mariette Sully in the leading part. Melba herself contemplates appearing in the leading rôle in his second opera, *Leila*. De Lorey had made some most adventurous expeditions, including one with Pierre Loti in Caucasia, and he was such a brilliant raconteur of his adventures that I asked him why he did not make a book of them. He replied that the travel-book is not the institution in France which it is in England, and that though he spoke English fluently, he could not write a book in English. Finally we decided to collaborate as related in a later chapter.

We had many Asiatic visitors, but no Africans, I think, unless one counts Englishmen who had won their spurs in the dark continent, like Sir Frederick Lugard. Decidedly our most interesting Asiatic visitors were Japanese like Yoshio Markino and Prof. Nakamura. Prof. Nakamura was for three years a pupil of Lafcadio Hearn. He came over to England for the Japanese Exhibition, and remained here a few years, studying educational methods for the Japanese Government.

He said that Lafcadio Hearn would see nothing of his pupils because he was only interested in the Old Japan, and was afraid of introducing modern ideas if he saw much of any Japanese who were not absorbed in the same studies as himself. I remember Bret Harte pleading much the same objection to revisiting California.

Yoshio Markino has been one of our most intimate friends for years. I cannot say in what exact year he first came to 32 Addison Mansions. I know that I first met him through M. H. Spielman, who wrote to me telling me all about Markino's powers as a black-and-white artist, and asking me to get my editor friends to give him some work, of which he stood in need.   Not until he published *A Japanese Artist in London* at my suggestion, and with a preface written by me, a few years after, did I know how badly he stood in need of that work; Japanese etiquette prevented him from intruding his private affairs upon a stranger.   I was successful in getting him a little illustrating work, and I got him some translating work, better paid, I suspect, than original contributions of men like the late Andrew Lang to the great *Dailies*.   It came about in this wise : I was anxious to include in *More Queer Things about Japan,* a translation of a Japanese life of Napoleon, which had come into my hands.   There were five volumes of it with extremely amusing illustrations.   Neither I nor the publishers knew what a small amount of words can make a volume in Japanese. The publisher looked at the volumes and thought that he was making a very shrewd bargain when he offered five pounds a volume as the translator's fee.   Each volume proved to contain about a thousand words, so Markino got five pounds a thousand, when the publisher meant to offer him about five shillings.

After this I lost touch of Markino for a long time, till Miss E. S. Stevens, who had been my secretary, and was then doing work as a literary agent, invited us to meet him at her Club.   Very soon after that I was at the annual soirée of the Japan Society with Miss Lorimer and another girl, and my cousin, Sampson Sladen, who was then only third in command of the London Fire Brigade, when we ran across Markino, who remained with us all the evening. He invited myself and the members of our household to the exhibition of the sketches which he had painted to illustrate *The Colour of London.*   From that time forward his visits were very frequent till we left London, and on two separate occasions he went to Italy with us for several months.

It was on the first of these occasions, while we were all staying at 12 Piazza Barberini in Rome, that he showed me a letter which he had written to Messrs. Chatto & Windus about the second of the volumes he illustrated, *The Colour of Paris.*   The letter was as brilliant, as interesting, as amusing, as one of Robert Louis Stevenson's or Lafcadio Hearn's. I saw that he was a born writer, and from that time forward did not rest until I had persuaded him to write his first book, *A Japanese Artist in London*. I got him the contract from the publisher for this book and wrote the preface.

While we were in Paris he brought us an invitation to dinner from the brilliant Parisian who was afterwards our dear friend, poor Yvonne, who died the other day after months of suffering. When we arrived she had a terrible headache, and we had to have our dinner without her, presided over by her niece, a gay and pretty child of thirteen, who made as self-possessed a hostess as any grown-up. We talked a great deal that night over Italy, and a great deal more when Markino came to see us at the little Citè de Retiro, near the Madeleine, and the result was that he decided to do a book on Italy with Miss Olave Potter, he supplying the pictures, and she the letterpress—the book that took form as *The Colour of Rome*, which Messrs. Chatto & Windus promptly agreed to commission, and of which I shall have more to say elsewhere. That winter and the summer of another year we all spent together in Italy, and the painting of the illustrations for *The Colour of Rome* led indirectly to Markino's writing *A Japanese Artist in London*, and the beginning of his brilliant literary career.

Markino's writings achieved such an instant popularity with English readers that I feel sure that they will like to know his habits of work, which I had the opportunity of observing during the two long visits he paid with us to Italy. For a painter of architecture and landscape his method is unique. Take, for instance, the story of the illustrations to Miss Olave Potter's book, *The Colour of Rome*. First of all, since he was a stranger to Rome, and knew neither its beauty spots nor its most interesting monuments, we took him walks to see all the most illustrable places. He selected from them the number he had promised to paint. Sometimes he took more than one walk to a place before he commenced the study for his picture, but intuition is one of his gifts, and he was seldom long at fault in discovering the best standpoint.

Having chosen this, he took his drawing-pad to the spot and made a rough sketch of it with notes written in Japanese of the colours to be used, and any special things he had to remember. Sometimes, where there was a great deal of detail, or of sculpture, he used paper with crossed lines on it, so as to preserve his proportions. But Markino, beautifully as he can paint detail, resents it, and prefers subjects unified by a haze of heat or mist.

He never took his paints out with him, and never did a finished drawing in the open air. He took his notes home with him and ruminated over them, till the idealised picture presented itself to his brain. Then he set to work on it, taking little rest till it was finished—always absolutely faithful to colour and effect, though the picture was painted entirely indoors.

That was his method of painting. He did no writing in Rome. But he came constantly to our flat when he was writing *A Japanese Artist in London*, *My Idealled John Bullesses*, and *When I was a Child*. Sometimes he liked to talk over his chapters before he began to write them, when they were slow at taking shape. But more generally he brought the chapters written in the rough to his Egeria, and read them over to her. They had blanks where he could not remember the English word which he wanted to use. It was in his mind, and he would reject all words till he found the word he was thinking of.

As he read the chapters aloud, the wise Egeria made corrections where they were necessary to elucidate his meaning—to clarify his style, but never treated any Japanese use of English as a mistake, unless it made the sense obscure. That is how the fascinating medium in which Markino writes took shape.

Take, for instance, Markino's omission of the *articles*. The Japanese language has no articles. Markino therefore seldom uses them, and his English is written to be intelligible without them, just as a legal document is written to be intelligible without punctuation. Again, if he used a word in a palpably wrong sense—*i e.* with a meaning which it had never borne before, or was etymologically unfit to bear

—she left it if it helped to express in a forcible way what he intended.

The result of this respectful editing was to produce a most fascinating and characteristic type of English, which has won for Markino a public of enthusiastic admirers. He has, as Osman Edwards said, *the heart of a child*, when he is writing, and he combines with it a highly original mode of thinking and expressing himself, but their effect would have been half lost if he had not found in his Egeria an adviser with the eye of genius for what should be corrected and what should be retained of his departures from conventional English.

When the chapters were corrected thus, Egeria typed them out, making any corrections or additions which were necessary to the punctuation, and generally preparing the manuscript for the press.

I am encouraged to think that these details of the way in which the books were edited will interest the public, because J. H. Taylor, the golf champion, once cross-examined me on the subject, as we were walking down the lane from the Mid-Surrey golf pavilion to his house. He had been reading *A Japanese Artist in London*, and was so delighted with it that he wanted to know exactly how this wonderful style of writing was born.

And there is no doubt that it is a wonderful style of writing. It is not pigeon-English; the Japanese do not use pigeon-English, they abhor it. It is the result of a deliberate intention to apply certain Japanese methods of expression (like the omission of the article) to the writing of English, in order to produce a more direct medium, and the result has been a complete success. Markino's English is wonderfully forcible. It hits like a sledge-hammer. He has a genius for discovering exactly the right expression, and he thinks on till he discovers it. As a reason why his English is not broken English, but a medium using the capabilities of both languages, I may mention that he has been living in America and England for nearly twenty years.

Besides Japanese, we had many Indian visitors.

THE MOORISH ROOM AT 32 ADDISON MANSIONS

CHAPTER VIII

OUR AT-HOMES : THE YOUNG AUTHORS WHO ARE NOW GREAT AUTHORS

OF all the men who used to come to 32, Addison Mansions from our having met them at the Idler teas, none were more identified with the success of Jerome's two periodicals *The Idler* and *To-day* than Arthur Conan Doyle and Israel Zangwill. Doyle had been writing for ten years before he achieved commanding success. Be that as it may, he was undoubtedly the most successful of the younger authors who were familiar figures in that Vagabond and Idler set. Doyle, who was the son of that exquisite artist, Charles Doyle, and grandson of the famous caricaturist H. B., and nephew of Dicky Doyle of *Punch*, ought to have been granted a royaller road to success, for he had enjoyed a very early connection with literature, having sat as a little child on the knee of the immortal Thackeray. Thackeray's old publishers, Smith, Elder & Co., have been his, but he had travelled to the Arctic regions and to the tropics and practised for eight years as a doctor at Southsea before he charmed the world with his famous novels *The White Company* in 1890, and *The Refugees* in 1891, and astonished it with the *Adventures of Sherlock Holmes* in the latter year. He was a doctor at Norwood when I first made his acquaintance. He was a little over thirty then, and a keen cricketer, being nearly county form (indeed, he did actually play once for Hampshire, and might at one time have played regularly for Hampshire as an Association back). It was not until late in life, however, that he found time enough to get much practise at games. Then for some years he played occasional first-class cricket, having an average of thirty-two against Kent, Derbyshire and other good teams; in the last year he

played for the M.C.C. That was after the war, when he was
over forty. He played a hard Association match in his
forty-fourth year.

From an early stage in his literary career he enjoyed
the admiration and the deepest respect of all his fellows in
the craft, and for years past has undoubtedly been morally
the head of the profession. Upon him has fallen the mantle
of Sir Walter Besant. In saying this, I am not instituting
any comparison between the merits of his various lines of
work, which in their own line are quite unexcelled, and
those of the other leading authors, but he is not only
among the handful who may be called the very best authors
of the day, he is the man to whom the profession would
undoubtedly look for a lead in any crisis.

Say, for instance, that the idea, so often debated recently,
of authors combining with publishers to fix the price of a
novel at ten and sixpence, and refusing to work for or sell
their goods to any one who would not abide by this decision,
were put to a vote in the literary profession, what Doyle
thought would count most. The profession as an army
would range themselves under his banner. Suppose
a question, like the insurance question which has been
threatening the livelihood of thousands of doctors, were to
arise for authors, they would look to Doyle for a lead. If
the decision which he made benefited authors as a whole, but
cost him half or three-quarters of his income, and a syndicate
approached him with a huge offer to abandon the camp,
nobody could suppose for one moment that Doyle would
listen to them. His moral courage, his loyalty, his generosity,
his patriotism, added to his wonderful literary gifts, have
confered upon him a commanding position. Of his gifts
I shall speak lower down. It is as the patriot that one must
always consider him first. He is not naturally a party man,
though he happens to have contested Edinburgh as a Liberal
Unionist, and the Hawick boroughs as a Tariff Reformer.
There have been moments when he has been openly opposed
to some measure of the Unionist Party. He really belongs
to the Public Service party. He made notable sacrifices
for his country at the time of the Boer War. First he gave

SIR A. CONAN DOYLE
Drawn by Yoshio Markino

up his literary work to serve unpaid on the staff of the Langlam Field Hospital and afterwards to write the pamphlet on *The Cause and Conduct of the War*, an attempt to place the true facts before the people of Europe, which brought him nothing but great expense and the undying gratitude and respect of his fellow-countrymen. That he cares nothing for popularity where principles are concerned is shown by the attitude he took over the famous horse-maiming case, or his acceptance of the Presidency of the Divorce Law Reform Union.

His sturdy character is reflected in his physique, and there are few people in London who do not know that unusually big and strong frame, that round head, with prominent cheek-bones, and dauntless blue eyes, the bluff, good-humoured face: for his sonorous voice is frequently heard from the chair of public meetings where some protest for the public good has to be raised, or at a dinner table on the guest nights of clubs. Sir Arthur, for he was knighted in 1902, is a most popular speaker; hearty, engaging, amusing, in his lighter moods, most trenchant and convincing in a crisis, of all the authors of the day he merits most the title of a great man.

The curious thing is that although every one knows how much he respects Doyle as a great man, and every one is aware that he is one of the most popular, if not the most popular, of the authors of the day, not every one has analysed the soundness of his literary fame. In my opinion, of all very popular authors, Doyle deserves his popularity as an author most. No man living has written better historical novels, judged from the standpoint of eloquence, accuracy or thrill. Doyle has carried the accuracy of the man of science into all his studies, and his power to thrill with eloquence and incident is beyond question. His detective stories are equal to the best that have ever been written. His history of the South African War is not only the best history of the war, but it is a model of contemporary history, always the most difficult kind to write, because only the eye of intuition can distinguish respective values amid contemporary incidents. He has been highly successful as a playwright too. His *House of Temperley* is the best Prize-Ring play in the language, as his novel, *Rodney Stone*, which had no lady-love heroine, was the best Prize-Ring novel, and his play on Waterloo, produced by Sir Henry Irving, has become a classic.   I have alluded elsewhere to the dramatisation of his *Sherlock Holmes* which has been played thousands of times. Doyle not only was present at our at-homes at 32 Addison Mansions, but, living out of town, once stayed with us there, as we stayed with him at Hindhead on another occasion. But owing to his living out of town, he was a great deal less familiar figure at receptions than most of the other younger authors of the first rank, except Rudyard Kipling and J. M. Barrie, both of whom cordially hate " functions " of any kind.   Doyle, placed in the same circumstances as they are, forces himself to go to many functions for which he has less time than they have, for his literary output is infinitely greater, and he has so many other duties to perform, and always performs them.

When I asked Doyle what first turned him to writing, he said—

" All the art that is in our family—my grandfather, three uncles, and father were all artists—ran in my blood, and took a turn towards letters. At six I was writing stories; I fancy my mother has them yet. At school I was, though I say it, a famous story-teller; at both schools I was at I edited a magazine, and practically wrote the whole of it also.

" When I started studying medicine, the family affairs were very straitened. My father's health was bad, and he earned little. I tried to earn something, which I did by going out as medical assistant half the year. Then I tried stories. In 1878, when I was nineteen years old, I sent *The Mystery of the Sassasa Valley* to Chambers. I got three guineas. It was 1880 before I got another accepted. It was by *London Society*. From then until 1888 I averaged about fifty pounds a year, getting about three pounds a story. My first decent price was twenty-eight pounds from the Cornhill for *Habakuk Jephson's Statement* in 1886.   Then at New Year, 1888, Ward, Lock & Co. brought out *A Study in*

Scarlet, paying twenty-five pounds for all rights. I have never had another penny from that book; I wonder how much they have had? Then came *Micah Clarke* at the end of 1888, which got me a more solid public. It was not until 1902 that I was strong enough to be able to entirely abandon medical practice. Of course, it was the Holmes stories in the *Strand* which gave me my popular vogue, but *The White Company,* which has been through fifty editions, has sold far more as a book than any of the Holmes books."

Kipling I regard as the genius of the junction of the nineteenth and twentieth centuries, and England owes an incalculable debt to his patriotism and eloquence. If Doyle is the voice of the literary profession, Kipling is the voice of the country. He speaks for the manhood of England in a crisis. All through the African War a letter or a poem from Kipling was the trumpet voice of national feeling. No poet who has written in English has ever inspired his countrymen like Kipling. His poems, though they have not the poetical quality of those of our great standard poets, have the prophetical quality, which is just as important in poetry, in a higher degree than any of them. They are Rembrandt poems, not Raphael poems, and they will remain without loss of prestige, an armoury for every patriotic or manful writer and speaker to quote from. I reviewed Kipling's poems when they were first published in America for the leading Canadian paper. I am thankful that I hailed them as the work of genius, and it was a proud moment when I first shook hands with him in the early 'nineties. Though his short stories are the best in the language, I always think of him as a poet, because he is our *vates.*

It is best to mention Barrie, our other genius, here, though I have little to say about him. On the rare occasions when he speaks in public, he speaks admirably, and he enjoys universal respect. As far as literature is concerned, no man's lines have been laid in pleasanter places. Unlike Doyle, Anthony Hope, Stanley Weyman and others, Barrie did not have to wait for recognition. It is notorious that from the very beginning he never had the proverbial manuscript in the drawer; in other words, that he always found an immediate sale for whatever he wrote. He began as a journalist.

Anthony Hope I first met at an Idler tea. He was one of the brilliant band of younger authors whom Jerome was among the first to recognise. In those days he kept the distinction between " Anthony Hope " the writer, and Anthony Hope Hawkins the barrister, most rigidly. Being the son of a famous London clergyman, Mr. Hawkins, of St. Bride's, Fleet Street, a cousin of Mr. Justice Hawkins, a scholar of Balliol, and an eloquent speaker, his prospects at the Bar were very good. There was an idea that they would suffer if it were known that he indulged in anything so frivolous as writing love-stories. These were the days when he was composing his immortal " Dolly Dialogues " for the *Westminster Gazette,* and when he was just beginning the succession of witty and delicate novels which made his fame. He had, I have always understood, been writing for some years, before he could make any impression on the public, and even then he had no hope of making a living by literature. I made one of his early novels my book of the week in *The Queen,* in a most enthusiastic review, and incidentally mentioned his real name. His friends, perhaps they were officious, entreated me not to do it again, lest it should injure his prospects. A year or two afterwards there was no question off which profession he was to make a living, though as he coquetted with politics, and contested a constituency or two, he probably kept up the legal fiction of his being at the Bar for some time longer.

As he had enjoyed the distinction of being President of the Oxford Union, he was a practised speaker before he came to London. He had plenty of opportunities of exercising his skill without waiting for briefs, for he became a frequent speaker at Club dinners. The charm of his voice and his delivery, the polish and wit of his speeches were recognised at once, and his popularity as a speaker has been undisputed from that day to this.

It was noticed that, though he was so brilliant and fluent, when making a speech, he was rather a silent man at receptions, except where politeness demanded that he should exert himself. But this is a common trait in the more considerable authors. They are frequently not only rather silent, but ill at ease. In those days one could count the authors who were both brilliant socially and brilliant writers, on one's fingers.

One legal habit Anthony Hope retained; he went to chambers to do his writing as he had been accustomed, and lived in other chambers, and was regarded as a confirmed bachelor till he married. He came to Addison Mansions very frequently in the 'nineties. The incident I remember best was his loss of presence of mind when I tried to save him from a terrific American bore, a middle-aged lady. Somebody had brought her; I had not met her before, and she was having a systematic lion-hunt. She thought that A. H. H. was Anthony Hope, but she was not certain, and said to me, " Is that *Anthony Hope?* I must know *Anthony Hope.*"

Wishing to save him from the infliction, because he was always rather distrait with bores, I said, " That is Mr. Hawkins." I didn't think she knew enough about literature to be aware of the identity, nor did she, but he had unfortunately caught the words " Anthony Hope," and smiled, and started forward, and was lost. As he had unconsciously convicted me of falsehood, I left him to his fate.

Generous to needy brother authors, punctilious in the performance of the duties to the literary profession, which his eminence confers on him (in such matters as the Authors' Society and literary clubs), wonderfully patient and courteous, an admirable literary craftsman, who never turns out slipshod work, as well as a brilliant romancer and witty dialogist, Anthony Hope Hawkins deserves every particle of his popularity and success.

I have not dilated on his plays, though he has achieved great success on the stage, because dramatists tell me that he is not going to write for it any more.

The popularity of our at-homes was at its height before Frankfort Moore had decided to come over to England, giving up the editorial post he held in Ireland, to devote all his time to novel-writing. He and his delightful wife, the sister of Mrs. Bram Stoker, took lodgings at Kew, and were ready for many receptions, so that he might meet his fellow-authors in London. As Bram Stoker had then for years been Irving's right hand, they had an excellent introduction ready-made, but they brought letters of introduction to us, and, up to the time of his leaving London, he was among our most intimate literary friends.

Frankfort Moore's success in London was instantaneous, as well it might have been, since he was a brilliant and witty speaker, as well as a writer of brilliant, witty and very charming books. Hutchinson eagerly took up the publication of his works, and the literary clubs soon learned to depend upon him as one of the best after-dinner speakers. In about ten years he made a fortune, and retired to take things in a more leisurely way at an old house in Sussex, where he was able to adequately house his fine collection of old oak, old brass, old engravings and old china, in which he was a noted connoisseur.

His immediate success justified his giving up his lodgings at Kew, and taking a nice, old-fashioned house in Pembroke Road, which he soon began to transform with his panelling, and his collections. His retirement from London left a great gap in many social circles. He was a universal favourite —a man of real eminence, although he regarded his achievements so modestly.

One of the most valued of our visitors was the celebrated Father Stanton, of St. Alban's, Holborn, who introduced himself to me when he was on his way to Syracuse with F. E. Sidney, with whom he went to Seville on that expedition which resulted in the publication of the latter's *Anglican Innocents in Spain*, the book which aroused such anger among Roman Catholics. We were the only two occupants of a sleeping compartment on the Italian railways. He was not wearing clerical dress, and I had no notion who he was until the conclusion of our journey, when Sidney, who had joined us, informed me. We did a lot of sight-seeing in Syracuse together, especially in the cathedral (built into an entire Greek temple, ascribed to Pallas Athene). Both Stanton and Sidney were experts in old gilt, in which Sicily is very rich—the organ at Syracuse is an example. From that time until Stanton's death we constantly met at the house of Sidney, who has the best collection of sixteenth-century stained glass in England, and built a house in Frognal with the proper windows to receive it. Though Stanton and I did not agree in Church matters, we were yet staunch friends, and I was an immense admirer of one who did so much for the regeneration of the poor in one of the worst districts of London.

The greatest compliment we ever received at our at-homes was when Lord Dundonald, who had known us for some years, and had just come back from his famous relief of Ladysmith with his irregular cavalry, came and spent the best part of the afternoon with us. He looked worn and very sunburnt, but it was one of the events of our lifetimes to hear the stirring details of England's greatest military drama in this generation, direct from the lips of the man who had given it its happy termination.

G

CHAPTER IX

THE HUMORISTS AT OUR AT-HOMES

AMONG the crowd of humorists who honoured Addison Mansions with their presence it is natural to mention first the famous author of *Three Men in a Boat*. There is no author for whom I feel a greater affection, though, as he once said, " You and I are sure to have a diametrically opposite opinion upon almost any point which may turn up, because we were born the poles apart." I was at the time his chief and only book critic on *To-day*. I believe I was called the literary editor, though all the patronage of the position was exercised by himself. It is patronage which constitutes an editor; the sub-editor can perform the duties. I believe also that it was I who suggested the name *To-day*. At any rate, it was I who helped him to formulate the paper, and for the first year or so it was my duty to do all the book reviews in it, and my duty to receive all the ladies who came to see Jerome about the paper. Of course, they mostly came in search of work or fame: those who wished to be written about were very numerous, and expected to succeed by making what is called the " Glad Eye " at him. He was *terribly* afraid of the " Glad Eye "; it made him turn hot and cold in swift succession. He was unable to say " no " to a siren, and equally unable to say " yes " when he meant " no." He was also an intensely domesticated man, entirely devoted to his family, and without the smallest desire for a flirtation. So it fell to my lot to pick up the " Glad Eye," a very agreeable job, when you have not the power to give yourself away. I had no patronage to bestow upon them. The only thing I could do for them was to write about them if they were sufficiently interesting, which frequently happened in that age of personal journalism.

And, if they were quite harmless worshippers, without any ulterior designs, I occasionally induced Jerome to be worshipped for a minute or two. I made many lady friends at this period, especially from the Stage.

Jerome hardly ever answered letters. He used to say, " If you keep a letter for a month, it generally answers itself." But he did not keep them. He tore them up directly he had glanced at them. He knew at one glance—probably at the signature—if he wanted to read a letter, and, if he did not, he tore it up without reading it. He had a horror of accumulating papers. He sometimes asked me to answer letters, as he had faith in me as a soother. It was never part of my duties to write " yes," I had to gild " no." He prefered to word his own acceptances, so as not to say more than he meant. He did not even want me to read the manuscripts. He prefered to read them himself. It did not take him long, because if he did not come across something worth publishing by the second page, he did not read any further. " You must grab your reader at the beginning," he used to say.

He was a very pleasant man to write reviews for. He believed in generous criticisms. " You can have a page or two pages for your book of the week," he said, " according to its importance "—he decided that when I chose my book —" but you can only have a page for the rest of the books that come in, so you can't afford to waste your space on bad books. If you can't say anything good about them, you obviously can't afford them any space. You can praise things up as much as you like if you can be convincing about it : don't be afraid to let yourself go about the book of the week : I am sick of the *Spectator* and the *Athenæum*, you never get a full-blooded review out of them, unless it's to damn something. The more knowledge you can show about the subject of the book you are praising, the better. But above all things, recommend it in the paper just as you would recommend it to a friend : use the same language as you would to a friend : be natural. And, whatever you do, beware of the Club Man. When I read an article or a story, I always ask myself what a Club Man would think of it ;

and if I know that he would like it, I turn it down : his opinions are dead opposite to the Public's."

The likes and dislikes of the Club Man was one of the matters in which my opinion was dead opposite to Jerome's. The Club Man and the Man in the Street between them fill the ranks of the average patriotic citizen. It is they who pull the nation through in a crisis, and the City of London leads them. At ordinary times their voice is drowned by the noise of the Radical Party, and the giant Middle-class, to whom all appeals for national safety have to be addressed—the blind Samson sitting chained in the house of his enemies—cannot hear their warnings.

In any case, it is so hard for a book to be popular at clubs, where people go to be interested and amused, that if it is popular there, it will be popular anywhere, except with the Nonconformist Conscience.

Jerome had written *Three Men in a Boat* and *The Idle Thoughts of an Idle Fellow* before I met him, and was consequently in enjoyment of world-wide fame. He had established in the *Idler* a monthly which had no equal then as a magazine of fiction, and had a sale of a hundred thousand copies a month, when he started *To-day*. He started it not only to amuse, but to educate Public Opinion, when it had secured attention by its brightness, for he had very strong views which he was eager to preach.

He was more of a Conservative than a Radical in those days; he had not despaired of the Conservatives, then, though he was baggy about beastly little nationalities. Suffragism had not then begun its March of Unreason, and we were all in favour of giving woman a vote. But I am bound to register the conviction that, if Suffragism had been a burning question then, the paper would have been full of it, and enjoying a circulation of a million, or whatever number the adult women suffragists run to. I can picture Jerome, a man famous for his hospitalities, being reduced to a hunger-strike by the ardour with which he would have espoused the idea. He was always tilting against some abuse, always asking for litigation. And he got it—or I suppose he would be editing a newspaper now, instead of

delighting both hemispheres with his plays. I say advisedly
" both hemispheres," because he has a considerable public
as a dramatist in America.

One of the first books on which I let myself go, and wrote
an absolute appreciation, was that magnificent historical
novel of Stanley Weyman's, *A Gentleman of France*. Jerome
was delighted with the way I handled it.

Seeing Jerome so much in the office led to our being a
good deal at each other's houses. He was living at that time
in one of the nice old villas in St. John's Wood. The chief
thing I remember about it was its cattiness and its scrupulous
tidiness. When you stay with him in the country, you
cannot leave your stick and hat in the hall, handy for running
out, as you might at Sandringham or Chatsworth. They are
at once arrested, and are very lucky if they get off with a
warning from the magistrate.

One of my diametrical divergencies from Jerome is in the
love of cats. I cannot respect a cat. To me it is a beast of
prey, a sort of middle-class tiger, operating in a small way,
but at heart a murderer of the Asiatic jungle. Jerome loves
them, and makes dogs of them : he used to fill the *Idler*
with Louis Wain's human deductions from cats. He has
a telephone to their brains. I agree with Lord Roberts,
who knows by instinct when there is a cat in the room,
though it may be wholly concealed, and cannot enjoy himself
until it is removed.

Like most real humorists whom I have known, and I have
known many from Mark Twain and Bill Nye downwards,
Jerome is not a " funny man " in ordinary life. He is, on
the contrary, except when he is on his legs, before an audience,
or taking his pen in his hand, apt to be a very serious man,
though his conversation is always illuminated by flashes of
wit. He is much more apt to air strong opinions about
serious questions. The Jerome you see in *Paul Kelvin* and
The Third Floor Back is the real Jerome. He is the loyalest
friend and most tender-hearted man imaginable. His kindness and hospitality are unbounded. You cannot stay with
Jerome in his own house without being inspired by the deepest
respect and affection for him. He is an ideal husband and

father, a friend of the struggling, a just and generous master.
Like Conan Doyle, though he has never shone in first-class
cricket or golf, Jerome is very athletic in his tastes.   In spite
of his glasses, he is a fine tennis-player and croquet-player;
he is a fine skater also, and devoted to the river and horses.
It was partly a horse accident in which he and Norma
Lorimer were involved, and both showed extraordinary
courage, which made me feel for him as I do.

He is essentially an open-air man, whose thoughts are all
outside directly he has got through his statutory amount of
work with his secretary.

But though the serious man weighs down the humorist
in Jerome, you would not guess it from his personal appearance.   When he rises to speak, his bright eye, the smile
playing round his mouth, his cool confident bearing, the
very way in which he arranges his hair, which has not yet
a particle of grey about it, is more suggestive of the humorist,
the man who is accustomed to making hundreds roar with
laughter at his speeches, and scores of thousands with the
flashes of his pen.

Jerome has no love for London, though he has a town
residence and enjoys Bohemian society, and is very popular
in it.   For many years he has lived on the Upper Thames,
and he is in the habit of going to Switzerland for the skating.

I asked Carl Hentschel, who was one of the three who went
on the trip immortalised in *Three Men in a Boat*, to tell me
about it.   He said—

" It is rather interesting to look back to the days of *Three
Men in a Boat*.   Jerome at that time was in a solicitor's
office in Cecil Street, where the Hotel Cecil now stands,
George Wingrave was a junior clerk in a bank in the City,
and I was working in a top studio in Windmill Street, close
to where the Lyric Theatre now stands, having to look after
a lot of Communists, who had had to leave Paris.   Our one
recreation was week-ending on the river.   It was roughing
it in a manner which would hardly appeal to us now.   Jerome
and Wingrave used to live in Tavistock Place, now pulled
down, and that was our starting-point to Waterloo and thence
to the river.   It says much for our general harmony that,

during the years we spent together in such cramped confinement, we never fell out, metaphorically or literally. It was Jerome's unique style which enabled him to bring out the many and various points in our trip. It was a spell of bad weather that broke up our parties. A steady downpour for three days would dampen even the hardiest river-enthusiast. One incident, which, I believe, was never recorded, but would have made invaluable copy in Jerome's hands, happened on one of our last trips. We were on our way up the river, and late in the afternoon, as the sky looked threatening, we agreed to pull up and have our frugal meal, which generally consisted of a leg of Welsh mutton, bought at the famous house in the Strand, now pulled down, with salad. We started preparing our meal on the bank, when the threatened storm burst. We hastily put up our canvas over the boat, and bundled all the food into it anyhow. It got pitch dark, and we were compelled to find the lamp and tried to light it. After a while we found the lamp, but it would not light; luckily we found two candle ends, and by their feeble light began our meal. We had hardly begun our meal when I said after the first mouthful of salad, ' What's wrong with the salad? ' George also thought it was queer, but Jerome thought there was nothing wrong. Jerome always did have a peculiar taste. Anyhow, he was the only one who continued. It was not till the next day that we discovered that owing to our carelessness of using two medicine bottles of similar shape, one containing vinegar and the other Colza oil, the lamp and the salad were both a bit off.''

When I asked Jerome what first gave him the idea of writing he said—

'' I always wanted to be a writer. It seemed to me an easy and dignified way of earning a living. I found it difficult; I found it exposes you to a vast amount of abuse. Sometimes, after writing a book or play which seemed to me quite harmless, I have been staggered at the fury of indignation it seems to have excited among my critics. If I had been Galileo, attacking the solar science of the sixteenth century, I could not have been assaulted by the high priests of journalism with more anger and contempt. But the work

itself has always remained delightful to me. I think it was
Zangwill who said to me once, ' A writer, to succeed, has to be
not only an artist, but a shopkeeper '—and of the two, the
shopkeeper is the more necessary. I am not sure who said
that last sentence; it may have been myself.

" You write your book or play while talking to the morning
stars. It seems to you beautiful—wonderful. You thank
whatever gods there be for having made you a writer. The
book or the play finished, the artist takes his departure, to
dream of fresh triumphs. The shopkeeper—possibly a
married shopkeeper with a family—comes into the study,
finds the manuscript upon the desk. Then follows the selling,
bargaining, advertising. It is a pretty hateful business,
even with the help of agents. The book or the play you
thought so fine, you thought that every one was bound to
like it. Your publisher, your manager, is doubtful. You
have a feeling that they are accepting it out of sheer charity—
possibly they knew your father, or have heard of your early
struggles—and yield to an unbusinesslike sentiment of
generosity. It appears, and anything from a hundred to
two hundred and fifty experienced and capable journalists
rush at it to tear it to pieces. It is marvellous—their un-
erring instinct. There was one sentence where the grammar
was doubtful—you meant to reconsider it, but overlooked
it; it appears quoted in every notice; nothing else in the
book appears to have attracted the least attention. At
nine-tenths of your play the audience may have laughed;
there was one scene which did not go well; it is the only
scene the critic has any use for. Their real feeling seems
to be that the writer is the enemy of the public; the duty of
all concerned is to kill him. If he escapes alive, that counts to
him.

" I remember the first night of a play by my friend, Henry
Arthur Jones. There had been some opposition; it was
quite evident that the gallery were only waiting for him to
appear to ' boo ' him, as if he had been a criminal on the way
to the scaffold. I was standing by the gallery exit, and the
people were coming out. Said one earnest student to
another, as they passed me, ' Why didn't the little —— come

out and take his punishment like a man?' 'Cowardly, I call it,' answered the other. They knew what was in store for him in the next morning's papers; they knew that a year's work, perhaps two, had been wasted. I suppose that it would be asking too much to suggest that they might also have imagined the heartache and the disappointment. The playwright who does not succeed in keeping every one of a thousand individuals, of different tastes and views and temperaments, interested and amused for every single minute of two hours, must not be allowed any mercy.

" Yet for a settled income of ten thousand a year, and no worry, no abuse, and no insults, I do not think any of us would exchange our job. I suppose we are all born gamblers —it is worth risking the half-dozen failures for the one success.

" And the work itself, as I said—one only wishes one's readers enjoyed it half as much; circulations would be fabulous. *Three Men in a Boat* I started as a guide to the Thames. It occurred to us—George, Charles and myself— when we were pulling up and down, how interesting and improving it would be to know something about the history of the famous places through which we passed; a little botany might also be thrown in. I thought that other men in boats might also like information on this subject, and would willingly pay for it. So I read up Dugdale, and a vast number of local guides, together with a little poetry and some memoirs. I really knew quite a lot about the Thames by the time I had done, and with a pile of notes in front of me, I started. I think I had a vague idea of making it a modern 'Sandford and Merton.' I thought George would ask questions, and Harry intersperse philosophical remarks. But George and Harry would not; I could not see them sitting there and doing it. So gradually they came to have their own way, and the book as a guide to the Thames is, I suppose, the least satisfactory work on the market.

" I suppose, like Mrs. Gummidge, I felt it more. It must have been about five years before I succeeded in getting anything of mine accepted. The regularity with which the complimenting editor returned my manuscripts grew monotonous, grew heart-breaking. But, after all, it was *The Times* newspaper which accepted my first contribution. Some correspondence on the subject of the nude in Art made me angry, and I wrote a letter intended to be ironic. It attracted quite a lot of comment, and, fired by this success, I wrote to *The Times* on other topics. The *Saturday Review* praised their irony and humour, and Frank Harris invited me a little later to contribute. But we differed, I think, upon the subject of women.

" *The Passing of the Third Floor Back* I wrote for David Warfield, the American actor, and discussed the matter with David Belasco in the train, when I was on a lecturing tour in America. I read him and Warfield the play at the Belasco Theatre in New York. It was after the performance was over, and we three had the great empty theatre to ourselves. Then we went to Lamb's Club, and Warfield, I think, had macaroni, and Belasco and I had kidneys and lager beer, and discussed arrangements. Firstly Anderson was to draw sketches of the characters, and it was while he was doing this in his studio at Folkestone that Forbes-Robertson dropped in for a chat. Percy Anderson talked to him about the play, and Forbes-Robertson took up the manuscript and read it. Belasco was a little nervous about the play. I did not like the idea of forcing it upon him, and other small difficulties had arisen, so, having heard from Percy Anderson that he had talked to Forbes-Robertson about the play, I thought I would go and see him. He, too, was nervous about it, but said that he felt that he must risk it. We produced it at Harrogate, for quite a nice, respectable audience, and they took it throughout as a farce. One or two critics came down from London, and commiserated with Forbes-Robertson on his luck.

" It was the miners of Blackpool who put heart into us; they understood the thing, and were enthusiastic. Then we produced it at St. James', and, with one or two exceptions, it was besieged with a chorus of condemnation—deplorable, contemptible, absurd, were a few of the adjectives employed, and Forbes-Robertson hastened on the rehearsals for another play. A few days later, King Edward VII, passing through

London on his way to Scotland, devoted his one night in London to seeing the piece. He said it was not the sort of thing he expected from Jerome, but he liked it. And about the same time strange people began to come, who did not know what the St. James' Theatre was, and did not quite know what to do when they got there, and they liked it, too."

I first met Zangwill—Israel Zangwill—at one of the old pothouse dinners of the Vagabond Club. He had not long given up editing *Ariel*, and was already known for his biting wit as a speaker. When the lean, arrestive figure of the Jewish ex-schoolmaster craned over an assemblage, there was always an attentive silence. He had not yet immortalised himself by those inimitable etchings of Jewish life, in which the graver and the acid were employed so ruthlessly —the Tragedies and Comedies of the Ghetto. But he was in sympathies already a novelist, for on that particular occasion he was upbraiding Robert Buchanan for forsaking literature for the drama. His own eyes have wandered to the stage since then. The curly black hair—an orator's hair—the sallow complexion of the South, the pallor of the student, the eagle nose, the assertive smile, the confident paradox—how well I can recall them! He was a young man in those days.

Jerome was always a thorough believer in Zangwill. And he showed his judgment by making him his first serialist in *To-day*. He paid him five hundred pounds for the serial rights of the first of those remarkable novels of Jewish life, as much, I believe, as he paid for the serial rights of *Ebb-Tide*, the book R. L. Stevenson wrote in collaboration with his step-son, Lloyd Osbourne.

Zangwill was a very constant and much-appreciated visitor at our at-homes, as was that encyclopædia of knowledge, his brother Louis. And their sisters sometimes came with them. They all lived together in those days at Kilburn. I remember going to a party at their house to meet Sir Frederick Cowen, the musician, which had a most comical finish. There were six of us left, and only one hansom between us. Three got inside, two sat on the splash-board, and Heinemann spread himself on the roof in front of the man, and kept filling the skylight with his face, like a Japanese Oni. Phil May sat in the middle inside. He was very excited, and we were trying to keep him quiet, so as not to draw the attention of the police to the fact that the hansom was carrying more than it was licensed for. When we got to the Edgware Road, he began to yell for the police, and a stalwart constable signalled to the cabby to heave to. He advanced to the side of the cab. " What is the trouble, sir ? " he asked, preparing to rescue the artist from the literary men among whom he had fallen.

Phil gave one of his knowing smiles, and said, " I want to go to Piccadilly Circus, and they are trying to take me home."

But to return to our Zangwills. Louis Zangwill had not yet shown his strength as a writer, but any one who had tested it, marvelled at the width of his knowledge. In those days Israel Zangwill favoured Slapton Sands for his summer holidays. We met him there. He used to wander about in a black coat and white duck trousers, gathering inspiration. The sunshine and scenery inspired him to be a perfectly delightful companion. We once met him yet further afield—at Venice. Norma Lorimer and I came upon him and Bernard Sickert, the artist, in the Casa Remer, an adorable old palace, with an open courtyard and a processional stair, on the Grand Canal. It was quite unspoiled by repairs in those days. It contained a curio-dealer by the water's edge, and at the head of the staircase was a large room in which a very beautiful young Jewish girl sat sewing for some sweating tailor. We had landed and made an archæological excursion up the staircase, when we discovered her. She arose, and with proper presence of mind, and with a total absence of *mauvaise haute*, conducted us to the curio shop kept by papa. There we met Zangwill and Sickert. We were all of us tempted by some very beautiful mediæval iron gates, which would have been a glory in any nobleman's park, but as we none of us had a park, and even the six hundred francs he wanted for them, added to the cost of transport to England, would have been a considerable sum for any of us, we denied ourselves, and Zangwill gave a dinner

in honour of the event, at a tiny restaurant on a screwy little
canal behind the Piazza of San Marco. The food and the
wine were excellent, and we sat on till the moon was high,
and Venice, on those small old canals, looked like a theatrical
representation of itself for *The Merchant of Venice*. Then
we wandered back to the Piazza to Florian's, the café whose
proud boast it is that it has never closed its doors day or
night for four hundred years. If you are sleeping in Venice
on a summer night—and, in spite of its noise and its mosquitoes, is there anything more adorable than Venice on
a summer night?—you will find that the habit is not confined
to Florian's.

At Florian's we sat down to coffee. We could not get
a seat outside; the band was playing " La Bohême," and the
municipality was throwing red and green limelight on San
Marco in honour of a royal birthday. There was no waiter
either, inside, and Sickert amused himself with drawing
an almost life-sized head of Zangwill with a piece of charcoal
which he had in his pocket, on the marble table. It was a
bit of a caricature, but far the best likeness I ever saw of the
great Jewish novelist. When the waiter did come, without
waiting to take our orders, he went to fetch a damp cloth to
clean the table. *Ars longa, vita brevis*—I would not let
him touch it, and told the proprietor what a prize he had
as I went out. I have often wondered what the fate of that
table was. Zangwill, the apostle of Zionism, has always
been intensely proud of his nationality, so he has never
minded cutting jokes about it. He brought the house down
at a Vagabond Christmas dinner, where he was taking the
chair, by remarking in his opening sentence, " It's a funny
thing to ask a Jew to do." This was the dinner at which he
introduced to English audiences the story which had lately
appeared in a German comic paper. A carpenter was in
a crowd waiting to see the Emperor pass. He had an excellent
position, but he was very uneasy because he had promised to
meet a conceited young brother-in-law, and the brother-in-
law had not turned up.

" Will the Jackanapes never come ! " cried the carpenter.
A policeman promptly arrested him.

" I was speaking of my brother-in-law," gasped the poor carpenter.

" You said ' Jackanapes '; you must have meant the Emperor," said the policeman.

When I asked Zangwill what made him turn to book-writing, he said—

" I never ' turned ' to book-writing, because I never thought of doing anything else, and I have said all I have to say on that subject in the chapter of *My First Book*, published by Chatto & Windus, a book which should be a sufficient mine to you for all your friends.   I was told at the Grosvenor Library that the middle-class Jews boycotted all my books—in revenge for the Jewish ones—but the Jewish ' intellectuals ' have always rallied round me, for I remember that the Maccabeans gave me a dinner to celebrate the birth of *Children of the Ghetto*—a dinner, by the way, at which Tree announced, amid cheers, that he had commissioned me to adapt *Uriel Acosta*.   I never took the commission seriously, but I gave him a one-act play, *Six Persons*, which had a long run at the Haymarket (giving Irene Vanbrugh her first good part), and still survives, twenty years after, having been played quite recently at the Coliseum and the Palladium by Margaret Halstan as well as by Miss Helen Mar somewhere else.

" An anecdote I remember telling at this dinner was : A man said to me, ' My son has had typhoid, but he enjoyed himself reading your book.'

" ' Where did he get it from ? ' I asked, because it was the old three-volume days, and I knew he could not have bought it.

" Thinking of the typhoid, he replied, ' From the drains.'

" This theory of the origin of my book is, I believe, favoured in high ecclesiastical quarters."

I knew Mark Twain very well.   He and Bret Harte were, I suppose, the two most famous American authors who ever came to our at-homes at No. 32.   Bret Harte, though he was such a typically American writer, spent all the latter part of his life in England.   I first met him at Rudolph Lehmann's hospitable dinner-table.   No one could fail to be struck with Bret Harte. He was so alert, so handsome, and though his plumes—his hair was thick and sleek to the day he died—were of an exquisite snow-white, he had a healthy, fresh-coloured face, and a slender, youthful figure, always dressed like a well-off young man. He used to come to our house with the Vaudeveldes. Madame Vaudevelde, herself an authoress, and the daughter of a famous ambassador, kept a suite of rooms in her great house in Lancaster Gate for his use, whenever he was in London.

"Don't you ever go back to California nowadays?" I asked him once.

"No. I dare say that if I saw the new California, with all its go-aheadness and modernness, I should lose the old California that I knew, whereas now it has never changed for me. I can picture everything just as it was when I left it."

He retained his vogue to the end. Any magazine would pay him at the rate of a couple of pounds for every hundred words. They used to say that the Bank of England would accept his manuscripts as banknotes. He never failed to charm, whether he was telling some story at a dinner-party, or talking to some undistinguished woman, young and beautiful or old and plain, who had asked to be introduced to him as a celebrity—and a celebrity Francis Bret Harte certainly was, for he founded a whole school in English literature.

Mark Twain was also very kind, but when I was in New York he was living at Hartford, the capital of the adjoining State of Connecticut. He described himself to me as a "wooden nutmeg," in allusion to a former thriving industry of the State. I met him when he was engaged to entertain a ladies' school at New York. That did not cost nothing. The idea seemed to me very American, that an author at the height of his fame, as Mark Twain then was—for he was fifty-five years old, and it was twenty-one years since he leapt into fame with *The Jumping Frog*, should accept an engagement to "give a talk" in a private house. The school received good value for its fee. He not only gave them an hour's entrancing address, but he stayed on till quite a late train, having anybody and everybody introduced to him, and being cordial to them all. Nor was his cordiality short-lived. I had done nothing then, except publish a few books of verse. Yet we became and remained till the day of his death, twenty years later, familiar friends. This was before I received that memorable invitation from Oliver Wendell Holmes to be his guest at the monthly meeting of the Saturday Club at Boston, where Mark Twain proved that the English were mentioned in the Bible.[1] He told story after story in that address, but I don't remember any of them. They were all good in tendency, that was one thing; there was no making fun of anything that was good or noble or sincere with him. He was, like our own humorist, Jerome, intensely serious in his soul, and he was projecting a big book about the Bible—as a publisher, for he was already in the publishing firm of Charles L. Webster & Co., who were producing the huge *Library of American Literature*, of which E. C. Stedman was joint editor.

In order to make all great men authors, it had the idea to give the most famous sayings of historical Americans, where they had not written anything. In this way Abraham Lincoln became an author. I expect that it was that encyclopædia which years afterwards brought the house of Charles L. Webster & Co. down, though it was sold " on subscription," with thousands of copies ordered before the book was begun. Mark Twain found himself responsible for debts of fifty thousand pounds. I met him soon afterwards, and began condoling with him on his losses as a publisher. He replied, " I am no publisher, nor ever was. I only put the money up for them to play with."

To make up his losses to him, a leading American firm— I seem to recollect that it was the Harpers, but I may be wrong—made him a gigantic " syndicate " proposal for all rights, which brought in large sums of money.

When I met him then, he had just come off ship-board. I asked him how he was.

" Better'n I ever was in my life. I've gotten a new lease."

" How ? "

" Well, it's a long story. You must know that when I am

---

[1] When challenged to prove it, he read out the text, " For the meek shall inherit the earth."

staying in a hotel, or on board ship, I can't go to bed while there is one person left to talk to in the bar. This habit, I don't know what ways exactly, gave me a cough that I couldn't get rid of, till an old Auntie from Georgia told me to try drops of rum on sugar. It took away my cough, and I liked it fine. I went on taking it after my cough had gone; it grew to be a habit, and before I knew where I was my digestion had gone. I tried all the doctors I could hear of, at home, and in England, and in Germany, including Austria, to cure that. But it was not possible; all they could do for me was to find out what I liked best to eat or drink, and tell me to do without it. I was wasting to a shadow, so I sent for my own doctor, and said to him, ' Doctor, I can't stand this any longer; life isn't worth living, what there is going to be of it, and that doesn't seem to be much. I am going to commit suicide.' ' Maybe it is the best thing to do,' he said. ' Do you know what is the most painless form of death ? ' ' Yes,' said I, ' I am going to eat and drink everything I like best for a week, and according to all of you, it ought to take much less time than that.'

" So I did, and I assure you, Mr. Sladen, before the week was up, I was as well as ever I had been in my life."

He could reel off this sort of story by the hour, with that slow drawl of his, which was so mightily effective.

Frank Stockton, the kindliest and most delicate humorist of America, I knew very well, and any one who knew him intimately could not help regarding him with affection. He was a little man with a club foot, and rather a timid expression, which he made use of when telling his immortal after-dinner stories; he emphasised the timidity until the point came, and his face was wreathed with smiles. Stockton was a great gardener. His garden out at the Holt near the Convent station in New Jersey was large and beautiful, and the product of his own imagination. It seemed incredible that a garden like that should have no kind of a hedge or fence, but he explained that in America to put a fence round your garden is considered an insult to the democracy, who by no means always deserve to be trusted in this matter.

Stockton was so good-natured that his wife used to say

H

he would never have done any work at all if he had not had a dragon at his side to guard him. She was not much like a dragon. But on one point she was inexorable; when the time had really come for him to set about fulfilling a contract, she insisted on his going into New York to a hotel with as blank an outlook as possible, so that he should not waste time over gardening; he could not trust himself within sight of a green leaf.

Stockton was a wood-engraver to start with, and was thirty-eight years old before he abandoned it to do editorial work. A year later he became assistant-editor of *St. Nicholas*, the American children's magazine. It was not until 1880 that he gave it up to devote himself entirely to book-writing. Up till 1879, the year in which he published *Rudder Grange*, he only wrote children's books, and he did not publish his next book for grown-ups, *The Lady or the Tiger*, for another five years.

Another old member of the Vagabond Club, always a very intimate friend of Jerome's, who was often at our at-homes was Pett Ridge, the humorist whose knowledge of the East End of London is sometimes compared to Dickens's; indeed, many consider him unequalled as a writer of Cockney humour and an interpreter of Cockney humanity. Unlike Jerome, Pett Ridge, who also has very earnest convictions and has done a world of good, has the humorist in him always near the surface. He used to be a constant speaker at literary clubs, and most popular for his never-failing fund of humour, which was heightened by his demure delivery.

With Pett Ridge, it is natural to mention W. W. Jacobs, our best sea humorist. People used to be surprised that the small, slight, youthful-looking man, who was known to them as a clerk in the General Post Office, should be the delineator of those inimitable captains and bo'suns and hands before the mast of little sailing-craft which ply round our coasts. He was one of the men to whom the members of the general public, who strayed to literary dinners, were most anxious to be introduced. Their admiration made him shy, and it was a long time before he grew accustomed to do him-

JEROME K. JEROME
Drawn by Yoshio Markino

self justice in his public speeches, for he is one of our most genuine humorists. He owed his unique knowledge of coasting-craft and their navigators to the fact that his father owned a wharf on the Thames, and that it was one of his chief pleasures as a boy to go down to the wharf and make friends with the sea-dogs. After his marriage he went to live in Essex, but, as a bachelor living in London, he was a very familiar figure at our at-homes. To those who frequented literary gatherings in the days of which I am speaking, it is natural to think of H. G. Wells with Pett Ridge and Jacobs, but Wells was much less seen at these gatherings, because he lived out of town at Worcester Park. He was already married when I made his acquaintance, and had got through the first marvellous part of his career, on which he draws for so many of his books.

He and his wife found a great difficulty in coming to our at-homes, because they were such very late-at-night affairs. Once they stayed with us, sleeping at the Temperance Hotel round the corner, called rather inappropriately the " London and Scottish," because all our bedrooms were turned into sitting-rooms for the night. The pair of them looked ridiculously young. Wells was very boyish in those days; he was slight in figure and youthful in face, with thick, rebellious, fairish hair, and a charmingly impulsive manner. It seems odd to think now that then he suffered from such very bad health that he was not expected to live long. Those were the days in which he used to write about flying men and scientific millennia, most brilliant books which told the British public that a genius had dropped from heaven, whose crumbs were picked up by Mr. John Lane. Wells became a Vagabond at a very early date, but he disliked making speeches, and, in point of fact, hardly ever did make one in his early days, so his wonderful literary gift was not recognised so quickly as it would have been if he had been constantly making speeches before literary clubs and other large audiences.

A feature of Wells' writing is his marvellous versatility. He will make a hit on entirely fresh lines, indulge the public with a few other books on these lines, and then, before they have time to tire of them, break out in another fresh vein. It is hard to believe that the same man wrote *Select Conversations with an Uncle* and *Marriage*, though it is true that seventeen years elapsed between their publication, and there were many changes of style between the two. In those days he was only a brilliant novelist; now we recognise in him a profound thinker, a solver of social problems, even if we ourselves are Conservatives.

In the *New Machiavelli* and *Marriage* there is intuition in every page and almost every line. You can read them with sheer delight for the writing alone; they do not depend on the story, however excellent.

Another humorist who was a constant visitor was Max O'Rell—the genial and irascible Frenchman who, as Paul Blouet, the name to which he was born, was principal French master at St. Paul's School. Max O'Rell lived in a house with a garden at St. John's Wood. We were very fond of him and his pretty wife, and much shocked when the two blows fell so quickly upon one another. Max O'Rell fought for France against the Germans, and he always looked a fighting man, with his strong figure and belligerent moustache. He was a fine fencer, and had, I am sure, fought duels in his time; with his temperament he could not have kept out of them; he was up in arms in a moment. I remember how fiercely he turned upon Norma Lorimer for using the expression, " The British Channel."

" Why British ? " he asked.

But he was quite floored by the repartee, " Because of the weather."

Max O'Rell was always quick at repartee himself—except in America. Of America and Americans he always spoke in public with his tongue in his cheek, but in private he was " screamingly funny " about them. He should certainly have left a posthumous volume of unpalatable truths about America. It would not have hurt him in the Great Beyond, and it would have convulsed the English-speaking world. He must often have felt in America as he felt at Napier, New Zealand, where the audience at the Mechanics' Institute, or some such place, would have none of him.

"I am good enough for London and Paris," he said, speaking to me about it afterwards; "I am good enough for New York, Boston and Chicago; I am good enough for Melbourne and Sydney. But I am not good enough for Napier, New Zealand—Napier, with its five thousand inhabitants, etc., etc."

He had the same staccato style in his lectures and after-dinner speeches as he had in his *John Bull and His Island* and his other famous books, and he easily drifted into it in his conversations.

Other humorists of the little circle—it is to be noted how many there were—were Robert Barr, Barry Pain and W. L. Alden. Barr, as co-editor of the *Idler*, was a pivot of literary society like Jerome. But his home for a considerable portion of the period was a long way down in Surrey, too far for his friends to pursue him to it. This was not without design, for he was a man so fitted to shine in literary society, that his one chance of writing his delicate and delightful novels was to bury himself in the country.

He made his reputation as "Luke Sharp," the most brilliant humorist of the *Detroit Free Press*, at that time the most-quoted paper in America, and he was very American both in appearance and speech. His brusqueness and pugnacity were at times terrifying, but underneath them lay a gentle nature and a most affectionate heart. He was a man who inspired and returned the warmest affection. His grim humour was famous: it suited the handsome features, marred with smallpox, the close-trimmed naval officer's beard, the sturdy frame, the strong American accent, much better than his dainty love-stories did. There was no more popular speaker; his influence among his fellow-journalists was unbounded. He and his pretty and charming wife, an excellent foil for his pugnacious exterior, were frequent hosts at the Idler teas, and frequent guests at our flat. Barr was very biting about England's national foibles, but they never moved him to such outbursts of righteous indignation as the intermittent immoralities of the United States Government.

He remained faithful to his birthplace till his premature

death, for he called two successive homes of his in the South, Hillhead, after the district of Glasgow in which he was born. In his later days he was so much the editor, so much the novelist, that one forgot the humorist, except when he was convulsing a knot of friends, to whom he was talking at a reception, or the audience he was addressing across a dinner-table.

Barry Pain and W. L. Alden, on the other hand, were always humorists. Alden, who had a most whimsical mind, had been the American Consul-General at Rome, and had, in consequence, been made a Cavaliere by the Italian Government. His title was part of his humorous equipment. It seemed so droll that a typical, middle-class American like Alden, should be a cavalier. Both he and his wife were kindly and agreeable people, but most of his personality went into his writing.

Barry Pain, on the other hand, had a forceful personality. Whenever you meet this cheery cynic, with his bright dark eyes, you know that you are in the presence of a man who was born to be editor of *Punch*. He was a constant speaker at literary clubs, though I don't think that he liked speaking at first. His speeches were full of the same brilliant paradoxes as his books. His cynicism was tempered by overflowing good-nature. He was always such a hearty man. He was another of the people who soon flew into the country to get away from parties, and have time for his numerous contributions to weekly journals. But while he lived in London he was very often at our house. I made his acquaintance at the Lehmanns'—he married Stella Lehmann—soon after he had come down from Cambridge. At Cambridge he had been R. C. Lehmann's bright particular star in Granta, and Lehmann, who had wealth, good looks, and a brilliant athletic record to back up his very great abilities as a writer, had at once become influential in London journalistic circles.

CHAPTER X

To use the famous expression applied by Dr. Johnson to his College at Oxford, we had quite a nest of singing-birds at 32 Addison Mansions, for, to mention only three of them, William Watson, John Davidson and Richard le Gallienne were at the same time habitués of our at-homes, and Bliss Carman, the Canadian, was constantly with us when he was over here.

Sir Lewis Morris, who was considered likely to succeed Tennyson as laureate at a time when those young poets were in the nursery, sometimes walked down from the Reform Club to call on us, but he always came on odd afternoons, a tall man, with a gaunt red face, who in those days was inclined to put his poetical triumphs behind him, and be the Liberal politician. Personally, I much preferred the poems of Lord de Tabley, a delightfully dignified, gentle and affable personage. His poems have never received full justice; for Graeco-Roman atmosphere he must be classed with those who come just below Shelley, Keats and Matthew Arnold—above Horne's " Orion," I think.

Edmund Gosse, who introduced me to Lord de Tabley, introduced me also to the late H. O. Houghton, at that time head of the eminent publishing firm of Houghton, Mifflin & Co., the John Murrays of America, and to the late Richard Watson Gilder, editor of the *Century Magazine*, two men at whose houses I met all the most famous authors of Boston and New York respectively. Gosse, who had for his brother-in-law the late Sir Alma Tadema, lived in those days at Delamere Terrace, and at his house on Sunday afternoons you always met authors of real distinction, men like Lord de Tabley, Maarten Maartens, Austin Dobson, or

103

Wolcott Balestier, Kipling's brother-in-law, the type of genius in a frail body.   Edmund Gosse, besides being one of those poets, rare nowadays, who preserve the traditional grace of form, the distillation of thought which characterises the poetical masters of the " Golden Treasury," was instrumental in giving England Ibsen and the other Scandinavian giants of the generation.

Austin Dobson, a man who has the mild and magnificent eye of Browning's *Lost Leader*, the Horace of lighter English poetry, began life, like Gosse, as a Civil Servant, and, like Gosse, is as felicitous in his essays and his criticisms as in his poems.   But, since he lived at Ealing and had five sons and five daughters, he was very little to be seen at literary gatherings in the days of which I speak.

It is natural to mention Andrew Lang with them.   They were the three best lighter poets of their generation, but Lang had the advantage over the others of being one of the most brilliant scholars of his time—no man since the mighty Conington displayed such a mass of classical erudition, combined with a genius for popularising it, especially in the direction of translation.   Lang's prose translations can be compared with Conington's rhymed versions of Virgil and Horace.   He had also a passion for the occult, and was one of the best scholars in comparative occultology and mythology.

His tall, lean figure, mop of grey hair, and screwed-up scholar's eyes, were as familiar among golfers and anglers as at the Savile Club, and other literary coteries, which he deigned to honour with his presence.   He reduced rudeness to a fine art, and never showed his heart to any one old enough to understand it.   But he was nearly a big man as well as a big scholar.

One cannot think of Lang without thinking also of Frederic W. H. Myers, whom I met far earlier.   As a child he was remarkable; at thirteen, on entering Cheltenham College (where I was educated long afterwards), so precocious was his scholarship that he was placed with boys of seventeen and eighteen.   I doubt if there ever has lived another English boy who learned the whole of Virgil by heart for his own pure delight, before he passed the school age.   He won the senior classical scholarship in his first year at thirteen; besides gaining the first prize for Latin lyrics, he sent in two English poems in different metres, and both were the best and came out top !

At the university few men have won more honours. Myers was to Cambridge as Lang was to Oxford—and more also. He was greater in pure scholarship, and far greater as a poet, for he wrote " St. Paul," almost the finest quatrain poem in the English language. His later volume of poems, entitled *The Renewal of Youth*, is perhaps less well known, but this was the poem that he himself cared for most, and its compressed force and intensity of feeling and wonderful beauty of expression have gained it a steadily increasing public.

In his later years he became more absorbed in psychical research. The success of his famous work, *Human Personality, and its Survival of Bodily Death*, is well known. The epilogue, pp. 341–352, has become almost a classic, and the book has now been translated into nearly all European languages. This would have surprised Frederic Myers enormously. He wrote to a friend in 1900, " I am occupied in writing a big book which I don't expect any one to read, but I do it for the satisfaction of my own conscience." He laboured in this field up to his death, with the same ardour and strenuousness that he threw into all his work.

He was a wonderful personality—no one who ever saw his unforgettable eyes, and beautiful majestic head, and heard his marvellously eloquent voice, could ever forget him. Myers is buried just where he should be buried—by the side of Shelley and John Addington Symonds in the new Protestant cemetery at Rome, under the ancient cypresses which top the city wall. Close by, this wall of Aurelian is pierced by the gate through which St. Paul was led to his martyrdom. The people who stood on the wall where the author of " St. Paul " lies buried, could have seen the Saint pass out.

Myers and H. M. Stanley married two sisters. I always though it so appropriate that Stanley's brother-in-law, one of the greatest scholars Cambridge ever nursed, should have been so great an explorer in the Universe. A mutual friend told me that when Myers was on his deathbed, Henry Sidgwick, the philosopher, quoted to Mrs. Myers some lines in "The Renewal of Youth," the poem which Myers himself, and many of his Cambridge friends, thought the best of all his work—

> " Ah, welcome then that hour which bids thee lie
> In anguish of thy last infirmity!
> Welcome the toss for ease, the gasp for air,
> The visage drawn, and Hippocratic stare;
> Welcome the darkening dream, the lost control,
> The sleep, the swoon, the arousal of the soul!"

Sidgwick thought these lines, and indeed, the whole poem, wonderful, far finer than " St. Paul."

Of the younger generation of the poets, four of the most noted, William Watson, W. B. Yeats, John Davidson and le Gallienne, were at one time almost weekly at our flat. Watson, whose powerful clean-shaven face always reminded me of Charles James Fox, before that inventor of irresponsible Liberalism lost his looks by dissipation, I see still sometimes. It was only last year that he and his beautiful young wife asked me to visit them at their house in the country.

The sturdy Yorkshire stock of which he came is reflected in his poems. He is accustomed to think and write upon large national and international movements, and he has a splendid gift of sonorous and epigrammatic diction. I did not share the views he expressed, but that did not prevent me from admiring the way in which he expressed them. In my mind, there was no question but that the laureateship lay between him and Kipling. But at Oxford Bridges already had a reputation as a poet while I was an undergraduate.

When Yeats first came to our house he was a shock-headed Irish boy of twenty-six, without any regard for his personal appearance. He did not care whether he had any studs in his shirt or not, and once he came in evening dress without a tie. But we knew then that he was a genius, and the world knows it now. He has a fairy-like muse, whose quill is dipped in pathos. He had then only just given up the idea of being an artist, like his father. He was an art student for three years. His poems and plays will live.

Yeats was very naïve. I remember his complaining to me in the early days of the Irish Literary Society that it suffered under a grave disadvantage; its authors were unable to

write as " nationalistically " as they would have desired, ,
because the Irish never bought books, and the brutal Saxon
would not buy them if they went too far in denouncing him.
Those were not his exact words, but they give the substance
of them.   One might fancy that these young men and young
women, falling between the devil and the deep sea, took
refuge in playwriting, because the Englishman will go and
see a play which is sufficiently pathetic or sufficiently funny,
no matter how disloyal to himself its sentiments may be;
but his purse-strings are tighter with regard to displeasing
books. Yeats was always highly appreciated. When he
published *John Sherman* it was thought that he had a career
as a novelist before him, but he did not follow this up.

Another Irishman whom I may mention here is Dr. Todhunter, though he already had some silver in his beard twenty
years ago, and was the *doyen* of our poets, and at the beginning
the most considerable in his accomplishments. He had made
his name with " The Black Cat " and the " Sicilian Idyll,"
and belonged to an older generation.

English literature is much the poorer by John Davidson
having taken his own life, in despair at the scantiness of the
rewards which his genius could earn. Davidson was a man
I liked very much. His robust personality was reflected in
his brilliant eyes and colouring. His heartiness and sincerity
were transparent and he was a very vital poet. He came
often. Davidson was inspired ; there are lines of white
fire in " The Ballad of the Nun." His cheery, courageous
face and blithe smile did not in the least suggest a man who
would commit suicide; they were much more suggestive of
the bloods who lived in the piping times of King George III.
He was another Lane discovery, I think, and I suspect that
Lane brought him to our house, as he brought Beardsley
and many another man destined to be celebrated, W. J.
Locke among them.

Le Gallienne I knew better than any of them. He and his
brother-in-law, James Welch, were conspicuous features at
our parties, Welch because he was irresistibly funny, and in
the habit of exercising his wonderful gift of mimicry at odd
moments—we all believed in his future eminence.

Le Gallienne was even more conspicuous for his personal appearance and frank posing. He had a face like Shelley, and the true hyacinthine curls, if hyacinthine curls mean the rich, waving black hair which one associates with the Greeks of mythology. He was really a rather vigorous and athletic man, and he used to say in the most captivating way, " You musn't mind me letting my hair grow, and living up to it—it is part of my stock-in-trade. People wouldn't come to hear me lecture without it."

Undoubtedly his picturesque appearance made him one of the most striking figures in any literary assemblage, but he also had splendid gifts as a poet. I have always thought that his version of Omar Khayyam is one of the most beautiful, and has never received justice in comparison with other versions. Like Fitzgerald, he was unable to translate from the original, but that did not signify, because hardly any one in England, in or out of the Omar Khayyam Club, can understand the original, and the most popular version of the Rubaiyat is valued, not for what Omar put into it, but for what Fitzgerald put into it. Huntly McCarthy, who was only in our house once or twice, did, of course, actually make a translation of the Rubaiyat, but he is a literary marvel who has not yet come into his own, author of exquisite poems, and of some of the most brilliant and delightful historical novels by any living writer. His father, the genial leader of the Home Rule Party, who loved Ireland without hating England, and wrote history blindfolded to prejudice, that grand old man, Justin McCarthy, was a much more frequent visitor. I can see him now, with his long beard, and eloquent Irish eyes behind very conspicuous glasses, leaning on his daughter Charlotte, and I can hear his rich brogue. It was a great honour to be admitted to the intimate friendship of Justin McCarthy, and when he grew more infirm, and went to die at Westgate, where he lived on for a surprising time, he never failed to remember me with a line at Christmas.

I ought to mention Oscar Wilde here, who had a wonderful gift of poetical expression, and whom I met when we were both undergraduates at Oxford, where he used to call himself

O. O'F. Wills Wilde—Oscar O'Flaherty Wills Wilde. He was always known as Wills Wilde.

But our parties were too crowded for him; he prefered to come to see me on a chance afternoon, like Lewis Morris. He hated having people introduced to him, until he had expressed the desire that they should have the honour, and in meetings so Bohemian he could not have escaped it. He took a scholarship at Oxford, and won the University prize for the English poem, and I rather think he got a First Class, but one did not think of him *dans cette galère*. He had, even in those days, a desire to be conspicuous, and in those days æstheticism pranced through the land. Garments of funny-coloured green baize, with a Greek absence of any pretence at dressmaking, were the badge of the æsthetic female, who to take first prize was required to have red hair and green eyes, and a mouth like a magenta foxglove. And the idea was that men should wear black velvet knickerbocker suits, with silk stockings and black velvet caps like pancakes. I never saw them doing it, except in an æsthetic pottery shop in the Queen's Road, Bayswater, where they sold Aspinall's enamels, and on the stage, where Gilbert and Sullivan's *Patience* took the place now occupied by works of genius like Bernard Shaw's *Chocolate Soldier*. Wilde never wore the dress at Oxford, but he was quite courageous in adjuncts. At one time he banished all the decorations from his rooms, except a single blue vase of the true æsthetic type which contained a " Patience " lily. He was discovered by the other undergraduates of Magdalen prostrated with grief before it because he never could live up to it. They did what they could to revive him by putting him under the college pump.

But they applauded his wit, at the coining of a famous example of which I was privileged to be present. We were both in for a Divinity exam. at the same time. There was no Honour school in Divinity; it was simply a qualifying exam. to show that we had sufficient knowledge of the rudiments of the religion of the Church of England to be graduates of a religious university; we used to call the exam. " Rudiments " for short.

I went to the exam., like a good young man, at the advertised hour, nine o'clock; Wilde did not arrive till half-an-hour later, and when Spooner, the Head of New College, who was one of our examiners, asked him what he meant by being so late, he said, " You must excuse me; I have no experience of these pass examinations."

It was the morning of the *viva voce* examinations, and his being late did not really signify because W is one of the last letters in the alphabet. But the examiners were so annoyed at his impertinence that they gave him a Bible, and told him to copy out the long twenty-seventh chapter of the Acts. He copied it out so industriously in his exquisite handwriting that their hearts relented, and they told him that he need not write out any more. Half-an-hour afterwards they noticed that he was copying it out as hard as ever, and they called him up to say, " Didn't you hear us tell you, Mr. Wilde, that you needn't copy out any more ? "

" Oh yes," he said, " I heard you, but I was so interested in what I was copying, that I could not leave off. It was all about a man named Paul, who went on a voyage, and was caught in a terrible storm, and I was afraid that he would be drowned, but, do you know, Mr. Spooner, he was saved, and when I found that he was saved, I thought of coming to tell you."

As Mr. Spooner was nephew of the Archbishop of Canterbury, the insult was of a peculiarly aggravating nature, and he ploughed him then and there. As my name also came low down in the alphabet, I was a witness of the whole performance.

Herbert Trench, the poet, who, when he became a theatrical manager, discovered the " Blue Bird," often came, a very handsome Irishman of the blue-eyed and black-haired type. I met him when he and I were fellow members of the House Committee which discussed the poorness of the dinners at the old Authors' Club.

Frederick Langbridge, the charming poet, who was joint author of Martin Harvey's evergreen " Only Way," only came once or twice, because, like Dean Swift, he was exiled by an Irish preferment. He is Rector of Limerick.

Wilde once brought a friend with him, whose name was Barlass. He wrote poetry which Wilde admired, though it had no market, and claimed to be a descendant of the Katherine Douglas who barred the door with her arm when the bolt had been stolen, to save King James III of Scotland from his murderers, and was nicknamed Katherine Barlass. I have a volume of his poems still, but the thing I remember best about him was an episode which happened when we were both at Wilde's house in Tite Street one day. Upstairs in the drawing-room he had asked Wilde, " What do you think of George Meredith's novels? "

Wilde, having nothing effective to say at the moment, appeared not to hear him. But as he was going out of the front door, he said, " George Meredith is a sort of prose Browning," and when Barlass was halfway down Tite Street, he called after him, " And Browning also is a sort of prose Browning."

Bliss Carman wrote some of the most delightful poetry of them all. Born in Canada, where they have eternal sunshine in summer, and brought up in those parts of the Maritime provinces where little mountains and little lakes and little rivers and little forests combine with a bold coastline to make Acadia an Arcady, it was only natural that he should be able to transfigure in his poems the Old World Arcady, with Pan, Faun, Syrinx and Adonis, and all the lovely rabble of mountain, sea and woodland nymphs.

Carman could write from a typical Canadian inspiration also. He could make you see Grandpré, and the lives of the men who won Canada from the wilds and maintained a seignorial grace of life in the new France, which was born in the days of the Roi Soleil, and lived under the white flag till it went down in the glorious sunset on the heights of Abraham. Carman's poetry is rich in romance, and he was a romantic figure, for with his great stature and fair hair, and blue eyes, he looked as if he might have been one of the Norsemen led to the far north of the continent by Leif, the son of Erik, a thousand years ago, whose descendants were discovered roaming in the Arctic only the other day. As a matter of fact, he was descended from one of the most famous men among the United Empire loyalists, who left the United States when they could no longer live there under the British flag, and gave Canada her unconquerable backbone.

I should have mentioned ere this two dear friends of ours who are both dead—William Sharp and Gleeson White. White was one of my oldest literary friends. We knew him when we were living at Richmond before we went to America, and saw a lot of him during the three years we were there. We came home, I think, just before him. William Sharp introduced him to us. Sharp, who was the friend of nearly every well-known author of his time, began life as poet and critic. As general editor of the " Canterbury Poets," his name is a household word. There was no wider-minded critic, none who had a wider knowledge of the poetry and other verses of his day. But his chief contribution to literature consisted of the works of " Fiona Macleod," which were never acknowledged as his during his lifetime, though he never denied their authorship to me. We saw him frequently, not only at Addison Mansions, but abroad, for, like ourselves, he was an insatiable wanderer over Italy and Sicily.

Gleeson White did not write much verse himself, but he edited a volume of society verses under the title of *Ballades and Rondeaux,* in the " Canterbury Poets," which had a really public effect. It collected the best examples of the ballades and rondeaux, and verse in other old French forms, written by Gosse and Dobson, and Lang, and other well-known writers, in such a convenient form, and gave the rules for writing them so clearly, that everybody who had any skill in versifying set to work to write ballades and rondeaux, and bombard the magazines and newspapers with them. There was a rage of ballade-writing which can only be compared to the limerick competitions of *Pearson's Weekly.* Of Gleeson White's accomplishments as an art critic I have spoken elsewhere.

Edgar Fawcett, the New Yorker who was so often at our parties on both sides of the Atlantic, was one of the best American writers of ballades, though thousands of American writers, according to the sardonic Miss Gilder, turned them out by machinery.

Sharp himself was more inclined to the sonnet, as was our mutual friend, Theodore Watts (now Watts-Dunton), who lived with Swinburne at the Pines, Putney, and will always be remembered as Swinburne's greatest friend. Watts's sonnets in the *Athenæum* became as well known to literary people as Dr. Watts's hymns. They were among the best sonnets of the day. Watts was Swinburne's companion on his famous swimming excursions. Like the matchless poet who refused the laureateship, he was a magnificent swimmer.

Hall Caine was at that time the chief authority upon the sonnet, as he was one of the chief literary critics of the *Athenæum* and the *Academy*. He gave me about that time his *Sonnets of Three Centuries*, which I still keep.

Two other followers of the Muse who came to our parties were Mackenzie Bell and Norman Gale.

Adrian Ross—Arthur Reed Ropes—who so long carried on a dual literary life—a Fellow of King's, an Examiner to the University, and writer of text-books at Cambridge, while he wrote the songs for George Edwardes's musical comedies in London, was a friend of ours before he came to live in Addison Mansions, partly, I believe, because we lived there. He is an amazingly clever man; his general knowledge is extraordinary. He took various 'varsity scholarships and prizes at Cambridge and was the ablest of the clever journalists with whom Clement Shorter surrounded himself for his great move. He may also fairly claim to be W. S. Gilbert's successor as a writer of really witty and scholarly songs (which have also been amazingly popular) for the principal musical comedies from *A Greek Slave* till the present day. Adrian Ross, who is a Russian by birth, looks like a Russian with his big, burly form, and fair beard and glasses, when you see him taking the chair at some feast of reason like the Omar Khayyam Club. He is one of the chief Omarians, and might, if he devoted himself to it, write just such a poem as Fitzgerald's " Rubaiyat " himself, for he has the gift of form, the wit, and the width of knowledge, to draw upon. In the same way, if he had been born early enough, he would have written some of our best ballades and rondeaux. There, in addition

I

to his extraordinary facility, he had the advantage of being one of the best-read men in England on French literature, and one of the chief authorities upon it. He married Ethel Wood, an actress as clever as she is pretty, who, if she acted more, would be one of our most successful character-actresses.

Rowland Thirlmere was another dual personality. When he came to see us at Addison Mansions he was Rowland Thirlmere the poet, literary to his finger-tips; when he was at home at Bury he was John Walker, a Lancashire cotton-mill manager, an ardent Conservative politician, a " Wake up, England ! " man. Did he not write *The Clash of Empires,* a classic on the German peril?

Douglas Ainslie, the poet of the Stuarts, who has now established for himself a solid reputation in Philosophy, was still a diplomat when he first used to come to see us.

We had not so many poetesses. The chief of them was Lady Lindsay, whose *In a Venetian Gondola* went through many editions, a poetess of the same order and rank as the Hon. Mrs. Norton a generation before. Her poetry was strengthened by sincere piety and morality. They gave it the mysterious quality which attracts us in the old Sienese pictures.

Among the younger poetesses who came to us, two stood out—Ethel Clifford, Mrs. W. K. Clifford's daughter, who married Fisher Dilke, and Marguerite Radclyffe-Hall.

The charm of Mrs. Dilke's poetry is universally admitted, but Miss Hall's has not yet received anything like the recognition which it deserves.

She is a step-daughter of the famous musician, Albert Visetti, and much younger than any of the others. To see her, even to speak with her, one would think that she thought more of her hunting-box and her horses than of abstractions like poetry. At the time when I first met her, her winters were equally divided between travelling and hunting, and she appears to have gathered inspiration from both of these sources. Her outdoor life in one of our most beautiful counties has given her a deep love and appreciation of the country pleasures only to be found in England. There is no one I know who writes more from inspiration.   I reviewed her first book, *'Twixt Earth and Stars*, with real enthusiasm. Since then she has published *A Sheaf of Verses*, *Poems of the Past and Present*, and *Songs of Three Counties and Other Poems*.   Of these three volumes, *Poems of the Past and the Present* shows her at her best.

Visetti was born a Dalmatian, but he has for thirty years been a British subject—and a very patriotic British subject. He had the celebrated composer, Arrigo Boito, for a fellow-student at the Conservatoire at Milan.   An even greater composer, Auber, introduced him to the splendid court of the third Napoleon.   Dumas père wrote a libretto for him. He was Adelina Patti's musical adviser for five years, and wrote " La Diva " for her.   He was admitted to the personal friendship of both the late King Edward and the late Duke of Edinburgh.   He was the first professor appointed to the staff of the Royal College of Music.   He has written lives of Palestrina and Verdi.

" Dolly Radford," a writer of delicate and sympathetic verse, and her husband, Ernest Radford, used to come to us in those days.   So, very occasionally, did two Irish poetesses, Mrs. Shorter and Katherine Tynan.   The former, wife of the editor of the *Sphere*, has won herself an assured position by Celtic ballads of a highly imaginative order. She is Yeats's closest rival.

I first met Mrs. Clement Shorter when she was staying with Miss Katherine Tynan (Mrs. Hinkson) at Ealing, where Shorter first met her.   Mrs. Hinkson thus recalls Miss Dora Sigerson, as she was then, in her *Reminiscences*—

" I was the means of introducing Dora some years later to Mr. Clement Shorter, whom she married.

" We were all possessed with the common impulse towards literature.   We were all making our poems and stories.   Dora Sigerson, who was then a strikingly handsome girl, was painting as well, making statuettes and busts, doing all sorts of things, and looking like a young Muse.   Dr. Sigerson was, as he is happily doing to-day, dispensing the most delightful hospitality.   His Sunday-night dinners were, and are, a feature of literary life in Dublin, chiefly of the literary life which has the colour of the green. At the time there was no Irish Literary Society, as there is now, with Dr. Sigerson for its President. The best of the young intellect of Dublin was to be found at Dr. Sigerson's board."

Mrs. Shorter has written several volumes of poetry, one with an introduction by George Meredith, novels and short stories. She also still paints in oils, and models; her country garden at Great Missenden has many examples of her talent in this direction.

Mrs. Shorter's poetry has an ample range. Some of her ballads are pitiful tragedies, told with a delicate sense of ballad simplicity, and an exquisite ear for the broken music which is so essential to ballads; and, at the other end of the gamut, she can also write songs in a lighter vein that deserve a composer like Bishop to set them to music—such songs as the poem called " The Spies " in her *Madge Linsey* volume.

Katherine Tynan, who had married H. A. Hinkson before we ever met personally, though years earlier she had given me introductions to Louise Imogen Guiney, the American poetess, and other valued friends among the writers in America, is the author of short lyrics, human and graceful, which ought to find a permanent place in our anthologies, as well as a popular novelist, and has lately written a charming volume of her *Reminiscences*.

I have left Sir Edwin Arnold, Thomas Hardy and W. E. Henley to the end of this chapter. Arnold, whom I used to see daily when we were both living in Tokyo, was too infirm to come to us much in Addison Mansions in his last days.

While he was in Japan, he lived in a native house in Azabu outside Treaty limits, receiving permission to do so under the legal fiction that he was tutor to the daughters of the wealthy Japanese who lent him the house under a similar fiction. It was just outside the Azabu Temple, a favourite resort for holiday-makers, and had delightful bamboo-brakes, which rustled rhythm to Arnold in his garden. The house had its proper paraphernalia of shifting wooden and paper shutters, thick padded mats of primrose straw, flat cushions to kneel on, flat quilts to sleep on, tobacco-stoves, finger-stoves and kakemonos. It was so native that you always had to take off your boots when you went to see him.   Here he wrote the *Light of the World,* and he used to read it to me batch by batch as he finished it.   His manuscript was most edifying; he wrote a beautiful scholarly hand, full of character, rather like the hand of Lanfranc, who was Archbishop of Canterbury in the reign of William the Conqueror.   He did very little sight-seeing or bargaining. His time was taken up with receiving Buddhist abbots and the sages who, by extraordinary abstinence and striking concentrations of mind and will, had acquired supernatural powers, just as Hall Caine used to see the leading Mohammedan *ulema* in Egypt.   They had a profound respect for him.   I always fancy that Arnold had in his mind some *magnum opus* on those Eastern superhumans, which he never gave to the world.   He wrote a good deal of poetry in those days besides the *Light of the World,* chiefly translations, adaptations and imitations of the Hokku and other Japanese forms of verse, in which he excelled.   He not only had the natural charm, he could put his mind on an Eastern plane of thought.   He looked quite Oriental when he was in Japanese dress; his dark skin, his Oriental type, the deep reserve which lay behind his affability, all suggested the child of the East.

Thomas Hardy (who honoured us with his presence very rarely) I must mention in this context as a poet and not as a novelist, though he is the head of the novelists' craft to-day, undoubtedly.   I am not certain that he is not also our truest living poet, except Kipling.   He has certainly come nearer to finding a new poetical form than any modern poet except Yone Noguchi, the marvellous Japanese, who has written some of the finest contemporary poetry in our language, for Walt Whitman's psalm forms are not suited for any country but America, or for any writer who is not one of the people working with his hands.   His crudities would not be tolerable in an educated man.   But Hardy struck out entirely fresh forms.   Hardy shook off the ancient trammels of rhyme and metre, while preserving a rich rhythm and a scholarly elegance, in poems inspired with a broad humanity.

Henley, who, like Gray, wrote a few gems, which will find

their place in every anthology, was never in our flat at Addison Mansions, though he was a friend of mine; he could not have climbed so many stairs if he had tried.

I remember two sayings of his specially. In those days I wrote verses; and he was good enough to read my books of verse and advise me on them. He said there was some hope for me because I wrote short pieces, and, in his opinion, the perfect poem should never contain more than three stanzas. But I have long since abandoned verse writing.

The other was a thing which he said to me when he was giving me some introductions, on the eve of my departure for America. I thought it was a joke then, but subsequent events threw a light on it. He was urging me after I left America to go on and see Stevenson at Samoa. He said that Stevenson would be my inspiration, and as he was handing me the introduction he said to me, with what I considered unnecessary emphasis, " And when you see him, tell the beggar that I hate him for being so beastly successful."

Years afterwards Henley wrote of Stevenson with an acidity which his friends regretted very much, and which proved to me that what he had said to me as we were parting was one of those outbursts of candour for which Henley was famous.

It required a big man like Henley to confess that he was envious, and perhaps there was good reason why he should be, for considering the way their careers began, and Henley's magnificent intellect and gift of expression, one would not have prophesied in the beginning that Henley would only be appreciated by the critical few, and Stevenson by all the world, gentle and simple.

I never did see Stevenson. We meant to have taken Samoa on our way back from Japan to San Francisco, but the Japanese boat which should have taken us there broke down, and we could not wait for the next.

CHAPTER XI

THE great " Miss Braddon," who is now one of the most valued of my friends, and a not infrequent visitor, never came to 32 Addison Mansions. She achieved fame before any living novelist. She had published *Aurora Floyd* and *Lady Audley's Secret* more than half a century ago, in 1862, while Thomas Hardy did not write *Under the Greenwood Tree* and *A Pair of Blue Eyes* till ten years after that. Her powers are undiminished. Her *Green Curtain*, published fifty years later, is one of the finest books she ever wrote.

Nor did I ever meet Miss M. G. Tuttiett, who, since she wrote her great *Silence of Dean Maitland*, has been known to all the world as " Maxwell Gray," until I became her neighbour at Richmond. These lost years have deprived me of a great pleasure, because, apart from my admiration for her novels, I share two of her hobbies—her enthusiasm for her garden and her enthusiasm for Italy.

I used to esteem it an honour and a privilege when dear old Mrs. Alexander—Mrs. Hector was her real name—used to toil up the stairs to our parties. Her books were delightful, and she was one of the earliest of my literary friends, for I met her at Louise Chandler Moulton's before I went to America.

Still more, on account of her infirmity, did I appreciate it when Mrs. Lynn Linton came. My intimacy with her arose from two facts. When my novel, *A Japanese Marriage*, came out, she wrote to me in the warmest terms about it. She not only was enthusiastic about it as a novel, but thought it an unanswerable piece of advocacy for the relief of the Deceased Wife's Sister (now happily accomplished). After that I was a frequent visitor at her flat in Queen Anne's

Mansions, and later we met as fellow-guests at Malfitano, the beautiful villa of Mr. and Mrs. J. J. S. Whitaker at Palermo. She looked the grande dame, and she was a great woman as well as a great writer, admired in both capacities by all the great writers of her day, which was a long one—long enough to include Walter Savage Landor. Her championing of *A Japanese Marriage* came as a very complete surprise to me, because she was noted for severity as a moralist, and the marriage of the hero and the heroine by the American Consul, after the clergy had refused to marry them, in the eye of the Law was no marriage at all, since neither of them was an American subject—it was a mere manifesto that they meant to live together as man and wife. That letter of hers was the beginning of one of my most delightful friendships.

I don't remember when I first met Mrs. Croker or Mrs. Perrin or Flora Annie Steel, though they have all been valued friends for many years. As they are all Anglo-Indians, I suppose that I must have met one of them through some member of my family in the Indian Army or Indian Civil Service, and the others through her. My family have been much connected with India. To mention only two of them, my cousin, General John Sladen, was a brother-in-law of Lord Roberts, and actually kept house with him in India for a year, and his brother, Sir Edward Sladen, was the British resident who played so great a part in Burmah, and whose statue has the place of honour in the Burmese capital.

Of one thing I am certain, that the marriage of Mrs. Croker's beautiful daughter—the belle of Dublin—to one of the Palermo Whitakers, was not the introduction, for Mrs. Croker has never been to Palermo, and I remember her asking me all about the Whitakers' famous gardens in Sicily. Captain Whitaker did not live there; he was with his regiment.

It is natural to mention Mrs. Steel, Mrs. Perrin and Mrs. Croker together, for they long divided the Indian Empire with Rudyard Kipling as a realm of fiction. Each in her own department is supreme.

In the days when we first knew her, and she was living

in Ireland, it used to be like a ray of sunshine when pretty Mrs. Croker, with her blue eyes and her bright colour and her delightful Irish tongue, paid one of her rare visits to London. As I write these words, I am about to pay a visit to her in her Folkestone home. She is exactly the type you would expect from her irresistible books.

When I asked Mrs. Croker what first gave her the idea of writing, she said—

" My very first attempt at writing was in the hot weather at Secunderabad. When my husband was away tiger-shooting, and I was more or less a prisoner all day owing to the heat, I began a story, solely for my own amusement. It grew day by day, and absorbed all my time and interest. This was *Proper Pride*. With reluctance and trepidation I read it to a friend, and then to all the other ladies in the regiment—under seal of secrecy. Emboldened by this success, I wrote *Pretty Miss Neville*, and when I returned home with the Royal Scots Fusiliers, I had two manuscripts among my luggage. These went the usual round, but at the end of a year I received a small offer for *Proper Pride*. It came out in August 1892, without my name, and was immediately successful—principally owing to long and appreciative notices in *The Times* and *Saturday Review*, both on the same day. Three editions went off in a month, and I must confess that no one was as much surprised by this success as I was. Subsequently I sold the copyright of *Pretty Miss Neville* for one hundred pounds, and though now a lady of thirty, she still sells, in cheap editions. I attribute my good fortune to the fact that my novels struck a new note—India and army society—and that I received very powerful help from unknown reviewers. I like writing, otherwise I could not work. I believe I inherit the taste from my father's family, who were said to be ' born with a pen in their hands ' ! " Mrs. Croker tells me that it was I who first introduced her to London literary society. I consider this one of the most charming successes of my literary career.

Mrs. Perrin, on the other hand, since she came back from India, has played a continuously prominent part in London

literary life.   She has been a leading figure at literary clubs
and receptions, and has been a pillar of " the Women
Journalists."   As story-teller and psychologist combined,
she has no superior.   Those of her wide public who know her
in private life know a brilliant and charming woman of the
world, with a proved capacity for managing literary affairs.

When I asked Mrs. Perrin what started her in a literary
career, she said—

" I think I took to writing from sheer need of occupation.
When I married my husband in India, as a girl of eighteen,
we were sent to a place in the jungle where he had charge
of an enormous aqueduct which was under construction.
He had several Coopers Hill assistants under him, not one
of whom was married, and I was the only English woman
in the locality.   There was no station—or permanent settlement; our houses were temporary erections of mud, and
we were miles from the railway.   The landscape consisted
of a sea of yellow grass about the height of a man, and there
was only one road, which lay behind our bungalow—the
grand trunk road that is the backbone of India.   I began
to write here, just to amuse myself, and then when we went
to less isolated spots, I gained confidence and used to send
little articles and turn-overs to the *Pioneer*—the principal
Indian daily paper.   These were nearly always accepted,
and so I took courage and wrote a novel called *Into
Temptation*, which ran through that prehistoric magazine
London Society, long ago defunct.   The book came out in
two volumes and had very fair notices.   Then I wrote
another called *Late in Life*, which ran serially in an Indian
weekly, off-shoot of the *Pioneer*, and in England through
the *Belgravia*, and then came out in two volumes.   So you
may imagine—or rather, realise—how long ago I began !
Both these novels are now to appear revised and corrected
in Messrs. Methuen's 7d. series.

" However, I did not receive the financial encouragement
I had hoped for from these first efforts, and I lost heart.
For nearly ten years I wrote nothing but a few Indian short
stories.   Then when my husband was offered an appointment at home, and we retired before we had ' done ' our

full time in India, I collected these stories, and they came out under the title of *East of Suez*. The book was a success and since then I have written and have been published steadily.

"I am deeply interested in India, in the people and their religions, and histories and social systems, and as I was sixteen years in the country I had an opportunity of receiving lasting impressions, and of gaining invaluable experience. I come of a family which has been officially connected with India for five generations. My great grandfather was with Lord Cornwallis, on his staff, at the taking of Seringapatam, and the surrender to Lord Cornwallis of Tippoo Sahib's two little sons as hostages. He was afterwards Chairman of the old East India Company—known in those days as John Company.

"I cannot think of anything more anecdotal in my experience as a novelist—I can only remember the disappointments and the difficulties of what success I have made, at which, perhaps, I may now bring myself to smile, but I do not think they would be interesting if related!"

A few years ago Mrs. Steel was also one of the most prominent figures in London literary society. She had written *On the Face of the Waters*, one of the finest historical novels in the language; she was a hard and earnest worker in all sorts of movements, and as a fighting speaker there were few to match her. She could make a good set speech, but her set speeches were nothing to the oratory of which she was capable if, when she was totally unprepared, indignation stung her into springing to her feet to denounce the offender. Then her words came as blows come from a man who hits another man because he is incensed beyond endurance. A face full of life and expression added force to her words.

Since Mrs. Steel settled down on an estate in Wales, she has been little in London. But in those days she had a sort of country-house on the Notting Hill slope of Campden Hill. She is a keen politician, and not long ago sold the opening page of *On the Face of the Waters* as her subscription to the Women's Cause.

Another author lost to London is Sarah Grand. She used to be our neighbour; she shared a flat in the Abingdon Road with her step-son, Haldane McFall, the art critic, and author of that remarkable novel, *The Wooings of Jezebel Pettyfer.* I met her soon after the success of *The Heavenly Twins*—a young woman with indignant blue eyes, very reserved, but with a rare charm of manner behind her reserve. I was introduced to her, I think, by Heinemann, who was often at our at-homes. He had, as I understood, purchased *The Heavenly Twins* from her ready printed, copyright and all for a hundred pounds, but when the success came had torn up the agreement, and substituted a royalty agreement, paying the royalties from the beginning. She had already, I gathered, received twelve times the original sum in royalties.

Alfred Walford often came to see us—his wife, Mrs. L. B. Walford, more occasionally, since she was the mother of a large family as well as many books, and they lived in Essex. Alfred Walford used to chaff himself about his connection with literature being to produce the paper on which it was printed. He was a paper-maker; and she, at that time, was the favourite novelist of the Colonies. She was the daughter of that Colquhoun of Luss who wrote that famous book *The Moor and the Loch.*

The gentle-faced " Miss Thackeray," the great novelist's daughter, now the widow of Sir Richmond Ritchie, I did not know in those days, but I used to meet her afterwards at Lady Lindsay's. There was a time when her *Old Kensington* was my favourite novel.

And here I must say something about my old and dear friend, Lady Lindsay, who has so recently passed away, and whose lameness prevented her from toiling up the stairs to our at-homes very often. For many years I was constantly at her house, both at her famous dinner-parties and running in to have a talk about books when I was sure of finding her alone, for she was good enough to be much interested in my work.

The daughter of a Cabinet Minister, the Right Hon. Henry Fitzroy (son of the first Lord Southampton), a descendant of Nathan Meyer de Rothschild, who founded

"MISS BRADDON"

Drawn by Yoshio Markino

the fortunes of his House, and sister-in-law of the Loyd Lindsay, V.C., who became Lord Wantage, she knew nearly every noted person of her time, and those whom she did not know, she generally could have known but for some prejudice against them. At her dinner-parties you met men like Tennyson and Gladstone and Layard of Nineveh—great politicians, great nobles, great authors, great painters, but hardly any one from the theatrical world. I was nearly always the least important person present. Eight was her favourite number, though sometimes there were a dozen at her famous round table. The conversation used to be brilliant; the company was arranged with a view to that— naturally the chief guest often got possession of the table, and we sat and chronicled the historic scene in our hearts.

Afterwards, when one went up into the drawing-room, our eyes rested on pictures by Sandro Botticelli and Titian, sixteenth-century Italian wedding-chests, and other inheritances of the great. She wrote more than one volume of poems which went into several editions.

It is natural to mention beside her another great lady who was in touch with all the notabilities of her time, Walpole's descendant, Lady Dorothy Nevill, who married a descendant of Warwick the Kingmaker's elder brother, the Baron of Abergavenny. Her husband was at one time the heir-presumptive of the Marquis of Abergavenny. She happily gave her reminiscences to the world, as Lady Lindsay always meant to do, so readers know her connections, though she was too modest to show how Disraeli leaned upon her advice. Among the most interesting things which I remember in her house in Charles Street, Berkeley Square, were the unique mementoes of her ancestor, the tremendous Sir Robert Walpole, the Asquith of the eighteenth century. It was she who told me that Nelson was called Horatio because Horace Walpole presented his father to the living of Burnham Thorpe, which is still in the gift of the Earls of Orford.

Lady St. Helier, another great London hostess, at whose house I have met some of the most celebrated people of the day—Lady St. Helier and her daughter, Mrs. Allhusen, never came to see us till we had left Addison Mansions for the

Avenue House, Richmond. No woman has been more integrally a part of the life of her time than Lady St. Helier, who wrote an admirable volume of reminiscences. Mrs. Allhusen has the inspiration of owning a house where one of the masterpieces of literature was written—Gray's *Elegy*. For the house in which Gray wrote it after the inspiration, which came to him as he was leaning over the gate of Stoke Poges Churchyard, has been enlarged into Stoke Court, and the room in which Gray wrote out the *Elegy* forms part of Mrs. Allhusen's writing-room.

Marie Corelli, like Hall Caine, has a dislike of literary receptions. I cannot remember if she ever came to Addison Mansions, though we have been friends for many years, and I remember going to brilliant dinner-parties at her house in Longridge Road. Her stepfather, Charles Mackay, who adopted her, was one of my earliest literary friends.

Her stepbrother, Eric Mackay, author of the famous *Love-letters of a Violinist*, lived with her, and he came to our at-homes so frequently that I think she must have come with him sometimes. They were a very musical family. It is always said that Marie Corelli, had she so chosen, could have won as much fame in music as she has in literature. Her books illustrate Hall Caine's axiom that the greatest novels are those which deal with the elemental facts of human nature. Her grasp of human nature has won her countless readers in both hemispheres.

It is not universally known that Marie Corelli is an admirable speaker—so lucid, so convincing, able by perfect elocution to reach the furthest corner of the large hall of the Hotel Cecil without raising her voice. Though she lives at Stratford-on-Avon, and is identified with all its functions, she is frequently to be seen in London at places like Ranelagh or dancing at the great balls at the Albert Hall.

Almost alone of the chief lady novelists of that time, Mrs. Humphry Ward was never at Addison Mansions. The most interesting thing I remember in conversation with her was her confession to me one day when we were at Mrs. W. K. Clifford's that she enjoys handling the character of a person who is a failure better than the character of a person who achieves success. Heroes apparently do not appeal to her.

Mrs. W. K. Clifford was often at Addison Mansions. She is a very old friend of mine, and a great personality. Mrs. Clifford is an admirable example of the modern woman, breezy, wholesome, warm-hearted, clear-visioned, lucid in expression, interested in all questions of the day, and withal one of our best novelists. Early in life she suffered a loss which would have overwhelmed most women, for she lost her husband, Prof. W. K. Clifford, F.R.S., who was already reckoned the third mathematician in Europe, at the same age as Wolfe fell at Quebec, thirty-three, when they had only been married four years, and she was still a girl. He was the most brilliant Fellow of Trinity (Cambridge) of his day, and the youngest Fellow of the Royal Society. There is nothing he could not have done and would not have done if he had lived, for there was no side of life which did not appeal to him. People of every rank and of every shade of thought came to see him, and no matter how little they agreed with him, they were always hypnotised for the hour.

He had wonderful dark-lashed blue eyes, like his daughter, and a wonderful soul seemed to be looking out of them.

But she did not allow her loss to prostrate her, and she has lived to see her house one of the Meccas of literature in London, and her daughter, Mrs. Fisher Dilke, a recognised poetess.

Talking of Mrs. Clifford reminds me of the chequered career of *The Love-letters of a Worldly Woman*. It was published just twenty years ago, and though the first edition sold out immediately, no second edition was published in England, but in America, where it was non-copyright, it sold enormously. There were a dozen pirate editions of it, including a marked edition, which means one with the most popular passages indicated. Such a height of popularity did it reach that it was actually sold at street-corners in New York! But I have heard that Mrs. Clifford only got fifteen pounds royalties off the whole dozen editions.

The first batch of love-letters in this volume appeared

anonymously in the *Fortnightly,* and were generally attributed to Oscar Wilde. As a piece of poetical justice when Housman's *An English-woman's Love-letters* were published seven years later, they were attributed to Mrs. Clifford. *The Love-letters of a Worldly Woman* was a remarkable book, and fully deserved its American popularity.

Mrs. Clifford is, above all things, an idealist and a lover of good work. She has said, in one of her books, " in good love and good work lie the chance of immortality for everything that is worth having or being; and yet, though I've aimed at the sun, and longed to put into the beautiful world something worthy of it, I have never hit higher than a gooseberry bush, or achieved anything that gave me satisfaction. And I've been so full of enthusiasms and dreams . . . perhaps one of the dreams will come true some day—who knows? For if I live to be ninety, I shall still feel, as I do now, that the soul of me is as young and fresh as ever; and it is a sense of the beauty of things, of the kindness that underlies human nature, even when it's choked with weeds at the top, that gives one courage, and helps one to do."

Beside Mrs. Clifford I should mention Margaret Woods, whom I first met when I was an undergraduate at Oxford, and her husband, the present Master of the Temple, was my tutor, engaged to her while I was his pupil. I remember his asking me and other undergraduates to meet her in his rooms. I do not think he told us why, but we knew. She was one of the few charming women that the monastic Oxford of that day contained. Her father, afterwards the famous Dean of Westminster, was master of University College; I used to go to his Socrates lectures. He was dissatisfied with the progress we were making, and boldly—it was very bold at Oxford—charged us with paying too much attention to athletics, and it was then that he made his famous mot, that he had never taken any exercise in his life, except by occasionally standing up when he was reading. I have heard that it is equally true of Mr. Chamberlain, but it was Dean Bradley who said it. The Bradleys were an excessively clever family. The Dean had a brother or a half-brother a great philosopher, a don at Merton, and another,

Andrew Bradley, a Fellow at Balliol, who became Professor of Literature at another University. I forget what his sister, Emma Bradley, did, but she was famous. Three of his daughters, Mrs. Woods, Mrs. Birchenough, Mrs. Murray Smith, are authoresses, Mrs. Woods being one of the best novelists of the day, and in my opinion the best of all poetesses in the English language. When Tennyson died there was a movement in favour of her being made the laureate, and no woman has ever had .such claims for the post. She made her mark very young with *A Village Tragedy* and *Esther Vanhomrigh*, and has written notable books ever since. Beautiful workmanship, singularly broad humanity, and truth to life are the characteristics of her prose. In poetry she has the gifts of both Brownings. She lives in an ideal home, the panelled Master's House at the Temple, which has, however, one drawback, that the only way out of it to a cab on a wet night is to be carried in a sedan chair; a sedan chair of the eighteenth century is kept in the hall for the purpose, and passes from one Master of the Temple to another.

Charles Kingsley's daughter, Mrs. St. Leger Harrison— the "Lucas Malet" of fame—used to come to us sometimes before she went back to live at Eversley, immortalised by her father; and once her cousin, the famous African explorer, the other Mary Kingsley, came. Lucas Malet is all that one might expect of Charles Kingsley's daughter and the writer of *Sir Richard Calmady*.

It seems natural to mention the author of *Concerning Isabel Carnaby* beside the author of *Sir Richard Calmady*. The two books made a stir about the same time, and the public mixed their titles with great impartiality. The author of the former, Ellen Thorneycroft Fowler, now the Hon. Mrs. Felkin, with her sister, Edith Fowler, was a good many times at Addison Mansions. I have told the story of her becoming an authoress in my chapter on the Idlers and Vagabonds.

I should have mentioned Beatrice Harraden before. When you see this small, slight, delicate-looking woman, with her bright eyes, you are forcibly reminded of the invalid heroine

K

of *Ships that Pass in the Night.*   But Beatrice Harraden is a public school woman; she was at Cheltenham College—the ladies' College—and has taken the liveliest interest in all the interests of women since.   She was cured, I fancy, of some pulmonary disease by going to California.   She now has one of the most unique flats in Hampstead.   I do not remember how I met her, but it was a long time ago, and I was very elated, because I always thought *Ships that Pass in the Night* one of the best-written short novels in the language.

Helen Mathers has for many years been a dear friend of ours.   She was another of the authors whose acquaintance it elated me to make.   Although she is much about the same age as myself, she made her two successes with *Comin' Through the Rye* and *Cherry Ripe* when I was a boy at school. Her husband, Henry Reeves, the eminent orthopædist, was one of the very first doctors to make practical use of the X-rays.   She had a son in the army who promised to be her worthy successor in literature had he lived, as the writing which he achieved proved.   Her real name was Mathews. She was a cousin of the Estella Mathews who married my near neighbour, George Cave, K.C., M.P., who was in my team, as was Mr. Justice Montague Shearman, when I was Captain of the Public Schools Football Club at Oxford, and who now occasionally plays golf with me when he can get a day off from the Courts, and from the case against Home Rule.

Frances Hodgson Burnett I first met in Washington, where she was the wife of a well-known doctor, and the mother of two beautiful boys in velvet Patience suits, locally called Fauntleroy suits, in honour of her book *Little Lord Fauntleroy.* But she was not an American; she was an Englishwoman born in Manchester, who had made her fame with a book about the north of England, called *That Lass o' Lowrie's.* Eventually she came back to live in her native England, first of all in a house in Portland Place and afterwards in a manor house in Kent.   Her gigantic success with books and plays did not turn her head; she was always the same gracious human woman she had been when she was making her way.

John Oliver Hobbes, on the other hand, though she lived so much in England, and wrote all her books over here, was an American-born, the daughter of John Morgan Richards, who was at one time Chairman of the American Society in London, and had as much to do with *entente cordiale* between England and the United States as any American Ambassador at the Court of St. James'. He was, as it were, a sort of social ambassador. The great house in Lancaster Gate in which he lived till he retired from business was a focus of entertainment for both branches of the Anglo-Saxon race.

Mrs. Craigie was a friend of our present Queen. She was extraordinarily clever and extraordinarily charming. She always gave every one to whom she was talking the knowledge that for the time being nobody else existed for her. In intellect she was the equal of any contemporary woman writer; added to this, she was very pretty, very engaging, very well dressed, and certainly proved the truth of the proverb " Whom the gods love, die young." She had the gift of bringing out the wit as well as the best qualities of others.

Another American authoress who has spent most of her life and done all her writing in England is Irene Osgood, who came here as a very beautiful young bride of fabulous wealth, and rented a house which was one of the shrines of English literature—Knebworth, the home of Bulwer Lytton. She did not write *Servitude*, the book by which she will be remembered, there, but at Guilsborough, in Northamptonshire, another seat which she took for the hunting.

Yet another American authoress, who was also young and beautiful when she came to England, was Amelie Rives, who was at that time wife of J. A. Chanler, a great-grandson of the original Astor, but is now Princess Troubetzkoi. The daughter of a Virginian country gentleman, she simply leapt into fame with a book called *Virginia of Virginia*, which took the Americans by storm. She was irresistibly clever, and very striking-looking, with her pale gold hair, clear dusky complexion, and big blue eyes.

Gertrude Franklin Atherton, a remarkable-looking Californian with the same pale gold hair and rather the same complexion as Amelie Rives, whose mother was a great-grandniece of Benjamin Franklin, was at one time a very frequent visitor of ours. She was a long time getting her recognition, and then suddenly leapt into her full fame. But those who used to meet her socially knew from the first that she was a woman of commanding intellect. She had an odd trick of wearing a quill thrust through her hair.

Mr. and Mrs. C. N. Williamson are among my oldest literary friends. I made Williamson's acquaintance when he was sub-editor of the *Graphic*, and asked me to write an illustrated article on Adam Lindsay Gordon. Alice Livingston was an American girl, who came over to England to spend a year with some friends, and has never been back in her own country for more than three months at a time since. She had a letter of introduction to C. N. Williamson, who introduced her to a number of London editors, and thus gave her a chance of success in story-writing. After their marriage she wrote many serial stories, some of which appeared in book form; but the first great " Williamson success " was *The Lightning Conductor*, suggested by their earliest motoring adventures in France and Italy. C. N. Williamson having expert knowledge as a mechanical engineer (he intended to be one, before he determined to become a writer), it was easy to mingle amusing mechanical details of motoring with the story, a feature which appealed to lovers of automobiles in the days, ten or eleven years ago, when the sport was an uncertain adventure.

They both love story-telling—Mrs. Williamson used to " print " stories when she was six years old, before she could write—and have written a good many popular travel novels since *The Lightning Conductor*. They love also to see the far corners of the world, though they contrive to spend two or three months each winter in their Riviera house, and a month or two in summer among their friends in London.

Next to travelling, they love to build houses, and make them beautiful. If they see some land on a hillside with a splendid view, they can hardly resist buying it, and planning exactly the sort of house which ought to exist there. This means that they sell their last house, and begin another, with a different sort of garden, but there must always be a bull-dog in it, rejoicing in the name of Tiberius, or " Tibe."

Madame Albanesi, one of the most successful novelists of the day, and wife of the well-known musician, is an old friend of ours. She had long been one of the most successful writers of serial fiction in popular journals, but it was not until after her marriage with Signor Albanesi that she turned her attention to novels—one of the earliest of these books receiving remarkable reviews. She conceived the idea of advertising these reviews herself, with the result that she was approached by a number of leading publishers for her next book, and happily followed with the book which established her name—*Susannah and One Other*, a book which has been running for over ten years, and is still selling. The book-reading public only required to have its attention adequately drawn to her novels, to see what admirable stories they were—faithful to life, pulsing with human nature.

I asked Madame Albanesi what first made her write. She said that she could not remember when she had not tried to write in some form or other, and that happily for her, when she was quite a girl circumstances threw her into a circle where her gift of imaginative writing was warmly encouraged, and opportunities were found for turning this gift to the most satisfactory results. I remember Madame Albanesi telling me that an interesting fact in connection with her earlier writing was that her imagination was so fertile that she used—before she was twenty years old—to keep three or four serials running at the same time. She never had less than two going at once, and wrote them in instalments from week to week, and never took a note. Everything was published anonymously, and a new serial would begin before the old one was finished. Madame Albanesi regards her serial work as being the very best training for telling a good story.

I ought to have mentioned earlier, since she belonged to that generation, John Strange Winter, a shining light in Bohemia at the epoch of which I am writing. She made her first success when I was at Oxford, with *Bootles' Baby*, and *Hoop-la*, but she had lost her vogue before we went to live at Addison Mansions, though her name remained a household word, and she continued to publish a number of popular books. She was then living in an old house at Merton near Wimbledon, but shortly afterwards came to live at West Kensington, because she found Merton too far out.

She was a woman of inexhaustible energy, and had a very kind heart. She was exceedingly good to young authors and journalists; she made their cause her own; she welcomed them to her house, and visited theirs. She was a sister-in-law of George Augustus Sala. She was unfortunate in losing her public; she would have it again if she were alive now. But at that time a wave of preciousness and morbidness, which left her stranded, was passing over the country.

"George Egerton" and "Roy Devereux," very pretty and clever women, were at the top of that wave among women, the former with books like *Keynotes*, the latter, and George Egerton's beautiful sister, Miss Dunne, with brilliant and virile journalism in the *Saturday Review*, the *Pall Mall* and elsewhere. Lane was their publisher, Beardsley was their illustrator, H. G. Wells headed the list of their male rivals, followed by Arthur Machen, H. D. Lowry and others. I have all their books—such slim books for novels. Fisher Unwin had another school of them, headed by John Oliver Hobbes, as daring from the sex point of view, but lighter in touch, which he published in long slim books with yellow paper covers at eighteenpence each. *Some Emotions and a Moral* came out in this series, which I heard some one ask for at Smith's Library quite seriously as *Some Morals and a Reputation*. These were Wells's *Time Machine, Stolen Bacillus*, and *Wonderful Visit* days.

I asked George Egerton, who was in camp at Tauranga during the Maori war as an infant, and as a child was in her uncle Admiral Bynon's fleet while he was bombarding Valparaiso, and who I knew was intended for an artist, what had made her turn writer. She told me—

"Why I wrote? Because I had to. Why I wrote as I did? Because I felt woman could only hope to do one thing in literature—put *herself* into it. Write not in breeches, but in corsets. That I took the name of George Egerton was partly because I did not think any publisher would take stories of that kind written by a woman, partly to see if my sex would make itself felt. *Keynotes* went into seven languages in two years. I am not dead abroad. At the Goethe Centenary in Weimar the Dr. Professor who gave the lecture on literature of the century, spoke of Rudyard Kipling and George Egerton as the two who had introduced a new note, a new method, into English literature ' in our time.'

" I gave up writing books when I found that authors are ' unsecured creditors '—not worth the candle unless one can reel off popular stuff. I can't. I go to America with plays. I make any money I make there. I shall arrive here to. I am doing a big book now, and I am starting a book of recollections. If one attaches credence to the fortune-tellers, I am to live to be an old woman. It might be amusing, if only to demolish the men and women of straw one has seen lauded to the skies, in one's memory."

Marie Belloc, who had not then married Lowndes of *The Times*, was a constant visitor. She belonged very much to the Idler and Vagabond set of which we saw so much, and was already longing to write novels, though many years were to go by before she was able to fulfil her wish. She is a sister of Hilaire Belloc, the free-lance M.P. of the last Parliament, one of the wittiest writers of the day, who has the further distinction of having been a driver in a French artillery regiment and a Scholar of Balliol afterwards. It should be added that he was twenty-three when he went up to Oxford.

Marie Stuart Boyd, of the same set, the wife of the well-known *Punch* and *Graphic* artist, did not begin to publish her delightful books till nearly ten years later, though she was a regular contributor to important Reviews.

Mrs. Frankau (" Frank Danby "), who came with her sister, Mrs. Aria, had at that time dropped writing for engraving, and did not resume it till some years later. *Pigs in Clover*, and her other successes in fiction, belong to a much later date.

One of the most daring and witty of women writers, Violet

Hunt, was constantly at our at-homes.   With a father who was a well-known artist, a Fellow of Corpus Christi, Oxford, and a friend of Gladstone's, and a mother who wrote novels of repute; and brought up in the brilliant set which gathered round Burne-Jones and Ford Madox Brown, it was no wonder that she should be extraordinarily clever, and no one was surprised when she produced scintillating books like *The Maiden's Progress* and *A Hard Woman*.   South Lodge, their house on Campden Hill, was a Mecca for distinguished literary people.   It was there that I first met Andrew Lang, Robert Hichens, Somerset Maugham, Katherine Cecil Thurston in a crowd of writers of high calibre.   It was one of the few houses where Lang was natural without being rude.

I now come to a group of able women writers whom I met at clubs like the Pioneers and the Writers', though they mostly came often to our at-homes afterwards.   First among them I may place that brilliant and delightful writer, Mrs. Alfred Sidgwick, who published her early novels under the pseudonym of "Mrs. Andrew Dean."   Her husband, Mr. Alfred Sidgwick, is the author of well-known works on logic, and one of the earliest of the modern school of philosophers, known as the Pragmatists.   He is a cousin of Mr. Henry Sidgwick (d. 1900), the distinguished Professor of Moral Philosophy at Cambridge, who married Mr. A. J. Balfour's sister, the guardian spirit of Newnham.

Mrs. Sidgwick's novels have always been full of verve.   She has steeped herself in the literature of three countries, and until she married knew the world better from the Continental point of view than from the English.   But her marriage took her amongst English people, so that she has had unusual opportunities of understanding two nationalities intimately.   In those days we saw a good deal of her because she lived at Surbiton, but for many years past she has lived in Cornwall.

At the same club I met Miss Montrésor, whose delicate health has prevented her seeing much of London literary society, though she lives in South Kensington.   With her *Into the Highways and Hedges* she leapt into fame at a single bound. Miss Montrésor is a genius. Her intuition enables her to describe with fidelity phases of life with which she cannot have had any acquaintance. When she wrote *Into the Highways and Hedges*, my friend Sheldon, who was the London manager of D. Appleton & Co., gave me five pounds to write a careful opinion of it, to see whether his firm, to whom it had been offered, should publish it or not. I gave them a long opinion, in which I told them that they could not possibly refuse such a book. But they did refuse it, because almost any American publisher will refuse any novel which is not by a novelist who has already made a great name. Some other New York firm took it, and it was the book of the year in America.

At a club, too, I met Annie Swan (whose husband, Dr. Burnett Smith, was last year Mayor of Hertford), twenty years and more ago, a woman completely unspoiled by success, which came to her early and without stint, and remained. She stands at the very head of the writers of the wholesome school of fiction. In those days she lived at Hampstead, in a house called "Aldersyde," after the novel which gave her her fame. She is one of those people whose obvious sincerity charms you the moment you meet them. I don't know whether she is interested in spiritualism, but I did on one occasion meet Florence Marryat and Dora Russell together at her table.

Of Florence Marryat (Mrs. Francis Lean), the daughter of the immortal Captain Marryat, I saw a good deal at one time. She was a very regular attendant at a dining club called the Argonauts, which Frankfort Moore and I got up because the Vagabonds would not then admit ladies to their banquets. Spiritualism played an immense part in her life. She was also a very voluminous writer. I remember her telling me that she had written more than seventy novels. She was a tall, striking-looking woman, whose eyes suggested intimacy with the occult.

The Leightons, who are among my most valued friends, I certainly met at some club—Marie Leighton is the best newspaper serial writer of the day—a story-teller born, and, like her husband, a great authority on dogs. One at any rate of her thrilling stories has been dramatised and others are sure to follow, as the managers of the melodrama theatres recognise how immensely dramatic her stories are.

"Lucas Cleeve," another frequent visitor at our house, wife of Colonel Kingscote, and daughter of Sir Henry Drummond Wolff, M.P., who made with Mr. Balfour, Lord Randolph Churchill, and Sir John Gorst the celebrated Fourth Party, had an extraordinary facility for writing novels of a certain merit, and, like her father, was a great linguist and traveller. Sir John Gorst introduced me to her. I met him at Castle Combe, which now belongs to him, and then belonged to his brother, the late Edward Chadwick Lowndes. I was staying with my brother-in-law, Robert Watkins, the agent of the estate, which is one of historical interest, for its archives prove it to have been irretrievably wasted by Sir John Fastolfe, Knt., Shakespeare's Falstaff, who had married the widow of the last of its Scroop owners, and managed the estate for her. He built the chancel arches in the church, fine and early Perpendicular. The Scroop and Falstaff house has long since disappeared, while the Cromlech of a British Chief, and a Roman Camp, continue almost perfect. I was often the guest of Sir John's eldest son, Sir Eldon, when I was in Egypt, and his younger son, Harold, and his charming wife, have been our intimate friends for many years. Mrs. Harold Gorst, who was a Miss Kennedy of the famous Shrewsbury School family of scholars, has an extraordinary knowledge of the life of the poor in London, and her novels reflect it with a fidelity which should have won them ten times their circulation.

Quite a prominent place among the authoresses who used to assemble on those evenings at Addison Mansions is occupied by novelists who began as my secretaries, and whom I trained to write.

I have been singularly fortunate in my choice of them. Not only have they given me so much satisfaction as secretaries that I have only had to send one away for inefficiency, and none for any other reason, but they have made such good use of the opportunities they had for observing the ways of book-writing, that in the twenty-seven years since

the first came to me, they have between them had more
than twenty-seven books published and paid for by leading
firms like Hutchinson, Heinemann, Methuen, Hurst &
Blackett, Constable & Co., Chatto & Windus, Eveleigh
Nash, Mills & Boon and Stanley Paul.

My first secretary was 'Norma Lorimer, who came to us
in her teens, before our memorable journey to America,
Canada and the Far East. She has accompanied us on
every important journey we ever made in Europe, Asia,
Africa and America since I returned from Australia. When
typewriting came in, she ceased to be my secretary, because
she was never a typist, but she continued to live with us,
and act as hostess, since my wife's health has never permitted her to undertake the strain of managing the large
literary, artistic and theatrical receptions which we held
weekly for a good many years.

During that period Miss Lorimer made an immense circle
of friends, which included practically every one in our
acquaintance. Men like Fisher of the *Literary World*, and
Robert Barr urged her to write a book for years before she
could persuade herself to put pen to paper, though seeing
so many of my books put together, and transcribing when
they were finished, had familiarised her with the process
of book-making, and though she had assisted me at every
stage, in sight-seeing with an armful of guide-books, in
making copious notes, in studying all the available authorities
on the subject, and in digesting and arranging the information
if it was a travel-book, or in giving her advice about the
story if it was a novel. She must have been with us quite
ten years before she published her first book, *A Sweet Disorder*.
Since then, besides the two books in which she collaborated
with me, *Queer Things about Sicily* and *More Queer Things
about Japan*, she has brought out *Josiah's Wife, Mirry-Ann,
By the Waters of Sicily, Catherine Sterling, On Etna, By the
Waters of Carthage, The Pagan Woman, By the Waters of
Egypt, By the Waters of Italy, The Second Woman, A Wife out
of Egypt*, and *By the Waters of Germany*.

It gives me great satisfaction to think that she was my
pupil in writing, for most of these books will stand reading

again and again for the admirable sayings and analyses of
life with which they are strewn, as well as for their stories,
and the knowledge displayed in them. They are redolent
with the atmosphere of the Isle of Man, Japan, Italy, Sicily,
Tunis and Egypt, and one of them, *Josiah's Wife*, contains
a brilliant picture of America, where she lived with us for
nearly three years.

Miss Lorimer comes of a very clever family. Her uncle,
James Lorimer, was Professor of International Law in the
Edinburgh University, and wrote some of the standard
books upon the subject. He was a man of international
reputation. His hobby was the restoration of Kellie Castle
in Fifeshire, which he acquired from Lord Kellie and Mar,
and, as the Latin inscription sets forth, " rescued it from the
bats and the owls." Living at Kellie was the inspiration of
three of his clever children. His youngest son, now Sir
Robert Lorimer, has become the most famous living Scottish
architect. He had the high honour of building the Chapel
of the Knights of the Thistle in St. Giles' Cathedral, Edinburgh. His second son, J. H. Lorimer, the Scottish
Academician, is recognised as one of the soundest painters
of the day. One daughter, Lady im Thurn, caught the trick
of the beautiful moulded plaster ceilings at Kellie, done by
a wandering band of Italian artists in the seventeenth
century, and was entrusted with the execution of the moulded
plaster ceilings which Lord Bute had made for his House of
Falkland. Another daughter is an author, and the other
married Sir David Chalmers, the only man who ever earned
two pensions as Chief Justice of two tropical colonies.

My next secretary was Miss Maude (Mary) Chester Craven,
who had quarrelled with her stepfather, and was seeking to
make her own way in the world.

She was a singularly clever girl, very much interested in
literature, with a great sense of humour, and a great idea
of " copy." Had she come to me later, when I was writing
the various volumes of *Queer Things* series, I should have
been able to make better use of her help. She was most
generous and self-sacrificing, and when she had thrown
herself into the subject, you could hardly get her away

from the papers. And she was very well read on certain subjects.

A few years after she left me she wrote an excellent book called *Famous Beauties of Two Reigns*. Since then she has found a niche all to herself in book-producing—teaching people who have led interesting lives, and have good stories to tell, but have had no literary experience, how to put their biographies together and editing them herself. The books produced in this way have proved some of the greatest sensations of our times. Lady Cardigan led off, followed by the adventurous ex-Crown Princess of Saxony, and Lord Rossmore's racy recollections came as an *entr'acte* to the drama of Meyerling as narrated by Countess Larisch.

Editing these books has made Miss Craven—she is now Mrs. Charles ffoulkes, wife of the Master of the Armour of the Tower of London—an admirable raconteur, and she told me that the late M. Charles Sauerwein, directeur of *Le Matin*, had offered her a large sum to write her reminiscences of her " sitters," but conscientious scruples prevented her from accepting the tempting offer, as to disclose all she knew would have caused trouble in London and elsewhere.

The ex-Crown Princess of Saxony, for instance, was a most ingenuous person, who would have written a chapter, had Miss Craven permitted her, on "why the royal honeymoon bored her to tears," and much more that would have caused endless scandal and heartburnings to the Saxon court.

" Our Louise," as she was termed by her subjects, had a positive mania for cleanliness, and she told Miss Craven that once when she was travelling with her mother the water supply gave out and she was in despair how to wash her hands. But necessity originated a brilliant idea, and at the next stop Louise rushed to the buffet, and returned with a waiter staggering under many bottles of mineral water, with which she performed her ablutions. " Surely," remarked the Grand Duchess of Tuscany, " there is no accounting for your vagaries, Louise ! "

Miss Craven asked the Princess what she most desired to do when the dullness of palace life obsessed her. " To post a letter in a pillar-box like any one else," was the reply.

Once, coming from the Continent, she overheard some fellow-passengers discussing her rather freely, and entering into the spirit of the adventure, Louise joined in the conversation, and for once saw herself as others saw her. " Well," said she, as the train slowed into Charing Cross, " you've had an opportunity of meeting that terrible woman—I am the ex-Crown Princess," and when the horror-stricken occupants of the compartment saw her name upon her small luggage, they realised that the pretty, vivacious, fair woman was none other than the former wife of the King of Saxony.

Lady Cardigan (whose recollections " Labby " described as a classic) disliked the blue pencil, for she saw no reason why you should not say what you like in a book. She was a most brilliant anecdotist, and Miss Craven said she could tell good stories for a fortnight without repeating herself. One, which related to a well-known Bacchanalian member of the aristocracy, is worth recalling. The gentleman in question once kissed a pretty housemaid, who made a decidedly original protest. " I wonder, my Lord," said the girl, " that a nobleman like you don't drink champagne. Brandy *do* colour your breath."

Lady Cardigan held the opinion that sauce for the goose was sauce for the gander. " Men fall in love with ballet-girls, barmaids and servants," she once remarked, " so why shouldn't women fall in love with men of inferior station if it amuses them ? "

Maude Craven could tell of flutterings in the dove-cotes of Mayfair, and of many skeletons in ancestral cupboards whose bones must have rattled in dread of what Lady Cardigan's marvellous memory could have recalled about them.

The lady who followed Miss Craven had only been with us for a short time when the doctors told her that she could not live in England. She went to California and got married. Miss Marie Ivory, who followed her, married a famous artist.

Miss Ethel Phipps, the next, was with us for several years, and accompanied us to Italy and Sicily, and inaugurated the system of tissue-paper scrap-books, which I have found so useful in collecting the materials for my books of travel. And she was an excellent typist, the first excellent typist

we had had, though I took up the use of the typewriter quite
early.   The first I ever had was a Remington which I bought
in 1883 in Sydney from a man named Cunningham who
reported law cases for the *Sydney Morning Herald*.   He
sold it to me for half the price he had given for it (I paid
him about fifteen pounds, I think), because the judges would
not look at his notes when they were in typewriting.   He
had bought the instrument under the idea that the extra
legibility would be received with acclaim.   The judges
thought that the machine might not write down what the
reporter meant it to—they credited it with the powers of a
planchette, which was then very fashionable.

Miss Phipps wrote a very amusing little book called
Belinda and Others, which Warne bought from her and
published both in England and America.

When she left us because she was needed at home, her
place was taken by a very clever and interesting girl fresh
from school, who has made a great name for herself in fiction
—Miss Ethel May Stevens, whose pen-name is Ethel Stefana
Stevens.   We took her to Sicily almost directly she came to
us, and Italianised her surname into the nickname Stefana,
by which even her own relations grew to call her.

The moment I saw her I was struck by her brilliance and
intelligence, and I did not require to learn that she had
carried everything before her at Miss Douglas's famous
school in Queen's Gate, to know that she was much the
ablest of the ladies who answered my advertisement when
Miss Phipps had to leave us.

At various times she travelled all over Italy and Sicily
with us, and visited Tunis and Carthage.   She was with us
for several years, and a great worker.   On her fell the almost
incredible labour of typing out and keeping sorted the
immense mass of materials accumulated chiefly from Italian
sources, for the Encyclopædia called *Things Sicilian*, which
forms the bulk of my *Sicily, the New Winter Resort*.

She had studied a great deal before she came to us, and
besides a good knowledge of French and German and music
(she played the violin charmingly), had a strange accomplishment—she spoke Romany, the Gipsy language, so fluently

that when she made up a little, even gipsies took her for a gipsy. She had learnt it in the New Forest, which was near her home. She began before she had been very long with us the gipsy novel, which now, after many years, she has taken up again. It was a story with a strong love interest in it, but it gave no promise of the admirable gift of writing which she has shown in her published works like *The Veil* and *The Mountain of God*. In the large amount of reviewing which she did for me—against time, it was true—she had a habit of introducing stock phrases and introductory periphrases, such as " the worst of the whole matter was that," " that redoubtable," " the venerable form of." Her criticisms of books were in judgment very good, but in expression they were verbose and lacking in distinction. She was always studying in the fine library which I had collected as a reviewer. Besides gipsy-lore and music she was especially interested in everything connected with occultism and amulets, and the Black Art generally, and everything connected with the Orient. It was in the three excellent chapters which she wrote for my *Carthage and Tunis*, where they are signed with her own initials, E. M. S., instead of the E. S. S. she uses now, that Miss Stevens first showed what she could do when she tried. The chapters are Chapter VI, Volume I, " The Lavigerie Museum at Cairo" ; Chapter XVIII, Volume II, " Superstition in Tunis "; Chapter XX, Volume II, " A Tunisian Harem, and the Tombs of the Beys."

It was when she was visiting Tunis with us that she first heard the " East a-callin'." She found it absolutely irresistible. In the short time that we were there she began to learn Arabic, and acquired quite a good knowledge of Arab amulets, and the Egyptian amulets in the museum at Carthage. She afterwards paid another visit to Tunis before she wrote her memorable book, *The Veil*, one of the most successful novels of its year.

In search of a fresh Oriental subject, she next went to Haifa, the Syrian seaport, where she was lucky enough to live in the little colony which surrounded the present head of the Bahai movement, and to see a great deal of the inner working of that movement, which is said to count half the Shia Mohammedans (chiefly Persians) among its secret adherents. So high an opinion did Abbas Effendi form of her abilities, that he invited her to stay in his house and gave her a special course of instruction, which lasted over many months, in the philosophy of the sect.

Her stay at Haifa also supplied her with the materials for her second novel, *The Mountain of God*. Since then she has published several able and successful books, just as *The Earthen Drum*, *The Long Engagement*, *The Lure* and *Sarah Eden*, for the material of which she paid two visits to Jerusalem.

My next secretary, who was with me for seven years, has also had three books published by leading firms.

It is not by any means an uncommon thing for authors' secretaries to become authors. One of the most conspicuous examples is Mary E. Wilkins, now Mrs. Freeman-Wilkins, who was for a long time secretary to Oliver Wendell Holmes. I well remember the day when he stopped me in the street in Boston (U.S.A.), to say, " I have a hated rival. My secretary, Mary Wilkins, has just published a novel—a much better one than I ever wrote."

L

CHAPTER XII

WHEN we came back from the United States in 1891,
besides our wide American circle, most of whom were in the
habit of frequently visiting England in the season, we soon
found ourselves in the heart of a Bohemian society, which
met almost daily at one or other club or reception. Receptions had become the order of the day among London literary
people, artists and actors. The epidemic came over from
America at the same time as the habit of personal
journalising. Certain popular newspapers devoted columns
and columns every week to giving every species of good-
natured gossip about the biographies and home-lives of well-
known people. It was this movement which culminated
in the production of *Who's Who*. Interviewing was a feature
of the day. From living like hermit-crabs, English authors
suddenly began to realise the value of publicity in the sale
of their wares.

They had always in a decorous Victorian way met at the
Athenæum Club, but that did not open its doors at all. The
pleasant Garrick and the Savile had an almost equal dread
of literary burglars. The National Club had only a select
few authors who liked its fleshpots. But their younger
rivals saw in receptions a fresh element of interest to attract
and benefit members. The Arts Club, the newly founded
Authors' Club, the Hogarth, the Savage, the Vagabonds,
and the Playgoers, to all of which I had been elected, were
free and fearless in their hospitalities, and here, and through
friends I met in these clubs, I acquired the friendship of many
of the world's workers.

The Arts Club in those days was a jolly place; charming
and distinguished men could be found dining there almost

every night, and after dinner you played pool with the Royal Academicians, or talked scandal about the way that artists were elected, and pictures selected, to the Royal Academy. These were most enjoyable evenings.

At the Hogarth, not far off, the artists who were not in the Academy or in the Academy set, used to assemble. It is the artist's habit to work till daylight is gone, and then to waste his time in conversation or the billiard-room. The talk, when it was not shop, was all what they call in theatrical circles " gag." Some of their shop was quite interesting, because it ran upon new men and new methods. I liked the latter best. Artists, unlike authors, are generally more ready to detract than to praise. They wish to mount over the bodies of the slain; they do not hold out a hand to those who are lower down the hill. But they were very kind to each other with money, though they were so unkind to each other's work, and none of them seemed to stay at home to read after they had done their work.

The Authors' Club had been established recently enough for me to come in as an original member. The Vagabonds Club, which had been in existence for a good many years, had not yet expanded into the New Vagabonds Club, nor had the White Friars organised banquets. The old Playgoers had a good many literary members, chiefly dramatists or would-be's. The Arts, the happy hunting-ground of famous artists, had a few; the Hogarth, the favourite meeting-place for less favourite artists, had a few more; the Savage, in spite of its traditions, and the Garrick not many more; and the editors of the *Idler* were in the habit of giving teas, which practically constituted a tea club without a subscription. I never was at the Yorick.

The Authors' Club at that time took the lead in receptions. Sir Walter Besant, who founded it, made it his mission in life to bring authors together, both for the enjoyment of each other's company, and for the defence of their common interests. For these purposes he originated both the Authors' Club and the Authors' Society, which had, in 1891, the same secretary, and himself for chairman of both, but which were technically unconnected.

The Authors' Club owed its success, and especially the success of its meetings, to Oswald Crawfurd, not less than to Besant himself. Crawfurd had written a book or two, but he had no eminence in literature, beyond having put enough money into Chapman & Hall to become chairman of the company and editor of its review, the *Fortnightly*. But Crawfurd was rich, and at Eton, and as a Consul-General, he had won the friendship of half the well-known people in London. He used his influence, his energy and his money, prodigally, in making the new Club go. He entertained possible members both at the Club, and in his own home and at favourite restaurants; he wrote an enormous number of persuasive letters; he kept the thing going generally. The Club was his protégé as much as Besant's.

Besant, with whom I had been in correspondence before I went to America, at the moment that he recruited me for the Club, was interested in introducing American methods at its meetings, and as I had just returned from America, the directors made me honorary secretary for this purpose.

I spent three years in America, and during that time enjoyed the hospitality of all the leading literary and Bohemian Clubs in New York, Boston and Washington. Washington, as far as I remember, had only one of any importance, but Boston and New York were rich in them, and I brought over ideas from them.

I explained to Besant what seemed to me the best features of American literary gatherings, and he evolved from them a programme for our weekly dinners at the Authors' Club; but he thought that reading a paper, followed by a discussion, or entertaining a great author, whose health was proposed and who had to make a reply, was more suited to an English audience than telling anecdotes. I think he was right; telling anecdotes is not an English art. The American expects boundless patience from his audience while he elaborates the gist of the story; the longer he prolongs the agony, the better his audience likes it. He has made a fine art of story-telling, and does it well enough to take the place of a curtain-raiser at a theatre. The Englishman only does it in private—generally to the distress of his family—or intro-

duces it incidentally into one of his speeches. Except
barristers, and politicians, and clergymen, most Englishmen
are afraid of the sound of their own voices in public, though
Englishwomen often do not suffer from this disability. There
is really some justification for the story of the man who was
asked to give a definition of *woman*. He began, "Woman
is, generally speaking . . . " "Stop there!" said his
friend. "If you went on for a thousand years you would
never get so near it again."

Englishwomen as a class are much better speakers than
Englishmen.

We got along comfortably at the Authors' Club with entertaining eminent persons, and expecting them to speak in
recognition of the compliment, until Sir Augustus Harris
was asked to propose the health of Isidore di Lara, whose
opera he had just presented at Drury Lane. Harris made a
long speech, in which he told us all that he had done for grand
opera, how much money he had spent, what singers, male and
female he had discovered and the rest of it, and was very
pleased with himself, and after about half-an-hour sat down
without making the slightest allusion to di Lara. Oswald
Crawfurd, I think it was, who noticed the omission, and,
springing to his feet, proposed the toast.

After this it was felt that we ought to do something to
strengthen the programme, and Besant proposed a form of
entertainment which had come up in the United States since
I had lived there. A man with the eminent name of Luther
had hit upon an idea for giving authors a fourth profit on
their works, and making them all contributors to his own profit.
He called it "Uncut Leaves." Under this name he offered
all the most eminent authors in America a generous price
if they would read their productions in a lecture hall before
they were published serially, so that they received money
for recitation as well as for serial rights, book rights and
dramatic rights. I believe it went very well in America for
a while, but in London it was impossible to persuade a Meredith
or a Hardy to listen to such a proposal. To start with, only
a funny man had a chance of getting an English audience
to listen to him reading his own productions.

Later on we did try the anecdotes with some success at informal dinners.

In any case the Authors' Club dinners and entertainments became a great success. It was the most popular literary institution of the day, both at its temporary first home in Park Place, and afterwards at its proper house in Whitehall Court. Some of the most eminent men were its guests. Among them, besides great authors, were great prelates, great generals, great admirals, great politicians, who enjoyed being entertained by the Authors' Club better than at public banquets, because they only had to speak to fifty or a hundred men instead of addressing huge assemblies, and the formal part of the proceedings lasted such a short time that they might chat afterwards in the smoking-room or the billiard-room with their hosts, who always had among them men whose books they had been admiring for years. While Besant lived he was a great inspiration, and when he died his place was taken by others who had sprung to the forefront of literature in the interval.

The Authors' Club differed from the original Vagabonds Club because only the Speaker or Speakers of the evening spoke, and the dinner was a more luxurious one. Most of the literary Vagabonds went to the Authors' Club too, but at the Authors' you met a fair sprinkling of the older authors like Sir Walter Besant, and, occasionally, Thomas Hardy. The gatherings were much larger. The Club contained many more members, and the bringing of guests was much more usual. Besant and Oswald Crawfurd brought a great many, generally distinguished men.

If the names of everyone present at some of those dinners were published now, people would be astonished to see what a high percentage of them have become household words.

Among them were John Hay, the greatest man the United States ever sent us as an Ambassador; the old Lord Chancellor; the old Lord Chief Justice; Lord Avebury, who invented the " bank-holidays " known as " St. Lubbock's-days "; Lord Strathcona, the father of the Canadian Pacific Railway, and the synonym for patriotic munificence in these latter days; Lord Wolseley, then Commander-in-Chief;

CHARLES GARVICE
Drawn by Yoshio Markino

Sir Ian Hamilton, who won the important battles of Wagon
Hill and the Diamond Hills in the South African war; Sir
Edward Seymour, the great Admiral, who won as much
reputation by daring to be a failure on his march from Tientsin
to Peking as he did by all his successes; Admiral Sir
William Kennedy, the wittiest speaker in the navy; Admiral
Sir Hedworth Lambton, now Sir Hedworth Meux; and
Admiral Sir Percy Scott, who saved the situation in the
South African war by converting his 4·7 ship guns into
field guns to meet the Boers' "long Toms"; Bishop Creighton,
and Bishop Ingram, of London; Bishop Gore, then of Worcester; Sir Robert Ball, the astronomer; Sir Leslie Stephen,
the father of *The Dictionary of National Biography;* Sir
Alma Tadema; Sir George Otto Trevelyan, Macaulay's
nephew, who wrote two of the greatest biographies in the
language, *The Life of Macaulay* and *The Life of Fox,* and has
sons who rival him; Sir William Ramsey, F.R.S.; two famous
brothers, the late Rt. Hon. Alfred Lyttleton, the greatest
of all the giants of sport on record except C. B. Fry (who made
the same impression on Parliament as he had made on his
Eton schoolfellows by his loftiness of character), and his
brother Edward, almost equally great in cricket, the head
master of Eton; with authors like Rudyard Kipling, Ian
Maclaren, Doyle, Barrie, Anthony Hope, Augustine Birrell,
and Henry Arthur Jones.   There are others equally eminent,
if I could only remember them.

The greatest favourite we ever had among our guests at
the Authors' Club was "Ballahooley"—Robert Jasper
Martin of Cromartin, better known as Bob Martin—a magni-
ficent-looking Irish squire of the Charles Lever type, who
bubbled over with natural wit.

Bob Martin was a brother of Violet Martin of Ross, and
cousin of Edith Œnone Somerville the lady M.F.H., who
collaborated in *Some Reminiscences of an Irish R.M.* and
other famous books of Irish life and character, and though
he did not write much, he had the same limitless fund of
humour.

The first time that ever I took him to the Authors' Club
the late Lord Wolseley was the guest of the evening, and an

admirable guest of the evening he was—illustrious, interesting, urbane, a brilliant talker.   He and Martin were old friends, and after Lord Wolseley's health had been proposed and he had responded in a speech which told us all about his literary work—like Moltke, he was an author by instinct—Martin got up to tell us some of his inimitable Irish stories.   The first was one about Lord Wolseley himself.   In the days when he was only a colonel, a sergeant-major came to him for a day's leave to help his wife in doing the Company's washing.

" I've been speaking to your wife, Pat," said Colonel Wolseley, " and she begged me, whenever you came to me for leave on her washing-day, to refuse you because you get in her way so."

The man saluted, and turned to leave the room, but when he got to the door he turned round and saluted again, and asked, " Have I your leave to say something, Colonel? "

" Yes, Pat."

" Well, what I wish to say, sir, is that one of us two must be handling the truth rather carelessly, because I haven't got a wife."

True or untrue, Lord Wolseley did not deny the impeachment.

That same night " Ballahooley " told us of his first experience of the Castle at Dublin.   He was asked to stay there the first time he ever came to town, and he was not used to town ways.   When his jaunting-car pulled up at the door of the Castle, he told the footman to give the coachman a drink, which was the custom of the country at Cromartin.   The footman stared at him.

" Didn't you hear what I said? " he asked.

" Yes, sir, I heard," said the footman slowly, and disappeared to fetch the drink because Martin swore at him so. When he came back, he brought a liqueur-glass of Benedictine on an immense silver tray.   The coachman took the glass and smelt it—doubtfully.

" It's all right, Pat, it was made by the Holy Fathers."

Thus encouraged, Pat drank it off.   He made a wry face.

" Don't you like it, Pat ?   It's very good."

" Oh, it's good enough," said the Jehu, "but what I'm thinking is that the man who blew that glass was mighty short of breath."

That same evening he told us of the first election to a District Council which was ever held on his estates.   The place was a hotbed of Nationalism, and Bob Martin was very anxious to have a friend of his, who was a Conservative, elected on to the Council.   So he assembled all his tenants, and said to them, " I wish you'd elect this man.   I've never asked you to do anything for me before, and I've made more money out of one rotten song (' Ballahoolcy ') than out of the whole blessed lot of you ever since I came in for this place."

Their Irish minds were so struck by this piece of special pleading that they returned his candidate unopposed.

Bishop Creighton was a very entertaining guest.   Just because he was so great and so potent as an administrator, he could be perfectly natural when he was dining with a couple of score of authors.   One could not imagine the present Bishop —whom I remember in the days when he was at Keble—he was a very plucky player at football, which he had learned at Marlborough—blurting out like his predecessor that the first thing he asked about a parson who was recommended for a living in his gift was " Is he a hustler ? "   Nor can one imagine him fencing with the late Father Stanton of St. Alban's, Holborn, over the use of incense.

I wish I had not forgotten the name of that club to which he and Balfour and I forget what others of the greatest in the land, a dozen or twenty in all, mostly great politicians or prelates, belonged, who dined together at the Grand Hotel once or twice a month, and quietly enjoyed themselves like the *Dilettanti*.   I suppose that it exists still.

Bishop Gore was delightfully human the night that we entertained him at the Authors' Club.   He said that he felt quite shy of replying to the toast of his health—that generally, when he was speaking, he was addressing an audience upon subjects on which he was entitled to speak with authority, and upon which his audience were very anxious to hear what he had to say, but that on this occasion he was going to talk about a subject which interested no one, meaning himself, and he was quite at a loss what to say.

Sir Evelyn Wood, one of the few men who have ever won the V.C. both as a sailor and a soldier—he was a midshipman before he was a soldier, and made a famous ride with dispatches —and he has been called to the Bar since—supplemented his speech in reply to the toast with a selection of rattling anecdotes.

Sir Ian Hamilton, the General who saved Ladysmith by his victory at Wagon Hill, described the touch and go of his battle, which saved Ladysmith, in the slang of ordinary conversation, which made it extraordinarily impressive. It was very appropriate, too, for slang was the language of the brief council of war which Sir Ian held with the Colonel of the Devons before they launched the charge which saved the day.

One of the most interesting dinners we ever had was the dinner we gave to Zola in the Whitehall Rooms. We had other guests, varying from Stepniak, the Nihilist, to Frank Stockton and Bill Nye, the American humorists. Stockton told one of his characteristic American after-dinner stories of the " lady or the tiger " sort. Nye was really wonderful. He said that he himself belonged to an old French family— that the Nye family used always to spell their name Ney, but they changed it because one of the family was unfortunate. This allusion to the bravest of the brave brought the house down, but it took about a quarter of an hour to explain it to Zola.

Henry Arthur Jones was extraordinarily interesting— Jones, if you catch him in the right mood, can make a really fine speech, full of imagination.

One man whom I first met at the Authors' Club, and whom I afterwards got to know better, though I have not seen him for many years—Lucien Wolf, had an extremely original way of working. Besides his ordinary press work, once a month he contributed a presentation of the foreign politics of the world to one of the principal Reviews. As foreign editor of a daily paper, he had the subject at his fingers' ends, but it troubled

him in a subject so full of tangled threads to break off his
work for meals and to go to bed.   Writing that article took
about forty-eight hours, and during that time he hardly left
his study; he did not go to bed at all; like the Admiral who
gave them their name, he had sandwiches brought to him
where he sat.   He apparently felt no ill-effects from this
tremendous effort of will-power and industry, though, of
course, he looked very tired.   His articles on foreign affairs
in the monthly Reviews took the premier place.

Poulteney Bigelow was a character at the Authors' Club
in those days.   The son of an American Ambassador—
minister, as they were then called—he was, for some reason
or another, an intimate personal friend of the German Emperor,
with whom he constantly stayed, and of whom he treasured
many anecdotes.   He once nearly persuaded the Emperor to
dine at the Authors' Club.   He disappeared for a while, and
went out West in the United States again, from which he
came back very full of the shooting exploits of Theodore
Roosevelt, another of his friends.

Bigelow always maintained that the Spanish-American
war was the best thing which ever happened for the relations
between Great Britain and the United States.   He said that
the garrison, who died like flies in the Philippines, were mostly
drawn from the South-Western States, where the hatred
of England had been liveliest, and their colonial experiences
made them understand how considerate the English were to
subject peoples, and how very inconsiderate subject peoples
were apt to be to their rulers.

We had quite a bevy of leading editors among our members,
some of whom put in an appearance pretty constantly, but
it never was a very active editor's club; I think they were
too afraid of would-be contributors.

William Sinclair, the Archdeacon of London, who was the
principal figure at London functions for nearly a generation,
was a pillar of the Club.   He was a constant attendant at
its house dinners, and apart from his influence and position,
was a brilliant raconteur.   Sometimes, like a true Scotsman,
he told a story against himself, as when he told us why he was
such a popular preacher at the Guards' chapel—because the

men said that he was the only person who ever preached to them with a voice like a sergeant-major.

Sinclair had met everybody of any importance in his time. He had one beautiful story of a Scotsman who suddenly became a Cabinet Minister on four or five thousand a year, and sported a butler. Sinclair, who was staying with him, in all innocence asked what the man's name was, and his hostess said, " I don't know; we always call him waiter."

After Besant's death, the two men who were most prominent at the Authors' Club were certainly Conan Doyle and Anthony Hope—Doyle especially, because he was for a long time chairman of the Club, and a frequent attendant at the dinners. I wish I could remember only a tithe of the interesting and amusing things he said at that dinner table, for Doyle always says something memorable in his speeches. But once I was so interested that I kept a note of what he said written down on my menu card. It was about his famous pamphlet— *The War; its Causes and its Conduct.* He told his audience that it came to him in an instant, like all great things in life, which hit on the head like a bullet. He was reading some peculiarly diabolical misrepresentations by the German editors. " Yet these men," he told himself, " were, in the ordinary affairs of life, honest men. Many books have been written from our standpoint; but, in the first place, a German editor cannot buy a book which costs six shillings or more, and in the second place, he has not got time to read through it. The only thing is to give him free of cost something which he can read in an hour. My materials were all to hand. I know how humane Tommy Atkins was to his enemies, and I had been flooded with letters on the subject in reply to an advertisement I had inserted in the newspapers. Half-a-dozen things which have occurred to me in my life must have been foreordained.

" At a small dinner that night I sat next to ——. I explained my project to him. ' How will you get the money ? ' he asked. ' From the public.' ' Well, I'll get a thousand pounds for you.'

" Chance had thrown me against the man who knew everything I wanted to know. He could even tell me the names of the people who could translate it into the various languages. Five months later I had the book on my table in twenty languages. Rich men gave their fifty pounds to the scheme, poor people scraped together their half-crowns to do their widow's-mites' worth for England. I sent that pamphlet to every man in Europe whose opinion counted. Leyds gave me the cue. It is astonishing how few people govern the public opinion of the world. In two countries an honest second edition was called for—Hungary and Portugal. In the latter, our old ally, there was a most kindly feeling for us, a genuine anxiety to learn the true facts of the case. In Germany the whole twenty thousand copies were distributed; twelve thousand of them gratis, and eight sold. The Swiss actually printed an edition for themselves."

He told us this on the night that we entertained him and Gilbert Parker in honour of their knighthood, and he told us how that morning a letter of congratulation from his gunsmith had arrived, addressed to " Sir Sherlock Holmes." The best thing he ever told us about *Sherlock Holmes* was its fate when he made a play of it, and sold it to a famous actor. The actor stipulated that he should be allowed to alter it as much as he liked, and when Doyle went to the rehearsals, he found that there was practically nothing of his play left except the title. That was all the actor really wanted to buy; he had made his own play out of the Sherlock Holmes stories before he went to Doyle.

It was at an Authors' Club dinner that Hall Caine made his awful disclosure about Londoners' insides. He said that no family could live in London for more than three generations unless its members went away for a change of air, and that the smoke-charged state of the atmosphere turned their insides from a healthy red to a slaty black. It was that same night that he recited his poem " Ellan Vannin " to us.

I remember, in the early days of the Authors' Club, J. M. Barrie telling the Club a story in the American story-teller's fashion. I don't suppose for an instant that it had actually happened. I expect it was just a *ben trovato*, but it was none the less amusing. He apologised for being late. He had been to the wrong club. He had never been to the Authors'

Club before, he said (though he was a member of the committee), so he asked a policeman the way. From the way
in which he pronounced the word, the policeman thought
he meant Arthur's, which was quite near the Authors' Club
when it was in its temporary premises in Park Place. When
he got there he found it a very grand place, he said. The
club porter looked him up and down, and said " The servants'
entrance is round the corner."

It took the moral courage of a Scotsman to tell that story
—true or untrue. It was inimitably funny, told in the broad
Doric of *The Little Minister*.

Jerome actually had an experience of this sort in New York.
But it was not due to the obtuseness of the club porter.
He received a straight-out invitation from the servants of
one of the great New York clubs to spend the evening with
them. I suppose they have their story-tellers' nights like
the members. He said that he never enjoyed himself more
in his life.[1]

But the Club could never rise much above three hundred
members. Many a time have G. Herbert Thring, the
secretary, and I discussed with our board, consisting from
time to time of Besant, Oswald Crawfurd, Lord Monkswell,
Tedder, the literary executor of Herbert Spencer, Conan Doyle
Anthony Hope, Hall Caine, Frankfort Moore, Morley Roberts,
and Percy White, projects for bringing in more members.

[1] The Authors' Club, before it was reconstructed, contained a number of very
representative members. Among them were Sir Walter Besant, Conan Doyle,
Frankfort Moore, Hall Caine, Lindsay Bashford, R. D. Blumenfeld, F. T.
Bullen, W. L. Courtney, S. R. Crockett, Sir Michael Foster, secretary of the
Royal Society, J. Foster Fraser, Sydney Grundy, Charles Garvice, F. H.
Gribble, H. A. Gwynne, the editor of the *Morning Post*, Major Arthur Griffiths,
Rider Haggard, Cutcliffe Hyne, Anthony Hope, Clive Holland, Joseph
Hocking, E. W. Hornung, Sir Henry Irving, J. K. Jerome, Henry Arthur
Jones, Edward Jenks, who wrote that famous book *Ginx's Baby*, and was
once M.P. for Hull, Rudyard Kipling, Otto Kyllman, Archdeacon Sinclair,
Norman McColl, editor of the *Athenæum*, Prof. Meiklejohn, father of the V.C.
who was killed in putting a horse that could not jump at some railings in the
Park to avoid running over a child; A. W. Marchmont, Bertram Mitford,
J. Eveleigh Nash, Gilbert Parker, Barry Pain, J. M. Barrie, Max Pemberton,
Sir J. Rennell Rodd, British Ambassador at Rome, Morley Roberts, Algernon
Rose, who reconstituted the club, Bram Stoker, M. H. Spielmann, Prof. Skeat,
the great etymologist, H. R. Tedder, the librarian of the *Athenæum*, Herbert
Trench, Horace Annesley Vachell, W. H. Wilkins, Percy White, Lacon Watson,
Horace Wyndham, and others.

The change from the temporary premises in Park Place behind St. James' Street, to the pleasant rooms overlooking the river, did something for us. But we were faced by a dilemma, which was that we had to widen the basis of our membership to get enough members to pay the huge rent of the premises, which we had taken for a term of years. If, instead of having these premises, we had hired a reading-room, and a smoking-room, and a dining-room in a hotel, we could have got the accommodation for a hundred a year, and as only a tithe of the Club ever used it, except on the nights when they were brought together by notice for the Club dinners, any premises would have been large enough; the hotel would always have lent us a room of any size which we could fill for a dinner. The Whitefriars principle would have suited us admirably, and the Hotel Cecil would have made a good venue. But we had these premises on our hands, and we wanted a larger membership, not to fill them, but to make financial arrangements easier. I myself in my time enlisted no fewer than a hundred members for the Club. But that did not fill up the wastage.

Thring saw the need of widening our basis as clearly as I did, but we never could carry our board with us to make an enlargement of the franchise sufficiently drastic, because they wished to be guided by the feeling of the men who used the Club most, and their feeling was decidedly against it—mainly, I believe, because they thought that the extra members we wanted to relieve the finances would make the Club too full to be restful. So in one way and another the old Club was drifting on to the rocks when Algernon Rose (with Charles Garvice as his chairman, and Cato Worsfold as honorary solicitor) took the matter in hand as honorary secretary. I did not see the throes. I was out of England on one of my wander-years.

Rose, with a clear-sighted policy, boundless energy and self-sacrifice, and inexhaustible tact, not only pulled the Club out of the fire, but has made it one of the most flourishing organisations in London, with two hundred town members, three hundred suburban members, five hundred country members, and six hundred oversea members. He could easily have a thousand town members if he wanted them, but the town membership is strictly limited to two hundred, and the suburban to three hundred, because that is the limit of habitués which the premises can accommodate. Unfortunately you can't have five-day members at an Authors' Club like you do at a Golf Club.

And nowadays members use the Club in a way they never did when I was the honorary secretary and we exhausted our ingenuity in efforts to make the club more inhabited through the week. The increase of attendance at the Monday night dinners is one of the most wonderful things of all. Week after week they have enormous dinners, and Rose provides a brilliant succession of famous guests of the evening. The other Tuesday I read a report of an Authors' Club dinner in the *Daily Telegraph* which filled three columns.[1]

The Club retains practically all its old outstanding names, including that of Thring. Thring for many years was the Authors' Club personified. He not only conducted its business; he peopled the club. Men went to lunch there because they knew they would meet Thring. They dropped in after business hours because they knew that Thring, at any rate, would be there. He kept the social life of the Club, as typified in the Club pools, and so on, going, and he was the friend of all the members, except those who desired to remain unsociable. And, in consequence, he always had his finger on the pulse of the Club.

The questions of club discipline which came up before the board in its early days were some of them of the most extra-

[1] Among the guests of the evening at the Authors' Club since Rose took it over have been musicians like Sir Charles Villiers Stanford, Sir Walter Parratt, Sir Frederick Cowen, Mr. William H. Cummings, Sir Hubert Parry; supreme scientists like Sir George Darwin, F.R.S., Sir Oliver Lodge, F.R.S., Sir William Ramsay, F.R.S., Sir William Crookes, F.R.S., Prof. Schäfer, F.R.S.; great lawyers, like Lord Chancellor Halsbury, the late Lord Chief Justice, and Lord Justice Fletcher Moulton; men who have been great outside the Empire like Sir Robert Hart, and Dr. G. E. Morrison of Peking, and Mr. F. C. Selous, the mighty hunter; great politicians, like Lord Milner, and Lord Wemyss; great explorers, like Sir Ernest Shackleton; great artists, like the late Sir Hubert von Herkomer; distinguished foreigners, like the American Ambassadors, Whitelaw-Reid and Page; well-known literary men, like Harold Cox, secretary of the Cobden Society, Maarten Maartens, Sir Owen Seaman, Sir Sidney Lee, W. B. Maxwell; and great actors, like Sir Herbert Beerbohm Tree.

ordinary nature. One man hated hearing clocks tick, and whenever he was left alone in a room always stopped the clock. Somebody else wished to have him turned out of the Club, but the Chairman said he did not see how it could be regarded as ungentlemanly behaviour, and proposed that no action should be taken, but that we should take it in turns never to leave the honourable member alone !

The Rev. John Watson, who, under the pen-name of "Ian Maclaren," suddenly burst into fame with *Beside the Bonnie Brier Bush* when he was forty-four years old, was a Liverpool clergyman, the minister of the Sefton Park Presbyterian Church. He had long enjoyed a reputation in his circle in Liverpool for story-telling and as a public speaker. His speeches were as good as his stories, and admirably delivered. His personal charm was as great as the respect in which he was held. He was very humorous. He told us one night, when he was our guest at the Authors' Club, that his boy at Rugby had said to him, " Father, I suppose that your books are all right to some people, or you would not be able to do so much for us. But couldn't you write something which would be good enough for me to show the other chaps ? "

One wonders if this was the boy who is now the head of Nisbet's great publishing house. If it was, how pleased he would be to have the publication of some of the books that were not good enough " to show the other chaps ! "

CHAPTER XIII

LITERARY CLUBS : THE IDLERS AND THE VAGABONDS

AT the beginning the Authors' Club had no exact rivals, but there were two institutions, very much intertwined, which came near it in a way—the Vagabonds Club and the Idler teas. The Vagabonds Club, in its conception, had been a little coterie of authors who met in the rooms of their friend, the blind poet, Philip Bourke Marston; but before I came back from America Marston was dead, and the coterie had been turned into a small dining-club, which used to take eighteen-penny dinners at cheap restaurants, and in theory drank beer and smoked clay pipes. The committee included Jerome, C. N. Williamson and F. W. Robinson, and the Club had among its members, besides those just mentioned, Conan Doyle, Israel Zangwill, Anthony Hope, Bernard Partridge, Dudley Hardy, Phil May, Hal Hurst, Rudolph Blind, Pett Ridge, Joe Hatton, Robert Barr, Coulson Kernahan, W. L. Alden, Hall Caine, Sir Alfred East, E. W. Hornung, Sir Gilbert Parker, J. M. Barrie, Barry Pain, Arthur Morrison, Solomon J. Solomon, and, of course, George Burgin, the original and indefatigable secretary.

Of these people Jerome and Barr were editors of the *Idler*, Burgin was sub-editor, Doyle, Zangwill, Pett Ridge and Anthony Hope were its favourite contributors. The *Idler*, in those days published by Chatto & Windus, was edited in a flat in Arundel Street, Strand, and there every week, on Wednesday afternoons, as far as I remember, the editors gave a tea at which they welcomed their contributors, and any friends whom contributors chose to bring with them, and the friends of these friends thereafter. It was like the snowball system of selling umbrellas in the United States.

The teas were of the simplest. I do not think we had anything except bread and butter and tea, but nobody wanted more; it was sufficient that here was the common meeting-ground for men and women, where you might, and often did, meet the ablest young authors of the day. I should say that the Idler teas were the first literary gatherings in London attended by Weyman and Crockett, and they certainly were the first attended by Anthony Hope, W. W. Jacobs and Frankfort Moore.

We received the warmest welcome at the Idlers, because there were many literary Americans in London just then, and both Jerome and Barr were insistent that I should bring as many as possible of them to their teas.

At those teas the principal occupation was introducing every freshcomer to as many people as possible, as the hosts do at American at-homes; and Jerome made a good many of his arrangements for articles and illustrations with the people who came to the teas. It was characteristic of the Idler and Vagabond gatherings to talk shop and do business without any pretence of concealment.

Hal Hurst and Dudley Hardy were two of Jerome's favourite illustrators. Other artists who were there a great deal were Robert Sauber, John Gülich, Lewis Baumer, Fred Pegram, James Greig, Paxton, A. S. Hartrick, Louis Wain, who almost always drew cats with human expressions, a little man named Martin Anderson, who called himself " Cynicus," and had an allegorical vein of humour. He won himself undying popularity here by bringing to one of those teas a charmingly pretty young American, who was soon to feel her footing as a writer. She had not yet written *The Barn-stormers*. This was Alice Livingston, who is now known to all the world as Mrs. C. N. Williamson. Townsend, the present art-editor of *Punch ;* Chris and Gertrude Hammond, who were among the most charming book-illustrators of that day; Seppings Wright, the naval war correspondent; Holland Tringham, Melton Prior, Fred Villiers and many other artists came constantly.

The great advantage of those Idler teas was that women as well as men could be present, and in those days women were not considered worthy to be admitted to authors' banquets, except at the annual function of the Authors' Society. Of course, you had the chance of meeting women authors at the at-homes of the Pioneer, Writers', and Grosvenor Crescent Clubs, because they were all ladies' institutions. But at their entertainments you met only a very few men of any importance, and not particularly many women of literary importance, other than journalistic. They were more interested in women's movements—the Pioneer might almost be called the ancestor of the Suffragettes.[1]

The conversations at the Idler teas were very shoppy. I remember being introduced to Ellen Fowler as the woman whose witty sayings had long been the delight of the exalted circles in which she moved, and who had been induced by the various leading authors whom she knew to write a book. This is the sort of laudation which we professional authors often hear and usually distrust. But the book happened to be *Concerning Isabel Carnaby*, and when I learned that the circle which she had dazzled was the circle in which the Liberal leaders moved, since she was the daughter of Sir Henry Fowler, M.P., afterwards Lord Wolverhampton, I understood that she certainly would have received an encouragement to write books from the authors and critics who were admitted to Front Bench Liberal dinners.

Mona Caird, whom we met often at the Women's Clubs afterwards, did much for the emancipation of women in those days, for she was not only clear-sighted and convincing in what she said and wrote, but she had a winning personality which commanded the sympathies of those who were not predisposed to share her views.

It was at an Idler tea that I first met George Bennett Burgin, with whom I was to be so intimately connected for so many years as joint Hon. Secretary of the New Vagabonds Club. He was the sub-editor of the famous *Idler Magazine*, and his tact and geniality were constantly in requisition, for the pugnacity of his chiefs was proverbial, and some of the best contributors were equally pugnacious.

---

[1] Among the eminent women whom I remember seeing at the Idlers were Marie Corelli, Mona Caird, Mrs. Sidgwick (Mrs. Andrew Dean), Mrs. Campbell Praed, Mrs. Humphry Ward, Mrs. Lynn Linton, Mrs. Alexander, Mrs. Meynell, Miss Montresor, Lucas Malet and Ellen Thorneycroft Fowler.

I forget if it was a recognised part of the proceedings at the Old Vagabond dinners to have a set subject for discussion. Some one always did get up and make a short speech, and in a club which had men like Jerome and Zangwill and Barry Pain to draw on, the speaking was always witty, unless the subject forbade it. The chief difference was that people did not discuss the speech by getting on their legs to fire witticisms at the speaker. They discussed it where they sat, sometimes talking to each other about it (or anything else), sometimes raising their voices to question the man who had been speaking, or to argue with him.

There was much less discussion of the subject than there was talking of shop. The point of the gatherings was that a number of brilliant young authors and artists dined together fraternally once a month.

It was a great boon to me suddenly to be received into the intimacy of some of the busiest and best-known authors and editors and black-and-white artists of the day, to hear and take part in their " shop." [1]

Burgin, the hon. secretary of the Old Vagabonds Club, who was once private secretary to Sir Samuel Baker in Constantinople and Asia Minor, and has been a great traveller in recent years, was sub-editor of the *Idler Magazine* until 1899. Since then he has given himself up to novel-writing, gardening and the control of literary clubs. One of his novels, *Shutters of Silence*, has been through thirty editions. His books are distinguished alike by uncommon vivacity and by exceptional skill in using local colour. They are very good indeed, and if they had their rights would be among the most popular books of the day.

I have made several attempts to discover when the original Vagabonds Club was actually started, and the best account I have had of it was from Kernahan, one of the oldest members. I certainly did not join it till about five years later.

[1] This Idler and Vagabond set included, besides those mentioned above, Anthony Hope, Frankfort Moore, Israel Zangwill, Eden Phillpotts, C. N. Williamson, F. W. Robinson, Joseph Hatton, Coulson Kernahan, George Manville Fenn, G. A. Henty, W Pett Ridge, H G Wells, Frederic Villiers, Henry Arthur Jones, Francis Gribble, Rudyard Kipling, Arthur A. Beckett, William Watson, John Davidson, H. Breakstad the Norwegian, and Carl Hentschel, the founder of the old Playgoers Club.

He writes—

"Marston died February 14, 1887, Valentine's Day. Yes, I was one of those who visited his rooms, 191 Euston Road. When he founded the Club I do not exactly know. I fancy it had only just been started when, at his invitation, I joined in 1886. We dined at Pagani's and then adjourned to his rooms, keeping it up very late. After he died the Club practically ceased, as it was he who ran it. Then I think Herbert Clark proposed that we should continue meeting and call ourselves the Marston Club—not a good name, as I always held, for it gave the idea that it was like the Browning club or society, for the study of his poems, whereas it was merely a gathering of Marston's old friends. All the same, lots of interesting men came to it. His father, Dr. Westland Marston, for one. So things went on for a long time, and the thing was dropping to pieces for want of some one to work it, until you came along, put us in the shop window, and, lo and behold, the old Club became a new force."

It was not so very long after I joined the Club that it fell on evil days, not, I hope, because I joined it, but because it contained Socialists, who are apt to wreck things. The course they took was most revolutionary. There were two of them on the committee, and they insisted on having committee meetings, which insisted on having a voice in the management of the Club.

The Club would not stand it; it transformed itself into a New Vagabonds Club without the offending members. I took a leading part in the transformation. I became associated with Burgin in the honorary secretaryship because I persuaded a hundred well-known men, like Crockett and Weyman and Reginald Cleaver, to join the Club, and we retained the old committee, minus the impossibles, and strengthened by the inclusion of Frankfort Moore and Joe Hatton. And this was a well-behaved committee, because I do not think it met once during its whole existence of not far short of twenty years. Burgin and I were the honorary secretaries and managers, and we used to decide everything, without even thinking of the committee, who, as reformed, had only one idea in their heads, which was that they were not to be bothered unless there was some real necessity for it.

Our most successful dinner, at which about six hundred people were present, was held in honour of Field-Marshal Lord Roberts—the idol of the nation. Lord Roberts has a wonderful memory, not only for faces, but for the records which go with the faces. When I met him the other night at the Authors' Society dinner, of which likewise he was the guest, he took me by the arm, and whispered, " Isn't *Who's Who* getting very fat ? " which was his way of showing that he remembered that I was the author of *Who's Who* in its present form—or, rather, in the form which it bore from 1897 to 1899, when its figure was not so middle-aged.

That Vagabond dinner to Lord Roberts was in honour of the publication of his celebrated *Forty-One Years in India,* and the Authors' Society dinner to him was also in its honour, though so many years later.

Jerome took the chair to Lord Roberts at the Vagabonds. He was very interested in *Forty-One Years in India.* He had commissioned me to write the long review of it in the *Idler*, and I am sure that he and the Field-Marshal, V.C., though looking at everything from an exactly opposite standpoint, got on like a house on fire.

The dinner to Lord Roberts was the very largest we ever had, though the lunches to Sarah Bernhardt and to Sir Henry Irving were about as numerously attended. Irving made himself perfectly charming, but when he came to reply to the toast to his health, the audience were confronted by the curious phenomenon that the first actor in Europe was totally unable to make himself heard even half-way across the hall, and if they could have heard what he said, they would have been confronted by the equally curious fact that he was no speaker. That, however, is nothing—very few actors can speak, always excepting my friend, Tree, who, if he is in the mood, brings the house down time after time with his naïveté.

There were few eighteen-carat dramatic celebrities whom we did not entertain at the Vagabonds—Irving and Sarah Bernhardt, Wyndham and Mary Moore, the Trees and Mrs.

Patrick Campbell, the Bourchiers and the Maudes, the young
Irvings, and Lena Ashwell, occur to me first.

Sarah Bernhardt's appearance was a very memorable one.
Mr. Balfour was in the chair. He was Prime Minister at
the time, and had important business at the House of Commons that afternoon. Sarah was three-quarters of an hour
late. I, who had charge of the guests, while Burgin was
making sure that all his orders for a banquet of five hundred
people had been carried out, felt more nervous than I had
ever felt in my life at the slight which was being offered to
so great a man. I racked my brain for adequate apologies,
but Mr. Balfour said, with his perfect manners, " Please don't
worry yourself about that, Mr. Sladen. Tell me about
Japan."

If Sarah was as great as he was in other respects, she
certainly was not as great in this respect, for a day or two
afterwards, T. P. O'Connor asked Sarah and Mortimer Menpes,
and Norma Lorimer and myself, to have tea with some
M.P.s on the terrace of the House of Commons. We duly
arrived—even Sarah was fairly punctual—and were herded
in the lobby of the House, like people waiting to see the
editor in a newspaper office, while a search was made for
T. P. O'Connor. He could not be found anywhere, and a
long time passed. I do not know how long it was, but it
seemed years, because Sarah was so angry. She had expected
to be met at the door with due ceremony—perhaps the leaders
of both parties, the Lord Chancellor, and the Speaker—but
nobody met her at all, and none of us could speak French
well enough to understand the unmeasured language she was
using about O'Connor. Finally, she lost her temper altogether, and though she had told me on several occasions that
she could not speak English, she was quite equal to telling
us in our own language what she thought of T. P. Finally,
some wholly unsuitable member of the Irish party—Dillon,
or somebody just as gloomy—came, waving a telegram.
O'Connor, it appeared, had been caught in a railway accident
coming back from the Henley Regatta, miles from a telegraph
office. As soon as he got to a place where he could telegraph
from, he did telegraph, but Sarah was not appeased, even

though Menpes offered to go to her island off the coast of Brittany and arrange a Japanese room for her.

I remember a similar contretemps, almost equally amusing, when George Cawston, one of the directors of the Chartered Company, gave a great supper at Willis's rooms in honour of a South African millionaire. He invited a number of eminent people to meet him—politicians, soldiers, authors, actors, artists and public people generally, most of whom knew each other. The millionaire, who was very " swollen-headed," was shamelessly late. So, finally, Cawston decided to begin without him. The people made up parties, and sat down at the various little tables, and enjoyed the munificent supper, and finally went away not knowing or caring whether the millionaire had been there or not. They had most of them never heard of him.

Sarah came to us a year later to a huge afternoon reception, which we got up in her honour, and she honoured us by giving us a long and magnificent recitation from *L'Aiglon* (which she had just produced), in which she was supported by her leading man.

We entertained other famous soldiers besides Lord Roberts, such as Lord Dundonald, when he came back from the great exploit of his life, the relief of Ladysmith, and Sir Ian Hamilton. Cecil Raleigh, I remember, took the chair to Sir Ian Hamilton, and showed his versatility by making a really admirable speech. I do not remember who it was who took the chair to Lord Dundonald, but he told a characteristic story of Lord Dundonald in his earlier service in Egypt.

When the news of the fall of Khartum reached the army which might have relieved Khartum, if Sir Charles Wilson had pushed on, taking the risks as Lord Roberts would have taken them, after the victory of Abu Klea, the General asked for an officer to volunteer to carry the dispatches to Sir Redvers Buller at the base. It was necessary to have some one with a knowledge of astronomy, because he had to find his way across the desert, to avoid the great loop of the Nile above the Second Cataract. There were many men who would have risked the dangers of meeting wandering parties of dervishes, but there was only one of the force who was not only prepared to take the risk, but possessed the requisite astronomical knowledge, and that was Lord Cochrane, a subaltern in the 2nd Life Guards, the future Lord Dundonald. He carried out his mission, and in an incredibly small number of hours presented the dispatches to Sir Redvers, whom he found sleeping under a palm tree. As soon as he had delivered them, he collapsed with exhaustion.

He is a grandson, of course, of the immortal frigate Commander, the fighting Lord Cochrane, the Almirante Cochrane who was the liberator of South America, and is a distinguished inventor. He invented the pocket heating apparatus for soldiers to carry when doing sentry work in cold climates, the extra light carriages used for machine-guns in the Boer War, and the apparatus for enabling cavalry soldiers to turn out ready for duty as quickly as firemen.

From time to time we entertained distinguished ecclesiastics such as the late and the present Bishops of London and the ex-Bishop of Ripon. Creighton was much the best guest of the three, for he had a most saving gift of humour.

For some reason or other, on the night that he was with us, at the conclusion of his speech returning thanks for the way in which his health has been proposed, he had to propose the toast of journalism, coupled with the name of the editor of *The Times*. He said, " I do not know much about newspapers; I read so few of them. I have only one test for them, and that is their suitability for wrapping up shooting boots. And, judged by this standard, *The Times* is the best newspaper."

It was not easy to get the better of Creighton, with his humour to back up his wisdom and firmness. But my dear old friend, the late Father Stanton, who was a frequent visitor to Vagabond entertainments with F. E. Sidney, once got the better of him, and he was very amusing in telling the story of it.

Creighton, it appears, went to a service of Stanton's, because he wished to wean him from certain ritualistic practices. After the service was over, they had a talk in the vestry, which was quite cordial, because Creighton knew the essential greatness and goodness of Stanton's character.

Stanton, who was very astute and tactful about getting his own way, and yet avoiding trouble with his Bishop, adroitly kept the conversation away from dangerous points, and finally the Bishop gave up, and called for his carriage. Stanton escorted him to the carriage door, and as he was driving off. Creighton got out what he had come to say.

" I don't like that incense of yours, Stanton."

" Nor do I, my lord, it's wretched stuff—only three and sixpence a pound, but I can't afford any better."

" Do without it, Stanton, do without it altogether," said the Bishop.

Lord Charles Beresford was another of our guests, and so was Admiral Lambton. Both of them made a violent attack on *Bridge*, which they said was sapping the energy of the nation by the awful waste of time to which it led.

Beresford was very amusing. He said, " The Navy is the finest thing in the world for a man. If I hadn't been in the Navy, I should have been in prison."

I only once saw Beresford seriously put out, and that was when he had to speak after that great man, Seddon, the Premier of New Zealand, whose patriotic attitude about the Boer War counted for so much in making the democratic colonies support the mother country so splendidly against the Boers. Seddon, like other New Zealanders I have known, could make a great speech, but did not know when he had used up all he had to say. In the first part of that speech for the Vagabonds, he began with great éclat, and then maundered on and on about " Womman," as he pronounced her generic name, while Beresford grew so impatient that when his turn came to speak he excused himself with a few witty sentences about their having heard so much good speaking.

Seddon brought two charming daughters with him, and one of them made a felicitous retort to a maladroit person who condoled with her on her father's not having been knighted like the leader of the Conservative Opposition in New Zealand, Sir William Russell, whose name had appeared in the Gazette of the day before.

" I don't mind," she said; " Billy's a darling."

Norman Angell, the apostle of peace, in books like his

famous *The Great Illusion*, and also the *Daily Mail* correspondent of Paris, was our guest on one occasion.

The most unexpected turns happened at times. One night we had an athletic dinner, with C. B. Fry and Eustace Miles for our chief guests, and Pett Ridge in the chair. There was hardly a word talked about athletics the whole evening, for Pett Ridge is most interested in work among the poor, and so are Fry and Miles, and the speeches related almost entirely to the serious side of the humorist and the athletes. The world at large did not know how earnest Fry is about good works until he refused to go to Australia in the all-England Eleven because he could not leave his work on naval training for boys until a certain sum was raised for the training-ship. In those days it regarded him merely as one of the greatest batsmen ever seen, and the only man who had ever had five blues at the university, and been captain or president of the university in three different kinds of games. Some of them remembered too, that he was a Scholar of his College, and got a First. None of them, I am quite sure, knew that he would have been unable to go to Oxford at all, because he had no money to go on, except his scholarship at Wadham, if he had not borrowed the money, and repaid it out of his own earnings after he left the university. Could anything be more magnificent than that the man who holds the record of all Englishmen, and for that matter, that of all recorded men, for achievements in games, should have paid for himself at the university? Yet there were some people in the Club that night who expressed their disapproval to me at the Club's entertaining a mere athlete!

But there were many more who expressed their disapproval of our entertaining Christabel Pankhurst as our guest of the evening—most of them ardent Radicals, who disliked the practical jokes of the suffragettes upon Cabinet ministers. We Conservatives felt no more sympathy for people who do idiotic damage, but were more tolerant. I did not propose the toast, although I was in the chair, and have always desired to give the vote to women with the proper qualifications. I called upon an old friend, a very successful barrister, whom I suspect of being an ardent Liberal, though he is

an ardent suffragist—Fordham Spence—to propose it. He
made the kind of points which could not fail to enlist the
sympathies of a popular audience—asking which of the men
who were present would have the pluck to go to prison and
starve themselves for a principle, as these women did. He
pointed dramatically to our guest, a pretty, slim girl, who
hardly looked out of her teens, and told us what she had done.
He was the clever advocate all through; he begged the question almost as flagrantly as Miss Pankhurst herself, when
she got up to reply to the toast.

I prefer to hear the arguments of the suffragists stated in
the dispassionate way in which Mrs. Fawcett states them,
pure appeals to reason and justice, stated without any attempts to draw red herrings across the trail—in fact, stated
by a judge, instead of pleaded by an advocate. I think they
would be difficult to resist. The weak point of the militant
suffragettes is that they not only do things of which moderate
people cannot approve, to attract the public attention, but
they have no consideration for our commonsense; they talk
to us like Socialists talk to a mob in Trafalgar Square, not
as a great Scientist, like Lord Kelvin, would address the
British Association. That is the convincing way.

I do not know if Miss Pankhurst made many converts to
the cause that night; she certainly made many personal
friends. An hour or two later I met her at a supper given by
Mr. and Mrs. Stanley Mappin at the Savoy, and had the good
fortune to sit next to her once more. She was off duty then,
and saying that she really must begin to play games again to
keep her " fit " for her work.

Two of the most successful dinners we ever had were to
Captain Scott, the Antarctic explorer, and Ernest Thompson
Seton. At the Scott dinner the great hall of the Hotel
Cecil was packed to its utmost limits, though it was not due
to any premonition that he might not come back. Before
Scott perished the world had got into the idea that Arctic
and Antarctic exploration was not really so dangerous as
going out with a friend who was learning to drive a car. But
Scott had such an irresistible personality; he looked the very
type of man whose courage and resourcefulness and indomit-

able endurance would get him and those who depended on him out of the tightest place. And he would have got his party through if the supplies in the hut had been left at their proper strength. Scott was one of those blue-eyed men who can meet any danger with a smile, and are absolutely devoid of fear. I never knew a man for whom I had a more instinctive liking, or to whom I should so naturally turn for support when facing death. Few men are such an asset to their race as he was.

Ernest Thompson Seton held his audience as no other Vagabond guest has ever done. The born naturalist and the natural orator are combined in him. He made a lecture, which had probably done duty several times as a lecture, do duty for his personal reply to the proposal of his health; it did not betray its origin, and yet it was a moving plea for the whole brute creation; he invested the lower animals, probably unjustly, with all sorts of human traits and human feelings, and made the audience feel for them as they feel for the hero or heroine in a tragedy. It was really wonderful; I never heard such a mixture of ingenuity and eloquence, or a speech more thrillingly delivered. He is the apostle of animated Nature.

I was abroad when the Club entertained Lord Curzon and Winston Churchill and Lord Leighton, but I was present when Lord Willoughby de Broke made such a popular guest. The position was rather a difficult one; not having noticed the views which Jerome had been expressing on the House of Lords to the local yokels, I asked him to take the chair, because he was the most successful playwright in the club— he had just produced *The Third Floor Back*—and our guest was one of the best amateur actors. Jerome's speech was not marked by his usual verve; like Balaam, he had come to curse, and he was so won over by the splendid manliness of the guest that he was unable to do anything but bless. Lord Willoughby de Broke would doubtless have given us a much more entertaining evening if Jerome had spoken of him to us as he spoke of his fellow-peers to the yokels, for no one is so ready with a retort. Who does not remember his retort at the meeting which he was addressing in favour of Mr. Balfour.

G. B. BURGIN
Drawn by Yoshio Markino

He was saying something in praise of him, when a voice at the back called out " Rats ! " He smiled sweetly—" I was speaking of Mr. Balfour," he said, " not of the first Lord of the Admiralty."

Later on, at that same meeting, a heckler asked him where he got his title, and was told " just where you got your d——d ugly face—from my father."

He gave us some pretty flashes of wit that night, but not of the scathing order which makes him one of the protagonists who fight against Home Rule. With his physical strength and activity, his dauntless courage, and his power of swaying great assemblages with his speeches, he is a born leader.

There were few well-known literary men and women in the London of the time who were not guests of the Vagabonds Club. The best speech we ever had from a woman author was, I think, from Flora Annie Steel, who, contrary to the habit of most speakers, explained to start with that she was likely to make a very good speech because we had taken her unexpectedly, and she was very angry with the last speaker— whom she proceeded to mince.

But charming Mrs. Craigie, " John Oliver Hobbes," made us a very fascinating one when she was our guest of the evening. That was the night on which she complained that people persisted in identifying her with her heroines, especially with the kind of heroine whom a woman does not wish to be suspected of drawing from herself, like her " Anne " (I think in *The Gods, Some Mortals, and Lord Wickenham*).

Anthony Hope, who was the next speaker, complained that he had never had such luck, that he had been hoping ever since he wrote *The Prisoner of Zenda* that somebody would confuse him with Rupert of Hentzau, but that no critic had ever obliged him.

Once, at any rate, he was the guest of the Club, and he occupied the chair, I should say, nearly every year during its existence. I wish I had kept a record of the *bons mots* which never failed to adorn his speeches. One of them comes to my mind as I write these words; he said that the reason why England and the United States were not better friends arose from their inability to understand each other's humour.

He and Conan Doyle were the mainstays of our chair at the New Vagabonds. Doyle may have taken it even oftener than he did. He was the chairman we instinctively chose for a great occasion, like that on which we had Lord Roberts for our guest, though he did not actually take the chair that night, for we could rely upon him to say the generous and dignified words which would express the feelings of the Club, as he did in proposing the health of Lord Roberts at the Authors' Society dinner, when he said that Lord Roberts was the one guest who, short of royalty, must always take the first place in any gathering of his countrymen, the first, not only in rank and distinction, but in the grateful love and veneration of Englishmen.

Doyle was in the chair at the farewell dinner which the Club gave in honour of Burgin and myself at the Connaught Rooms, and said just exactly the right things to make us feel very proud, and to voice the regret of the Club at meeting for the last time. The Club did not exactly die, because it was amalgamated with the O.P. Club.

Carl Hentschel was a very prominent member of both clubs, and when Burgin and I were unable to carry on the Vagabonds any longer, he very kindly came forward, and was willing either to take over the honorary secretaryship of the Vagabonds, or to amalgamate the two clubs. Finally, seeing that Bohemians had more dining clubs than they had the leisure to attend, we decided in favour of amalgamation, and there is some talk now of the Playgoers combining with them both.

George Grossmith was one of our best members. We had him as a guest, and he often gave us an entertainment. One of his most felicitous efforts was when he proposed his own health, and was very sarcastic about himself. But that was a favourite vein of humour with him. Those who were at the great party which he and Weedon gave at the Grafton Galleries will remember the story of the clergyman's wife who was getting up a bazaar, and suggested that they should ask George Grossmith to give them a performance, because he was such a fool—" You can always get him to do things for nothing," she explained, and added, " The best of him is that he can be humorous without being funny."

She was right about his being generous; that was always characteristic of George Grossmith.

Bill Nye distinguished himself in an equally original manner when he was the guest of the evening. It was Independence Day, and he had enjoyed such a reception from the American colony that he was sleepy, to say the least of it, before he reached the New Vagabonds. Not one word could the chairman get out of him during the dinner, but no sooner had the chairman said, " Gentlemen, you may smoke," than Nye got up and returned thanks for all the handsome things which had been said about him. He spoke at great length, and with the greatest fluency, and it was only with considerable difficulty that he could be stopped. He is the only man I ever remember to have come to one of the dinners so tired, though I have seen others unbend as the evening grew old; and it was entirely due to the accident of his arriving in London on Independence Day. And, as poor Phil May said, of course, your tongue does sometimes run away with you, when you are on your legs.

Arthur Diósy (the son of that Martin Diósy who was secretary of the Hungarian Revolution), who was chairman of the Japan Society for years, had talked so learnedly about Japan, and had mouthed the Japanese names so lovingly, that every one imagined that he had been in Japan for at least half his lifetime. Most people went further, and, not knowing that the Hungarians were Mongols who conquered parts of Europe a thousand years ago, imagined, from the Mongolian type in his features, of which, as a Hungarian, he was so proud, that he was a Japanese. Even the name did pretty well if you spelt it wrong. When he did go to Japan for the first time, and received an enormous welcome from the Japanese authorities as the founder of the Japan Society, and the practical originator of the Anglo-Japanese Alliance, we, his fellow-members of the Vagabond Club, gave him a dinner in honour of the event.

I am an original member of the Japan Society, and had the honour of giving them their opening address in the season of 1912.

We had a very interesting guest in Sir George Scott Robert-

N

son, the doctor who was knighted for his successful defence of Chitral when the combatant officers were all *hors de combat*. Robertson not only wrote his name on the golden roll of the besieged who have endured to the end and who have prevailed, but he gave us one of the best speeches we had ever heard at the Club. He told us marvels of his other claim on his country—his exploration of Kafiristan, a country which had kept its population pure from other strains, and had preserved unique monuments until, in our own generation, the Afghans began to absorb it, and he proved himself a great orator, with a well of biblical English flowing into his impromptu speech.

Sir Edward Ward we entertained for his share in another and yet more memorable defence, for it was to him, more than anybody else, that England owes the preservation of Ladysmith. He foresaw what was coming, and before it was too late got on the track of everything edible and potable in Ladysmith; he made the horses, which were not going to be of any use, into chevril, a horsey form of Bovril, and if the siege had gone on much longer, he would have found a way of making *suprêmes* out of old boot-soles. He made the provisions last by his foresight and administrative capacity, and he was almost as invaluable with his indomitable pluck and cheeriness. He was for years Permanent Secretary of War, and it is a mighty pity that he is not Secretary of State for War, for which his unparalleled knowledge of Army administration and his robust commonsense would make him the ideal appointment. No detail is too small for Ward to attend to it; no person is too small for him to listen to courteously and patiently. He made a great impression on the Vagabonds, for he has an Irishman's wit in speaking, and is most soldierly looking, a man of Herculean build.

Sir George Reid, the High Commissioner of Australia, is one of the best speakers we had at the Club; he is very witty when he is witty, and from time to time turns serious with marked effect. I had known him many years before he came to the Vagabond dinner; I made his acquaintance in the early 'eighties, when I held the Chair of History in the

University at Sydney, and he was the only Free-trader of any influence in Australia. Since then he has been the Premier of Federated Australia, and now most worthily represents the Commonwealth, for he has impressed on the Government that he is a force to be reckoned with, even where the colonies are only vaguely affected.

In decided contrast to him was the Princess Bariatinsky—Lydia Yavorska, the Russian actress who married a cousin of the Czar. We entertained her as a recognition of her splendid acting in Ibsen's *Doll's-House*, where her foreign accent was no drawback, and her tragic power had scope.

There are other Vagabond dinners which, I remember, went off with much éclat, though I cannot recall their incidents—dinners to great sailors like Lord Charles Beresford and Lambton, now Meux, and Shackleton of Antarctic fame, dinners to great soldiers like Sir Evelyn Wood; dinners to great artists like Lord Leighton and Sir Alma Tadema and Linley Sambourne, all, unfortunately, now dead, and J. J. Shannon, still with us and still young; dinners to great actors like Ellen Terry and Tree, Wyndham and Mary Moore and the younger Irvings and the Bourchiers and the Asches and Forbes-Robertson and Lena Ashwell; and dinners to great authors like Doyle, Mrs. Humphry Ward, Hall Caine, H. G. Wells, Mrs. Burnett, Jerome, W. L. Courtney and Robert Barr. They were all great occasions, with two, three or four hundred present, but readers will wish to be spared the details of dinners to perfectly well-known people unless they brought out some fresh trait, or some priceless anecdote.

It is to be hoped that the Vagabond dinners will come to life again, not on the huge and expensive scale which is going out of vogue, but little meetings of really eminent people gathered at some restaurant in Soho, to eat a dinner which reminds them of joyous Bohemian days in Paris or Italy, and to enjoy the pleasures of a general conversation upon the topics of Bohemia, such as we used to have in the days when we met as men only (which we will never do again), before we were reformed Vagabonds.

The Argonauts, a little dining club which Frankfort Moore and I founded, before the Vagabonds allowed ladies at their dinners, to dine every Sunday or every other Sunday at Mrs. Robertson's tea and luncheon rooms in Bond Street, where we had our club-room, would give a good example to follow. We seldom had a guest or speeches. A number of well-known people used to dine together for the pleasure of each other's company. We left our places as soon as we had finished dinner, and broke up into little knots to converse. There you really could see your friends, and introduce interesting people to each other.[1]

At these Vagabond dinners, the ordinary procedure was for two or three or four hundred members, male and female, to assemble to do honour to a famous guest. As soon as dinner was over, the chairman proposed the health of the King, and made the stereotyped joke about any lady, who wished, being permitted to smoke. He had this excuse at the Vagabonds, that many of the men smoked before they had received permission. Then he proposed the health of the guest, and the guest replied. All guests made the same jokes about the name " Vagabonds." I rather think that they must have been supplied to them by the toast-master at the Hotel Cecil, who always " prayed silence " with special gusto for " Mr. Hanthony 'Ope," because no other name gave him the same chances.

When the guest had finished his speech, which was usually a very good one, because we chose them for their speaking,

[1] The members of this club, as far as I can remember, were : Conan Doyle, E. W. Hornung, Justin McCarthy, M.P., J. K. Jerome, S. R. Crockett, Anthony Hope, Gilbert Parker, Oswald Crawfurd, W. H. Wilkins, J. Bloundelle-Burton, Frankfort Moore, Moncure D. Conway, Rudolf Lehmann, Edward Heron Allen, Barry Pain, Arthur Playfair, Arthur Diósy, Reginald Cleaver, G. A. Redford, Lewis Hind, Herbert Baily, Walter Blackman, G. W. Sheldon, Edward Elkins, Edgar Fawcett, Louis F. Austin, Bernard Partridge, John Charlton, Sir James Linton, Mortimer Menpes, Basil Gotto, Emerson Bainbridge, M.P., Sir J. Henniker-Heaton, M.P., Penderel Brodhurst, C. N. Williamson, Arthur A'Beckett, H. B. Vogel, Horace Cox, Grant Richards, Joe Hatton, Percy White, Clarence Rook, Henry Arthur Jones, Adrian Ross, Herbert Bunning, Judge Biron, Grimwood Mears, Rudolph Birnbaum, Ben Webster, Mrs. C. N. Williamson, Flora Annie Steel, John Oliver Hobbes, Florence Marryat, " Iota," Mrs. Campbell Praed, Annie Swan, Arabella Kenealy, George Paston, Norma Lorimer, " Rita," Mrs. Stepney Rawson, Violet Hunt, May Whitty, Rosalie Neish, Mrs. Alec Tweedie, Mrs. C. E. Humphry, and Mrs. Oscar Beringer. To these I must add one of the two famous Greenes who were singers; I cannot find the initial. It will be observed that there was hardly a person in the club whose name was not well known.

unless they were very eminent, we retired into the adjoining
hall for an entertainment of singing, story-telling and con-
juring, which I always thought spoilt the evening, much as
I appreciated the performances of men like Churcher and
Harrison Hill and Bertram, or Willie Nichol, or Reggie
Groome, for when you had a number of eminent people
collected together, far the best form of entertainment was
to introduce them to each other. I remember the positive
pain I felt at Lady Palmer's, when, a few minutes after she
had introduced me to George Meredith for the first time,
Johannes Wolff, the violinist, played a thing of Beethoven's
which was as long as a sermon. I wanted to hear George
Meredith so much more than him, having regarded him as
one of the greatest masters of literature all my life, and wishing
to surrender to the extraordinary charm of his way of speaking.
I sympathise with a famous tenor, who told me that the first
time he heard Handel's *Messiah*, when they came to the
Hallelujah Chorus, he said, " Let's get ' oot,' there's going
to be a row."

Personally, I used to try and induce the most interesting
people present, except the guest of the evening, to stay
outside, and have whiskies and sodas. They generally
hadn't the good taste to prefer singing to whiskies and
sodas; I hadn't, either, though I don't drink whisky.

But the Hotel Cecil, where we held the Vagabond dinners,
was not as bad as the Savage Club. In the old days there,
if you did not wish to spend your evening glued to one chair,
listening to singing, you had to stand in a tiny bar, the size
of a scullery, and hear the same jokes from the same steady
drinkers, just as you would have heard the same songs every
Saturday evening if you had stayed in the room all the
time. The Savage is a much more literary club now, and the
accommodation is better arranged. I do not want to say
anything against the old Savage. Those performances were
good enough for anybody to listen to once, even King Edward
VII, who, when he was Prince of Wales, dined there, and
said that he had never enjoyed himself so much in his life.
What I objected to was the constant repetition of the same
performance Saturday after Saturday, without having any

place for members to sit and talk if they did not want to
hear the music. But I have been to many Bohemian
dinners in my time, and I have not met many men, except
Walter Besant, who confessed that performances made him
feel, as they make me, that he would have a nervous break-
down if he listened to them for half-an-hour longer. I have
noticed that most men, when they go to a club of this kind,
where there are a number of really eminent people in the
room, have no objection to listening to one vapid song after
another, instead of being introduced to, we will say, Lord
Kelvin, or Tennyson, or Sir Henry Irving, and this though
they could have an equally good performance any night of
their lives by paying for a seat in the promenade of a music-
hall. When will people understand that the two sorts of
entertainments ought to be kept separate—that the great
object of a literary dinner is for one to meet men who write,
or the people whom all the newspapers are writing about?
You can go to a concert by paying for it; you cannot meet
these people by any other means except introduction, and
the hour or two after you have done eating at a public dinner
is all too short a period for the chance of introduction to the
world's workers.

CHAPTER XIV

LITERARY CLUBS : THE SAVAGE CLUB

I WAS for a number of years a member of the Savage Club, and I was an honorary member there for a long time at an earlier period, when I first came home from Australia and the waiting list was full.

I sometimes hinted to the then secretary that I had out-lived my month of honorary membership several times over. His answer was invariably the same : " Rules are intended to be enforced against disagreeable people." I remained an honorary member till I went away to America in 1888. Some years afterwards, when I returned from America, I became an ordinary member.

At first I loved the Savage. There were not many author-members, it was true, who ever put in an appearance, except Christie Murray and Patchett Martin—Barrie was a member, but he was never there. The Club did not run to authors. What celebrities there were were chiefly actors and artists. But it was a club that consisted more of the admirers of the arts than their professors, men who packed the dinner-table every Saturday night, and made an enthusiastic audience for the actors and musicians and reciters, who did " turns " to amuse the company and get their names known to the public, if they were not already popular favourites, like W. H. Denny, Fred Kay, Odell, Willie Nichol and Reggie Groome.

I have known the Savage Club long enough to remember Brandon Thomas and Seymour Hicks being regarded as brilliant amateurs, who never would be anything more. But both were very favourite performers at giving sketches accompanied by the piano. Penley was often there, but never would perform. One of the favourite *jeunes premiers* of musical comedy—I forget which—used to sing " I'll sing thee Songs of Araby " every Saturday night.

Before I went to America, while I knew hardly any one in Bohemia, and it was all new to me, I loved those Saturday nights.   We had a bad half-crown dinner, in which I generally sat between quite uninteresting people—well-off furniture dealers and that kind of thing, who were most of them, however, keen and intelligent patrons of music and the drama, and belonged to the Savage for that reason.   Most of them, too, were old members, with a large number of friends at whom they fired good-humoured banter across the tables.   I found them willing to take one into their good-fellowship in the readiest manner, and occasionally one was rewarded by finding oneself near an affable celebrity.

But the conversation was seldom in the least bit intellectual.   Books were treated as non-existent in the Savage of that day.   There were hardly any, even in the library, except poems given by the poets themselves.   I was always heartily glad when the dinner was over, and the fusillade of ordering drinks was over, and the performance began.

The club-house was situated then, as now, in Adelphi Terrace, a fine row of Georgian houses standing on a sort of marine parade above the bank of the Thames.   If you looked over the railings on the opposite side of the road, you would expect to find a beach like Brighton's.   I have never yet looked over these railings, so I don't know what there is below, but there must be vaults, which are used for something, under the road, in such a valuable locality.

The room where we held the dinners and these brilliant club concerts was only separated by a wall from David Garrick's dining-room.   He made the mistake of living in the wrong house.

The theory why we dined at 6.30, was that popular actors and singers could dine with us, and give us a turn before they went to their theatre.   In practice, they very seldom came, unless they were having a holiday, voluntary or otherwise.   But there were always enough of them " resting " to give us a brilliant evening.

For some little time after dinner the Club did not settle

down sufficiently to make its favourite performers willing to give their turns. It made too much noise over diluting whisky with soda, and manœuvring to get the waiter's attention. This gave the new aspirant his chance. If he was timid and low-voiced, he did not always get the attention of the room, but it was not difficult to get the chairman to call on him. I know by experience how difficult it was to get any old " hand " to sing first. I called upon the bores first, when I was in the chair. There were several of them, whom the Club had grown into the habit of tolerating every Saturday night, so they had earned a right to be called on. They all said that they had colds, and afterwards, when the performance was at its height, sent round notes that they felt better, and would try to give a turn if I called upon them now. But I ignored the notes so long as I had any one else to call on. They were mostly reciters; almost any kind of song will go in a club which takes up a chorus.

Some of the humorous reciters were very good. The club was never tired of hearing Robert Ganthony give a scene in a Metropolitan Police Magistrate's Court; or that youthful octogenarian, Fitzgerald, the artist, mimicking a rehearsal at Astley's in the old days; or Odell, the idol of the Savage, going through his wonderful repertoire. Early in the evening, Walter Hedgcock, the Crystal Palace organist, would give us the song he never could publish, because he was blocked by an earlier setting—Kipling's " Mandalay." It was delightful music, and was eventually published as the " Mousmee," with words which I wrote for him in the metre of " Mandalay." Hedgcock did not mind coming on early, because he could always pick up the audience with the first bars of " Mandalay."

Townley, who was Registrar of Births and Deaths at St. Pancras, I think—except on Saturday nights and Sundays—was our funniest singer; he was a natural comedian. The Club always insisted on its favourites singing the same songs. He had to sing a song called " Hoop-la," or something of the kind. Willie Nichol had to sing " Loch Lomond "; Cheesewright had to sing " The Three Jolly Sailor-Boys "; Denny, who was afterwards our honorary secretary, did generally

give us something recent from the music-halls. But the old
" hands " eyed him half resentfully while he did it.

I soon came to regard Odell as an oasis, because, though
the Club made him sing and recite the same things Saturday
after Saturday, he had a blessed gift of gag. In the midst of
his ballad about the Fleet, the one Warham St. Leger wrote
for *Punch*, he stopped one night to tell us how he lost his
last engagement. It was in a piece based on the wreck of the
Princess Alice, the Thames steamer in which so many lives
were lost. Odell played the part of captain of the steamer,
and all went well till one night, as he expressed it, just at
the fatal moment, when the people in the stalls were taking
off their coats because they were so perspiring with excitement, he could stand the tension no longer, so he took out his
watch and said, " It's just five o'clock. I wish I had gone
back by the penny 'bus." The audience rose in their places,
and stoned him with whatever came handy, and he pretended
that after that he never could get an engagement.

As I don't drink after dinner, and don't smoke at all,
I began to find these concerts very tiring as soon as I knew
all the performances by heart. But there was no other
place of meeting except the bar. We badly needed a smoking-
room, adjoining the dining-room and the bar, where those
who had brought interesting people with them could introduce
them to interesting Savages, without losing touch with the
evening, as they did if they went up to that melancholy
library, which has probably been given over to some legitimate
purpose, like *Bridge*, long ago.

I frequently agitated for this smoking-room, and I believe
that they got it eventually. The bar did too good a business;
you did not see people getting intoxicated; its habitués
carried their liquor too well. But I have seen one man
drink as many as thirty-three whiskys-and-sodas in a single
evening, and I saw him the other day—twenty years afterwards—looking as fit as possible.

Gradually I came to the conclusion that as there were
so many other interesting things happening on Saturdays,
it was not wise to give my Saturday evenings up to the
Savage, and there was " nothing else to " the club in those

days. It had not then become the favourite lunching-place of the great editors, an important venue for authors.

So I retired from the Savage, as I retired from the Devonshire a few years afterwards. When one of the committee of the Devonshire asked me why I retired from it, I said that I only used it for funerals, and that I was retiring because they had made that an extra. This was a fact. The windows of the Devonshire Club are one of the best places for seeing a royal funeral—or, of course, any other royal procession. The committee discovered this, and put on a charge of ten pounds a seat, to pay for the decorations of the Club. So many people wanted these seats that they had to be balloted for. The action of the committee was justified. But, as I had not used the Club since the funeral of Queen Victoria, when I found that I could not see the funeral of King Edward from its windows without balloting for the privilege of paying ten pounds for it, I sent in my resignation, and paid a guinea for a seat from which I could see the funeral for the whole length of Oxford and Cambridge Terrace. I went with Norma Lorimer and Markino, who painted a wonderful picture of it. The people on whose roof we hired the seats from the contractor, asked us to lunch, and became quite intimate friends. They proved to be Mr. Sanderson Stuart and his daughter—the youthful genius of sculpture.

We used to get most notable guests at the Savage—was not the list headed by Albert Edward, Prince of Wales. I was in the chair the night that Nansen was the guest of the evening. It was on the eve of his departure for the North Pole, and I hammered the table and asked the Club if they would allow me to invite our guest to write his name on the wall behind his seat, to remain there till he came back again. They assented with rapturous applause, and the name is there still, glazed over. I have told in another chapter what he said to the "Savage" who wished to accompany him to the Arctic Circle.

The Savage Club is, undoubtedly, one of the institutions of London, and every literary visitor to these shores should see one of its Saturday nights.

CHAPTER XV

I MUST allude briefly to my long connection with journalism.

When I settled in London in 1891, I had already done a good deal of journalism in New York and San Francisco. In the latter my writing had chiefly lain in travel-articles on Japan, to which San Francisco, as the Pacific Capital of the United States, naturally looks. In New York I had written on travel—much of my *Japs at Home* appeared in travel-articles for the McClure Syndicate. But I also wrote a number of literary and personal articles for the *New York Independent*, the *Sun*, the *World*, and so on, such as my *Reminiscences of Cardinal Newman* told in the first person. In doing this I found that what America demanded was the personal reminiscence.

When I came to England, I naturally sought work on the same lines, and had no difficulty in finding editors who saw the opening for this comparatively fresh line in British journalism.

I turned first to Fisher, of the *Literary World*, whom I had met at the Idler teas, and who had invited me to do some reviewing for him. He had *Table-Talk Notes* as a feature, and here my first journalism appeared.

When I was helping Jerome to formulate *To-day* in 1893, I suggested to him that we should have a book of the week, in which we told as much about the author as we knew, and that biographical gossip about authors and artists and actors should be one of our chief features. He was completely in favour of it, and I wrote a good deal for him, especially about authors.

About the same time, Lewis Hind became editor of the now defunct *Pall Mall Budget*, and I carried out the same idea for him in a regular *causerie,* to which we gave the name of the *Diner-Out,* and which I signed " St. Barbe "—the family name of my maternal grandmother.

Between these three papers I was pretty fully occupied. But my mind was turning towards a more congenial form of journalism—the travel-article. Percy Cox, a son of the Horace Cox whose name appeared on the *Queen* as its publisher for so many years, was anxious to develop its travel side, and while the late Sievers Drewett was organising the wonderful travel department, which now has its annual *Queen Book of Travel,* he employed me to write a series of articles on my travels in Greece and Turkey, and a regular travel-serial on the trans-continental journey across Canada, which I amplified and brought out as *On the Cars and Off.*

While I was doing these, Clement Shorter, who had been a sort of literary editor to the *Queen*—all the important books being sent to him, and he writing a sort of *causerie* about them—became too busy with his offspring, the *Sketch,* to do any more work for the *Queen,* and I was offered his place. My suggestion that we should have a signed " book of the week " for the most important book—unsigned minor reviews to be worked in anywhere about the paper—and that I should do my *Diner-Out* column for the *Queen,* instead of the *Pall Mall Budget,* was accepted, and I began my literary connection with the *Queen,* which lasted for so many years. I kept the *Diner-Out* for biographical gossip about authors chiefly, and for announcements of forthcoming books, which could be made interesting by personal gossip. Actual reviewing I kept as far as possible out of that column. In those days, though the *Queen* was and always had been the chief ladies' paper, it had not nearly so many departments of feminine interest as it has now, so there was plenty of space for book-reviewing, which became a very important feature of the paper. I was only responsible for the *Book of the Week* and the *Diner-Out,* though I did perhaps a page of unsigned minor reviews, which were never attributed to me.

I had one faithful reader in her late Majesty, Queen Victoria. I learned this quite incidentally. I had taken a *manoir* in Brittany for the summer, and at the house of Mrs. Burrowes, a niece of the late Lord Perth, met the lady who filled the post of reader to Her Majesty; Queen Victoria prefered having books and newspapers read aloud to her. This lady informed me that Her Majesty had my *Diner-Out* column in the *Queen* read to her every week, and was most amused by it.

As the woman's side of the paper developed, the space for reviewing became more and more restricted, and the *Diner-Out* became simply a column of small reviews, without any of its own features, and finally, I think, the name itself very often dropped out.

While I was doing the reviewing for the *Queen*, we were travelling a great deal in France, Italy, Sicily and Egypt. The books which I published on these countries were, as far as the travel portion of them was concerned, largely drawn from these articles in the *Queen*—beginning with *Brittany for Britons*. Some of them, such as the Normandy articles, I never did re-publish, and I contributed to the *Queen* enough articles on Italy to form another volume, besides those which have already appeared in my books on Italy and Sicily.

I still do some reviewing for the *Queen*, but I do little other journalism now, except when I am approached by some newspaper to do an article on a subject upon which I have special knowledge.

The fact is, that in recent years I have employed my journalistic faculties on the preparation of books like *Who's Who, Sladen's London and Its Leaders* and *The Green Book of London Society*, which need much the same kind of gifts as personal journalism does.

The Green Book was a sort of one-line *Who's Who*, which only mentioned the leading people in each walk of London life, except the bearing of a title. The selection of the chief personages and experts in each line—say, for instance, shooting or fishing or golf or writing books—was not made by any correspondence with the people themselves, but was entrusted to the chief expert in each line. Golf was by a runner-up for the Amateur Championship, fishing by the

SIDNEY LOW
Drawn by Yoshio Markino

fishing editor of the *Field*, exploration by the secretary of the Royal Geographical Society, and so on.

Who's Who itself must form the subject of a separate chapter.

I have no older friend in journalism than Sidney Low. We went to Oxford, I think, on the same day—he was a Scholar of Balliol and I was a Scholar of Trinity—and we certainly knew each other very well there, and have been intimate friends ever since. His ability received early recognition. Before he had left Oxford ten years, he was editor-in-chief of a great London daily, and he has written books which have become standard works, like the *Dictionary of English History*, which has been through half-a-dozen editions. Since he gave up editing he has represented the leading papers on the most important special missions. He has been an alderman of the London County Council, and he has been one of the chief forces in literary society. If I were asked who had introduced me to the largest number of eminent persons, I should say Sidney Low—without hesitation. No man passes saner or more moderate judgments on the great questions of the hour. Indeed, I should say that Low stands in journalism for what a man who was at Oxford with both of us—George Cave, K.C., M.P.—stands in politics—for moderation in statement, combined with great firmness of principle and judgment.

With Low's name I must couple that of the late Samuel Henry Jeyes, who was his colleague both on the *St. James's Gazette* and the *Standard*. He was a beloved friend of us both, but my intimacy with him began much earlier. He was my greatest friend at Trinity, Oxford, and one of the Oxford men of whom I saw most in after life. We were elected Scholars of Trinity on the same day; we had rooms on the same staircase; we went to all the same lectures till we passed mods., and I taught him to play billiards. It was the only game of manual skill which he ever did play. He lashed the adulation for sport which prevails at Oxford with the gibes of which he was such a master. When we had only been up at Oxford for a few days, A. J. Webbe, who was the special idol of Trinity because he was captain

of the 'Varsity Eleven, asked all of us Trinity freshmen
to meet some of the lions of the Oxford Eleven. All of us
except Jeyes were vastly elated. We all, except Jeyes,
talked our best cricket shop to make a good impression on
the demigods. At last he could stand it no longer, and,
waiting till there was a dead pause in the conversation, he
said, "This b——y cricket!" I can remember the tableau
still.

His reputation as a wit came up with him from Uppingham.
All Uppingham men could remember how, when he was
caught cribbing with a Bible on his knee at a Greek Testa-
ment lesson, and his class-master had said to him triumphantly, "What have you there, Jeyes?" he said, "A book,
sir, of which no man need be ashamed," and how when
Thring, the greatest head master of his time, had asked him
how he came to be ploughed in arithmetic for his Oxford
and Cambridge certificate, he replied from Shakespeare,
"I cannot reckon, it befits the spirit of a tapster"—a
readiness which Thring would have been the first to appreciate.

Among the best things I remember him saying at Oxford
are his definition of the Turks in a great debate over the
Bulgarian atrocities, as a people "whose morals are as loose
as their trousers, and whose vices are as many as their
wives." And it was he who said, "I don't want to go to
Heaven, because Gore (now Bishop of Oxford) is the only
Trinity man who will be there, and I'd rather be with the
rest."

Jeyes never spoke at the Union—he despised it—or he
would have been as great a success as the miraculous
Baumann or Freeman, now Rector of Burton-on-Trent.
I never remember hearing Cave speaking at the Union,
though perhaps he did.

One of Jeyes' wittiest retorts was to "Bobby" Raper,
at that time Dean of Trinity, who was "hauling" him
for some meretricious disregard of College discipline. The
glib excuse was not wanting, but Raper was stern. "No
no, Mr. Jeyes, that won't do. You told me the exact
opposite of that last term." "I know I did, Mr. Dean,
but that was a lie."

He owed the Dean one, for the first thing he did when he went up to Trinity had been to go and call on the Dean and tell him that he had conscientious scruples against going to chapel.

" Morning chapel, you know, Mr. Jeyes," said the Dean, " is a matter of discipline and not of religion, but if you really have conscientious objections, I'll put on a roll-call for you at 7 a.m."—Chapel was at 8 a.m., so Jeyes swallowed his nausea.

But Jeyes' wit was tireless. He was a fine scholar—he made his pupils write wonderful Latin prose when he became a don at University—I presume during the undergraduacy of Lord Hugh and Lord Robert Cecil. But he tore himself away to be a journalist, and became in time an assistant-editor of the *St. James's Gazette,* and later of the *Standard.*

As a journalist he was distinguished by incorruptibility of no common sternness. Though he had always spoken as a Liberal at Oxford (very likely out of malice, because all his friends were Conservatives), he was one of the pillars of Conservative journalism. He knew all the chiefs of the Conservative party, and enjoyed great influence with them. He was so rugged and unbending. I never knew a harder editor to " work." He wrote a Spartan life of Chamberlain, for whom he had a great admiration, except in the matter of Tariff Reform.

He married an old friend of ours, the beautiful Viva Sherman, an American nearly related to the Senator-Vice-President and the General. Both before and after his marriage he was a frequent visitor at our house, and we often met at Ranelagh and elsewhere. He enjoyed a discussion with Norma Lorimer. Her wit provoked his, and their conversations were most brilliant to listen to.

At last poor Jeyes was struck down with cancer—aggravated, I believe, by cigar-smoking, in which he was a noted connoisseur. He bore it with magnificent fortitude, and for a long time kept it a secret. Even I did not know that he had been mortally ill till he was dead. But I was one of the three old Oxford friends who stood by his grave—his oldest friend, except H. B. Freeman, who read the service.

o

Sidney Low was the other. Charles Boyd was there too, but he belonged to a much younger generation.

If Jeyes had known that his life would be so short, he would perhaps have devoted more time to book-writing. It is a pity—except for his country and the Conservative party—that he gave up so much of his life to necessarily ephemeral journalism. I always heard that but for a flaw in a will he would have been owner of one of the greatest provincial journals in England.

Peace be to his ashes. He was a merry soul, and if the theosophists are right about our astral bodies meeting the spirits of the departed, there is no one with whom I should so much enjoy an astral conversation as Jeyes. He would be such a volatile spirit. I can imagine the naïveté with which he would describe his experiences.

The Rev. Herbert Bentley Freeman—the Rector of Burton-on-Trent—a cousin of the historian, and a descendant, I believe, of the mighty Bentley of Phalaris renown, came up to Trinity from Uppingham in the same term as Jeyes. Freeman and A. A. Baumann, who was afterwards Conservative M.P. for Peckham, were the two most brilliant speakers at the Union in my day. The undergraduates said that both wrote their speeches beforehand, and learned them by heart and practised their delivery.

Years afterwards I met Baumann when he had given up his safe seat at Peckham and unsuccessfully contested a seat in the North, I think at Manchester.

" What made you give up Peckham? " I asked. " They would have gone on electing you there as long as you lived."

" My dear chap, life isn't worth living when you are member for Peckham. I live in South Kensington, and while I was member for Peckham I used to find my hall full of constituents by the time I came down for breakfast, and by lunch-time you'd have thought that I was having an auction of my furniture."

But of all the men who were at Oxford with me, no one has been so prominent, then and now taken together, in intellectual circles as W. L. Courtney. Courtney was then a rather young New College don, who had the distinction

of being married to an extremely smart-looking wife. That
would have been a distinction by itself in the Oxford of
that day, for few were married in a way suitable to impress
undergraduates. Added to that, he cut the most eminent
figure in athletics of any don in Oxford. He was the
treasurer of the University Boat Club, while the dons respected him as the ablest man in Oxford at philosophy.
I was not there when he gave it all up to come to London
and be literary editor of the *Daily Telegraph* and editor of
the *Fortnightly Review*, but I can imagine the consternation
which fell upon that ancient seat of learning when their
bright particular star, the admiration alike of don and
undergraduate, " chucked it," as they say, for journalism.
Of course he did wisely, for in an incredibly short space of
time he had as distinguished a position in London as he had
had at Oxford. His influence on literature has been immense.
He has stood for the combination of scholarliness and up-
to-dateness. His own books range from essays on the verge
of fiction to some of the most important works on philosophy
published in his generation. Incidentally, the creator of
Egeria is our best dramatic critic, and a writer of plays.

Both the late and the present editors of the *Field*, William
Senior and Theodore Andrea Cook, came to our Addison
Mansions receptions. That delightful man, William Senior,
the " Red Spinner " of fishing journalism, and his wife
came very often to us. Theodore Andrea Cook is the ideal
editor for a great sporting paper like the *Field*, for he had
not only been editor of a great daily, but he had rowed in
the Oxford boat, and been a Scholar of his College, and he
had captained the all-England team in the international
fencing matches at the Olympic games which were held
at Athens. He has also written very sound books on an
unusual variety of subjects (one of which, his book on
The Spiral in Nature and Art, was most widely discussed);
and is one of the most delightful writers we have of travel-
books on France. Of course, everything which he has written
upon sport is *ex cathedra*.

Walter Jerrold, who lives a little higher up the river than
I do, in an old house with a great garden, a very old friend,

and a much older Vagabond than I, often came with his wife to us at Addison Mansions. Jerrold is a grandson of the famous wit, Douglas Jerrold. He was for more than a dozen years sub-editor of the *Observer*. But fortunately he found time for editing of another nature as well, which will help his own books to give him a permanent place in our literature. He is one of our best editors of nineteenth-century classics; his biographical and bibliographical introductions are the most useful of their kind—just what you would expect from the grandson of a man who was a star in the firmament of which he writes.

Clement Shorter, who married the Irish poetess, and was editor of the *Illustrated London News* when we met at Rudolph Lehmann's in the "nineties," is another editor of books as well as papers. The Brontës are his special protégés. He is the acknowledged Brontë expert, and every one has read his new book on George Borrow. He has been great at founding—he not only founded the *Sketch*, the *Sphere* and the *Tatler*, but he was one of the founders of the *Omar Khayyam Club*, beloved of Radical litterateurs, though it deals not with English politics, but English Persics. Here you are always sure of good speaking—Mr. Balfour and Mr. Asquith, and all the important Cabinet Ministers and ex-Cabinet Ministers have spoken there on occasion. I have never heard Shorter speak himself, but I understand that he is a very good political speaker, and I can picture him telling a Lincolnshire audience how wrong it is to have an income not half as great as his own, for Shorter has been deservedly prosperous. He is a great journalist—one of the pioneers of modern journalism. He was a Civil Service clerk when in 1890 he became editor of the *Illustrated London News*, and only a couple of years had passed before he started the *Sketch*, the model of a new class of paper, for the same office, and continued to edit both papers till 1900. Then he thought that he would like to have a paper of his own, and raised a hundred thousand pounds to found the *Sphere* and the *Tatler*, with which he has been associated ever since, as editor of the former and director of both. They are rightly among the most popular illustrated papers of the day, for they have reduced the handling of the personal element to a science, and Shorter always was a brilliant editor. His success has been largely due to his colossal energy and industry. He has taken a minute interest in every detail of the production of both papers.

In the midst of all his journalistic labours, Shorter has found time to write some admirable books, and has made himself with two books a specialist on Napoleon in his period of exile at St. Helena.

Herbert White, the present editor of the *Standard*, is one of the best informed of all the English newspaper editors about Continental politics, because he went through such an arduous schooling in Austria and Germany, and knows German as well as he knows English. He married the niece of an Austrian political leader, and after war-corresponding in the Græco-Turkish war of 1897, represented leading English, American and French newspapers at Vienna from 1897 to 1902, and Berlin from 1903 to 1911. Besides this he has taken twenty special journalistic missions in every country of the Continent except France and Russia.

I should be accused of sycophancy if I said all I should like to say of Robertson Nicoll, of whom I saw a good deal before we were both such busy men. But there are some things about Nicoll to which nobody can be blind, besides the position of respect which he enjoys in the literary community. He makes a *bona fide* attempt to educate his party in politics, and his public in a spirit of commonsense and toleration instead of appealing to their prejudices, and no man has done more in the way of securing the publication of the books of unknown authors of merit, who have justified his expectations and given the world great books. Nicoll has been the sincere and enthusiastic friend of merit. I can say this without prejudice, because his firm have published nothing of mine.

Similarity of name, and their common friendship with the A. S. Boyds, makes me mention here James Nicol Dunn, whose editorship of the *Morning Post* was marked by such an advance in the political weight of that paper. Dunn was managing editor of the *National Observer* in its prime. For solid efficiency as a journalist, he had no superior in the country. It would have been a bad day for England when he left it to edit the *Johannesburg Star*, if it had not been so important that the chief organ of the Transvaal should be in such brave, moderate and judicious hands, at such a critical period in the history of South Africa.

T. P. O'Connor is a very old friend of mine. I met him first when we were both in America in 1888–1889, and we have been on terms of Christian names ever since. Though we differ strongly in politics, it has never affected our friendship, for T. P. is very fair to his enemies, except when he happens to have a special hatred for them. He has founded four papers—the *Star*, the *Sun*, *T. P.'s Weekly* and *M. A. P.*— but I am not sure as to how far he is still interested in any of them.

T. P. is to me a fascinating personality. He is so generous and genial. The swift recognition, the ready smile, the warm affectionate manner, have endeared him to hosts of friends, and every one recognises that he has a golden pen which invests everything he touches with interest, and an acute intelligence—acute enough to sift even the Humbert mystery and present a clear analysis of it, as witness his *Phantom Millions*.

He is a golfer too, and once upon a time used to play with W. G. Grace, who, it seems, in spite of his being the best cricketer that ever lived, always hits his shot along the ground except from the tee, though he drives and puts pretty well. I got this egregious piece of journalism from him when we were sitting next to each other at the dinner given by M. Escoffier, at that time, and probably still, cook at the Carlton Hotel, who gave a gourmet's feast on the occasion of the publication of his book on cookery, published by Heinemann. Heinemann invited me. The chief thing I remember about the feast is that the wine Escoffier selected was *Pommery Naturel*, and that the *tour de force* was lamb stuffed with sage and onions to replace the usual mint sauce.

John Malcolm Bulloch, the editor of the *Graphic*, who gave me such immense assistance when I was writing *Adam*

Lindsay Gordon and His Friends in England and Australia, is an author whose father and grandfather were authors before him. His specialities are the ancient University of Aberdeen, of which he is an M.A., and the great house of Gordon. He edited the *House of Gordon* for the New Spalding Club, and has written many pamphlets on Gordon genealogy besides his book on *The Gay Gordons.*

I happen to enjoy the friendship of the editors of both the *Bookseller* and the *Publishers' Circular.* George H. Whitaker, who is a doctor by profession, saw a good deal of the world as a ship's doctor when he was a young man. Now the world sees a good deal of him as head of the firm which publishes *Whitaker's Almanack*, as well as editor of the *Bookseller*—famed, as a trade-organ ought to be, for the justice of its reviews.

R. B. Marston, who edits the *Publishers' Circular*, edits the *Fishing Gazette* also. He founded the Fly Fishers' Club. The Marstons are famous fishermen—his father, Edward Marston, who has just died at a Nestor's age, had been one of Izaak Walton's chief followers both with pen and rod. R. B. is, besides writing books on fishing and photography, one of the chief writers on our food supplies in war, an energetic and patriotic public man.

My oldest acquaintance in journalism, except Sidney Low, is Penderel Brodhurst, the editor of the *Guardian.* We used to meet at Henley's in the days before I went to America, which was in 1888. He was in those days the walking encyclopædia of the *St. James's Gazette*, and afterwards edited the long-defunct *St. James's Budget.* He was, as he is, a man wrapped up in his work : he could, if he had chosen, have been a personage in literary society on his very historical name, for he is a descendant of the Penderel who saved King Charles II in the oak at Boscobel, and enjoys a pension therefor, probably one of the oldest pensions still running in England, and he is, though he does not use his title, an Italian marquis (Penderel de Boscobel, created 1782).

Lindsay Bashford, being literary editor of the *Daily Mail*, has only had time to write one book—*Everybody's Boy*— but that was a very good one. But he has a sufficient literary record apart from that, for he was lecturer on English literature at a French university.

J. A. Spender, the editor of the *Westminster*, is another author-editor. I have known him for many years. He comes of a brilliant family, for he is a son of Mrs. J. K. Spender, and brother of Harold Spender. He was an Exhibitioner of Balliol, and Harold was an Exhibitioner of University College, Oxford. Both of them are authors of half-a-dozen books, and both of them are wonderfully clever and well-informed men, real powers in journalism.

Sir Owen Seaman, of *Punch*, who was Captain of Shrewsbury School, and took a First in the Classical Tripos, and the Porson Prize at Cambridge, can best be described as the modern Calverley, for no one since Calverley has written such brilliant satirical lyrics. He was the " O. S." of the *National Observer*, and who does not remember " The Battle of the Bays," " In Cap and Bells " and " Borrowed Plumes " ?

H. W. Massingham, of the *Nation*, the most conspicuous political journalist on the Liberal side, one of the few Liberals who dare to try and lead their party against its will, has only written a couple of books, both rather technical, *The London Daily Press* and *Labour and Protection*.

Sidney Paternoster, the assistant-editor of *Truth*, is well known as a novelist, as is Adcock, of the *Bookman*, but, taken as a whole, editors of great newspapers are not writers of books.

Ernest Parke, director of the *Daily News and Leader* and the *Star*, was at one time a regular attendant at the Vagabond banquets, as was his sub., Hugh Maclaughlan. Parke and I saw the Coronation together from a seat in the triforium of Westminster Abbey right over the little square of Oriental carpet on which His Majesty King George V was crowned, so we had a splendid view of the Archbishop of Canterbury and the Garter King-at-Arms, addressing the North, South, East and West as witnesses, and of the Dukes of Beaufort and Somerset, towering above Lord Kitchener as he walked between them, an object lesson which I suppose was not unintended. Parke is a great journalist, and made the *Star* a force in literature. Leonard

Rees, of the *Sunday Times*, who shines as a literary critic as well as a musical critic, with whom I have had much correspondence, I have never met personally. But Vivian Carter, who was on the staff of the Institution of Civil Engineers till only a dozen years ago, and has in the last five years edited the *Bystander* with such conspicuous success, is a mutual friend of the C. N. Williamsons and myself. We meet there.

J. S. Wood, the founder and managing director of the *Gentlewoman*, and one of the real founders of the Primrose League, was often from the beginning at our at-homes, with his pretty Italian wife, and his daughters as they grew up. We used to meet them in the season at Ranelagh, too. Wood has been much more than a founder and 'editor of newspapers, for he has been connected with the management of several of our most important charities, and has himself been instrumental in raising a quarter of a million for them.

All the Kenealys (Arabella and Annesley, both authors, Edward and Noel, both editors) were frequent visitors at our flat, except Alexander Kenealy, the editor of the *Daily Mirror*, who was in America for twenty years before he became news editor of the *Daily Express*, and, later, editor of the *Mirror*. More than any of the others, Alexander Kenealy inherits the splendid abilities of his father, the famous Dr. Kenealy, Q.C., M.P., one of the greatest lawyers of his time, who took up the case of the Tichborne claimant when others had abandoned it as hopeless, and almost pulled him through.

Another of our editor friends was Edwin Oliver, at that time editor of *Atalanta* and subsequently of the *Idler*, and, since 1910, of the widely influential *Outlook*.

I cannot conclude my chapter on journalism without reference to Sir Hugh Gilzean-Reid, whose pet plaything was the Institute of Journalists. He used often to come to our house with his charming daughters. Sir Hugh, who had made a considerable fortune out of journalism, large enough to let him live in Dollis Hill, the house near Willesden which Lord Aberdeen lent to Mr. Gladstone, never forgot the working journalist, and it was he who engineered the agitation which defeated the intention of two of the great London dailies to issue Sunday editions like the American *Sunday World* and *Sunday Sun*. As Herbert Cornish was the creator, he was chief founder and first President of the Institute of Journalists also. He used to give large garden-parties at Dollis Hill, chiefly to people who appreciated its having been consecrated by the residence of Mr. Gladstone, though there were others, like ourselves, who went because we liked his family so much. He was a philanthropic man, and did an immense amount of good.

The first paid journalism I ever did was writing articles on public school life for the *Educational Reporter* when I was a boy at Cheltenham. About the same time I wrote a story for *Bow Bells* called " Douglas Thirlstaine's Wooing," which was not paid for, and soon after that I supplied unpaid notes about Cheltenham College to a Cheltenham paper, which had never been able to get them, as a favour to the late Frederick Stroud, who had got me out of the libel action brought by the editors of the *Shotover Papers*. I wish I could find that libel now. It was a small pamphlet of a few pages, published under the title of *Overshot* by a printer in Turl Street, Oxford. I saw about the printing of it when I was up in Oxford competing for a scholarship at Trinity or Balliol, lodging with Ray, who was afterwards to be my scout, in one of the sixteenth-century cottages which now form part of Trinity.

In Australia the only money I made in journalism was five pounds which I received from the *Queenslander* for the serial rights of a novel which I have never re-published, and a guinea which I received from the *Illustrated Australian News* as a prize for the best poem on Federation.

When I got back to England, the first paid journalism I did was, for the *Illustrated Sporting and Dramatic News*, edited by A. E. T. Watson, who now edits the *Badminton Magazine*, and who projected and edits the *Badminton Library*, and is a member of the National Hunt Committee—one of the chief sportsmen in journalism. The subjects on which I wrote were Australian cricket and Australian poetry, like Gordon's, and on both subjects I was the chief authority until I went to America, odd as it may seem now. I also wrote on Gordon for the *Graphic*, and had a long historical article in the *Cornhill*, and a serial novel—*Trincolox*—in *Temple Bar*.

When I went to America, I wrote a good deal for papers and magazines, but almost entirely in verse, except a series of articles which I had to telegraph from Montreal about the Carnival to a great American daily. I remember thinking that the telegraphing was such a useless expense for such unimportant stuff.

In Japan I wrote a good deal for the *Japan Gazette*, but my contributions were gratis, because there the editor, Nuttall, now one of the editors of the *Daily Telegraph*, was expected to write the whole paper himself. I used to help him, and he exerted himself to get various permissions for me. He was a very capable man, who kept his paper interesting though he had to make his bricks without straw.

However, when I got back to America from Japan I commenced journalism in real earnest. I wrote a good many articles at four pounds a column for the *San Francisco Chronicle*, and, as I have said, wrote for many papers in New York, and when I returned to England I introduced the American biographical journalism to many papers, and at one time was fully occupied with it, until I diverted the capabilities I used for it to the founding of *Who's Who*.

CHAPTER XVI

THE WRITING OF MY BOOKS : PART I

My active literary career dates from my return from America. Hitherto, with the exception of the *Handbook to Japan* and the potboiler for the North German Lloyd, and a shilling shocker, published anonymously, and the two series of articles on Japan executed for the *San Francisco Chronicle* and McClure's Syndicate respectively, my literary aspirations had all been poetical. I had published volumes of my own verse entitled : *Frithjof and Ingebjorg, Australian Lyrics, A Poetry of Exiles, A Summer Christmas, In Cornwall and Across the Sea, Edward the Black Prince, The Spanish Armada, Lester the Loyalist,* and four anthologies, *Australian Ballads and Rhymes, A Century of Australian Song, Australian Poets* and *Younger American Poets,* one of which, *Australian Ballads,* had a very large sale, though I only had ten pounds for doing it.

But in America I had been under the necessity of making money, because my private income was unequal to the increased expense of living in America. The articles for McClure and the *San Francisco Chronicle* were the outcome of this necessity, and having found that I could add materially to my income by writing about travel when in America, I conceived the idea of making my articles on Japan, a country then but little known in England, into a book. I went to Mr. A. P. Watt, then not many years established, and he procured me a commission from Hutchinson & Co.—the first of a series of commissions which has gone on from that day to this. That book was *The Japs at Home,* the most successful, in point of sales, of all my books, for not less than a hundred and fifty thousand copies of it have been sold by various publishers. Hutchinson & Co. brought out editions of it at eighteen shillings (two), six shillings, and

THE DINING ROOM AT 32 ADDISON MANSIONS.

(From the Painting by Yeshio Markino)

three-and-six, and then, having got through four editions of it, and believing the sale at an end, gave the book up to me. Another publisher sold fifteen thousand copies of it at half-a-crown, and then exchanged the book rights with me for the serial rights, and since then there has been a shilling edition, an enormous sixpenny edition, and a threepenny-halfpenny edition; the shilling and the threepenny-halfpenny editions are selling still.

Following *The Japs at Home* came *On the Cars and Off*, the success of which was ruined by having illustrations which took six weeks to produce. It was a guinea book, and a first edition of a thousand copies was sold directly. But the second edition was not ready till nearly two months later, and by that time the interest in the book was dead.

My next book of travel was *Brittany for Britons*, published as one of the familiar little half-crown guides of A. and C. Black, of which a great number of copies were sold. I cannot say how many, because I parted with the copyright.

After this my energies were diverted from travel-books for a while, because I wanted to try my hand at novel writing. The result was *A Japanese Marriage*, which, after *The Japs at Home*, has been my most successful book in sales. About ten thousand copies of it were sold in octavo form, and as a sixpenny various publishers have sold a hundred and twenty thousand.

For two years after our return from America we confined ourselves to short excursions to the milder parts of England —Hampshire, chiefly round Norman Christchurch; Devon-shire, in the nook of Dartmoor round Drewsteignton, and on the gloriously wild coast round Salcombe; and the woods of the Isle of Wight. During this period I finished *The Japs at Home*, and wrote *On the Cars and Off*, which was not published till 1895, about our double journey across America from Halifax to Vancouver's Island.

Then a new interest came into my life—we were persuaded in 1895 to spend a summer and autumn at St. Andrews, and there I acquired the inevitable taste for golf, which has kept me interested and amused and healthful and unaging. Certainly this was one of the most fortunate inspirations we ever had for a holiday, since, after being devoted to games at school and College and in Australia, I had left off football and cricket and tennis, and even shooting, as soon as I settled in London.

Poor old Tom Morris never had a worse pupil, for I play everything wrong, and owe the prizes and medals I have won at golf to the straightness of eye which helped me to win every shooting challenge cup at Cheltenham and every shooting challenge cup at Oxford. At St. Andrews I not only had a glorious spell of golf, but fell deeply in love with romantic and historical Fifeshire. There are few places which combine so many attractions as St. Andrews. It is the capital of golf; its cliffs capped with old houses, and its ancient port, are beautiful enough for Sicily, and its great ruined castle and its immemorial cathedral make it architecturally the most interesting place in Scotland after Edinburgh and Stirling. Nor does it yield to many in historical interest. I should live there if it had a climate like Naples.

It gave us such a hunger for old architecture and romantic scenery that in the following summer we went to the old Breton towns on the Gulf of St. Malo. We stayed at St. Servan in a seventeenth-century *manoir* called La Gentillerie, which we had from the chaplain, my school-friend, William Vassall, who stayed with us as our guest in his own house.

From a point close by we could look across the harbour to St. Malo, with its mediæval walls and crane's-bill steeple, and on the other side were no further from Dinan. From St. Servan we went on for a month in Normandy, which I much prefer to Brittany. Towns like Rouen and Caen, Coutances and Bayeux, Evreux, Lisieux and Falaise, are citadels of mediævalism.

During this holiday I wrote my third travel-book, published in England, *Brittany for Britons*, issued a year later, and put the final touches on my first acknowledged novel, *A Japanese Marriage*.

It was my two books on Japan, *The Japs at Home* and *A Japanese Marriage*, which helped me to gain a literary position; both went into several editions in their first year. Between them they have sold more than a quarter of a million copies.

But I was on the verge of a book-success of another kind, which could hardly be called a literary success, though more people connect my name with this than with any of my books. Messrs. A. & C. Black, who had published *A Japanese Marriage* and *Brittany for Britons*, approached me to know if I would expand *Who's Who*, of which they had just purchased the copyright.

They showed it to me, and asked me if I could turn it into a book of reference—a sort of cross between the old *Who's Who* and *Men of the Time* was the idea which shaped itself from our discussion.

The two visits which we paid to Salcombe in Devon, the second of them with Reginald Cleaver, have not yet furnished me with any subject for writing.

The year 1896, in which I compiled the new *Who's Who*, was also a notable year for me from the travel point of view. At last I faced the exertion of taking my family to Sicily, which had been my ambition for exactly ten years. It was not such a stereotyped journey as it is now. I began to make inquiries about it when we reached Naples, and could not find an Englishman in the place—even the Consul-General—who had ever been to Sicily. But the Consul-General made inquiries, and said that he did not think travelling in Sicily was very difficult or dangerous. He, however, asked me if I had a revolver, and recommended me not to take out a licence for it at the Consulate, because in Sicily a licence is not available for the whole island, but only for one province, and there are seven provinces. He also told me that he was quite sure that no Sicilian ever took out a licence, though they all carried firearms. As for malaria, he did not know; he never troubled about it; he always spent the summer in or near Naples, and never felt any the worse for it. This Consul was my great friend, Eustace Neville-Rolfe, who had lately sold his ancestral estate of Heacham in Norfolk. Nelson students will remember allusions in the great Admiral's letters to his uncle Rolfe at Heacham. But my friend hated the climate of Norfolk, and hated its politics, and settled at Naples, where a good many years afterwards they made him Consul-General for the unconstitutional reason that he knew more about Naples than any living Englishman. He had the unique distinction of joining the Consular Service as a Consul-General.

When we got to Sicily we found it perfectly easy and safe. The Whitakers of Palermo, to whom he gave us an introduction, at once became our friends, and told us all we ought to see and all we ought to do in the island. On that trip we paid fairly exhaustive visits to Palermo, Taormina, Syracuse, Girgenti, Marsala, Trapani, Selinunte, and Segesta, and flying visits to Catania and Messina.

Sicily is an adorable country. Grass, flowers and fruit-trees grow right down to the edge of the sea, where there is any soil, for half the island is rock. There are no brigands on the sea-coasts, and nearly every monument worth visiting is in sight of the sea. There is not a place in the island from which you cannot see a mountain. It is the land of the orange and the lemon; and possesses the rare charm of ancient Greek and mediæval Arab architecture.

Sicily inspired me to write the largest of all my books, *In Sicily*, and inspired a publisher to produce it in an *édition de luxe*, whose two volumes weighed fourteen pounds, and contained four hundred illustrations. I called it *In Sicily* because it was not until several years afterwards that I considered that I knew enough about the island to write a book with the more pretentious title of *Sicily*. A great French author paid me the compliment of appropriating my title, and a good deal of my information, a few years afterwards. I began to write *In Sicily* in 1896, but it was not published till 1901.

We spent the spring of 1896 in Sicily, and the summer at Lulworth, on a little round cove in South Dorset. We went there partly because it was said to be the mildest place in England, partly because Thomas Hardy told me that he had laid the scene of one of the chief episodes in *Tess of the D'Urbervilles* in an old farmhouse near the station which served Lulworth; it had a hopelessly unromantic name—Wool.

In the following summer we went to Ostend for the season, because I wanted to see the gambling and the fashions. The morals of the Ostend of that day may be gathered from this. A friend of mine who was staying at the principal hotel with her husband, was asked by the proprietor if they were properly married. She was most indignant, and said that of course they were.

" Very well," he said coolly, " then I think you ought to go to some other hotel, because you are the only people in mine who have been married."

That same hotel manager considered that things were no longer what they were, for an Indian Maharajah had that morning complained at being charged two pounds for a chicken—that the English and Americans were no longer fools, and, in fact, that the only fools left were the Austrians.

The late King of the Belgians was in residence at the chateau, and had not one, but three, notorious French actresses staying with him.

Apart from its *plage* and its gaming-tables, I should have found Ostend a dull place if it had not been for Henry Arthur Jones, who was there, off and on, writing a new play, and ready to discuss it. He had had a play at the St. James's which had not gone too well, and he asked me if I could account for it. I suggested that allowing a hospital nurse to frustrate an elopement was more calculated to gratify the gallery than the stalls, and that the St. James's was a stalls theatre.

Jones had one curious habit—whenever he felt at a standstill in writing his play he used to say he must have a change of air, and then fly away to Homburg or some other place which took many hours to reach. He was much interested in gambling, though he did not gamble seriously. I imagine that he found the gaming-tables full of " copy."

In the winter we went to Sicily again, and in the summer to Salcombe again.

In the following winter my connection with *Who's Who* ceased. My agreement with the publishers was only for three years in case the book was a failure, and the publishers pronounced it a failure.

Almost immediately afterwards I had an attack of jaundice, brought on, or not brought on, by the incident, and after a short stay at Brighton, went to recruit my health at Nice, from which I paid many visits to Monte Carlo, though I did not gamble much.

On our way back from Nice we did what not one Englishman in a hundred, among the thousands who winter in the Riviera, does, got off at Tarascon, and wandered about the cities of Troubadour-land, such as Tarascon, Arles, Nîmes, ·

P

Avignon and Les Baux, the deserted capital of a dead principality, where the houses, instead of being built, are hewn out of the face of the rock.   Provence is full of ancient Roman buildings, and of Romanesque buildings, hardly to be distinguished from them; and, in our day, in spite of the law against it, they used the Roman amphitheatres for the modern equivalent of gladiatorial games—bull-fights.   Bull-fighting always began on Easter Sunday.

I registered a resolve, which I have never kept, to write a book about Provence.

That summer we spent at Cookham on the Thames. Since we were unable to go abroad, we went on the river, as being the most frankly " Continental " place in England. We had perfect weather, and Ostend itself did not give us more pleasure than the reach of the river between Cookham and Maidenhead.   I found lying in a punt outside the lock at the Cliveden end conducive for finding incidents for fiction.

And I had not done sufficient creative work since I began *Who's Who*.   Indeed, *The Admiral*, my novel of the love of Nelson and Lady Hamilton, which I finished at Ostend, had been nearly my whole output, for *Trincolox* had been written ten years before, and published in *Temple Bar*.   I was, of course, working at the materials for *In Sicily* all the time, and in the spring of 1900 we paid another three months' visit to Sicily to see that all my facts were up to date.

We were at Syracuse during the darkest days of the Boer War.   About half the people in the house were Germans, who were openly pleased at the succession of disasters which had befallen the British arms before they could get proper forces out to South Africa, to fight an enemy who was prepared in every single detail before he forced on the war.   It seemed as if the disasters never would stop, and these amiable people told us so every day.   But one fine day a British battleship, one of the largest then afloat, steamed into the great harbour of Syracuse, and anchored in the waters where the Athenians were annihilated in their last sea-fight against the Syracusans.   We were down on the quay, and so was nearly every other foreigner in Syracuse, when a launch put off from H.M.S., and made towards us. The Captain, a typical sea-dog—it was Callaghan, now one of our chief Admirals—was in the stern. As he stepped ashore he said : " We have just had a wireless from Malta— Kimberley is relieved." It was most dramatic to have the news brought to us by the biggest battleship in the Mediter- ranean, how French had introduced a new feature into warfare by raising a siege with a dash of five thousand cavalry riding all day as hard as they could. I shall never forget it.

We returned to Rome in time for the Papal Jubilee, the sixth centenary of the original Jubilee established by Boniface VIII in 1300. Some of the ceremonies were extraordinarily interesting, and the procession of Leo XIII in St. Peter's was one of the most impressive things I ever saw. I think it was that which inspired me to write *The Secrets of the Vatican*, though I did not complete it for publication till nearly seven years afterwards.

That summer again we went to Cookham, which had serious results, for my son was thrown into contact with some charming boys who had just passed into the Army, and were spending their vacation from Woolwich at Bourne End, a mile up the river from Cookham. Nothing would do for him after this but to go into the Army. I did not oppose it, because he was an absolutely idle boy at school, and it seemed such a good thing that he should want to pass any exam., and further, I was almost as much under the glamour of those dear boys—poor St. John Spackman, who was afterwards killed in the polo-field, was one of them—as he was.

That inspired me to write *My Son Richard*, which is a story of river life and boys who want to serve their country. I took him to Captain James, the leading Army crammer, and said that he wanted to get into the Army. In a few home questions, James discovered that he had never done any work at school, and said he had better go into the Artillery —he could not get into the Line. I looked incredulous, and he explained that in the Artillery exams. there are papers in more subjects which boys do not learn at school, so that a boy who has not done any work has not lost time over this—such things, for instance, as " fortification " and " military topography."

My son amply fulfilled his prognostications by securing ninety per cent. of the marks in the military subjects, and only sixteen marks out of two thousand in Latin. Still, he passed, but, to his great disappointment, was not allowed to go out to the war which had just begun, because he was too young.

In this year, 1901, in which both my big book *In Sicily* and my novel *My Son Richard,* first saw the light, I had plenty to do, for I was finishing and attending to the publication of *Queer Things about Japan,* which was the best received of all my books of travel. It owed its success largely to the timely moment at which I wrote it. Knowing Japan well, I was convinced that there was going to be a Russo-Japanese war, and Sidney Dark, the brilliant literary editor of the *Daily Express,* as alive a journalist and critic as there is in London, was at that time manager of the firm of publishers to whom I offered the book, because they had recently taken over the publication of the sixpenny edition of *A Japanese Marriage.* It was not hard to convince him that there was war in the air for Japan, and he commissioned the book with the happiest results. Much of it appeared serially in the papers connected with the Tillotson Syndicate, which at that time had Philip Gibbs for its editor. He accepted my offer to write him eight long instalments about Japan for the Syndicate. Just as I had finished and dispatched them, he wrote to tell me that he did not think that Japan was a sufficiently live subject, and asked me not to write the articles.

No sooner had he written the letter than he received the articles. He read them and thought them so good that he sent me a telegram cancelling his letter, and used them. They form the backbone of the book. He had asked me to be as humorous as possible. Other editors thought them very amusing, and when the approach of war made Japan the topic of the day, showered commissions on me.

Norma Lorimer, who was all through Japan with us, was of great assistance to me in recalling our life there, and I got her a good many commissions for articles, which were afterwards collected with some of the articles that I wrote during the war into *More Queer Things about Japan.*

In this same year, 1901, Hutchinson & Co. published *My Son Richard,* which, as I have said above, was a novel about boys who had just passed into the Army, and girls of the same age, spending the summer on the river at Cookham. As an instance of rapid printing, I may mention that Hutchinson got me all the proofs of this book in seven days, but he recently, in 1913, eclipsed this by making the printer give me all the proofs of *Weeds* in six days.

My Son Richard was very popular. A Duchess wrote to a newspaper which was collecting statistics about the popularity of books, that this was the nicest book she had ever read, and when it came out as a sixpenny, the village grocer at Cookham ordered hundreds and told me that every maid-servant for miles round was buying it. I wish they would buy all my other sixpennies. To reach the servant class is a most difficult achievement.

As Miss Lorimer had broken her leg that year and still could not move about much, we went for August to Baveno on Lago Maggiore, to an hotel with a garden on the lake, where she had a room looking right over the exquisite Borromean Islands, Isola Bella and Isola dei Pescatori. Italy has always been her favourite subject for writing. She corrected the proofs of her *By the Waters of Sicily* here, which is as popular as ever, though it has been out for twelve years.

Baveno had the happiest effect on her. The air is lovely, and her window looked right over the finest sweep of Lago Maggiore, with the islands in front and the snow-tipped Alps behind. Heavy square-prowed barges with junk sails used to glide slowly across the eye-line, and light high-prowed fishing-boats with hoods like Japanese sampans darted about near the shore, which had long pergolas over-hanging the lake and Passion-vines sweeping over every shed.

A month's rest at Baveno made her leg quite well, and then we were able to spend a fascinating September in the mountain city of Bergamo; Brescia, with its history and monuments of a thousand years; and Venice, which is always most adorable in summer. The Feast of the Redentore in July is the crown of the year at Venice. We had learnt, and we have often made use of our knowledge since, that Italy is at her best in summer.

I do not seem to have published any books in 1902 or 1903, though I was writing steadily all the time, and had

a couple of serials running in a magazine, but I was collecting
materials hard for the biggest piece of work I have ever
accomplished. Those who take up *Sicily, the New Winter
Resort,* a small octavo, and *In Sicily,* two immense quartos,
will be surprised to hear that the smaller book contains a
far greater amount of reading matter than the larger—half
as much again, I should say—though the one costs five
shillings net and the other three guineas. The Directors of
the Rete Sicula, for whom I compiled the smaller book,
stipulated that it was to be cheap in price and handy in
form. This book is an encyclopædia of Sicily. It itemises
every monument of any importance, every custom, every
piece of scenery noted for its beauty, every railway station,
and gives information about every name which comes
prominently into the history or the mythology of the island.
It also gives directions how every monument and beautiful
piece of scenery is to be reached.

Nineteen hundred and two was the last summer which
we spent at Cookham. My son was then at Woolwich, and
we stayed at Cookham so that he could have his week-ends
on the river. That winter and spring we again spent in
Sicily and Italy. But that summer we spent at Tenby for
the first time, because my son had now been gazetted to a
Company of Artillery which was stationed at Pembroke Dock.
Tenby I consider one of the most beautiful coast-places in the
United Kingdom. It stands on a rock over the sea, and still
retains a considerable portion of walls and towers built in the
reign of the third Edward, and restored during the Spanish
Armada scare in 1588. It has also a magnificent Gothic
church, and one Gothic house. Its position is hard to beat,
for its rock stands between two splendid stretches of sand,
and when the wind blows on one side you are out of the wind
on the other. On the north sands is a green bluff. If you
walk inland it is easy to find deep woods, and if you walk
across the golf-links (there is very good natural golf) you come
on to noble downs with gorgeous precipices sheering down to
the sea, and rich in the ruins of historic and prehistoric
men—literally historic, for there is Geoffry of Monmouth's
castle of Manorbier, and far beyond, my ancestor Aylmer
de Valence's castle of Pembroke, which, like the castle of

the Carews, rises out of the windings of the great haven of the West.

Such is Tenby, round which, under the name of Flanders, I built a romance in my novel, *The Unholy Estate*.

The golf-links served both Tenby and the naval and military officers at Pembroke Dock. Nearly every day I used to meet the Gunner and Infantry subalterns and captains disporting themselves on the links, and I was often over at Pembroke in the barracks. It was there that I picked up my knowledge of young soldiers, which I put into use in *The Unholy Estate, The Tragedy of the Pyramids* and *The Curse of the Nile*.

The winter we generally spent in Italy, except the winter and spring of 1906, when we were once more in Sicily, and went across from Sicily to visit Tunis and Carthage.

In 1904 I was busy putting the finishing touches on two books about Japan, *More Queer Things about Japan*, the book in which I collaborated with Norma Lorimer, and *Playing the Game*, which in the cheap editions has had its name changed to *When We Were Lovers in Japan*. This book has been running serially in *Cassell's Magazine*. It never had half the popularity or circulation of *A Japanese Marriage*, though it had much more value as a study of Japan and the Japanese, for it deals with the transition of Japan from a weak Oriental nation to one of the great powers of the world, and gives an acid picture of the futility of the diplomats to whom Great Britain entrusts her interests.

In this same year, 1904, Methuen brought out *Sicily, the New Winter Resort*. In 1905 I turned my attention to Sicily once more, working up the serial which had appeared in *Cassell's Magazine* into the volume which the publishers insisted on christening *A Sicilian Marriage*, to try and lend it some of the popularity of *A Japanese Marriage*, which it never acquired, and the world never discovered that it was an excellent popular guide-book to Palermo, Girgenti,Syracuse and Taormina.

In the same year I brought out *Queer Things about Sicily*, a companion volume to *Queer Things about Japan*, with Norma Lorimer.

CHAPTER XVII

THE WRITING OF MY BOOKS : PART II

In 1906 I was busy writing two books into which a good deal of history came, *Carthage and Tunis, the Old and New Gates of the Orient*, and *The Secrets of the Vatican*, the former of which I published at the end of that year, and the latter at the beginning of the following year.

We were hovering between Italy in the winter, and Tenby in the summer, and taking uncommonly little out of our rent at 32 Addison Mansions.

I had always been mightily interested in Carthage. I hated Carthage being beaten by Rome, partly, perhaps, because history has invested the career of Hannibal and the fall of Carthage with such undying romance. When we were in Sicily in 1906 we suddenly made up our minds to go to Tunis, of which Carthage is practically a suburb, just as when we were at Vancouver we suddenly made up our minds to take a trip to Japan.

Carthage is disappointing to those who wish to see Punic remains. Of the mighty walls described by Polybius, there remains hardly one stone upon another. Its impregnable naval harbour and arsenal have dried up into mere ponds—in fact, there is nothing Punic about it, except subterranean tombs, which you can only reach by being lowered in a basket, and the gorgeous coffins and ornaments which came out of them, and are preserved in the museum of the White Fathers.

But of Roman Carthage there are plenty of remains—an amphitheatre, and a theatre, and mighty underground cisterns, and the foundations of immense churches. In that amphitheatre a most interesting lot of saints were martyred, St. Perpetua herself among them.

No ruins have been discovered connected with the career of St. Augustine, the Carthaginian to whom the White Fathers attach so much more importance than to Hannibal or Hamilcar; and all memories of Dido have hopelessly disappeared. Any remains that there might have been of the citadel so desperately defended against Scipio, have been obliterated by the erection of a cathedral on the site, the consummation of the life-work of Cardinal Lavigerie. That there is not one human being for a congregation, except the White Fathers in the monastery, does not appear to signify at all. The cathedral is there, just on the spot where you want to forget it most, and think of the tremendous human tragedy to which that hill is sacred.

I loved wandering about the site of Carthage, ruminating upon history; I found the study of the saints of Carthage fascinating, and gave a good deal of my book to them when I came to write about Carthage, in which I also gave translations of the very extensive passages which Virgil devotes to it, without apparently having possessed any antiquarian knowledge at all upon the subject.

History is very ironical here. You sometimes meet wandering, or encamped about the site of Carthage, Berbers, lineal descendants of the aborigines dispossessed by Dido and her Phœnicians when they founded Carthage, who lasted as a race to see Phœnician Carthage perish, and the Christian and Roman Carthage, which rose upon its ashes, perish likewise before the invading Arabs, and the Arabs, after temporary subjugation by this or the other invader, finally conquered by the French. Their language, too, has survived, though it was in danger of extinction till French scholars made its preservation and study a hobby.

It must not be forgotten that when Carthage came to life again she had her revenge on Rome, for the Vandal King of Carthage captured Rome, and carries its empress in chains to Carthage, with the Table of the Shewbread, the Ark of the Covenant, and the Seven-branched Candlestick captured by Titus—trophies to which the Romans had ever since attached superstitious importance.

In the last half of 1906 and the spring of 1907 I was

unusually busy. We spent the summer for the fourth year in succession at Tenby. Eustache de Lorey was there with me collaborating in *Queer Things about Persia.* I planned the outline of the book; I suggested subjects for the chapters; I extracted some of them by cross-examination; I wrote down others when he was in an anecdotal vein. And some he wrote in French, and we translated them together. Had he been able to accumulate a book in English unaided, there was no reason why he should not have written it all himself. His careful, slightly foreign English was very effective. But I may take this credit to myself, that the book would never have been conceived without me, and even had it been conceived, it would neither have been begun, nor, having been begun, would it have been finished, without my professional industry. I enjoyed writing it very much indeed. De Lorey was such a delightful companion, and I learnt so much about Persia by writing a book on it. This sounds like a paradox, but it is a universal truth.

Simultaneously I was engaged on finishing my own book on Carthage and Tunis. In this book I had to rely almost entirely on French materials, because the two main sources of information are the official publications of the French authorities, and commercial firms interested in the exploitation of Tunis, and the publications of the White Fathers out at Carthage, about its site and its remains.

I was also finishing a book upon which I had been at work for some years—*The Secrets of the Vatican*, in which I enjoyed the assistance of his Eminence the Cardinal-Archbishop of Westminster, in the chapter which dealt with the Church crisis in France.

When I went to ask him to help me, he asked me what I was going to call my book. I replied, *The Secrets of the Vatican*. He said, "Doesn't it sound rather——"—instead of giving me the word, he gave a sniff. I shall never forget that sniff—it expressed the whole situation. I hastened to explain that the Secrets were all archæological secrets, and he handed me the materials for my chapter.

Some time before this, he had asked our mutual friend, Cortesi, Reuter's agent at Rome, to tell me a story of the

Pope, in connection with my *Sicily, the New Winter Resort.*
Cardinal Bourne had taken a tour in Sicily, using my *Sicily*
as his guide.   When he got back to Rome, he showed an
anecdote in the book to the Pope.   The anecdote was about
Cardinal Newman, who had told me an extraordinary experience he had had in Sicily.   It was at Castrogiovanni, where
he lay for some weeks between life and death, suffering from
a fever, which was the result of his being totally robbed of
sleep by fleas when he was making a tour round Etna.   The
greatest affliction with which he had to contend was the
incessant ringing of church bells—Castrogiovanni, the Enna
of Ceres and Proserpine, has more churches for its size
than any city in Sicily.   Poor Newman's only chance of
sleep, which meant life to him, was to keep his head under
the bedclothes in that semi-tropical climate.   The inhabitants went about aghast, saying that he had a devil.   The
Pope thought the idea of the future Prince of the
Church (Protestant though he was then) having a devil,
was ludicrously funny, and laughed till his sides ached,
like an ordinary man.   When Newman did recover from
the fever, and was on his way from Sicily to Sardinia in
a fruit boat, he wrote his famous hymn, " Lead, kindly
light."

The Secrets of the Vatican formed one half of a book which
I began as a commission from Eveleigh Nash some years
before.   The numerous changes in non-papal Rome, and the
important excavations of its pagan monuments, which were
announced, but postponed and postponed, made me despair
of ever getting the book finished, and finally I decided to
publish the part which related to the Vatican in a volume
by itself.   This, after going through three editions, has
been, for further publication, divided into two parts.   The
personal matter about the present Pope, and the information
about the ceremonies which relate to the election, coronation,
death and burial of a Pope, and about the composition of
his court, are still published by Hurst & Blackett, with
certain additional information on the subject, under the
title of *The Pope at Home*, while the part which relates to
the history, architecture and collections of the Vatican, is

now published by Kegan Paul, Trench & Co., under the title of *How to See the Vatican*.

The Secrets of the Vatican was published in 1907, a few months before we began our memorable expedition to Egypt, which has played such an important part in my writings ever since.

Having to study economy in our travels, we determined to break the journey to Egypt in Italy, and with that idea went to Lake Como in the last days of July 1907.

Anything more beautiful than Lago di Como in August it is difficult to conceive. All the way up its west side the lake is fringed with crimson oleanders in full blossom. Though the days are cloudless, and the nights encrusted with stars, by perfect summer weather, there are no mosquitoes. It is a land of peaches, and of old villas with gardens, which look as if they had come down from the ancient Romans, with their vases and pavilions and terraces and broad flights of steps leading down into the clear water of the lake—this is the lake from Arconati to Cadenabbia.

Here we spent a month under the acacia and tulip trees, revelling in fruit and flowers, before we went south to Como City; and east to Sermione, in the reedy shallows of Lago di Garda, dominated by the castle of the Scaligers, which loses not one ray of sunshine from sunrise to sunset; to storied Mantua in its marches; to Verona, half ancient Roman, half Gothic, and wholly romantic, and to Venice the matchless.

Venice is a stone city conjured up from the sea. In the city proper there is no more earth than you might have in roof-gardens. There are no horses, no motors. You seem to be living on the roof of the sea. The palaces, which rise from the water in such unending succession, were mostly built in the Middle Ages, when Venice had the sea-trade of the world. The finest of them line the Grand Canal from side to side for a mile from its mouth, and at its mouth are the most beautiful buildings in Europe, which have been standing there three and four and five hundred years at the head of the stately flight of steps where the world once came to the feet of Venice—St. Mark's, the Doge's Palace, and the Library, surrounding that Piazetta of smooth white flagstones.   You feel that they are too beautiful to be true, that they must be the airy fabric of a vision, which will presently pass away, and leave not a wrack behind.

I never go to Venice without wondering why I can live away from it.   Yet I have never published my tribute to it, except in periodicals, and in the pages about it which come into my *How to See Italy*.

I have to say the same of Florence, to which we moved from Venice on our progress through Italy to Egypt.   Like Venice, I have visited it many times, and I find Florence one of the most inspiring cities in the world.   The Venetian, unless he be a guide or a gondolier, is silent to foreigners; he takes no account of them; there are few foreigners living in Venice.   But in Florence there are five thousand foreigners, who talk about the glories of Florence every day, and all the inhabitants seem to be children of the Medici Florence, who think that every foreigner's mind should be in the Florence of the Middle Ages.   You talk pictures or history all day long.

From Florence we went on to Rome and Naples, where we were to take ship for Egypt.   Of Rome I have written much in *How to See Italy*, as well as in *The Secrets of the Vatican*, which contained the fruit of years of study.   I have also published in periodicals enough to fill another book about the parts which belong to the kingdom of Italy, as the Vatican belongs to the Papacy.   To Rome I go back regularly.   About Rome I intend to publish a book like *How to See Italy*, and *Sicily, the New Winter Resort*, combined, to make use of my street by street study of the Eternal City.   I know Rome far better than London.   Rome has always appealed to my historical enthusiasm, in the one point where Florence leaves me cold, for Florence was, as it were, at the back of the door while kingdoms were being carved out of the unformed mass of Europe during the Middle Ages, while Rome gave the world laws, language and civilisation, collated from the wisdom of the ancient world.

Naples itself is not an inviting town, but it slopes up from one of the most beautiful bays in the world, and it is rich in outstanding objects—Capri in front, Vesuvius on the left, the hill of Posilippo on the right, and the three great castles, St. Elmo, del Ovo and Nuovo, which make the points of a vast triangle from the sea to the mountain-top, while in the centre is the rock of Parthenope, now called the Falcon's Peak, the site of Palæpolis, the old city, which came before Neapolis, the new city.

The outskirts of Naples are of the highest interest, for on the south side the disinterred ruins of Pompeii and Herculanæum lie under their destroyer, Vesuvius, the most interesting volcano in the world; and on the other are Cumæ, the first settlement of the Greeks in the virgin lands of Italy, which was their America; and all the volcanic phenomena, which furnished Roman mythology with the details of its Hades.

Pompeii is of undying interest to me, especially since the new custom has come in of leaving any fresh treasures which are discovered, *in situ*.   There is no place where, if you study it in conjunction with the collections in the museum of Naples, you can so easily picture the life of the Greeks and Romans as at Pompeii.   I have many times thought of writing upon Pompeii.

CHAPTER XVIII

THE WRITING OF MY BOOKS : PART III

IT was Benton Fletcher, one of the " identities " of Egypt, equally well known as an artist who does valuable work in connection with excavations and does delightful landscapes, which are the fashion with " winterers " in Egypt, who first put into my head the idea of visiting that matchless country. Egypt is literally matchless; there is no country in the world which has such a winter climate, and no country in the world which has monuments so ancient and so perfect, so close together and so accessible. Every monument which is not in an oasis is on the Nile, and the Nile in Egypt is like a railway in other countries.

Fletcher not only worked up my enthusiasm to the point of going there, but met us on our arrival in Cairo, and initiated me in the secret beauties of the Arab city. But for him *Oriental Cairo* would never have been written.

I was also much influenced by the photographs published by Leo Weinthal in *The African World* and *Fascinating Egypt.*

We sailed from Naples to Alexandria in the November of 1907. We did not delay an hour there, but took the next train to Cairo.

At Alexandria Egypt is Roman, and the monuments which have yet been excavated are not, with the exception of one marvellous late tomb, very interesting. But Alexandria is an unexcavated Pompeii, and when some Schliemann among its leading merchants decides to devote his energies and his fortune to excavating the vast mounds which still bury Roman Alexandria, we may expect finds of astonishing interest. In the desert, about thirty miles from Alexandria, is the city of St. Menas, an early Christian Pompeii, where there has already been excavated a wonderful Basilica founded by the Emperor Arcadius.

Except for a few articles in the *Queen*, I did little writing in Egypt beyond taking copious notes. But these I did more completely than I ever had done before, and as my secretary was with us, they were typed out every evening, and are now bound together into a sort of diary-journal of our entire visit. To make them more complete as journals, I took eight hundred photographs, and certainly bought as many more, and as complete a collection of postcards as I could form. Therefore I was in a very sound position for writing my various books upon Egypt after I had returned home. The first book I wrote upon our visit was *Egypt and the English*, consisting partly of what we saw while we were staying in Cairo, Alexandria, Luxor, Assuan, the Fayyum, the Great Oasis, and while we were journeying up the Nile to the second cataract, and down the Nile to its Rosetta and Damietta mouths, and over the Desert Railway into the Sudan; and partly of the result of my inquiries about the political condition of Egypt. When the book came out, many reviewers took up the attitude that what I said was too alarmist, but when Mr. Roosevelt repeated it to the letter, the Government took the warnings seriously, and appointed the best possible man, Lord Kitchener, to take the place of Sir Eldon Gorst, whose policy of scuttle and kowtow may have been dictated by the Government which appointed him.

I knew that my facts were sound, because I had not only sucked as much information as I could out of British officials and editors, and the Leader of the Egyptian Bar, but also from the leading Syrians and Armenians, who see much more behind the scenes than the English, because Arabic is their business language, and the Arabs associate with them freely in private life. Among Syrians especially I had repeated conversations with Dr. Sarruf and Dr. Nimr, the proprietor and editor of *El Mokattan*, the most important Arab paper in Egypt, to whose opinions Lord Cromer had always attached the greatest importance, and they had told me how to meet such of the Nationalist leaders as spoke English. These were actual Egyptians, so *Egypt and the English* did give

HALL CAINE
Drawn by Yoshio Markino

native opinion both directly from the mouths of Egyptians, and indirectly through Syrians and Armenians.

I wrote *Egypt and the English* for a commission to write *Queer Things about Egypt*. The then chairman of Hurst & Blackett, when he saw the political chapters in the book, considered them so interesting and important that he asked me to hold over the humorous chapters for another book. Which I did. But in the interval he sold the business of Hurst & Blackett to my old friends Hutchinson & Co., who published my real first success, *The Japs at Home*. They were quite ready to take another book on Egypt from me, and we decided to make these chapters the nucleus of that book to be published under the original title of *Queer Things about Egypt*. This book gives the humours of the native city in Cairo, and the humours of travel on the Nile. The parts of the book which attracted most attention were those which dealt with Arab life in Cairo in the native quarters round the Citadel, and with Arab architecture and art, so Hutchinson asked me to do another large volume on Egypt, devoted entirely to *Oriental Cairo—the City of the Arabian Nights*. For that part of Cairo is almost as much an Arab City of the Middle Ages as was Granada in the days of the Moors, and the stories of the Arabian Nights were made into a book by a Cairene in the sixteenth century.

Egypt and the English was published in 1908, *Queer Things about Egypt* in 1910, and *Oriental Cairo* in 1910.

In 1908 I also wrote, and Hurst & Blackett published, *The Tragedy of the Pyramids*, which has been one of the most successful of my novels. It was written as a counterblast to Hall Caine's *White Prophet*, which at that time was running as a serial in the *Strand Magazine*. I considered that Caine was giving an entirely incorrect impression of our army in Egypt. The book is now in its ninth edition, and was an imaginary picture of the revolution which would have overtaken Egypt, if Sir Eldon Gorst's scuttle and kowtow policy had been persisted in. I had a great deal to say about the Senussi in this book—the battle of the Pyramids was fought against a great host of invading Senussi. The British public had then heard little of the Senussi. But in the Turko-

Q

Italian war the Senussi have proved a far more dangerous enemy to Italy than the Turks, as they are very hardy and move with great rapidity. They are said to own many *zawia*, or convents, in Egypt, and to have established a network of wells at twenty-four hours' distance from each other all over the great desert of the Sahara—also to have twenty-five thousand swift camels accumulated against any invasion of their country, which is almost conterminous with the great desert. Boyd Alexander, the famous explorer, is considered to have fallen a victim to his intrusion upon their territory, which they openly forbid to Christians, on pain of being assassinated. But their Prophet refused to join forces in any way with the Mahdi when he had possessed himself of the Egyptian Sudan.

The Tragedy of the Pyramids was published in 1909, *Queer Things about Egypt*, and *Oriental Cairo*, in 1910, the same year which saw the publication of *The Moon of the Fourteenth Night*, the romance which I wrote in collaboration once more with Eustache de Lorey. As it had so much of the travel-book about it, it was not brought out in the form of a novel. It was, in fact, the biography of a dashing young French attaché, who is still alive, pretty faithfully told. He had no objection to our using it if we killed him off in the book, to throw the girl's relations off the track, in case they should try to kill him in real life. The public never realised that it was actually reading a romance of real lfe, that there had been such a person as Bibi Mâh, that the escapades of Edward Valmont were not imaginary, but episodes in a career of gallantry. The book comes very near to being a journal of life in the Persian capital at the beginning of the revolution.

In the autumn of 1908 we went back to Itay to spend the six cold months in Rome, hoping that we should have one of those winters which you sometimes get in Rome, as full of sunshine as spring—only cold when you are in the wind and out of the sun. Yoshio Markino spent that winter with us at 12 Piazza Barberini. I got my friend Percy Spalding, one of the directors of Chatto & Windus, to give him a commission to do the illustrations for *The Colour of Rome*, and as I knew Rome so well, I conducted him to nearly all the beauty-spots which furnished the subjects of his illustrations. I showed him many others which did not appeal to him, for Markino will not begin a picture until some *motif* in the locality has appealed to his artistic temperament. He is an artist to the finger-tips. His fidelity is all the more extraordinary when you take into consideration his method of painting a landscape.

In those days he had written nothing but a short chapter in *The Colour of London*, and *The Colour of Paris*, but he used to show me the letters he wrote to Spalding and Ward, of Chatto's, about the book,—most brilliant some of them were, and I saw that he was a born writer. I suggested to him as early as this that he should write his life in Japan—I had not then grasped what a story he had to tell of his life in England.

He felt the cold in Rome very severely. He used to consume quantities of the childish substitutes for fuel provided in Roman hotels.

In that first visit which he paid to Italy, he was not much interested in the architecture or the art, just as he never visited the Louvre while he was in Paris painting *The Colour of Paris*. And the scenes of historical events interested him little more, though often they played an important part in the history of the world. He was absorbed in the novel lines of buildings; the gay colours of Italy; the strangeness to him of the atmospheric effects of Rome; the subtle and ceaseless humours in the life of the Italian poor. And their clothes delighted him, with their gay, faded colours, their rags, and the fine abandon with which they were worn.

We were in Rome collecting materials for my book on *How to See Italy*, and I was writing the *Tragedy of the Pyramids* mostly in bed, before I got up in the morning. Between five and eight a.m. is a favourite time for writing with me. I seldom begin later than 5.45; I have a cup of tea brought to me at 6 a.m. I also wrote a good deal in periodicals about the great earthquake at Messina. The Italian papers were naturally full of details, which had not been telegraphed to England, and we used to get wonderful cinema films, which made one quite an eye-witness of the events. In Italy you can go to the cinema for twopence.

I was about to make a tour of the earthquake scenes in South Italy and Sicily, and to go on to Malta, where my son was then quartered, when I was suddenly called home by the alarming illness of my father, who was given up by the doctors, though he recovered and lived for nearly two years afterwards.

We re-visited a few favourite spots, such as Pisa and Lucca, on our way up, as we did not hope to see Italy again for some time.

As it chanced, it was little more than a year before we were back in Italy again, on the most interesting tour which we have ever spent in that country. I had a commission from Kegan Paul, Trench & Co. to write for them *How to See Italy*, which was destined to be so popular, and there were forty-five cities in Italy which I wished to visit or re-visit before writing this book. I wrote it for the Italian Government, as Kegan Paul, Trench & Co. were aware, and they had offered me many facilities. They had the blocks made for the illustrations. I went over their entire collection of photographs in making my choice, and where no photograph existed, they sent their special photographer to take one. Also they allowed me to travel about on their lines wherever my wish took me free of charge, so I was able to wander about Italy in a way in which the expenses would ordinarily have been too great for any book.

Markino went with us again on this journey, which lasted from July to November. This time I had got him a commission from Constable & Co. to illustrate a book by Miss Potter, which was published under the title of *A Little Pilgrimage in Italy*.

We visited all our cities, starting from Genoa, and proceeding to Florence, Arezzo, Cortona, Perugia, Deruta, Todi, Siena, St. Gimignano, Passignano, Monte Oliveto, Asciano, Chiusi, Città della Pieve, Assisi, Foligno, Spoleto, Spello, Bevagna, Montefalco, Trevi, Clitunno, Gualdo Tadino, Gubbio, Urbino, Rimini, Ravenna, San Marino, Ancona, Loreto, Terni, Narni, Orvieto, Viterbo, Ferento, Bagnaja, Monte Fiascone, Rome, Tivoli, Milan.

As soon as we had left the mountain heights of Arezzo and Cortona, the Etruscan eyries from which the Romans marched

down to their red fate on the shores of the lake Trasimene,
we learned how hot mid-Italy can be in midsummer. Even
on the rock of Perugia, fifteen hundred feet above the sea,
you could not walk on the sunny side of the street without
an umbrella on account of the risk of sunstroke, and the
heat was almost unendurable as we drove across the hills
the thirty or forty miles to Todi, a little city which the Gods
of the Middle Ages have kept to themselves.

Perugia was always defiant, from Etruscan times. With a
man like Duke Frederick of Urbino to rule and lead its fierce
citizens, Perugia would have been more potent than Urbino,
or Rimini, or Mantua, or Ferrara, perhaps a city of the first
rank, like Milan or Florence. Its rock made the whole city
a citadel, and it sits astride the road from Rome to the Alps,
with the fertile Vale of Umbria to provision it.

The Vale of Umbria below Assisi is only rivalled by the
shores of Lake Trasimene in the beauty of its women—we
know them from the pictures of Raphael, Perugino, and
Pinturricchio. I wish I could put its magic into words—
the nobility of its farm-houses, the soft grace of its orchards
and olive-gardens, its antique hermitages.

Summer in the Vale of Umbria was perfect, and certain of
its beauties were such as could only be seen in summer, like
the translucent sources of the Clitumnus, which, with their
lawny banks, remind you of the Twenty-third Psalm. I
would rather go and see them, below the tall poplars which are
a landmark across the plain, than the graceful little Roman
temple above them, which is a landmark for travellers.

Foligno is only a walk from exquisite Spello, a city which
is a hill covered with Gothic houses. Foligno and the cities
on the hills round it are rich in great pictures by small
masters; but Spoleto is, after Perugia, the prize city of Umbria.
It is rich in monuments of all ages; in its walls it has
prehistoric masonry of three ages; it defied the assaults of
Hannibal; you can still see the house of Vespasian's mother,
and other Roman monuments of the classic age; it is rich
in the handiwork of the forgotten centuries which followed;
it has a church built like a pagan temple in the fourth century
after Christ; it has the most stupendous aqueduct in Italy,

carried across a valley from the hill of Groves, on arches two hundred and fifty feet high; and a unique cathedral, planted in the valley, like its other great church; it was the capital of the only King of Italy who bore the title before Victor Emmanuel. Standing on the hillside, embosomed in groves, looking over the plain, in an amphitheatre of mountains, Spoleto is a place which never leaves the memory.

We went straight from it to most famous cities—Gubbio was not its equal, except when the sunset fired the façade of its city hall, six hundred years old and three hundred feet high; and Urbino, on its dizzy height, crowned with the fantastic palace of Duke Frederick, is a prosaic place beside it; Ravenna, for all its mosaiced churches, built by Justinian and his successors, when the first millennium was half spent, has no glory of site, nor has Rimini; Ancona has only its site and its glorious Byzantine cathedral, on a green hill between two seas.

We wandered from town to town such as these; we drove all day from Rimini to San Marino, the castled eagle's nest, which is still an independent Republic; we went to Loreto on the Virgin's day, and saw peasants, who had come in ox-carts from the recesses of the Apennines. We stood below and above the stupendous waterfalls of Terni, the most stupendous in Europe. But we saw no naturally nobler city than Spoleto.

All that summer we wandered about the byways of Tuscany, Umbria, Latium, and the March of Ancona. We hardly ever saw an English face. We stayed for the most part in humble native inns. It was a hot summer, even for Italy, but we were not frightened by the heat from going where we meant to go, nor by the fetish of malaria, for we stayed a week at Ravenna in September. We never enjoyed ourselves more in our lives. We tested an Italian summer fairly on the hot plains and sun-baked hills. I needed the experience to write *How to See Italy*.

It was a guide-book on a new principle. While I was writing of the cities and scenery of Italy, generally I grouped them in provinces, but I devoted other chapters to the hobbies of travellers. I told the lover of paintings where all the best paintings in Italy are to be found, and which places have the richest galleries. I did the same for the lovers of architecture, sculpture, mosaics, and scenery. I told the traveller how to see all the principal sights of Italy by rail, without going the same railway journey twice, and I tried to convert English travellers to the delightful native inns of Italy, and I gave them the prices of inns all over Italy.

The idea of the book was, briefly, to enable any one to see at a glance which parts of Italy he ought to visit in pursuit of his special studies. And I had three special chapters on the changes in Rome, which have made all the old books on Rome out of date.

When we reached London in the late autumn, I found a sad change in my father, who had reached the great age of eighty-six. He had lost much of his memory, and very often did not care to speak. He gradually failed, until one night between Christmas and the New Year he passed away quite peacefully, holding my hand.

I sold the house on Campden Hill—Phillimore Lodge—in which he had lived for nearly fifty years, to Sir Walter Phillimore. The estate was so burdened with legacies, made while he was a much richer man, that I should have lost by accepting my inheritance if I had not sold all the real estate.

I had no wish to live there. For years it had been my intention to leave London when I no longer had my father to consider. I wanted to go to some rural spot just outside London, where I could have pleasure in being at home in the summer months, because I like going abroad in the winter, and you must make use of your house some time during the year. At Addison Mansions we were only at home for a month or two in some years.

I set about looking for a new house almost immediately, and after nearly taking an old Queen Anne mansion in the Sheen Road, finally settled on the Avenue House, Richmond, which stands in the north-west corner of the old Green, with its front windows looking down the Avenue, and across the Green to the Old Palace, and its back windows looking over the old Deer Park and the Mid-Surrey Golf Club to the trees of Kew Gardens. In the winter we can see a mile or two of grass and trees from those windows, and the river when the tide is high. The house suited me perfectly; it had a charming old-fashioned garden, with ancient trees, a cedar of Lebanon, a mulberry, and an arbutus, which covers itself with flowers and fruit, among them, besides two great wistarias and many flowering laburnums, lilacs and hawthorns.   I added rockeries in the Sicilian style, and **various** features of a Japanese garden.

The house had the further advantage of being only a few minutes' walk from the railway-stations, from golf at Mid-Surrey, and from one of the most beautiful reaches of the Thames.

Here I have written the present book, *The Unholy Estate*, *The Curse of the Nile*, and my parts of *Adam Lindsay Gordon and His Friends in England and Australia*, and *Weeds*; **and** I was here when *How to see Italy* was published.

I was sorry in a way to say good-bye to Addison Mansions, which had been my home during the most interesting years of my life.   I liked the rooms; I should have liked to transport them to Richmond.

CHAPTER XIX

OF all the books I have written, none have attracted more attention than *Who's Who*.

Various biographical dictionaries of living persons were in existence before the new *Who's Who* appeared in 1897— *Men of the Time, People of the Period*, and so on. But none of them were annual, and none of them were published at a popular price. I myself had attempted to get a cheap annual biographical dictionary published, before A. & C. Black came to me with their proposal about *Who's Who*. I put the idea into the hands of a literary agent for sale. It was very much on the lines of *Who's Who*, but not on so ambitious a scale, and I thought that Sell, who has a Press directory, might be likely to buy it. No one did buy it, and when I told an interviewer, who came to get "copy" out of me about *Who's Who*, about it, that agent was wrong-headed enough to think that I was trying to libel him, instead of trying to claim originality for my idea.

However that may be, Adam Black, one day, when I was talking to him about my novel, *A Japanese Marriage*, which A. & C. Black had published, produced a copy of the old *Who's Who*, an insignificant pocket-peerage, of which he had just purchased the rights, and asked if I could make anything of it for the firm. Having made a synopsis of my own idea for that literary agent to sell, I had it cut and dry, and it was settled that I should do the book as soon as the agreement could be drawn up. As events proved, it was drawn up too hurriedly, for I signed it without insisting on the clause which has gone into all my other agreements of the same kind —that, in case the publishers wished to be released from the agreement because the book was not as successful as they hoped, the book should become my property. I do not say that the Blacks would have consented to the insertion of this clause, but it is certain that I ought never to have signed it without, because I put into it ideas, whose originality and value has abundantly been proved since. It was agreed that I should edit it for three years certain, but that if the book was not successful by then the agreement should terminate. At the end of the three years, they determined that the book was not a success, and terminated the agreement. At the time that I wrote this book there was no one in London with the same knowledge as I had as to who should be included in the book, because my three years' work in New York papers had made me take up biographical journalism—a profession which did not exist in London till I brought it over from America, and which never took permanent root in England. In fact, it very soon withered out of existence.

It is an odd fact that this book in its dried pippin form, which went on for about half a century before it was expanded, never struck the world as having a specially good title, till Adam Black recognised its value, though now its title is regarded as a stroke of genius.

" But how are you going to get the information ? " he asked, when I had detailed my formula for the biographies, much the same as that which is used for *Who's Who* now, with the exception of the details about telephones and motors, which were not part of English everyday life in 1897, and a few other points which I ought to have thought of.

" I shall make the people themselves give it."

" But will they ever do it ? "

" I think so, if we give them proper forms to fill up, and get a well-known peer and a well-known commoner to fill up their forms as specimens before we send the others out."

" You'll have to tell them that you're going to use their biographies as specimens.   I wish nothing to be done of which anybody could complain."

In the matter of the special stationery provided for the purpose, the firm were extraordinarily liberal. They only studied attractiveness, just as they had special type cast for setting up the book because none of the small types offered to us were sufficiently beautiful. The selection of the long blue envelopes, opening at the side, has an almost public interest. Adam Black requested that we should leave the matter of envelopes over until the following week, when he was to meet Lord Rosebery on the yacht of his brother-in-law, George Coates. When Lord Rosebery was asked what kind of envelope he should treat with most respect in opening his correspondence, Lord Rosebery pronounced in favour of this particular form of long blue envelope, because it was used by the Cabinet for their communications. So we adopted it, and the first persons in official circles who received it may have experienced a strange flutter of expectation, because we did not in those days, I think, have the envelopes stamped *Who's Who*, lest they should defeat their object of being taken for Cabinet communications.

Then came the question of whom we should invite to write their biographies to be models for the biographies of other people. I selected the Duke of Rutland for the peers, and Mr. Balfour for the commoners. The Duke, both as Lord John Manners and as Duke, had occupied one of the first places in the eyes of his fellow-countrymen. He had filled his place in the Cabinet with distinction; he had been the typical aristocrat; his exquisite politeness had helped the democracy to forgive him for writing "Let Wealth and Commerce . . . die. But give us still our old nobility."

I wrote to ask him to fill the biographical form, which I had drawn up, to be the model for other members of the peerage, and with his usual consideration, he acceded. Then I wrote to Mr. Balfour to ask him to write his biography, to be a model for the untitled. The only title he bore was so proud that we usually, as I did then, forget to reckon it among titles— the "Right Honourable." Mr. Balfour, too, acceded, and he was particularly suitable, because, in addition to being the first man in the House of Commons, recreation had a real meaning in his case, since he was known to be an inveterate golfer.

The idea of adding "recreations" to the more serious items which had been included in previous biographical

dictionaries was adopted at one of the councils of war
which we used to hold in the partners' room of A. & C.
Black, at 4 Soho Square. And for selling purposes it
proved far and away the best idea in the whole book, when it
was published. The newspapers were never tired of quoting
the recreations of eminent people, thus giving the book a
succession of advertisements of its readability, and shop-
keepers who catered for their various sports bought the book
to get the addresses of the eminent people, who were, many
of them, very indignant at the Niagara of circulars which
resulted.

I wonder if many people remember the old *Who's Who ?*—
a little red 32mo, which looked something like the Infantry
Manual with its clasp knocked off. It was a sort of badly kept
index to the Peerage, as futile as an 1840 Beauty Book.
We turned it into a dictionary of biography for living people,
and we made it eternally interesting by persuading the people
whom we included in it to give us their favourite recreations.
I chose (from an un-annual biographical dictionary edited by
Humphry Ward) the type, which had to be specially cast
for it; I chose the people who deserved to be included in it;
I drafted the letters and the forms to be filled up, which were
sent to each person; and I persuaded those two very eminent
men to be the bell-wethers for persuading other people to
fill up their forms, an idea which was crowned with success.
The late Duke of Rutland's and Mr. Balfour's fillings up of
the forms were printed at the heads of the forms sent out to
other people, and few people objected to following where they
had led the way. But among these few recalcitrants were
Lord Salisbury and Mr. Chamberlain, and most naval officers.
Army officers, on the other hand, were generally very oblig-
ing. Architects and literary men filled up their forms best,
artists and actresses worst, though actors were almost as
bad. You would have thought that the actual formation
of the letters in framing a reply was a torture to artists,
actors and naval officers. The actresses, if you had compiled
the biographies by interview, would have asked for two columns
each.

Many people thought it necessary to write me rude letters,

demanding what right I had to intrude upon their privacy, and ordering me not to include their names. To one of them, the head of an Oxford College, I wrote. "Dear Sir, If you had not been head of —— College, no one would have dreamt of including you, but since you are, you will have to go in whether you like it or not."

The late Duke of Devonshire said that his recreation had formerly been hunting. One man said that he did not see how the ownership of four hundred and fifty. thousand acres made him a public person. A prominent authoress first of all refused to fill up her form at all. I wrote to tell her that in that case I should have to fill it up for her. She showed no concern about this until I sent her a proof of the biography, in which I made her out ten years older than she really was, and said that I meant to insert the biography in that form unless there was anything she wished to correct. She then corrected it, and added so much that it would have taken the whole column if I had inserted all she sent.

W. S. Gilbert wrote the rudest letter of anybody. He said he was always being pestered by unimportant people for information about himself. So I put him down in the book as " Writer of Verses and the libretti to Sir Arthur Sullivan's comic operas." He then wrote me a letter of about a thousand words, in which he asked me if that was the way to treat a man who had written seventy original dramas. Next year he filled up his form as readily as a peer's widow who has married a commoner.

Bernard Shaw said in 1897 that his favourite recreations were cycling and showing off, and informed the world that he was of middle-class family, was not educated at all " academically," and coming to London when he was twenty, for many years could obtain no literary recognition, even to the extent of employment as a journalist.

But the most humorous experience I had in connection with *Who's Who* was when I succeeded in bringing a certain actor-manager to book. He had repeatedly promised to fill in his form, and failed to do so, when I found myself next to him at a public dinner to which we had both been invited. " Why did you not send me that biography ? " I asked him, and he said, " Well, the real reason is that I thought I should have to say how damned badly I have behaved to my wife."

The book was a complete literary success; the newspapers gave it column reviews, chiefly consisting of the unsuitable recreations of prominent people.

When I edited it, *Who's Who* contained a great deal of information besides the biographies, such as lists of peculiarly pronounced proper names, keys to the pseudonyms of prominent people, names of the editors of the principal papers. Some of the real names were so unreasonable that people wrote to know why they were not included in the lists of pseudonyms; one of these was Sir Louis Forget.

Ascertaining the correct pronunciation of peculiar names was very diverting; there was such a divergence of opinion among people of Scottish birth about words like " Brechin." I was bewailing their egotism to the late Lord Southesk, when he said, " I have been collecting peculiarly pronounced Scottish names and their proper pronunciation for years. You can have my list."

I thanked him and gladly inserted them all.   A very good friend of mine, the late Hugh Maclaughlan, who was sub-editor of the *Star and Leader*, in reviewing the book over his own name, found great fault with my Cockney pronunciation of the Scottish names.   I do not know to this day whether he was serious, or, as schoolboys say, " pulling my leg," and in any case, I did not mind, but Lord Southesk was furious.

" Tell Mr. Maclaughlan," he said, " that I am the man whom he called a Cockney, and that my ancestor commanded the Highlanders at the battle of Harlaw."   Harlaw was the last great battle between the Highlanders and the Lowlanders, and was fought in the year 1411.

One of the funniest entries in the book was made by a famous authoress, who wrote in her biography " she is at present unmarried."

One of the most amusing experiences I had when I was editor of *Who's Who* was my receiving a message from a Mrs. Williams or Williamson, asking me to call on her upon a matter of great importance.   I imagined that at the very least Queen Victoria (Mrs. Williams was supposed to have influence in such matters) had deputed her to offer me a knighthood. At any rate, from the tone of her letter, it ought to have been a considerable advantage of some sort which was to be bestowed upon me. I was not much flustered because the lady had not the reputation of giving anything for nothing. But I own I was rather taken aback when I was shown into her den, and she said, " I sent for you because Mrs. Dotheboy Tompkins "—or some such name—nobody of the slightest importance—"wishes you to put her into *Who's Who.*"

I said, " The only answer I can give you is that I do not consider Mrs. Tompkins of sufficient importance. I don't know how you will break this to her. Good-afternoon."

It was such colossal impertinence, her sending for me instead of writing to me, though that would have been bad enough. that I was determined not to spare her.

CHAPTER XX

AUSTRALIANS IN LITERATURE

As I lived four or five years in Australia, and have written various books upon Australian poets, and as both my wife and my son are Victorians by birth, it is natural for me to devote a chapter to Australians in literature whom I have known, counting both people from the Old Country who became Australians by residence, and those who were born or educated in Australia, though their writing career has been in England.

I never met either Gordon or Kendall—Adam Lindsay Gordon and Henry Clarence Kendall, the twin stars of Australian poetry, naturally come first to one's mind in writing of Australian literature, because poetry in Australia, as usual, preceded prose as an art.

Gordon, whose nephew, Henry Ratti, living in London, had just placed himself in communication with me in a couple of long letters, and invited me to lunch when he died so prematurely, had been dead for nearly ten years before I landed in Australia. But Kendall did not die till I had been in Australia for nearly three years. I was in Victoria when he died; I think I had actually been appointed to the Chair of Modern History in the University of Sydney before it happened, so I missed him by a very narrow margin. So little stir did his death cause in Victoria that I never even heard of it, and imagined that he had been dead for years, though he wrote lyrics only excelled in music by Shelley's, Swinburne's and Poe's in the whole of English literature. Yet he had visited Melbourne, and was, in fact, there and in the company of Gordon the very day before his rival died. Kendall, unlike Gordon, was Australian born.

Far the greatest author born on Australian soil is, of course, Mrs. Humphry Ward, a Tasmanian by birth, though Australia had long passed out of her life before she wrote. " Tasma " was also a Tasmanian by birth, and " George Egerton," whose father, Captain Dunne, fought in the New Zealand war, was born in Melbourne.

- Mrs. Campbell Praed, on the other hand, was not only born in Queensland, the daughter of a prominent Queensland politician, Thomas Lodge Murray Prior, but has gone to her native land for the scene of her brilliant novels.   Ill-health kept her from coming often to Addison Mansions, where she had a double claim to literary homage, for, apart from her own eminence as a novelist, she has a matrimonial connection with William Mackworth Praed, the brilliant novelist and father of Society Poetry.

Rolf Boldrewood, though born in London, has been so long in Australia that he almost counts as a Colonial (Australian born) rather than a Colonist (settler).   He went to the old Sydney College in New South Wales more than seventy years ago, and though he spent the greater part of his life as a Police Magistrate and Warden of the gold-fields in New South Wales, began life as one of the pioneer squatters of Victoria.   His experiences gave him a rich equipment for writing tales of wild life in the old Colonial days, like *Robbery Under Arms*, with which he made such a huge reputation in 1888.   I remember him as a writer ten years before that, when he used to send a weekly *causerie* to the *Australasian*, admirably written under his famous pseudonym.   I believe that he used to call it " Under the Greenwood Tree."   He had already written and published the novel which he afterwards called *The Squatter's Dream*.   It was a thin paper volume, a sort of cross between our sixpennies and the French three francs fifty coverless novels, and it was called in those days *Ups and Downs*.   It was a true story; it dealt with the ups and downs of the famous Mossgiel Station, which made John Simson's great fortune, and the ruin by drought of the De Salis brothers who had the station before him.   It was published anonymously.   Rolf Boldrewood's real name is Thomas Alexander Browne.   His mother was a Miss

R

Alexander. Both the Brownes and the Alexanders were huge men; Rolf's brother, Sylvester Browne, was the tallest man in Australia, a couple of inches taller than my uncle, Sir Charles (who was just under six foot six, and I think may have owed some of his influence in the early days to his great stature). The Brownes were not only very tall, but very strongly-built men. Their adventurousness took them to West Australia, where they made large fortunes during the mining boom.

Guy Boothby and Louis Becke, on the other hand, both much younger men, were real Colonials, Becke having been born at Port Macquarie, New South Wales, and Boothby at Adelaide, where his father was a member of Parliament and his grandfather a Judge. That did not prevent him from leading the wildest life. At one time he was an explorer and crossed Australia from north to south. At another time he was stoker on a tramp steamer trading between Singapore and Borneo. He "struck oil" with the detective stories of Dr. Nikola, which the *Windsor Magazine* ran in opposition to Doyle's Sherlock Holmes stories in the *Strand Magazine*, and at one time was making nine thousand a year out of his writing. I remember his chartering an eight hundred ton steam yacht, and he had some wonderful prize dogs at the Manor House, close to the Kempton Park racecourse, in which he lived.

Becke was never so fortunate in his earnings, though he was a far superior writer. He acquired his wonderful knowledge of the Australian coast and the South Sea Islands as supercargo of one of the schooners which trade between the islands and Sydney.   He was one of Fisher Unwin's discoveries, and came very near achieving a *Kidnapped* and *Treasure Island* success, for which, as far as first-hand knowledge was concerned, he was infinitely better equipped than Stevenson.

Frank Bullen, Becke's rival in South Sea knowledge, was not an Australian, but born in Paddington. Like Becke, he was in the Merchant Service. I have more to say about him in another chapter.

Ada Cambridge, who was for a long time the best-known

novel-writer in Australia, was born in Norfolk, and spent all her time in East Anglia till she married the Rev. J. F. Cross, and sailed with him to Australia in 1870, the year of Adam Lindsay Gordon's death. She published her first novel about seven years later. Cambridge was her maiden name.

Ethel Turner, Mrs. H. R. Curlewis, is another of the few Australian authors living in Australia who have had large publics in England. As a reviewer, I hailed with delight her first books, *Seven Little Australians* and *The Family at Mis-Rule*, and prophesied the wide and continuous success which she has attained with her stories of child life in Australia. Mrs. Curlewis was born in Yorkshire, but she has lived in Sydney ever since I can remember.

Frances Campbell (Mrs. Howard Douglas Campbell), the author of *Love the Atonement*, *The Two Queenslanders*, and other novels, married a cousin of the late Duke of Argyll, who was out in Queensland, and commenced writing at his Grace's suggestion. In point of fact, she came to us with a letter of introduction from him. Since then she has been an active and successful journalist, doing several special journeys abroad as correspondent for the great London dailies. She is not to be confused with Mrs. Vere Douglas Campbell, the mother of Marjorie Bowen, who is also a novelist. I made the mistake myself once.

Mrs. Mannington Caffyn, who under the pseudonym of " Iota " wrote the famous *A Yellow Aster*, was a beautiful and spirited Irish girl, the daughter of a country gentleman, who took to hospital nursing as a profession, and married a doctor, whose ill-health drove him to Australia. Her life there was full of hard experiences, but she did not make a mark in literature till her return to England. Andrew Lang was struck with the extraordinary ability of *A Yellow Aster*, and urged with all his influence one of the old classical publishing houses to bring it out, but in vain. Hutchinson saw his opportunity, accepted the book, advertised it with genius, and made a colossal success of it. Other successes followed, so real that she was able to send her growing boys to a crack public school. Another novelist not born in

Australia, but resident there for some years, was " Rita," who was educated in Sydney.

The Countess von Arnim, author of a delightful series of books from *Elizabeth and Her German Garden* to *Fraulein Schmidt and Mr. Anstruther*, was an Australian born, the daughter of Mr. Herron Beauchamp.

Haddon Chambers, one of my earliest literary friends in London, though I have seen little of him for many years, I met because we came from Australia at about the same time. He was born near Sydney, of Irish parents, and was for a while in the New South Wales Civil Service, like his father before him. Feeling, as I did, that Australia was no place for a literary career, he visited England when he was twenty, and returned to England for good when he was twenty-two, a handsome, alert, indomitable Australian boy. He looked very boyish in those days. Beginning life in England as a journalist and story-writer, he suddenly took London by storm with his play, *Captain Swift*. Captain Swift was one of the greatest parts which Beerbohm Tree has created, and from that time forward Chambers became one of the dramatists who count.

To my mind, the best author living in Australia at the present moment is the Rev. William Henry Fitchett, President of the General Conference of the Methodist Church of Australia, editor of a magazine and a weekly newspaper, and Principal of a ladies' college in Melbourne. He made his name with a series of remarkable books about the exploits of the British army—writing at first under the pseudonym of " Vedette." Few men have ever written so brilliantly or so sympathetically on the subject as the author of *Fights for the Flag* and *Deeds that Won the Empire*.

A. B. Paterson, the poet who wrote " The Man from Snowy River," is an Australian by birth and residence. He is another of the few Australian authors who have a vogue in England without ever having lived there. He is recognised not only as one of the chief poets of Australia, but as a publicist. He is a solicitor by profession.

W. H. Ogilvy, the best living Australian poet, was not born in Australia, nor does he live there now, but he spent many years in the Australian bush, and caught its spirit better than any poet except Adam Lindsay Gordon.

The Countess of Darnley, who wrote some fiction a few years ago, was the beauty of Melbourne when I was there in the 'eighties.   Lord Darnley met her when he came out to Australia with one of the English cricket elevens.   He was then the Hon. Ivo Bligh, a name which will never be forgotten in the history of sport.

The charming and elegant Eleanor Mordaunt, author of *Lu of the Ranges*, the best novel ever written about hardships in Australia, is English by birth.

"*Lu of the Ranges*," says a *nil admirari* Australian newspaper, whose editor could not have known that she was born in England, "is a notable contribution to Australian literature. . . . It is solidly constructed, finely written, frank to the verge of brutality, and inherently Australian.   Lu, pictured on the cover by the fool illustrator as a charming English maiden, is a drab and very human girl of the backwoods, who, to the end of her life, could not speak grammatically.   Her language is the sort that looks neater printed with a dash; and she has a temper of her own.   A hard, glittering, valiant personality, whom life teaches to take care of herself ' on her own.'

"A veritable child of the bush, she was inured alike to heat and cold, to hard work and a spare diet, to an almost incredible isolation. . . . For the children of the bush are, above all things, old, like the primitive forms of vegetation, the wistful-eyed, prehistoric animals which are with their fellows.   When they grow up and find their way to the cities, they blossom into a splendid youth, which never again quite leaves them; or else, scared and bewildered, they creep back again to the wild places whence they came.   But to the irresponsible gaiety of childhood they are for ever strangers."

It was the outcome of the seven years of struggles, more than once coming perilously near starvation, which she had in the colony of Victoria.   Some of her short stories are good enough for Rudyard Kipling.   That she has not assumed her place in the front rank of novelists is due only to the immense barriers to recognition which have to be surmounted owing to the mountains of fiction which are cast up every year, and stand between the new writer and fame.

When I asked Eleanor Mordaunt about her life in Australia she said—

" In Australia I edited a woman's paper, and made gardens, and blouses for tea-room girls, and worked in an engineer's shop at metal work, and was four times carried into public hospitals for dying. I never had a penny in the bank—and more than once not in the world. Once I lay in bed for three days because I had nothing to eat. Then came thirty pounds for a manuscript of essays from *Lothian* of Melbourne (published 1909 under the title of *Rosemary*), and seven pounds a woman owed me for painting her a set of silk curtains, and two pounds for *The Garden of Contentment*, and I got up and went out and bought a pound of chops, and cooked and ate them all. I did all my housework at night, and all the washing.

" In Leek this time I lived on fifteen shillings a week with the weavers, and knew no one else except the two daughters of the Trade Union secretary, and never had so much love and kindness in my life. The book comes out next autumn, and is called *Bellamy*."

Mary Gaunt, the novelist and traveller, was born and brought up in Victoria. Her father was a well-known judge in the Colony. She had met with considerable success in journalism before she left the Melbourne University.

Dr. George Ernest Morrison, who made himself so famous as correspondent of *The Times* in Peking, was, as I have said elsewhere, a fellow-student and friend of mine at the Melbourne University, and has been a great friend ever since. It was I who persuaded Horace Cox to publish his *An Australian in China*, the only book he has ever published, though I myself conveyed to him an offer of a thousand pounds on account for a book about China before the Allied Powers invaded it. He was unwilling to enter into a contract, and the matter dropped. He has since then resigned his position on *The Times*, and become English adviser to the Government of China. His book on China, whenever it does come, will be read all over the world, because no European has ever understood Chinese politics as well as he has.

His knowledge of the country Chinese, the two hundred million toiling agricultural poor, is just as extraordinary. His gigantic journeys across China have given him a chance of seeing them as no other Anglo-Saxon, and probably no other white man, ever has seen them. His first journey was from Shanghai to Rangoon by land in 1894, which he accomplished at a cost of eighteen pounds, and on which he went unarmed, as usual. That is the journey described in *An Australian in China*. His second was from Bangkok in Siam to Yunnan city in China and round Tonquin in 1896; his third across Manchuria from Stretensk in Siberia to Vladivostok; his fourth from Peking to the border of Tonquin; his fifth from Honan city in Central China across Asia to Andijan in Russian Turkestan, nearly four thousand miles.

Morrison, whenever he came back to England from the East, used to come straight to Addison Mansions. One night he turned up about 10 p.m.

" How long have you been in London? " I asked.

" About two hours."

The hero of so many striking adventures (in which most people would feel inclined to include the siege of Peking, for he was badly wounded in it, and without his leadership the city would have fallen) is, though his bushy hair has turned snow-white, singularly youthful-looking. His rounded clean-shaven face has not a line or a wrinkle from its long sojourn under Eastern suns. His blue eye has a merry twinkle in it which gives his face a humorous expression when it is not hardened for action. Those who have seen him in a crisis, know how stern and resolute and uncompromising it can be. He has a slim, active figure.

Just before he was appointed *Times* correspondent in China, I approached Sir Henry Norman, who was at that time one of the editors of the *Daily Chronicle*, and whom I knew, to try and get the proprietors of that paper to give him a similar appointment in China, or in some country where Spanish is spoken, for Morrison speaks Spanish fluently.

I enumerated all the qualifications which immediately afterwards led *The Times* to make the best appointment they made since De Blowitz. At the end of it Norman just said with a cold smile, " Oh, all your geese are swans," and changed the subject. I wondered if he ever let the proprietors of the *Chronicle* know what a goose they had lost, and whom they could have secured for quite a moderate salary. To his honour be it known, that Moberly Bell, of *The Times*, recognised Morrison's value the moment the young doctor approached him.

Morrison's middle fame was of a quite unusual sort. His walk across Australia without money and without arms had been a nine days' wonder. His gallant explorations in New Guinea, culminating in his being brought home with a barbed wooden spear-head inside him, and being sent on to Edinburgh because no one in Australia could extract it, made him a celebrity in Scotland as well as Melbourne. But when Prof. Chiene extracted the spear-head successfully, Morrison's exploits, for the time being, were lost sight of in those of the great surgeon, and he became known as "Chiene's case."

G. W. Rusden, the only important historian of New Zealand and Australia till Henry Gyles Turner's book appeared, I knew very well. We lived together, until I was married, at Cotmandene, Punt Road, South Yarra, a suburb of Melbourne. In fact, I was married from there. He had for many years been clerk of the Parliaments in Melbourne, and was actually engaged in writing his histories when we were living together. He was a strange mixture in his sentiments—a violent Tory in everything except where natives were concerned. But he was even more violent as an advocate for coloured people. At that time the Maories were giving a good deal of trouble in New Zealand, and Bryce, the Minister for Native Affairs, showed great resolution and capacity in dealing with them. This infuriated Rusden, who, partly from the yellow journals in New Zealand, and partly from Sir George Grey, who had been Governor and afterwards Premier of the Colony, gleaned a farrago of libels, accusing Bryce of murdering native women and children. He showed these reports to me triumphantly. At the risk of losing his friendship, for he was very touchy, I begged him not to make any use of these materials, which appeared to me patently false. But he persisted in inserting portions of them. Years afterwards, when both he and I were living in England, Bryce brought an action for libel against him in the London Courts on these very grounds. Rusden went to my uncle's firm, Sladen and Wing, as his solicitors, on account of his friendship with my other uncle, Sir Charles. My cousin told me about it. " Well," I said, " make him pay anything to keep it out of court. I was living with him when he wrote that part of his history, and saw the materials, and he hasn't a leg to stand on."

But Rusden was a great deal too stubborn to compromise —and the verdict against him was five thousand pounds damages.

Turner also is an old friend of mine. He was long manager of the Commercial Bank in Melbourne, and was one of the founders and editors of the *Melbourne Review*. He and the late Alexander Sutherland, who was a schoolmaster, wrote the excellent book on Australian literature which has been the foundation of all subsequent works on the subject, especially in the matter of our knowledge of Adam Lindsay Gordon.

And here I must mention my two closest Australian literary friends—Arthur Patchett Martin and Margaret Thomas. Margaret Thomas, who was brought up in Australia, though she was actually born in England, began life as a sculptor. She won the silver medal of the Royal Academy, and executed, among other public works, the memorial to Richard Jefferies in Salisbury Cathedral, and the memorials to various Somerset celebrities in the Somerset Valhalla, founded by the Kinglakes at Taunton. She was so successful also as a portrait painter that she was able to retire with a competency, and devote the rest of her life to travel and book-writing. She has written travel-books on Syria, Spain and Morocco, and hand-books on painting and sculpture. Probably no one living has such a wide knowledge of the picture-galleries of the Continent.

Patchett Martin was born at Woolwich, but went to Australia at an early age, and was educated at the Melbourne Grammar School and University. He helped to found, and edited the *Melbourne Review*, and was intimately associated with the theatre, because his sister married Garner, the principal theatrical impresario of Australia. He settled in London in 1882, and practically introduced Adam Lindsay Gordon's poems to their popularity in England, where they had been neglected except for the reviews and articles which appeared in *Baily's Magazine*, about the time of Gordon's death a dozen years before. While editor of the *Melbourne Review*, Martin was among the very first to " boom " Robert Louis Stevenson, who was his model in his own delightful poems and essays. His big, burly form and hot, good-humoured face were very familiar in the Savage Club in the 'eighties.

Australian authors in London centre round the Royal Colonial Institute, and the *British Australasian*, the editor of which, Mr. Chomley, is the secretary of the literary circle at the Royal Colonial Institute, which meets on Thursday nights, and has most interesting papers and discussions.

Both the former librarian (my old friend, J. R. Boosè, who is now the secretary) and the present, P. Evans Lewin, who was for a brief period the chief librarian of South Australia, have kept the track of nearly every book which has been published about Australia or by an Australian, and Australian authors and journalists make a regular club of the Institute when they are in London.

CHAPTER XXI

MY NOVELIST FRIENDS : PART I

By far the greater number of my literary friends have been novelists. I have counted no less than two hundred and seventy male novelists who have visited us at Addison Mansions, and I have no doubt that I have forgotten enough to bring the number up to three hundred.

Of Walter Besant, a short sturdy man, with a bushy brown beard and blue eyes behind spectacles, which could be very merry or very indignant, I have spoken elsewhere. Besant, who pronounced his name with the accent on the second syllable (it is said because people always pronounced the famous theosophist's name with the accent on the first syllable, though the recollection of its Byzantine etymology may also have guided him), was very outspoken. He could not abide the famous Annie Besant; he considered that she was a millstone about his brother's neck, and made no bones over saying so. That brother was a master at Cheltenham College when I first went there. But I do not remember if I ever saw Mrs. Besant there, though we saw the masters' wives as a body in the College Chapel every Sunday morning. Another matter on which he was outspoken was his repulsion for George Eliot—not her works, but her personality. He once said to me that her head reminded him of a horse's, and on another occasion said that no woman's face had ever struck him as more sensual.

His own personality was splendid. He was so genial, though such a fighter; he was so splendidly full of energy, so quick to catch on to ideas, so masterful and wide-grasping in carrying them out; so absolutely friendly; such a good enemy, and so astonishingly warm-hearted. I never had a greater personal feeling of respect and affection for any great man than for Besant.

251

All the world knows how much he effected for authors, and how much he sacrificed for them. He made as large an income as any great novelist of his time, but he might have made much more and lived another twenty years, if he had not slaved for his brother authors.

George Meredith, who succeeded him as head of the literary craft, was never at Addison Mansions, though his daughter came twice with Lady Palmer. I only had the privilege of knowing him towards the end of his life, when his time and his health were far too precious to be spent on going to at-homes, though he was very kind about having younger authors introduced to him at the parties which Lady Palmer gave in his honour when he was staying with her. Once seen, George Meredith could never be forgotten. You were delighted to find that a man who had created a literature within a literature, the writer who by common acclaim is the greatest of all English novelists, was so rare and impressive in his appearance and speech. His face was singularly beautiful in its old age, surmounted by a fleece of snow-white hair, and illuminated by bright blue eyes, absolutely clear. He was, of course, an excellent talker, and both his voice and his way of using it were strikingly emphatic. There are few old men whom I have met to whom I should so unhesitatingly apply the word majestic. The whole face, with its well-trimmed beard and unexaggerated features, reminded me of the bearded Zeus in the group of the three gods on the frieze of the Parthenon.

He was very gracious also to young authors, though it must have been a severe tax on him to have so many worshippers introduced to him. For George Meredith was not a man like Oliver Wendell Holmes. A lady whom I introduced to him began, " It must bore you terribly, Dr. Holmes, to have everybody who is introduced to you telling you how they admire your books."

"On the contrary, madame," he said gallantly, " I can never get enough of it. I am the vainest man alive."

On the same occasion Holmes told me that he had been unable to do any writing (except his short *Hundred Days in Europe*) for years, because his entire time was taken up with answering complimentary letters.

Hardy did come to 32 Addison Mansions, Hardy who has received the Order of Merit, and is proposed for next year's Nobel prize for literature, as the head of the literary craft, one of the great masters of English fiction. I am very proud to have known Thomas Hardy; he is not only so great, but so silent and reserved, that it is not easy to know him. I have met him often, but seldom seen him talking, except very quietly to an intimate friend. He has generally been on the edge of a crowd, observing—we have the fruits of that profound observation in his novels. That slight figure, that melancholy face, with the watchful eyes, was always a cynosure, for Hardy has been the object of unbounded admiration for many years. I remember his being the bright particular star about whom the late Lady Portsmouth was always talking at her house-parties at Eggesford, where I stayed, as far back as 1885.

I have a letter from him which is one of my most treasured literary possessions. He wrote it to me to explain his point in introducing the passage about the slaughtered pig after I had reviewed *Jude, the Obscure,* at considerable length and with minute criticism in the *Queen.* I have alluded to his almost equal eminence as a poet in another chapter.

It is natural to couple Hall Caine with Thomas Hardy, for both of them were brought up as architects, though they turned to literature, and reached the topmost rung.

Hall Caine has been an intimate friend of mine for many years. Our friendship began before he was a novelist, in the days when he was a critic of the *Athenæum* and the *Academy,* and an editor of poetry. His sending me *The Sonnets of Three Centuries* in the year in which he lost his housemate, the poet and artist, Dante Rossetti, was the beginning of our friendship. He began publishing novels in 1885, and two years later leapt into the front rank of novelists with his magnificent *Deemster.*

After my return from America I began to see more and more of him. He became a director of the Authors' Club, of which I was Honorary Secretary, and one of the chief speakers at the New Vagabonds Club.

In 1894 he reached, with *The Manxman,* the height of fame, at which he has since continued. I prophesied its enormous success in a long review of it, which I wrote for the *Queen*, which came out simultaneously with the publication of the book. We were in Rome together at the time that he was writing the *Eternal City*, and in Egypt together while he was writing *The White Prophet*.

No one could be in the presence of Hall Caine for five minutes without knowing that he was in the presence of a remarkable man. His resemblance to Shakespeare is extraordinary, not only in the dome-like expanse of his forehead and the Elizabethan slope of his beard, but in the burning eyes and the shape of the eyecups. He looks the genius that he is.

Hall Caine has always had the merit of being highly approachable and affectionate, and if his conversation is apt to centre round the work he is doing, it is always most interesting and pregnant.

At Rome, for instance, where I very often had lunch with him in his flat at Trinità del Monte, overlooking the city, and went for walks with him, he was very full of the Vatican, where he constantly went to see certain cardinals, who were most indiscreet in their confidences.

He was intimate with the Italian Government, too. I met various members of the Cabinet at his table, and one of them, Ferraris, then Postmaster-General, as well as editor of the *Antologia Nuova*, has done me many acts of friendship since.

Jerome's neighbour in those days, Joseph Hatton (than whom there could have been no more striking contrast to him), was one of his and my dearest friends. There were few men so dear to their friends as Joe Hatton. He had an enormous circle of them in literature, and on the stage, and so won their hearts with his geniality and loyalty that they forgot how eminent he was, and treated him as a brother. But Joe Hatton, in addition to the vast amount of work he did as editor and critic, wrote some of the best novels of his day. I can see him now as he so often came to our house, a rather small man with a brown beard, a lift of the chin, a ready smile, and such very bright sympathetic brown eyes. He used to bring his pretty little daughter with him before he was grown up. How proud he was of her first successes on the stage, and the fairy-book she wrote ! He had a house with a very nice garden in St. John's Wood, where he gave parties at which one met all the leading actors and actresses of the day. They could always spare time for a reception at Hatton's, as actors always stopped for a word with him at the Garrick Club on Saturday nights.

Of Doyle, Kipling and Barrie, Anthony Hope and Frankort Moore, I have spoken in another chapter.

Stanley Weyman was such a rare visitor to London that he was not often at our house. But I have corresponded with him a good deal. I knew when I made *A Gentleman of France* my book of the week in *To-day*, and hailed the author as an historical novelist of the first rank, on what a solid basis his work rested, for we were at Oxford at the same time, and he took his First in History almost in the same term as I took mine. He is a very fair man, with an eyeglass, much more like a soldier than an author.

Poor Crockett, a big tall man, with a fair beard, the type of the Saxons who fought against the Conqueror at Hastings, was not very often in London, but when he was there, he was a conspicuous figure at our at-homes. We had many tastes in common, including Italy. Crockett asked my advice when the question arose of his giving up the ministry. He was at that time Free Church minister of Penicuik, a little place in Midlothian, with a salary, as far as I remember, of a hundred or two a year, but as an author was making a thousand or two a year, and able to earn a good deal more if he could save the time which he had to devote to his clerical work. His congregation were aghast at the idea of losing their beloved minister just as he had sprung into Anglo-Saxon fame, and, with Scottish casuistry, represented to him that it would be wrong for him to neglect the work of the Lord for any worldly object. Crockett thought, and I agreed with him, and decided him, that he would be more certain of doing good if he allowed some man to whom the minister's stipend was necessary to be minister of Penicuik, while he did his teaching and his preaching with his pen.

F. W. Robinson's short, thick-set figure, and heavy moustache, were as conspicuous. It is strange how soon poor Robinson has been forgotten. His work was popular with readers, and treated with respect by critics, and he was one of the bigwigs at literary clubs and receptions, but with his death all memory of him seemed to pass away, except among his old friends.

G. A. Henty, on the other hand, though he has been dead for years now, seems to stand before us still, with his great beard, his great pipe, his great body, and his breezy personality. Henty loved clubs and literary gatherings. The Savage was his particular stronghold, when he had said good-bye to war-correspondenting in distant lands. He was the typical chairman there, with his Father Christmas beard, and his volumes of smoke, and his bluff personality. He had been as popular among his fellow-correspondents. Was it not Henty who lost his only pair of boots, when the British army marched into some capital (I think it was King Theodore's in Abyssinia), and took his place in the triumph in carpet slippers, riding on a pony?

Henty's work as a war-correspondent gave him the copy for those wonderful books which made him the boys' Dumas. He was a great personality, and, as I saw, on the only two occasions when I ran across him in a crisis, a born ruler of men.

He often came across from his house on Clapham Common to our at-homes, and looked like a strayed Viking, or a master-mariner, among the other authors and authoresses. Sailing was his hobby.

Speaking of Abyssinia, it is natural to me to mention Prince Alamayu—Ali, as we used to call him. He was sent to Cheltenham College, so that he might live in the house of Jex-Blake, then Principal of Cheltenham, and afterwards head master of Rugby and Dean of Wells. Of all the head masters of his time, Jex-Blake had the most considerable reputation as a courtier and a man of the world. Alamayu was brought to England after the capture of Magdala, and came to Cheltenham in 1872, when he was eleven years old. He was just a royal savage when he came to Cheltenham; if he was hot, he took his coat off and threw it on the ground, and left it. He had no tutor to go about with him; he just mixed with the boys in the ordinary way. And at first he had the cruelties of his bringing up; he once, for instance, pushed a small boy into the water to see the splash he would make. But he soon got cured of this, for Jex-Blake wisely left him to fight his own battles, and though a sense of chivalry made the boys very indulgent to the poor little orphaned black, they soon let him know that bullying was not to be one of his privileges, though almost anything else was treated as a joke.

When Jex-Blake went to Rugby, Alamayu went with him, and thence, when he was eighteen, he went to Sandhurst to qualify for the British Army. That was fatal. He was his own master there, with no one to make him take care of his health, or restrain himself in taking spirits. He soon contracted some deadly disease—pneumonia, I think—and died. Queen Victoria showed her regret by having him buried in St. George's Chapel at Windsor.

I knew him very well, because I was in the head form when he came to the school, and was often at Jex-Blake's house, and was asked by " Jex " to keep an eye on him. He was a nice little boy, with a very affectionate disposition, and not at all stupid. It was his misfortune to lose at a critical moment of his life the firm and tactful hand which had disciplined and protected him for seven years.

Green Chartreuse is almost as deadly as aeroplanes. I knew a man, a very well-known man, who went mad because he drank thirty-six green Chartreuses in one day.

It is natural to mention George Manville Fenn in the same breath as Henty. He was another old friend of mine, and of all the men I have known, retained his youth the longest. Fenn's hair remained golden and undiminished in its vigour, and his figure remained slim and upright till he was nearly seventy. He lived at the beautiful old red-brick house on the river at Isleworth, which stands at the gates of the Duke of Northumberland's park, and is known as Syon Lodge. There he turned out those wonderful boys' romances of his in a steady stream. Like Henty, I met him constantly at the Savage and Vagabond Clubs, and at my

8

own flat. He was very fond of meeting his fellow-craftsmen. His son, Fred Fenn, used to come too. At that time he was sub-editor of the *Graphic*, and I think he afterwards became first editor of the *Golden Penny*. In any case, he freed himself from the fetters of journalism by writing *Amasis*, that admirable Egyptian comic opera, in which Ruth Vincent won all hearts. He not only had the cleverness to write it, but formed the company which put it on, and stood an action at law about it triumphantly—a rare instance of grit.

Richard Jefferies never came to see me at Addison Mansions; he was dead, I think, before we went there. But I have a long and pathetic letter which he wrote to me some time before he died, setting forth the cross-fire of diseases from which he was suffering, and asking me if I thought the climate of the exquisite Blue Mountains of New South Wales would afford him any relief. One can picture how the genius of Jefferies would have blossomed forth amid that matchless gorge scenery (where you hear the bell-birds calling) and amid the natural history curiosities of a new land.

Grant Allen, who lived in a charming house in the Haslemere district, was a constant visitor to our flat. We had visited his people in Canada before we met him. His father was the principal inhabitant at Kingston, Ontario, the dear old-fashioned town which contains Canada's Military Academy. The old Allen had a fine house with a delightful garden, right on Lake Ontario. Grant Allen was a remarkable-looking man, with his long red beard, and keen, hawk-like face. He always reminded me of the gaunt, red-bearded faces one sees on knights and lovers in the great French tapestries of the fifteenth century. And he had the same spare figure as they have, and the same habit of arching his back. He was a remarkable man, who, famous as he was, never got his due as a writer. He was never an F.R.S., though half the Fellows of the Royal Society were his inferiors in scientific attainments, and he never reached eminence as a novelist, though he wrote some amazingly clever and powerful books. He had a great contempt for actresses on account of their want of conversation. He said they could not talk about anything but the stage. I once came away with him from a party at H. D. Traill's, where he had taken down to supper a woman who was beyond dispute the greatest actress of her time. He was complaining loudly about it; he said that he thought she was the most stupid woman he had ever met.

But he was happy in his friendships. His brother-in-law, Franklin Richards, father of the publisher, Grant Richards, was recognised as one of the soundest philosophers of his day at Oxford—I say this though his lectures were entirely thrown away on me. I had to attend them because he was a don of my College, but Philosophy was Chinese to me.

One of Grant Allen's greatest friends in the last part of his life was Richard le Gallienne, who went to live in that house in the wood beyond Haslemere to be near him. Le Gallienne had a sort of summer-house in the wood, a long way from the house, in which he wrote those charming poems, secure from interruption. I often went to see him in the days when he lived in the King's Farm at Brentford, which was not a very farm-like house. But I only once went to see him at Haslemere, and on that occasion I found him at the summer-house, dressed as carefully as if he had been in town, but with an eye on country effects. He had on a black velvet coat and waistcoat, and a rich black evening tie, but immaculate white flannel trousers; and I must admit that even in this costume he managed to look appropriate.

When we were living at Cherwell Lodge, Oxford, that delightful marine villa across the Cherwell from the Gothic part of Magdalen, Grant Allen brought his best friend to see us, Edward Clodd, the secretary of the London Joint Stock Bank, who, in the intervals of a business career, had written a number of great books, beginning with *The Childhood of the World*.

W. D. Howells only came once to see us at Addison Mansions, but I saw more of him when I was living in New York, when he used to come in at tea-time to that little hall-room we had for a sitting-room in that boarding-house in West Forty-second Street. It gave me pleasure to see him under my own roof, because I remembered how eagerly I bought and read his novels when I was at Oxford, and David

Douglas was bringing out *A Chance Acquaintance, Their Wedding Journey*, and so on, in the dainty little shilling paper volumes which were the fortunate precursors of the modern sevenpenny. Howells was rather a stout, bull-necked man, very capable-looking, and in those days had a thick mop of grey hair. In after years we knew his Italian books, written while he was a Consul in Italy, almost by heart. They are photographic in their fidelity.

George W. Cable was another American who came to the flat but once. Like Howells, he seldom honoured England with a visit. His books, and John Burroughs', too, I first knew in the little David Douglas Library, and I well remember reading his *Old Creole Days* all night, because I was so fascinated with it.

I was staying at the house of my sister's father-in-law, the Court Lodge at Yalding, at the time, and the month was June—I had just come down from Oxford. At some impossibly early hour—midnight seemed only just to have slipped past—the dawn streamed in, and made me blow my candle out, and the birds began their comment on the peach garden. Five-and-thirty or forty years have passed since then, but the delight of Cable's poetical touch remains still in my memory. Cable always rather reminded me of Hardy, though being a Southerner from New Orleans he is darker skinned. When he wrote *Old Creole Days*, he was the idol of the South, but later, when he took up the colour question on the other side, he would have been torn to pieces by the mob of New Orleans if they had got hold of him, so he took up his residence in Massachusetts.

I always slept in the haunted room in that house, a very old house, with a kitchen and vaulted cellars going back to the time of Edward III. It contained a very large cupboard, between the old-fashioned chimney-piece and the window, in which somebody is supposed to have been bludgeoned to death, the corpse afterwards being dragged across the floor, and when the window had been thrown up with a bang, flung on the flags below. At one particular season of the year, the noises which indicate this procedure plainly have been heard by various people. I have forgotten when it happened, but it must have been a very long time ago, for everything to have been done so openly.

I have slept in that room repeatedly, alone, and never heard the noises or thought about it being haunted, but I should not like to sleep in the kitchen, for it was only separated by a moth-eaten sort of door from the wickedest-looking cellars I ever remember, which, unless something has been done to them since then, lose themselves in pitch-dark spaces.

Another author, whose delightful essays on nature used to be brought out in those dear little volumes of David Douglas's, and whom I read with even more enthusiasm in those days, was John Burroughs, whom I visited in his home at West Park, on a broad reach of the Hudson. He told me that he wrote most of those essays when he was a clerk in the Treasury at Washington, where his duties were to sit opposite the safes, and see that no improper person had access to them. I have forgotten what safes, but I suppose they were those which contained the United States gold reserve. He used to project the scenes in *Wake Robin* and *Pepacton* on the blank doors of the safes in his mind, as the cinema projects dissolving views on the lecturer's sheet. The sedentariness of this pursuit gave him acute indigestion, and he was advised that nothing but manual labour and a vegetable diet would cure it. When I was with him, I think he lived entirely on asparagus, lentils and onions. He could eat about three pounds of asparagus at a sitting, as I suppose other people could if they weren't going to have any meat or pudding. He told me one thing which filled my soul with joy. As manual labour was part of the cure, he started a vineyard, in a position chosen with great care, on a steep sloping bank of the Hudson facing due south. His grapes ripened here three or four weeks before any one else's, with the result that he got a hundred pounds a ton for them instead of four pounds. Bravo, literature !

Henry James, in virtue of his long sojourn among us, belongs to England almost as much as he does to America. He still lives in London in the winter, but in the warm part of the year he retires to a delightful Georgian house on the crest of the hill at Rye, one of the most old-world places in England. Henry James's house and garden are exactly what you would choose for him—the most refined and dignified and subtle novelist in the language. The house is called "Lamb's House," but it has nothing to do with Charles Lamb, though it is exactly the house which he would have chosen, when fortune came to him. All the garden is adorable, but especially the Dutch court behind the house, and the kitchen-garden, surrounded by the most ancient cottages in Rye, with roofs red and chimneys bewitched. Between the garden and the kitchen-garden is a red-brick Georgian pavilion, facing the top of the street, as the Tempietto faces the long sloping lane which leads up to the Sculpture Gallery of the Vatican, and it is not less beautiful than the Tempietto.

Everything is appropriate; the novelist even bought the cottages at the back of the kitchen-garden, to prevent them being rebuilt, and thus ensured the permanence of a perfect setting. He has a singularly noble head and face, the type one would like to imagine for a Cicero.

Richard Whiteing, who leapt into fame at a comparatively late age, with *No. 5, John Street*, after having been one of the most important newspaper writers in England for many years, is another man whom you would pick out in any crowd for his splendid head.

Sir Gilbert Parker, who was a regular habitué of our at-homes before he went into Parliament and became such an overworked man, was in those days a slim, black-bearded Colonial, with noticeable blue eyes. He was born in Canada, the son of a British officer stationed out there, and knew Australia as well as Canada—in fact, I met him because we had both been in Australia. He was at that time a busy journalist and in the first flush of his success as a novelist, and no one could have deserved it better, for his novels had the historical fidelity and felicity of Francis Parkman, in addition to their graceful and romantic style. In spite of the solid work he has done in politics, he will be remembered as an author more than as a politician, though now we clap him on the back for the splendid spade-work he does for the Conservative Party. As a writer he fires the imagination, like the bugles in his famous story.

Henniker-Heaton, on the other hand, will be remembered not for his biographical dictionary of Australians, which was the precursor of *Who's Who*, but for his achievement in politics —a postal reform as far reaching as that of Rowland Hill, the father of the post-office. I prophesied his success in print nearly thirty years ago. He is a shining example of what a man who has a great ideal can do by singleness of vision; nothing could shake him from his ideal of a universal penny post; ridicule was poured on it; the big battalions were brought up against it; but he pursued it doggedly. He showed infinite patience, infinite good-nature, infinite tact. He brought his personal influence to bear on politicians of both sides. He went to conferences all over the world; he entertained delegates from all parts of the world; he collected and classified every species of statistic; he accumulated irresistible facts until he had a penny postage, not universal, because it does not bridge the twenty miles between Kent and France,[1] but universal for the possessions of the Anglo-Saxon nations, for the United States came into the agreement as well as the Empire. Nor did his activities stop at the post-office; for he has achieved reforms of almost equal magnitude in telegraphic charges. Now he is taking a well-deserved rest, and I cannot help thinking that he would take it very usefully if he had a flat in Berlin, and saw the Kaiser every day. A monarch of the force and intelligence of the Kaiser could not help seeing the irresistibleness of the argument that a letter ought to be taken from London to Hamburg and Berlin for the same price as it is taken to the heart of British Borneo, and if he once happened to notice it, he would brush away the cobwebs which impede it.

To Alfred Austin I was never attracted, except by his enthusiasm for gardens and Italy. He was made Laureate because he was a leader writer, not because he was a poet, and possessed neither the ability nor the affability for the post. Had he gone on writing about blackthorn and blackbirds, he would have left a greater name as a poet, and would not have been made the victim of the famous story which is told of a Scottish law lord, who, meeting him at a country house, said, " Well, Mr. Austin, are you still writing ' pomes ' ?"

---

[1] Now happily soon to be accomplished.

" One must do something to keep the wolf from the door,"
replied the poet, with official modesty.

" And is that what you use those ' pomes ' for ? " asked
the man of law, giving one visions of a small man with a
big moustache belabouring a wolf on the door-step with a
roll of manuscript.

I know of only one more malicious story, which relates to
the bestowal of a bishopric. While it was in the balance,
Lord Salisbury was suffering from one of his fits of insomnia,
and, as his custom was, sent for an M.P. son, whose speeches
were the only thing which could make him sleep. His son
bothered him all night to bestow the see—it was the premier
bishopric—on its present holder. At last Lord Salisbury
lost patience. " Oh! give it to him, and leave me. I
prefer insomnia."

It was à propos of insomnia that Lord Salisbury made his
finest retort in the House of Lords. A new Liberal peer, to
whom the leader was particularly acid, because, having been
a whip in the House of Commons, he was rather conscious of
his importance, was, in spite of the fact that his income arose
chiefly from a brewery, advocating Local Option, because he
said that the number of public-houses was a temptation to
drink. " Of course," said Lord Salisbury, " I do not enjoy
the same opportunities as the noble Lord does for knowing
the effect of the number of public-houses upon the amount
which is drunk, but I don't see his line of argument, because,
though I live in a house with forty bedrooms, I never feel
the slightest inclination to sleep."

The Irish Party, too, came in for his acid wit. Who has
forgotten his comment on the member of the Irish Party
who libelled him, and went to America, when he lost the action,
to escape paying the costs? Lord Salisbury only shrugged
his shoulders, and said that escaping was the forte of the
Irish, adding, " Some prefer the fire-escape, and some the
water-escape."

Harold Frederic owed some of his vogue as a novelist in
this country to Mr. Gladstone, who had an immense enthusiasm
for his great novel, In the Valley. Frederic, a big burly man,
with a burly moustache, was the ablest American journalist
in London, till the advent of Isaac Nelson Ford for the

Tribune, and Harry Chamberlain for the *Sun* and the Laffan Agency. Frederic represented the *New York Times*. He was a man coarse in his speech, and rather coarse in his fibre, and full of prejudices, but he had the gift of political prophecy, and, like Balaam, his utterances were dictated by the voice within him, and not by what he had come to say. His letters to his paper were splendid journalism. He used often to come to Addison Mansions, because he lived just round the corner in the old house on Brook Green. He might have been with us now, if he had not been a Christian Scientist. He was an enormous consumer of alcohol, though I never knew him the worse for liquor, and when he was taken with his last illness, the professor of Christian Science, who was called in by a woman who had great influence over him, was not able to insist upon banishing spirits as a regular practitioner would have done. The result was that he took stimulants (which were worse than poison to him) whenever he felt bad, and ruined his chance of recovery.

Rider Haggard I have spoken of elsewhere.

Frank Hopkinson Smith is a man I should have liked to see more of at Addison Mansions; he was one of the men I liked best among my friends in American literary clubs. He was an engineer by profession, who had carried out many important contracts. Writing, though he was one of the best writers in America, was an afterthought with him. Like Du Maurier, that delightful man and delightful writer, he stumbled upon his most brilliant gift.

Du Maurier became a novelist because he had become such a master of situation and polished dialogue in his pictures and their titles. Frank Hopkinson Smith grew to be a novelist out of the anecdotes which he told so brilliantly at story-tellers' nights at the Century Club. He had a fund of stories about the Italian labour which he employed in contracts. He always used to declare that engaging Italian labour was as simple as Kodaking, which had for its motto, " You press a button—we do the rest." He said that no matter how many men he needed, all he had to do was to ring up an Italian boss the night before, and tell him that he wanted so many men for a certain kind of job. Then they would be at any station in the city at seven o'clock the next :

morning, with the proper tools. He added that he always put a clause into the contract that if any of them murdered each other, the number was to be made up at once.

"That is their weakness," he said, "but they only practice it on each other. It's the only kind of labour I would undertake a contract with. They're better than the Irish, anyway."

"I don't agree with you," said Vermont, the sculptor; "they're so cruel."

"Cruel!" retorted Hopkinson Smith. "What price this? An Irishman named Larkin hired an organ-monkey from an old Dago for a dollar a day. The monkey was often badly bruised when he came back at night, and looked frightened to death when Larkin came to fetch him in the morning. So one Saint's day when the old Dago had a holiday, he determined to follow them up and watch them. The Irishman drove along till he came to the bridge over the railway at the bottom of Twelfth Avenue, where the coal carts all pass on their way up from the depot. Then he took the monkey out of the cart, and tied him to a post ten or twenty yards away from the bridge, but in full sight of it. Then he drove his horse and cart to a convenient place a little way off, and awaited events.

"Presently the coal carts began to stream across the bridge, and the monkey in terror ran up to the top of the post. The whole way across every carter took cock-shots at it with pieces of coal. Occasionally one hit it, and then the monkey screamed with rage and pain. As soon as there was a cart load of coal lying at the foot of the post, Larkin brought up his horse and cart and shovelled them in, first putting the monkey where he could not be seen, to show that the sport was over for the present. When he was loaded up, he hitched the monkey to the cart again, and drove into New York to the retailer who bought the coal from him.

"But the next morning, when he came for the monkey, he found not only that monkey, but every monkey in the organ-grinders' quarter, gone, and when he got down to the bridge, the place was looking like a zoo."

Suddenly the popular anecdote-teller wrote *Colonel Carter of Cartersville*, one of the best American novels of its generation.

William de Morgan, the other novelist who achieved his

first book success so late in life, was never at Addison Mansions, but I had the honour of meeting him at a much more interesting place—the little *atelier*, somewhere in the Kilburn district, where he made the famous lustre tiles by which he was known before he took to literature. George Joy, the artist who painted the famous picture of Gordon meeting his death at Khartum, took me to see De Morgan, knowing how enthusiastic I was over the famous Mazzara Vase, and the other pieces preserved in Sicily of the old Sicilian Arab lustre ware.

Of Bret Harte and Maarten Maartens I have spoken elsewhere.

Egerton Castle, whose *Young April* is the most delightful book of the romantic school, in which Anthony Hope, Henry Harland, and a few others have written with such charm, was a rare visitor. Any one could see that he had been a soldier. But the militariness of his active, upright figure is no doubt partly due to the fact that he is one of the finest fencers in the country. He has been a representative of England in the international contests. He is likewise, as his books show, a notable connoisseur, and he has ample means to indulge his tastes, not only from the wide popularity of the novels which he writes, mostly in collaboration with his wife, but from his having owned one of the chief daily newspapers, the *Liverpool Mercury*, which is now amalgamated with the *Liverpool Post*. The Agnes Castle who collaborates with him is, of course, his wife, not his sister.

Percy White was a constant visitor. He has been my intimate friend since he published his first novel, *Mr. Bailey Martin*, that merciless dissection of suburban snobbery. I used to write for him when he edited *Public Opinion*, and that was a long time ago. He was one of the handsomest men in literature, with his merry, boyish face, dark eyes, and bright golden hair. C. B. Fry, the greatest all-round athlete in the records of sport, is his nephew, and, though darker, reminds me very much of Percy White as he was. Florence White, who paints portraits, is his sister.

Percy White's books have never met with the circulation they deserve. If he had been born an American, they might have had the largest circulation in the world. He is just the writer whose circulation would have spread like wildfire, if he had lived in America, and written of American social life as he has written of ours. No one could have expressed the good and the bad in the American character with the same light touch and ruthless penetration. His is just the pen to depict the iron courage and the insight of genius which, with or without chicanery, lead to the amassing of millions— the selfishness, made endurable by grit and personal charm, of the American woman—the brilliant wit and pathetic lack of humour in Americans as a nation—the business side of sport.

Once upon a time I introduced him to a man whom I will call the Vidler, who ran a newspaper, and never paid anybody anything except by advertisements in that paper. He made periodical business journeys, collecting advertisements for his paper—my heart bled for the advertisers—and used to engage an editor to look after his paper while he was away. He chose Percy White for the honour on this occasion, and asked me if I could bring them together. I gave White his message, warning him that he would only be paid in promises, and was surprised to hear that he was willing to discuss the matter with the Vidler. The Vidler gave him a wonderful dinner at the Carlton, probably not paid for yet, and then took him back to his chambers to discuss the matter in hand. White sat up with him nearly all night, gravely taking down notes of his projects for the paper, but reserved his decision, which resulted in a negative. I met him the next day, and asked him how he had got on, and when I heard how late he had been kept, apologised for all the trouble to which I had put him, knowing how little chance there was of his getting any pecuniary advantage out of it.

" Don't apologise, my dear Douglas," he said; " I got a whole book out of him. He's the finest study I ever met in my life."

As Percy White did not take up the appointment, I set myself to find a man who was willing to take the post, and would not suffer for it. I found a man who was as sharp a diamond as the Vidler himself. He was duly engaged, and I always wondered which did the other in the eye. I have my suspicions, because when I met the Vidler a year or two afterwards at Monte Carlo, he did not allude to the finish.

George Gissing did not come often, though we had the great link of both knowing and loving the Ionian Sea.

If Gissing had not died, and there was no reason why he should have died if he had taken ordinary care of himself— he would only be fifty-six if he were alive now—he would have had a reputation like Barrie or Bernard Shaw by this time, for even during his lifetime people were just beginning to wake up to the extraordinary qualities of his writing. I am not comparing him to either of those two; I only make the comparison because everything pointed to his having popularity. Every now and then some excellent writer achieves popularity. No one knows why. His excellence is against his having a wide public, and it is very seldom possible to tell why one is taken and another left. As the Bible proverb says, " Two women shall be grinding at the mill; one shall be taken and the other left." .

Gissing had a genius for imparting romance to the sordid.

W. J. Locke often came in those days. He was secretary to the Royal Institute of British Architects, and combined with it the post of literary adviser to John Lane, the publisher —a collaboration which resulted in the publication of many notable books, of which none were more eventually successful than his own, except, I suppose, H. G. Wells's, and I think that it was he who advised Lane to bring out the works of Wells, and Harland's *The Cardinal's Snuff-box*, and Kenneth Grahame's *Golden Age*.

Locke was always one of the most distinguished-looking persons in a room, with his tall, slight figure, very well dressed, and his hair—golden, with a natural wave in it—beautifully valeted. His theatrical successes did not begin till much later, nor had he developed his powers as a public speaker. He published admirable and solidly successful books before he took the reading world by storm with *The Beloved Vaga-bond*, and his novels won the respect of his fellow-craftsmen from the first. In those days he lived in a modest flat at Chelsea, and was a pretty regular attendant at literary clubs and receptions

Coulson Kernahan was one of the most prominent figures in the set, because he had both a brilliant personality, and was producing a remarkable series of books, beginning with *A Dead Man's Diary*. Coulson is one of our oldest and most intimate literary friends. I met him again directly I came back from America. He was at that time literary adviser to Ward, Lock & Co.

When James Bowden split from his partners, Ward, Lock & Co., and started a publishing business of his own, Kernahan went with him, and continued his profoundly imaginative series with books about Heaven—long, thin volumes, longer and thinner even than the John Oliver Hobbes booklets, which Fisher Unwin was bringing out. They sold by the hundred thousand. They were the literary topic of the day, till Norma Lorrimer in despair said, " Kernahan is growing too chummy with his Creator."

In another line his imagination produced *Captain Shannon*, a mysterious and thrilling adventure book. But he was soon to find his *métier*, and leave thrilling fiction to Mrs. Kernahan. He became a lecturer, for which his brilliant personality, his eloquence, his gift of humour, and his conviction, had cut him out. He went to live in the country; he lectured; he became an officer in the Territorials. And now he has turned them all to account in the service of the Empire, to which he is so passionately devoted, by going round as a caravan-lecturer to make the youth of the country awake to the national peril from unpreparedness.

At a National Defence meeting, last summer, at which Kernahan was the chief speaker, with Rudyard Kipling in the chair, Kernahan told his audience of his last good-bye word with Captain Robert Scott.

The hero of the South Pole asked him what he was doing, and whether he had any new book on the stocks.

" No," was the reply; " I am neglecting my scribbling to work for Lord Roberts and National Defence."

" Good ! " said Scott, with unwonted warmth and enthusiasm. " Good ! I'm with you there ! "

Speaking of Lord Roberts, the grand old soldier is very appreciative of the work Kernahan is doing in this direction.

The veteran Field Marshal not only wrote a eulogistic introduction to the Territorial author's book on soldiering, but when the latter has been addressing great audiences on National Defence, has on several occasions sent telegrams to the chairman, asking that his thanks be conveyed to the speaker, and warmly commending Kernahan's patriotism and the work he is doing for his country. Kernahan is almost as widely known for his friendships as for his writings. He has known intimately many distinguished men and women—authors, actors, soldiers, artists, explorers and politicians. On the walls of his library are many signed and inscribed portraits of celebrities, as well as pictures inscribed to him by the painters. On his shelves are numerous books dedicated or inscribed to him by the writers. One takes up a volume of Swinburne and finds written in it, " To Coulson Kernahan, whom Swinburne dearly loved, and who as dearly loved him. From his old and affectionate friend, Theodore Watts-Dunton."

Another bears the inscription, " With the kind regards of Arthur James Balfour." Yet another, " To Coulson Kernahan, from his old chum, Jerome K. Jerome."

He is famous too, or I should say infamous, as " infamous " is the only word to apply to it, for the illegibility of his handwriting. His friend Harry de Windt, brother of the Ranee of Sarawak, tells a good story of this. It is to the effect that Kernahan once received a letter which ran as follows—

" Dear Kernahan,—Many thanks for your letter. The parts we could make out are splendid. We are using the rest as a railway pass. No one can read enough of it to say that it isn't a railway pass, and as life is too short for any one to find out what it really says, the collector has in the end to let us through."

Of Horace Annesley Vachell, one of those whom the gods love, well born, more than usually prepossessing in appearance and disposition, a sportsman, and one of the best novelists of the day, I saw a good deal when he first came back from California, and brought me a letter of introduction, asking me to help him to meet the literary people in London. I was immensely attracted to him, as attracted to him as I was to his books, for which he had a good foundation in the variety of life which he had led. He started with Harrow and the Rifle Brigade, and had been many things, from a rancher in California to an artist, before he found his vocation in literature. *The Hill*, his famous Harrow school novel, increased his popularity wonderfully, but he was an admirable writer from the first, both in story and style. I have heard it stated that on one of his great books his publishers made the sporting suggestion that he should receive no advance on account of royalties, but a thirty per cent. royalty from the beginning, and that he accepted the offer.

When I wrote to Vachell to ask him what had made him turn his attention to writing, he wrote back—

" MY DEAR SLADEN,

    " Bad times in California turned me to scribbling, although I had written some short stories for the magazines. I am rather proud of the fact that I burnt my first very long novel on the advice of a friend, who said that he could find a publisher for it, and yet urged cremation instead ! "

Vachell told me that one of the triumphs in his career which he valued most was the winning of the half-mile race for Sandhurst against Woolwich, which gave them the victory in the Sports that year, 1881. Later he was asked to run against Myers, the famous American, but wisely refused to do so.

He told me an amusing story of the hundred-pound prize which *T. P.'s Weekly* offered for the person who could discover most mistakes, typographical and so forth, in one of his novels, which he had been unable to revise himself. A parson wrote to him most indignantly, saying that there were no mistakes at all in the book, and that he was surprised that Vachell should lend himself to a cheap dodge for advertising a novel. He hinted that Vachell had obtained money from him—he had bought a six-shilling copy—under false pretences ! Vachell in return sent him one announcement of the result of the competition. The man who won the prize discovered nearly *four hundred* errors ! This sounds quite incredible, but it is true, as a most lengthy document in his possession proves. The knowledge of his works displayed by the winner fairly confounded him.

He had some strange personal experiences in California. A big cowboy rushed out of a saloon in the West, one day, followed by another cowboy brandishing a big six-shooter. The first cowboy took refuge behind the only cover in sight, a telegraph-post. He dodged round this, while the second cowboy emptied his pistol into the post. All six bullets were in the post! Afterwards, when he was chaffed by me for missing his man, he retorted, " Boys, the son of a gun shrunk ! " Both cowboys were full of sheep-herder's delight.

And he told me another amusing Californian anecdote.

" I met a pretty girl whom I had not seen for months. She informed me that she was engaged to be married, and when I asked for details, she replied, ' He is not very rich in this world's goods, but in morals, Mr. Vachell, he's a millionaire.' She married her moral millionaire, and about a year later I met her again. She was alone. Remembering her phrase, I said, ' How is your moral millionaire ? ' She replied instantly, ' He's bust ! ' I heard later that she had just divorced him."

And a short while ago he sent me one of the best newspaper bulls I remember, which appeared in the *Western Daily Press* review of *Loot*, on Dec. 19, 1918.

" Mr. Vachell, who is perhaps most widely known as the author of one of the best modern stories of school life, *The Hell*, in which Harrow is described," etc.

Another of those whom the gods love is A. E. W. Mason, who met with success very early. Mason was a Dulwich boy, and a Trinity, Oxford, man, and was on the stage before he took to literature, to his permanent advantage, for it gave him that practical acquaintance with stage-craft which hastened his success as a dramatist.

From the moment that he published *The Courtship of Morrice Buckler* it was recognised that Mason was a romance-writer with the charm of an Anthony Hope. And his reputation has gone on increasing. *The Four Feathers* was a book of genius. Unlike most authors, Mason has remained a bachelor, consoling himself with yacht-sailing among the Hebrides when he grows tired of social distractions and politics. For some years he represented 'the important

T

constituency of Coventry in Parliament as a Liberal. And he was one of the few Liberals who dared to be independent, which is probably the reason why he gave up politics. He was one of the most boyish-looking members in the House, blue-eyed, clean-shaven, fresh-coloured and slim. He has changed very little since he left Trinity. He is a charming public speaker, and his boyishness is one of his great charms in speaking. My friendship with Mason began on our first visit to Salcombe, the little Devonshire town on the wooded inlet which lies behind the Bolt Head. He had sailed into the inlet in a small yacht, and came to see me as an old Trinity man. Mason is one of the men who count.

Max Pemberton has had many successes in his half-century of life. Educated at Merchant Taylors, and Caius, Cambridge, he nearly got into the Cambridge boat. He started his literary life by editing one of the chief boys' papers and writing boys' books—his *Iron Pirate* had a prodigious vogue among future men. From this he soon passed to editing *Cassell's Magazine*, which occupied ten of his fifty years, and writing novels, with their scenes laid in romantic and half-civilised countries—what one might call " Balkan " novels. In these he has hardly any rivals, because to an instinct for construction, and skill in dialogue and description, he adds unusual ingenuity in contriving plots and selecting subjects, and accuracy in handling facts. Pemberton's novels present most vivid pictures of the far countries in which their scenes are laid.

I met him first at the Savage Club; we were sitting next to each other at dinner, and he introduced himself as the editor of *Cassell's Magazine*, and asked if I felt disposed to write a series of Japanese stories for him—the stories which were afterwards worked up to *When We were Lovers in Japan* (*Playing the Game*). I was very much flattered by his proposal, and from that day to this we have remained intimate friends. This series was followed by the series of Sicilian stories which were worked up into my novel, *Sicilian Lovers*. In both series I was to give as much local colour as possible.

After this we began to go to each other's houses, and I well remember the first time that we went to Pemberton's, before he had moved to Fitzjohn's Avenue. It was a Sunday evening, and he had asked us to meet poor Fletcher Robinson, who would have been one of the greatest journalists of the day if he had survived. He was born to it, for he was a nephew of old Sir John Robinson, who managed the *Daily News* for many years. He was, at the time of his death, assistant editor of a great daily, and he was one of the persons whose death was attributed to incurring the displeasure of the celebrated Egyptian mummy in the British Museum. He was a huge, fair man, with curly sandy hair; he was beloved of society, and a poet as well as an editor.

The popular account of his death is that, not believing in the malignant powers of the celebrated mummy-case in the British Museum, he determined to make a slashing attack on the belief in the columns of the *Daily Express*, and went to the museum, and sent his photographer there, to collect the materials for that purpose : that he was then, although in the most perfect health, struck down mysteriously by some malady of which he died. The ancient Egyptians certainly seem to have been able to protect the tombs and coffins and bodies of their dead by active spiritual powers, which I respect. But in any case, the adage of chivalry, *de mortuis nil nisi bonum*, ought to prevent people from behaving unkindly to anything that concerns the dead.

We continued to see a good deal of the Pembertons till Max took Troston Hall in Suffolk because he found that London gaieties interfered with his work. But a few years later he felt drawn back to London, and took chambers in St. James's, though he kept Troston on, and it was in those chambers that he wrote one of his great successes, the revue *Hallo Ragtime*—the best and most popular revue ever written.

Unlike so many of our leading authors, Max Pemberton, who is a distinguished-looking man—one would take him for a diplomat—is as interesting to meet as his books are to read. He shines in society.

A mutual friend of us both is Robert Leighton. Mrs. Leighton I have mentioned above. Leighton's gifts are of a serious editorial order, though he has written boys' books of wide popularity. The Leightons are among the most popular figures at literary gatherings—they are so lovable

that they have an immense circle of friends.   Robert Leighton
is recognised as having no superior as a writer on dogs.   They
have left their house in St. John's Wood now and gone to
live in an old-world house at Lowestoft.

When Arthur Morrison, who was already known as a
brilliant journalist, one of Henley's most incisive young men,
made such a success with his *Tales of Mean Streets* and his
Martin Hewitt stories, one imagined that he would pour
out a stream of books like other writers who have " boomed."
But he has been exceedingly moderate.   We had a bond of
sympathy which used to bring him to our house.   We had
a collection of very unusual Japanese curios of the humble
order, and he had one of the finest collections of Japanese
prints in the country.   We never saw as much of him as
we wished because he lived in Essex, and when the success
of his books enabled him to do his work where he liked, he
grew more and more reluctant to come to London.

Another man of that generation to whom we grew much
attached was Eden Phillpotts.   In those days he was struggling with ill-health and over-work.   London did not agree
with him, and he had to write his novels in the intervals of
journalism.   Though he told me that they seldom went out
elsewhere, he and his pretty wife were often at 32 Addison
Mansions.   They lived at Bedford Park in those days.   While
he was assistant editor of *Black and White*—that paper edited
by so many of our friends—it seemed to be a different one
every year, during its brief existence—he began to feel the
strain a good deal, and finally determined to burn his ships
and go back to his native Devon—he was a grandnephew of the
famous Bishop of Exeter—and depend entirely upon his novels.

The experiment was a complete success.   His health
improved in his native air, and directly he could give the
proper leisure to writing his novels, he sprang into almost
the first rank—alike for the extraordinary power of his stories,
for his intimate knowledge of Devonshire and Devonian
character, and for the individuality of his style.   Phillpotts
never deteriorates.   He is one of those men who carry the
stamp of intelligence and *simpatica* on their faces.   Now he
is following in the footsteps of the other great novelists and

getting a footing on the stage, where he will be well represented this year.

Robert Hichens is a very handsome and intellectual-
looking man—if his portrait had been executed by the steel
engravers of a hundred years ago it would have borne a
striking resemblance to the portraits of Lord Byron. He
has regular, clear-cut, refined features, of a very similar type.
I have not run across Hichens as often as might be expected
in Sicily and Egypt, though we have both been in these
countries, especially the former, so much. But I did meet
him one evening at Luxor, in the midst of one of those superb
Egyptian sunsets. He was on his *dahabea*, which he had
brought over from its usual anchorage near the bar on the
Thebes side. It was a luxurious and very Oriental-looking
dahabea. The saloon, separated from the cabins by heavy
Persian curtains, would have made a far more picturesque
scene for *Bella-Donna* on the stage than the steam-*dahabea*
which appeared in the actual play. He was living on one
of the old sailing-*dahabeas*, which are the most delightful to
occupy, though people generally do not sail up from Cairo
nowadays, but have them towed up to Luxor before they
join them, so as to have all their time in the picturesque,
temple-studded reach between Luxor and Assuan.

That meeting is riveted in my mind, because Hichens, in
thanking me for a long and enthusiastic review which I had
written over my signature in the *Queen* about his *Garden of
Allah*, said that though I had spoken in such terms of the
book, and brought out all its good points, he had a conviction
that in my heart of hearts I felt a sort of repulsion for it,
which was true. I thought the heroine's falling in love with
such a man at first, and her sending him back to his cell as
a monk afterwards, equally repellent; while I could not help
doing homage to the book, and revelling in its Eastern setting.

Some time after my return to England I was nearly brought
into a very close relation with Hichens.

One morning Sir George Alexander came post-haste to
call on me. I was not in. So at lunch a telegram as long as
a letter arrived—would I see him in the theatre after such
an act that night? The royal box was at my disposal if I

cared to see the play. I telephoned my acceptance to
Helmsley—a good actor, but far too good a manager to be
spared to take a part—and wondered what was up. When
I got to the theatre, I discovered what I was wanted for.
Hichens's *Bella-Donna* was coming on. All the preparations
were ready for his inspection, and Hichens could not be
found by telegram in Europe or Africa. Alexander asked
if I would superintend the staging. The fee fixed was a
liberal one. But I was in a quandary. I knew that neither
J. Bernard Fagan, who had dramatised the story, nor Alexander, had ever been in Egypt, and that the play and its
mounting, however well done, must be full of slips, to which
I ought to object. About Alexander I was not disturbed,
for I knew that his only idea would be to get the thing right.
But with Fagan it might be different. He would doubtless
have been studying the subject fiercely, and I should have to
reckon with his *amour propre*, and probably lose a friend—
who had been at Trinity, Oxford, like myself—that delightful
Sheridan-like person and personality, so I gave rather a
modified consent. I suggested that fresh efforts should be
made to find Hichens, but promised that if finally he
could not be found I would take his place in correcting the
Egyptianities of the piece.

Fortunately, at the last minute Hichens did turn up, and
I was saved from the responsibility. I was very grateful,
for when the first night came, and with it stalls for the
performance, there were many little points to which I should
have had to take exception, though they made no difference
to the enjoyment of such of the public as had not been in
Egypt. Still, I am sure that Fagan would have felt sore
about my correcting his scenes like a schoolboy's Latin verses.
As it happened, Alexander and Mrs. Patrick Campbell were
so magnificent in their parts, and the piece was so splendidly
produced, that the public did not bother itself about small
details, but flocked to see the play. It could hardly have
been a greater success than it was for any improvements
that I could have suggested. I never saw Hichens at his
residence in Taormina—we never happened to be in the
Sicilian Eden at the same moment.

W. B. MAXWELL
Drawn by Yoshio Markino

CHAPTER XXII

W. B. MAXWELL I hardly knew in those days, though I had met him years before, and, in the long and elaborate review which I wrote of his *Vivien*, had hailed him as a novelist who would rise to the very head of his craft.

Maxwell, of course, had heredity and atmosphere in his favour. His mother, the famous Miss Braddon, had written novels which took the world by storm long before he was born—it is more than half a century ago since an astonishing girl founded a new school of fiction with *Lady Audley's Secret* and *Aurora Floyd*—and he and his wife live with his mother in a stately old Queen Anne mansion in the Sheen Road at Richmond. Maxwell, who looks like a youthful judge—he is clean-shaven, and has a calm, judicial face, with an illuminating smile—has a judge's gift of scrutiny in reviewing life in his books. He is ruthlessly just with his characters; they cannot deceive him. His sentences are not too severe. But whatever their sentences are, the criminals leave the court moral wrecks. He is obliged to mete out just sentences, but he is ruthless in his summing up. His last novel, *The Devil's Garden*, is an excellent example of his great impeachments of wrong. His books have the Até—the Nemesis—tracking down their victims as ruthlessly as the Œdipus is tracked down in the tragedies of ancient Greece.

Another writer whose novels I admire immensely, and I have had to review a good many of them, is H. B. Marriott Watson, the New Zealander. He has a large public, and, in my opinion, ought to have a far larger one. As a writer of novels of adventure, I think he has no superior among the novelists of the day. For his adventures are most romantic,

and his writing is so good—so delicate where it ought to be
delicate, so strong where it ought to be strong.   Added to
which, he is scrupulous about getting his local colour and
" properties " correct.   In appearance he is a typical colonist
—a huge man, with a dark, resolute face.   When he first
became prominent in the literary world, you might have
thought that he was captain of the famous " All Black "
football team, rather than a writer.   Apart from his success
as a novelist, he has been a power in journalism.

Charles Garvice, whose novels have a greater circulation
than those of any other living writer, is now my neighbour.
We live exactly opposite each other, with the breadth of
Richmond Green between, with its old lawns, and tall elms
planted by dead kings.   He lives in one of the Maids of
Honour houses, built a couple of centuries ago, abutting on
the wall of the Old Palace of the Tudors, in which Queen
Elizabeth died, and those Maids of Honour served.   It has
some beautiful eighteenth-century painted panelling.   I look
out on its mellow brickwork, pointed with white stone, and
the fantastic Georgian ironwork of its gate, half-buried in
a tangle of swaying roses, from my study windows, just as I
look out on the crenellated wall and old perpendicular
archway of King Henry VII's palace on the other side of
the clipped yew and the great stone-pine.

When I first knew Garvice, twenty years ago, he was
farming his own lands in Devonshire, and just beginning to
find his public on this side, though he had long enjoyed an
enormous public in America.   He used to pay frequent
visits to the Authors' Club, where, since he had rooms
in Whitehall Court, he was more of a habitué than many
men who lived in London, and became extremely popular
for his genuine good-fellowship.   A few years ago, when the
Club was rather languishing, he became chairman of the
committee which undertook its reconstruction, and though
he had in the interval become one of the most popular and
hard-worked novelists of the day, lavished his time and
energies with happy results, so that now it has even more
members than the Athenæum, and far more than any other
literary club.   He is the central figure at its great dinners.

He wrote a delightful book about farming—not a literary exercise, but as the outcome of many years' practical work. Garvice, undoubtedly, has the largest sale of any novelist in the world. I have seen the figures. Last year's sales alone amounted to 1,750,000 copies—books of all prices. His romantic love-stories are conspicuous not only for their thrilling plots—Garvice is a born story-writer—but for their freedom from all deleterious influence. There is nothing goody-goody about them; they are just wholesome, straight-forward romances—an almost lost art. He is only the length of the Palace away from the river, where he keeps a sailing-boat, and he is fond of riding in Richmond Park. He needs recreations, for he is a very hard worker. Every morning he goes up to his office in London, where he spends the business day in dictating his novels, and he gives many of his evenings up to the Authors' Club, which, under his chairmanship, and the tireless secretaryship of Algernon Rose, has now a membership of 1,600. Garvice is a great reader of his brother-authors' books.

Feeling that the public would like to know the secret of one of the most remarkable literary successes on record—more than six millions of his books have been sold—one night when I had run in to see him, I got him to tell me his story over a pipe—he smokes hard all the time he dictates his stories, and cannot go on when his pipe goes out till it is refilled. This is what he told me.

"My first novel, though I had written a number of short stories before this, was about the last of the three-deckers. When it was revised and re-written quite recently, for a cheap edition, I understood fully why, in its first form, it was not the brilliant success I, a youth of nineteen, expected it to be. Quite early in my literary career I made the acquaint-ance, which grew into a warm friendship, of the proprietor of a weekly fiction periodical which had attained an enormous circulation. He was a clever editor, with a keen nose for good stuff; and he would buy nothing else, for he had hit upon the excellent idea that, if you gave the masses good stuff at a low price, they would jump at it. They jumped. I wrote the leading story for this paper for many years, and

was well paid.   The serials attracted the attention of George
Munro, the famous American publisher, who was running
a similar paper in New York.   He arranged for me to send
advance sheets for it, and he afterwards published the serial
in cheap book form.   They had an enormous—to me a
fabulous—sale, and are still selling.

"Munro started a sevenpenny magazine, asking me to
edit the English part of it, and to write a serial and a series
of short stories.   I worked nearly day and night, and was
so fully occupied and contented that, absurd as it may sound,
I never gave a thought to publishing the serials in book
form here in England;   notwithstanding that the books
were so popular in America that one of George Munro's rivals
hit upon the extremely ingenious idea of waiting until half
a novel of mine was published in serial form, getting some one
one else to finish it, and issuing it in volume form before I had
finished the story.   Of course, this was before the International Copyright Act.   Blessings on its name !

"One day, my friend, that brilliant journalist, Robert
Harborough Sherard, while sitting at my writing-desk, took
up the American edition of *Just a Girl*.   When I told him
it was not published in volume form in England, he asked
my permission to take it away and try to place it.   He took
it to Mr. Coulson Kernahan, who recommended it to the
publisher for whom he was reading.   It came out, and, to
my surprise and delight, proved a success.   The review
that, more than any other, helped me, was a very kind one
in the *Queen*.[1]   Then, again, the books were so fortunate as
to win the approval of Dr. (now Sir) William Robertson
Nicoll; and when he likes a book he does not fail to say so.

"The rest of my literary career, if the phrase may be
permitted me, is public property.   I may add that, in my
early days, I sold the copyrights of my stories.   Later on,
I got them back by the simple expedient of buying the
periodical, lock, stock and barrel, in which they had appeared; and I am glad to be able to state that I hold now
the copyright of everything I have written.   Some of the
books have been dramatised, and others are on their way to

---

[1] Written by myself.—D. S.

the stage; indeed, at an early age, I made a dramatic essay with a little play in two acts, which was produced at the Royalty Theatre, and obtained a success chiefly, if not entirely, owing to the splendid cast; amongst others, I was fortunate enough to have such actors as Richard Mansfield, who afterwards became so famous in America, that sterling player, Charles Denny, and Fred Everill, of the Haymarket. It would be a poor play such men as these could not pull through. Encouraged by my first effort, I might have directed all my attention to the stage, but fiction had got a firm hold upon me; it was safe and regular—and there you are! But I am making a new start, and ' you never can tell,' as Mr. Shaw says.

" The story of my lecturing is soon told. I gave a lecture, consisting of recitals linked together by biographical notes, for a Bideford debating society. An agent who happened to hear it, thought it good enough for the general public, and for some years past I have, during the winter months, appeared on the lecture platform. It is a change of work, which is good; and it is lucrative, which is also good, if not better.

" I have just been elected President of the Institute of Lecturers. The duties of this office will fill in my spare time—when I get it."

Sir Arthur Quiller-Couch (" Q "), another admirable writer, not only of novels, but of poems and essays, I have seen hardly at all since he left Oxford, where, sometime after me, he occupied my old panelled set of rooms at Trinity (of which he was a Scholar like myself, and A. E. W. Mason an Exhibitioner some years later), attracted probably by the fact that they had been Cardinal Newman's rooms when he was an undergraduate. Couch was a splendid example of the *mens sana in corpore sano*. He was stroke of the College boat, as well as the most brilliant Trinity man of his time intellectually, and he looked it. He had a lithe, active figure, and a humorous, self-reliant face, with light eyes— the type which takes so much beating. For a brief time he had a very successful journalistic career in London, but he quickly decided that it was not worth while to live in London

unless you were rich enough to do all the nice things which
came along, and returned to his native Cornwall to devote
himself to literature.   In Cornwall he not only wrote delightful books, but went in for sailing, and became a power in
local Liberal politics, and was knighted.   Recently he has
become Professor of Poetry in the University of Cambridge
—a post he was admirably fitted to fill, since the mantle
of Francis Turner Palgrave fell upon him as an anthologist.
His *Oxford Book of Verse* is simply delightful.

Couch had from the first been a stylist.   When congratu-
lated early in his career on the exquisite writing of a short
story, he deprecated its importance, because it was too
conscious an imitation of De Maupassant.   " My great
difficulty is not to imitate my models," he said.   In the light
of this saying, it is interesting to recall the fact that in 1897
he was chosen for the high honour of completing Robert
Louis Stevenson's *St. Ives*, which he did with absolute
success.   Stevenson must have been one of the models he
was trying not to imitate.   There is no reason why he should,
for no one could want a more delightful style than his own.
Hetty Wesley is an exquisite book.

Sir Henry Rider Haggard I ought to have mentioned long
before this, since he has been one of the recognised heads
of the novelists' profession for many years.   Haggard had
the good fortune for an imaginative man to go out to South
Africa when he and the South African question were young.
He was on the staff of Sir Theophilus Shepstone, the Official
Commissioner in the Transvaal, and actually assisted in
hoisting the British Flag over the Republic in 1887.   His
first book, published in 1882, was about South African
politics, but in 1884 he began as a novelist, with *Dawn*, and
in 1886 he achieved world-wide fame with *King Solomon's
Mines*, one of the finest romances ever written.   *She* came
out a year later, and confirmed the success.   He has written
many other famous novels.   For years he was always quoted
as the most successful novelist—but that was before the
days of " booming," a practice against which Haggard has
steadily set his face.   He told his agent that he would not
ever write to order, unless he was driven to it—that the bare

fact of having signed a contract to produce a given thing by a given time paralysed his pen. Besides writing novels of increasing seriousness, Haggard, like Doyle, has proved himself a patriot, with the deepest sense of his responsibilities as a citizen. He has twice tried to get into Parliament, with a view to legislation for restoring agriculture in England, and he has given his time lavishly, both to the investigation of the agricultural question and to serving on various Commissions, as well as to writing books on various subjects connected with the land. He came back from South Africa and went to live in his native Norfolk many years ago, but in spite of this he has done his duty in attending literary gatherings. His active figure, and close-trimmed beard, give him the cut of a naval officer.

His brother, Major Arthur Haggard, who has seen much service in Africa, and written well-known books, has done patriotic service for his country in another way by organising the Union Jack Club and the Veterans' Club for soldiers and sailors.

Another visitor to Addison Mansions in latter days was William Romaine Paterson, better known as " Benjamin Swift "—a man of extraordinary ability, whom I should not be surprised to see in a Radical Cabinet. The moment you meet him you are aware that you are in the presence of an intellect of the first rank, and an uncompromising personality. A deep reader and thinker, he has the gift of clear expression and glittering sarcasm. I have seldom heard a more effective speaker. He has already written a number of remarkable novels. He is a born leader, and he looks it, with his commanding figure, his face, of the eagle type, and his burning eye.

I ought to have mentioned Morley Roberts before, because he was a man of whom I saw much in those days. He was often at our at-homes, and nearly always in the Authors' Club when I went there. He was the greatest personality there in those days—not only as an author whose books every one in the Club admired, long before the public took them at their true value, but for his wide and deep knowledge, and for the adventures he had successfully concluded with

his splendid physique.   We always felt that Morley Roberts
was essentially a man, that the strength of his books was due
to the daring life he had led.   I have very seldom heard
Morley Roberts make a speech, but I have seen him hold a
whole room of brilliant men from his easy-chair beside the
fire, while he unfolded some curious piece of knowledge with
surprising power and interestingness.   It was he who said
that books of adventure are generally written by sedentary
cowards for sedentary cowards.

I met Morley Roberts first at a garden-party given by
Rosamund Marriott Watson, the poetess, whose husband
I have for many years considered one of the finest novelists
of the day.   She introduced us to each other because we
had both been to Australia, and I rather think that she
accused him as well as myself of having wooed the Muse of
Poetry (though there was no Muse of Poetry among the
immortal nine).   After that he came a good many times to
our house, though he never was fond of at-homes, and I
don't remember his ever coming back after his long illness.
A very strong man, six feet high, or thereabouts, with a
commanding face, and flashing dark eyes, he was always
one of the most conspicuous figures in the room.   He had
been a sailor before the mast, a navvy out west, a hand on
a ranch, and I don't know what all in his adventurous youth.

It seems incredible to think that Somerset Maugham, who
is barely forty, should have been a long time coming into
his own, yet ten years elapsed between the publication of
Liza of Lambeth and the production of *Lady Frederick*, and
in the interval he had written those delightful books *The
Merry-go-Round* and *The Bishop's Apron*.   He came to us
with a mutual friend in the year 1897, when he had just
written *Liza*.   I remember, when I read it, venturing, as
an old reviewer, to prophesy that such a writer must leap
into fame forthwith.   I was sure of it when I read *The
Merry-go-Round*, but the public did not quite answer to
my expectations.   I have always heard that *Liza of Lambeth*
was inspired by the gruesome sights and sounds which were
his environment when he was at St. Thomas' Hospital,
that he lodged in some street where, from his back windows,

could see the she-hooligans hitting each other with their
abies. He is, a rare thing for an author, an admirable dancer.

Another man born in the same year, 1874, who came to
is own through plays, and was even longer in doing it, is
dward Knoblauch, the author of *Kismet*, and joint author
' *Milestones*. Knoblauch, who is an American, born in
ew York, and educated at Harvard, and his sister, came to
; with Lena Ashwell a good many years ago. Knoblauch
as Lena's reader at the Kingsway, and collaborated with
ie Askews in *The Shulamite*, in which she created such a
)lendid character. He had already adapted *The Partikler
'et* for Cyril Maude. But he was writing plays for years
efore he had a single one accepted, and it was not until
)11 that he sprang into general fame with *Kismet*, quickly
)llowed by *Milestones*.

Louis Napoleon Parker, another old member of the Authors'
lub, is a very old friend of mine. I think it was Adrian
oss who introduced us, when he first came up from Sher-
orne School, where he was appointed Director of Music
pon leaving the Royal Academy of Music. Strangely
iough, one who has composed such delightful music is
xtremely deaf. For many years, of course, he has been one
f our leading and most prolific playwrights, and only a
iort while ago he composed the incidental music for his
rama, *Drake*. Parker, who was born in France, and might
most pass for a Frenchman, has been the translator of
)me of the most celebrated French plays which have been
Englished " for our stage—*Chanticleer*, *L'Aiglon* and
yrano de Bergerac* among them. He has had yet another
)here of activity in producing the series of splendid masques
hich are associated with his name. He is, indeed, practi-
illy the inventor of the masque in its present form, such as
ie Sherborne pageant, the Warwick pageant and the York
ageant.

CHAPTER XXIII

HENRY HARLAND, who justly made such a prodigious hit with that exquisite book, *The Cardinal's Snuff-box*, I knew well in America. Stedman introduced us at one of his at-homes. He wrote then under the pseudonym of " Sidney Luska," and was best known for some big action he had had with some firm of publishers in New York, the American Cassells, I think. He was a very opinionated man, and I did not at the time believe that he would ever write so fine a book as *The Cardinal's Snuff-box*, which breathes the very air of Italy, and is the most exquisite idyll of Italian life which we have in the language. But it is only just to him to say that Stedman, in introducing him, spoke of him in terms which should have made me believe this. He was born in St. Petersburg, and looked rather like a Russian. He would have been fifty-two if he had been alive. Lane always believed in him, and made him editor of the *Yellow Book*. He and his pretty little wife had a flat in Cromwell Road, and were popular in the " precious " section of literary society. His early death was a great loss to literature.

Frank Bullen is one of the most interesting personalities I have met in literature. He is so many-sided in his abilities and his experiences. After being an errand-boy, and everything up to chief officer on a sailing-ship, and a clerk in the meteorological office at Greenwich, he became a writer, an orator and a philanthropist. No one has done more for the men of the Merchant Service, for while he did all that man could for them practically, he enlisted the sympathies of the world for them in his books. A small, dark man, with very bright eyes, and a sympathetic manner, except when he is moved to indignation, he was born to dominate great audiences, especially when he is telling them of wrongs which need practical redress. The wonders of the Lord which he saw when he went down to the sea in ships, made such a profound impression on his imagination that they fill the pages of his books with eloquence and knowledge. With the exception of Joseph Conrad, he has no rival among living writers as a sea-novelist. I think I met him at the Idler first. I know that we became friends from the first day.

Dion Clayton Calthrop, that prince of light novelists, who is always finding fame by some new stroke of genius, was our neighbour for several years at Addison Mansions. He is such a distinguished-looking man that I used to watch him and wonder who he was, until one night I met him through a mutual friend. It is not surprising that he is so brilliant, because he is the son of John Clayton, the actor, and grandson of Dion Boucicault.

When I asked Calthrop, who started as an artist, what made him take up writing, he said—

" I really took up writing owing to a bout of insomnia when I was living in Paris, and as I was painting in the schools all day, I tried to write at night. I read the sketches to Norman Angell, a friend of mine (who wrote *The Great Illusion*), and through him met Manuel, the artist, and through him they were published in *The Butterfly*.

" I believe in many irons in the fire; people specialise too much, so I have books, plays, dress designs, or scene models, and a picture or two, all going at once, and it is a great cause for regret to me that I cannot write music. In the great days of Art, artists were so interested in life that they tried everything—why shouldn't we? I even have a rock-garden full of Alpine flowers on my writing desk— true, it is only four feet by one—but it is very interesting to see flowers grow as you work. As a matter of fact, I am writing against an Alpine crocus, trying to finish a book as it comes into bloom."

Desmond Coke, one of the most brilliant of our younger novelists, I met in 1904 through his mother, Mrs. Talbot Coke, who had been my colleague on the *Queen*, the wife of one of our generals in the Boer War. Mrs. Talbot Coke

U

was at the time—as she is still—one of the principal contributors to *Hearth and Home*, a paper which served as a literary cradle to Robert Hichens, whilst it was sub-edited by no less a personage than Arnold Bennett, who was just beginning to write his series of great novels about the pottery towns.

Desmond Coke, who, under the pseudonym of " Charbon," wrote the reviews in a lively strain, possibly sometimes more welcome to his readers than to the novelist reviewed, was at the time I speak of fresh from Oxford, which he had made his own in fiction with that delirious skit on feminine fiction, *Sandford of Merton*. Since then he has written a number of novels, distinguished for their original ideas. He has long been a keen collector, as his chambers in a backwater off Oxford Street show, and has of late turned his collecting to good account by writing the classic on *The Art of Silhouette*. He is very accomplished, and is one of the chief pillars of Chapman & Hall's publishing house. The announcement, however, that **Mr. H. B. Irving** has secured his three-act play, *One Hour of Life*, proves that here is yet another novelist who, given the opportunity, would gladly exchange the quiet covers of Bookland for the more adventurous and hectic boards of Theatredom !

E. H. Cooper was a very dear friend of mine, who came near being one of the conspicuous figures of his time. He had a short life and a merry one—merry, at all events, for his friends. He was, perhaps, too cynical ever to be quite merry himself, except with children. His father was a Staffordshire country gentleman, with an estate adjoining the Duke of Sutherland's, and the Duchess and her children and her nephews and nieces were much attached to that wayward genius. While he was still an undergraduate at Oxford, he contracted the taste for gambling on horse-races, which kept him a poor man, but enabled him to write one of the best racing novels of the language—*Mr. Blake of Newmarket*. That did not prevent him from writing delightful children's books, inspired by the Duchess's children. He was a very handsome and romantic-looking man, with wonderful iron-grey eyes, but, like Byron, was born lame.

For a brief time he edited the *Daily Mail*, as a *locum tenens*, I believe, and for a long time he was Paris correspondent of the *New York World*. Once, during that period, he made a big coup at Chantilly, and for some days pressed me with letters and telegrams to go and stay with him for a week at Paris and " paint the town absolutely red " at his expense. We were to stay at the Ritz. He said he was going to be really rich for a week, and it would supply me with the material for a whole novel. But if he was determined to waste his one stroke of luck, I was not going to be a party to it, and I not only refused, but did my utmost to wean him from the idea—unsuccessfully, I think. If Cooper had really given his mind to novel-writing and journalism, he might have made a great name, for he was brilliantly clever, and his distinction of manner made him an impressive figure in society.

We were drawing near the end of our time at Addison Mansions when I met Jeffery Farnol. Farnol, who is still young, is as likely as any one to rank among the foremost novelists of his time. His *Broad Highway* is one of the best books produced by the generation, and *The Amateur Gentleman* was a good successor to it. He is an Englishman born, but lived some time in America, where he made his living as a scene-painter. There he wrote his great novel, and after disappointments in searching for a publisher he sent it to Shirley Byron Jevons, at that time editor of the *Sportsman*, a relative of the celebrated Professor Stanley Jevons, the Political Economist, and brother of Dr. Frank Jevons, Vice-Chancellor of Durham University, he himself being now connected with literary journalism. Shirley Jevons at once recognised it as something like a work of genius, and taking it to the old firm of Sampson Low, Marston & Co., Ltd., told them that they must publish it. It made its way a little slowly at first, but then the public, led by the strong convictions of one man, swept him on to fame on an irresistible tide. Farnol was born in Birmingham thirty-five years ago. His parents came to London when he was seven, and he has made a suburb of it, Lee, in Kent, his permanent home, though business may take him to the United States for months at a time.

He married in his early twenties the daughter of Hawley, the scenic and architectural artist, an Englishman living in America. She was on a visit to relatives in England, and the rash young couple, soon after the birth of a daughter, their only child, resolved to try their fortunes on the other side of the Atlantic, the plucky and fascinating little wife sharing there his bad fortune as now she shares his good. The struggle was hard enough for a time, and, if Farnol cared to relate all that he went through in those years, the story would be a human document of great interest. At my house he met Yoshio Markino. I was about to introduce the already famous Jap to the coming young Englishman, when the impulsive Markino rushed at and fondled him, crying out in delight, " Why, it's Jacky ! " They had been fellow students at the Goldsmiths' Institute when both were younger, and both unknown to fame. There Farnol had shown welcome little kindnesses to the lonely, warm-hearted stranger from Nippon. Their ways had parted, neither thinking to see the other again, and least of all in this dramatic fashion and in these brighter circumstances. *The Broad Highway* has been dramatised for America, and is to be staged in England. *The Amateur Gentleman* is also to be adapted to the stage. His third important story—he has done many shorter things—is likely to be of modern times.

Francis Gribble is a very old friend of mine; we belonged to the same literary clubs, and met constantly at them, and he and his charming Dutch wife were often at Addison Mansions. Gribble, who is an Oxford First Class man, besides his very able novels and his biographies, which are recognised as classics on their subject, has made a neglected aspect of Switzerland his particular province. He is the authority on the Swiss towns, like Geneva and Lauzanne, where so much of the scenes of some of his biographies had necessarily to be laid. He now spends a good deal of his time in Continental travel. I remember his telling me that it was through his study of Swiss towns that he was led on to write biography. The connecting link was his accidental perusal of that wonderful book, *Benjamin Constant's Journal Intime*. He saw from it that the life of Madame de Staël

needed to be written from a new point of view, then he was
led on to cover the whole ground of the romantic movement
in French literature from Rousseau to Victor Hugo.

Frank Hird I have known many years. I met him first
as editor of some important journal—I forget what—with
which I was arranging a contribution, just as I met C. N.
Williamson first as sub-editor of the *Graphic*. I was astonished to find myself in the presence of a person who was
hardly more than a boy, very good-looking, very well-bred,
very well-dressed. Since then I have met him repeatedly,
and enjoyed the friendship of one who fully came up to my
first prepossession. I have met him most, I think, at the
hospitable villa of the Joseph Whitakers' in Palermo, where
he frequently stayed, and showed himself as good in private
theatricals as he is as an author. The place where he seemed
most in his element was when he was correspondent to one
of the chief London newspapers in Rome, and I used to
meet him in salons like the Countess Lovatelli's. The
Countess was the sister of the Duke of Sermoneta, one of
the highest of the Roman nobility, who has a similar position
to our Duke of Norfolk. The Sermoneta family have a
proud record in Italian archæology; the Countess herself
is an author, and, as a centre of public and literary life, the
Lady St. Helier of Rome. Her " salon " is said to be the
only one in which the " Whites " and the " Blacks " habitu-
ally meet. He was always the diplomatist, more than the
correspondent, though he was so excellent at his own work,
and would have risen high in diplomacy if he had made it
his career.

Edgar Jepson and his wife were often at Addison Mansions,
and I used to meet him constantly at the Authors' Club as
I now meet him at the Dilettanti. He is a man in whom
his friends believed from the first, and the quality of his books
and his speaking have amply justified them. Intellectually
he is a typical Balliol man, but that does not prevent his
being one of the delights of Bohemia, where his popularity
is unbounded. Experts are agreed that on his day, he is
the second best, if not the best, auction-bridge player in
England. He says of himself, that he is a walking warning

against writing fiction, since from his first book he made 0, from his second six pounds nineteen and nine, and from his third nine pounds ten and fivepence.

William le Queux has been an intimate friend of mine for many years. A Frenchman by birth, he is a strongly Imperialist Englishman by naturalisation, and in his writings and politics. He has led a most interesting life. He was once an artist in the Quartier Latin, but he deserted this for journalism, and was sent by *The Times* as a special correspondent to Russia, using the opportunity to acquire an extraordinary knowledge of the secret workings of the Nihilists, just as he has in recent years been very much behind the scenes in the Balkans and Turkey. For a while he was sub-editor of the *Globe*, which post he resigned as soon as his success as a novelist justified it. Since then he has travelled continually, and acquired a unique knowledge of the secret service of the Continental Powers. He is one of the most popular novelists of the day, the secret of his popularity lying in his brilliant handling of mysteries, and the use he makes of his knowledge behind the scenes in Continental politics. His books dealing with supposed invasions of England are masterpieces in their way, showing an extraordinary grasp of military details. A member of the Athenæum Club told me once that judges and bishops almost quarrelled with each other when a new William le Queux book came into the Club. His affable face, with bright, dark eyes, behind *pince-nez*, and an inscrutable expression, is familiar to frequenters of the Devonshire Club and the Hotel Cecil. The curious thing is that, though we have been such friends, and have been frequent visitors to the same places on the Continent, from the little republic of San Marino, of which he is Consul-General, upwards, we have never, so far as I remember, met out of England.

Bertram Mitford lived side by side with myself and " Adrian Ross " at Addison Mansions for years. He belongs to one of the oldest families in England. His father, the late E. L. Osbaldeston Mitford, of Mitford in Northumberland, which has been in the possession of his family since Saxon times, appearing in Doomsday Book, was a wonderful old gentleman; he lived to be more than a hundred years old, and, till a few years before his death, used to come up to London for first nights at his favourite theatres.

Bertram Mitford is a good sportsman, who has travelled and shot in the back parts of South Africa, and the wild lands bordering on India and Afghanistan. His travels have inspired novels which are splendid books of adventure. He has also been in Italy a good deal.

Guise Mitford, who has written one or two good novels, is his cousin, as is the stately Lord Redesdale, the head of a cadet branch of his family, who wrote the famous *Tales of Old Japan*. Miss Mitford, too, a once most popular authoress, was of the clan.

Mitford and I used to see each other constantly in Addison Mansions, and frequently at two or three clubs to which we both belonged, but I don't remember ever doing the journey between together, between them and our flats. He often walked both ways for the exercise.

K. J. Key, the great cricketer, who for many years held the record for the Oxford and Cambridge match, with his 130, and was afterwards Captain of the Surrey Eleven for years, one of my most valued friends, introduced me to Charles Marriott, of whose novels he was an immense admirer. Key is a great reader. Unlike most cricketers, who prefer to watch the game intently until they go in to bat, as if they were playing whist or bridge, and wanted to see what cards were out, he used to read a book or a newspaper till it was his turn to go in, and I have no doubt that he saved a good deal of nerve energy by doing so. I think he met Marriott in Cornwall, to which they are both devoted. Certainly, they are both fond of photography. Marriott made a considerable *succès d'estime* with his first novel, *The Column*. He is, or was until recently, the Art critic of one of the great London dailies, and is a most accomplished man, of wide knowledge, and one of the best novelists of the day. Living at Brook Green, he was a near neighbour of ours, and from the time that Key introduced us to the time that we left Addison Mansions, we saw a good deal of him. Key's wife has recently published a novel with a cricketer (not her husband) for its hero—*A Daughter of Love.* She is a sister of Lascelles Abercombie.

Compton Mackenzie first came to Addison Mansions as a small boy at St. Paul's School, where he was a friend of my son. They began to be men very early in my son's little cupboard of a study, overlooking Lyon's cake-factory. I did not see him after he made his fame as a novelist till we came to live at Richmond. He has, like myself, a passion for gardening. He is, of course, a son of Edward Compton, the actor, and Virginia Bateman, and his great-grandmother was a Symonds, aunt of John Addington Symonds, so there is one of the best strains of literary ability in the family. The famous Sir Morell Mackenzie was Edward Compton's cousin.

When I wrote to ask Compton Mackenzie, who is now indulging his passion for gardening by living in Capri and making landscapes round his house, what first impelled him to write novels, he said—

" I can remember shooting peas at your guests as they came in, and throwing cake, etc. I don't suppose we did it always, but I distinctly remember doing it once or twice. It is difficult to extract anything from the past and account for my writing novels. Yet I always had a passion for writing. In the Upper Sixth in 1896, I, with two other boys, ran a paper called *The Hectona*, of which, so far as I know, only two numbers are in existence. It was printed on gelatine, and all the contributions were copied out by myself in my execrable handwriting. Like many magazines since, it expired of illegibility. Later, at Oxford, I ran another paper called *The Oxford Point of View.*

" Gardening I took up to console myself for not being able to find a publisher for my first book. It toured round London for nearly two years, and I did not sit down and write *The Carnival* until *The Passionate Elopement* lay bound upon my table. This was according to a vow I had made. I started very early. *The Passionate Elopement* was printed just after I was twenty-five. It was originally—or some of it—a play which I wrote to console my father for having got married without warning or expectation. That was when I was twenty-two.

" *The Carnival*, I suppose, may be called the result of helping my brother-in-law, poor Harry Pelissier, with his Alhambra Revue. I used to rehearse the Corps de Ballet, and, I suppose, naturally made use of such an opportunity to make a book."

Lord Monkswell, who wrote a single novel, and whose sister, the Contessa Arturo di Cadilhac, born Margaret Collier, has written some valuable books about life in Italy, I met constantly as one of the directors of the Authors' Club. He was also my sponsor for another club. He was very regular in his attendances at the Board Meetings of the Authors' Club, which he occasionally illuminated with a naive outbreak, as in his dictum about the National Liberal Club. At one of our Board Meetings, I was advocating some change in the financial arrangements of the billiard-room, and quoted as an example to be followed the rule at the National Liberal Club.

" National Liberal Club ! " cried Lord Monkswell, who was at that time Under-Secretary for War in a Liberal Government; " why, I don't call that a club at all—I call it a railway station ! "

Richard Orton Prowse has won admiration in high places with his work. One of his novels ran as a serial in the *Cornhill*, and he had a play produced by the " Stage Society." He used to come to Addison Mansions because we were in the same small house at Cheltenham College—Gantillon's, in Fauconberg Terrace. There were only about half-a-dozen boys in the house, but we used to knock up a game of football on a waste bit of ground at the back of the terrace, with two small day-boys who lived in an adjoining house. There were not more than eight of us all told—I think only seven, and of the seven, besides Prowse and myself, there were the two famous Renshaws, and the two famous Lambs. The Renshaws were very small boys in those days, but so absolutely certain in their catching, and their drop-kicking, that they counted in football games with boys three or four years older. When they grew up, their extraordinary scientificness in games was proved in the lawn-tennis courts, because for years, until one of them died by his own hand, they were undisputed champions. As it happened, I never met either of them after they left school, but one day I was driving through a remote Buckinghamshire village, White Waltham or something of the kind, with a friend, when we observed a crowd, in the street outside the village pound, of persons whom you would not have expected in such a place. We inquired what the trouble was, and found that it was an inquest on a suicide—one of the famous Renshaws.

Curiously enough, there was the same element of tragedy in the history of the brothers Lamb—Captain Thomas Lamb and Captain Edward Lamb, were for years the finest shots in the British army. Edward Lamb was the only boy who ever won the Spencer Cup twice; when he was at school, there had never been such a shot at a public school. Thomas Lamb, who had the finest nerve I ever remember in any one, broke down in a match when he went over to the United States to represent England, and was so mortified that he shot himself on the way home.

I shall always remember with pride that I was the first person who ever put a rifle into the hands of those two Lambs. I taught them how to shoot, and did most of the explaining in that house in Fauconberg Terrace, Cheltenham. I was at the time Captain of the school shooting eight, and I had won the Spencer Cup myself in the Public Schools matches at the preceding Wimbledon Meeting. I rather despaired about Tommy Lamb; he was not quick at taking things in, but I knew that if he could learn to shoot, his nerve and his doggedness might carry him to any heights of success. The houses of Fauconberg Terrace were very high, and there was a high parapet about a foot wide on the roof. I have seen Tommy Lamb run along that parapet from end to end. He said, " If it was only two or three feet from the ground, instead of two or three feet from the roof, it would be nothing. Why should it make any difference? It is all the same to me."

Several feet from our study window, which had a storey underneath it, there was a railing of about the same width. He used to jump from our window on to that railing, and keep his balance. Anybody could do it, he said, if it was nearer the ground. Why should it make any difference?

And he was always ready to jump from a height of twenty or thirty feet, and never hurt himself.

The seventh boy in those football games was Frank Lamb, the youngest brother. I never heard if he did anything in after life, but we six, I am quite sure, had no thought beyond a football which bounced so unevenly on that piece of waste land.

Tommy Lamb was a very fine fellow, singularly modest about his achievements. Several years afterwards, when I first came back from Australia, I went down to Wimbledon to see the Public Schools Veterans' Match, in which I had captained Cheltenham three or four times. Lamb, who was then in the flower of his shooting, was very anxious that I should take his place in that year's team. He thought it so wrong that I should not be shooting. I had, fortunately, not fired off a rifle for at least three years, or I should have had great difficulty in dissuading him from effacing himself for me, and if I had been at my very best he would have been heavens above me in the form he showed. That was the sort of man he was. We were in the same house at Cheltenham for two or three years, so I knew him extremely well.

These chapters in no way exhaust the list of my novelist friends—they are merely reminiscences which I thought likely to interest readers about some of them. I have not mentioned, for instance, one of my greatest friends, that brilliant historical novelist, John Bloundelle-Burton; or Hornung, Doyle's brother-in-law, whom I first met out in Australia thirty years ago; or Richard Pryce, that dainty novelist and playwright; and I have passed by many other well-known authors whom I knew equally well and saw very often.

CHAPTER XXIV

OTHER AUTHOR FRIENDS

ONE is apt to let fiction speak for itself, as if it represented the whole of literature. But it does not. Several of the men mentioned below are novelists, but they owe their importance more to other books.

The late W. H. Wilkins, who was much at our house, is an example. Wilkins, who was the son and heir of a West Country Squire, was an extraordinary mixture—a man of fashion, who was at the same time an industrious museum-worker. He wrote admirable books on the Georgian Courts. But he will be best remembered as the editor to whom Lady Burton entrusted her manuscripts for publication. It was from him that I learned the irreparable loss which she inflicted on literature by burning a number of Burton's manuscripts because of the grossnesses which they contained. There was no reason why any of these grossnesses should have been published—the manuscripts could have been printed with lacunæ where these passages occurred, and the manuscripts could have been left to the nation in the British Museum on condition that the offending passages never were published. But the idea of burning unpublished works about Arabia, by the greatest of all explorers of Arabia and students of Arab customs, was too infamous. Wilkins put it down to her religion. She was a very ardent Roman Catholic.

He had a good deal to do with the *Ladies' Realm* in its early days, when it was published by Hutchinson, and I believe he had a good deal to do with the formation of the fortnightly part publications for which this house is famous. He certainly was a friend and constant adviser of Hutchinson's. His books enjoyed a considerable sale. The novel

300

he wrote in collaboration with Herbert Vivian was one of the last of the three-volumers.

Wilkins was a man of strong likes and dislikes, very affectionate to his friends. Like E. H. Cooper, he was a well-known figure in society as well as in literary circles— and, curiously enough, he, too, was lame.

Joseph Shaylor, the managing secretary of the Whitefriars Club, and the managing director of Simpkin, Marshall, Hamilton, Kent & Co., the largest wholesale booksellers in the world, I have known almost as long. It is interesting to note that Shaylor, besides being the largest dealer in books commercially, has a most intimate and discriminating knowledge of all the books which are worth reading, and issues delightful little books on books, including his dear little annual *From Friend to Friend*.

Every one knows his volume called *The Fascination of Books*. His career is a romance; it reminds one of Dick Whittington. He has himself told us that he is a self-made man—*i. e.* he has had nothing but his own intelligence and grit to help him. He was born in Stroud in 1844, where he was apprenticed to a bookseller named Clark. It was part of Shaylor's duty to fetch the London papers from the train in the morning. In 1864 he came to London, at once entering the firm of Simpkin, Marshall & Co. His diligence and business acumen generally was noted, and after a while he was given charge of one of the departments. It became increasingly evident to his employers that their confidence in, and judgment of, this young man from the country had not been misplaced, and within five or six years after the formation of the company, as it now stands, Shaylor was elected to the position of one of the managing directors.

Shaylor is an authority on the history of books and book-selling, and has many interesting stories to tell of how things were done in the trade years ago, when life was more leisurely. In those golden days, reviewers had some power; a good review in *The Times* sold two hundred thousand copies of *The Fight at Dame Europa's School*, timidly brought out in the very smallest way, and an article in *The World* sold four hundred copies of *Called Back*. How a book sells depends very much upon the original subscription before publication, of which Shaylor, as head of the world's biggest buyers, thinks it worthy.   Of him it may be justly said that he has his finger on the pulse of English literature and that his diagnosis is accepted by the world.

Ernest Thompson Seton—who took for his pen-name Ernest Seton Thompson—came to us first many years ago, when he became engaged to a friend of ours, the beautiful Grace Gallatin, daughter of the Speaker of the California House of Representatives.   A descendant of the last Earl of Winton, he went to Canada when he was only five, and lived in the backwoods for ten years.   Then he went to school and college in Canada, and had two years' art-training in London before he returned to Manitoba to study natural history, eventually becoming naturalist to the Manitoba Government.   In 1898, when he was thirty-eight years old, he published his *Wild Animals I have Known—the Biographies of Eight Wild Animals*, which went through ten editions in the first year, and was the foundation of his fame and large fortune.   He founded the outdoor-life movement, known as *The Woodcraft Indians*, which has a membership of nearly a hundred thousand, and in addition to his soundness as a naturalist, he is the most dramatic lecturer I have ever heard.   He lectures on the psychology of wild animals as if they were human beings, and is said to be the most popular lecturer living.   His books about wild animals have delightful sketches of animal playfulness and humanness in their margins, some of which are by himself, and some by his wife.

Dr. Dillon, whose articles in the *Daily Telegraph* on the Balkan question during the war formed the most illuminating comment on the subject, I have been meeting for years at Violet Hunt's.   He is an elderly man, who looks more the scholar and the recluse than the publicist with his finger on the pulse of all Eastern Europe.

Max Beerbohm, Sir Herbert Beerbohm Tree's brother, is recognised as one of the most brilliant wits and intuitive critics of the day, as well as our most inspired caricaturist. There are few educated people in England who are not familiar with his work.   I met him first at a dinner of the Women Journalists.   We were both guests of the Club, and

Mrs. T. P. O'Connor, who was in the chair, said to me, "You know Max Beerbohm, don't you?"

I did not know him, though I had always wanted to know him, because I was a great admirer of his work and his wit. I said, "No, I don't," and was about to add what pleasure it would give me, when he took the words out of my mouth by saying, "I refuse not to be known by Mr. Douglas Sladen." That was our introduction.

He was in splendid form that night. He and a man with an unpronounceable Polish name, who was one of the leading foreign journalists in London, were deputed to reply for the visitors. The Pole, who spoke very broken English, at interminable length, made Max Beerbohm very angry, because he hated the idea of speaking to a jaded audience, so when at length his colleague sat down, and he rose to make his speech, he began, "I, too, am a foreigner. I go about in holy terror of the Tariff Reform League."

The audience recognised that he was really alluding to the Aliens Act, and rocked with laughter.

I remember Mark Twain being similarly annoyed at a dinner of the American Society, when he had to speak after a number of verbose platitudinarians. He was quite dispirited when he rose, and confined himself to a few sentences. After the dinner was over, he told me this, and he went on to say, "But I was wrong, for the late Sir Henry Brackenbury spoke after me, and look what he did with the audience! He took them up in his hand, and moved them to tears and laughter, just as he pleased."

That speech of Sir Henry's certainly was magnificently eloquent. It was during, or just after, the South African War, and the phrases in which he alluded to the war swept the audience, though they were mostly Americans, right off their feet; they were as fine as John Bright's immortal allusion to hearing the angels' wings in his Crimean War speech. I only once heard a finer speech—the sermon preached in St. Paul's by the present Archbishop of York, then Bishop of Stepney, upon the centenary of Nelson's death. In that sermon over and over again the words were flames. There is nothing so inspiring as a supreme speech at a supreme moment.

Dr. G. C. Williamson, the art editor of George Bell & Sons, is one of the most potent figures in the world of art— in fact, there are few branches of art on which he has not got any reasonable information at his fingers' tips. He has written books which have met with wide acceptation on several of them, and has been a great collector and traveller.

I met him under curious circumstances. We were both, though I did not know him then, in St. Peter's, witnessing the Jubilee of Leo XIII. On occasions like this in Italy no one interferes with the liberty of the sight-seer, and as I was not, in the nature of things, likely to see the Jubilee of another Pope, and I had to write a description of it, I determined to seize whatever opportunity I could for seeing it, without any *mauvais honte*. The cathedral had been so packed for the past six hours that it was practically impossible to see anything unless you seized some coign of vantage. Williamson and I were standing close to one of the great piers of the nave, and the base had a projection some feet from the ground. I determined to stand on it, but he was between me and the pier. He very good-naturedly made way for me, and helped me to scramble up, calling out " *Viva il papa re ! Viva il papa re !* " all the time. I offered, of course, to share my giddy eminence with him, turn and turn about, but he was a devout Catholic, and though he saw no harm in my ambitions, which he furthered so nobly, he was quite content to be in the church, and worshipping. He did not want to see more than everybody saw without striving, when at last it happened—the carrying of the frail old Pope on his *Sedia Gestatoria*, supported on men's shoulders, between the snow-white *flabella*.

When it was all over, we exchanged cards, and that was the beginning of my friendship with the famous art-critic.

It certainly was about the most impressive sight I ever saw—that vast cathedral, packed with a hundred thousand human beings, with the nonagenarian Pope dressed in snow-white garments borne on his moving throne from the High Altar to the Chapel of the Crucifix.

It is not too much to say that literary London felt a shock when it heard that William Sinclair had resigned the Arch-deaconry of London which he had held with such conspicuous success for twenty-two years, and retired to a Sussex benefice. He had been one of the foremost figures in every London function of the time, since the Jubilee of Queen Victoria, and he had started life as a Scholar of Balliol and President of the Union—the University Debating Society at Oxford. Being a bachelor, there was no reason why he should restrict himself to dining at home, and, consequently, he was the most prominent figure at public dinners, of a patriotic, philanthropic or useful character, where he spoke comparatively seldom, considering what a good speaker he is. Being a connection of half the Scottish aristocracy—he is a cousin of the Lord of the Isles—he was equally conspicuous in country-house parties. A constant attendant at the functions of the Authors' and other literary clubs, his eminence as an ecclesiastic and a public man obscured the fact that his performances as an author were among the most distinguished of those present, for he has a gift of saying wise things in epigrammatic form. His *magnum opus* is a book on his own cathedral, and here I may incidentally remark that few archdeacons have ever exercised such influence on the Dean over the care of the cathedral. His great object was to emphasise the voice of St. Paul's as that of the nation in its religious aspect, and it was with this view that he prevailed on the Dean and Chapter and the Crown to install the Imperial Order of St. Michael and St. George in the Chapel of the Cathedral where they meet for annual commemorations. His loss, also, from the Sunday afternoon pulpit of St. Paul's has been distinctly felt. It was one of the institutions of London. He was a wise man to retire for leisure to write and travel while he was still in his prime.

Basil Wilberforce, the Archdeacon of Westminster, and son of the great Bishop, I came to know because we used to meet at dinner at Lady Lindsay's. It was there that I heard him declare his firm faith in the Holy Grail—I am refering to the vessel which had been discovered a short time before at Glastonbury Abbey, and which was believed to emanate a luminous *aura* at night, from time to time. The Archdeacon declined the honour of having it left in his bedroom at night to test the truth of the allegation, either because he thought his emotions might act on his imagina-

x

tion, or because he did not think himself worthy, but I understand that it was left in Sir William Crookes', the great F.R.S.'s room for three nights without his observing any phenomena.

I remember George Russell—the Rt. Hon. G. W. E. Russell, the editor of Matthew Arnold's letters, and Under-Secretary for India in Lord Rosebery's Government—who was present that night, interposing a jarring note of incredulity, which the Archdeacon very sweetly forgave in an old friend.

Until her prolonged absences from London for ill-health, Mrs. Neish, the wife of the Registrar of the Privy Council, was, on account of the remarkable rapidity with which she made her way in literature as well as for her beauty, a conspicuous figure in London literary society. She made her way so quickly because she was a born writer, and mingled the witty and the pathetic naturally. She was a daughter of Sir Edwin Galsworthy. There is literature in the family. She is a first cousin of the great novelist and playwright, John Galsworthy. Her husband's father was a Scottish laird, who in an inspired moment advanced the capital for founding the *Dundee Advertiser*. She has often done the *Saturday Westminster* and written many nature sketches.

One of the principal figures in literary society, and one of my most valued friends, is M. H. Spielmann, the great art critic who discovered and bought the lost Velasquez a year or two ago. Spielmann was for seventeen years editor of the *Magazine of Art*, and is an authority on *Punch* and its contributors, as well as on painting and sculpture. He is the author of several standard works, and has been juror in the Fine Arts' section of innumerable exhibitions. He is also a keen politician on the Conservative side, though he is the brother-in-law of the Rt. Hon. Herbert Samuel, and is an admirable speaker. But you always feel that it is not his accomplishments which count in Spielmann, though he has so many; it is himself—his shining character, his almost feminine gentleness and considerateness, combined with unusual firmness and principle. There are few men in London who could be so ill spared as Spielmann.

THE JAPANESE ROOM AT 3² ADDISON MANSIONS

(From the Painting by Yoshio Markino.)

CHAPTER XXV

FRIENDS WHO NEVER CAME TO ADDISON MANSIONS

I OUGHT to say something here of the interesting people I have known, who never happened to come to Addison Mansions, for one reason or another.

Distance prevented the great Dr. Boyd of St. Andrews—the famous A.K.H.B., of whom I saw a good deal in the long summer I spent at St. Andrews—from coming. Dr. Boyd possessed the most crushing powers of repartee of any person I ever met. One day, when he was walking with me along the street at St. Andrews, which leads down to the links, some one presented an American publisher, a partner in a famous firm, to him.

"I am very glad to meet you, Dr. Boyd," said the publisher. "I enjoyed your *Scenes from Clerical Life* so much."

"I did not write that book, sir," said the terrible Doctor. "I wrote *The Recreations of a Country Parson*—and you ought to know it, because your firm stole them both."

I once unconsciously helped him in using this talent, which happened in this wise. Dr. Boyd was a reformer as drastic as John Knox. The great humanising movement in the Scottish Church, which made its services and music so much more beautiful and its attitude so much less angular, was largely his work, for he was not only one of the most eloquent of the notable ministers who worked for it, but he had any amount of backbone. An old ultra-Protestant lady, having perceived this, paid an evangelist a thousand a year to go about Scotland preaching against him. One Sunday he was at St. Andrews, on the public space where the inhabitants used to practice archery, preaching against Dr. Boyd. His preaching was all " limehousing," an appeal to the coarsest

307

prejudice, most banal abuse and derision.   It was so ludicrous
that I took most of it down in longhand, in the intervals when
he paused for applause, as he did whenever he imagined that
he was scoring.   It so happened that I was having afternoon-
tea with Dr. Boyd, and that he was preaching in his own
church that evening.   I began to sympathise with him in
being made the subject of such a persecution.

" Were you there? " he asked.   I nodded.

" Do you remember at all what he said? "

I produced my notes.

" Do you mind reading them out to me? " he asked, after
a despairing glance at the writing.   I did.   He took no
notes; but he had an admirable memory, and he evidently
took it all in, for that evening, without having lowered his
dignity by being present at the evangelist's attack on him,
he turned the tables on the offender from his own pulpit,
with a dissection of his remarks which can only be compared
to throwing vitriol, though it was all done with beautiful
polish and observance of form.

He was never more amusing than when he was sympathis-
ing about the difficulties which he described Andrew Lang
as experiencing when he came to St. Andrews.   He was such
a master of innuendo.

Dr. Boyd wrote his books in handwriting so minute that
he could get two thousand words on to one foolscap page.
The firm who always printed them for his publishers had
large magnifying glasses fitted to the case on which his copy
was fixed for setting it up.   And Dr. Boyd was very proud
of it.

One of Dr. Boyd's sons has inherited his power as a writer
—my friend Charles Boyd, who acted for some time as
private secretary to Cecil Rhodes in South Africa.

Sir Charles Dilke, M.P., took a flattering interest in my
books, and was very friendly in his intercourse with me.
The most amusing reminiscences I have in connection with
him are à propos of a dinner at which we were both taken in,
though I was too obscure for it to signify in my case.

A dinner for a high-sounding object was given at Prince's.
Sixty important public men and leading writers and journal-

ists were invited, and Sir Charles Dilke was asked to respond to the toast of the evening.

His rising to speak was the signal for three great acetylene flares to be turned on, which reduced the scores of electric lights in the room to looking like the gas jets in the Richmond railway-station. This was taken as a compliment to Sir Charles, though it would have disconcerted any less practised speaker.

When his speech and the other speeches were over, the chairman electrified the assemblage by informing them that a new sort of gramophone would reproduce for them Tennyson's last words in the voice in which he spoke them. It was a most impressive moment. For a few minutes one did not realise the colossal impertinence of pretending that there had been a phonograph in Tennyson's bedroom on this solemn occasion. But, of course, the record might have been produced by a man who knew Tennyson's voice well enough to imitate it, as certain reciters imitate celebrated actors. We did not realise this at the time. The next day the dinner was duly reported, with the names of the makers of these wonderful lamps, and this wonderful phonetic record, and later on it transpired that these two parties had paid for the dinner, which was only got up to advertise them.

This is one of the two cleverest pieces of journalism I remember. The other happened on the night that King Edward died. A great London linen-draping firm had an elaborate intelligence system during the well-beloved monarch's last illness. They were well served. I happened to see the head of the firm about twelve hours before the nation was plunged into mourning.

" You may take it from me," he said, " that his Majesty won't live another twenty-four hours."

As he was in the habit of making impressive statements, I discounted what he said. But he was right, and acting on his information, he bought up all the available mourning in the market, and scored a huge business victory. I met him long afterwards, and alluded to the information which he had given me.

" I wasn't the only one who took pains to know," he said,

" for that night, at the hour the King died, I was driving from the hotel, where I had been dining, to my office, with the correspondent of one of the great French newspapers. As we passed the Palace, one of the top windows was opened, and a person came to it with a lighted candle, and blew it out. ' Did you see that? Do you mind driving me to the West Strand post-office? " said my French friend. ' Why, no,' I said; ' but what do you want to go there for? ' ' To send a cipher-wire to my paper that his Majesty is dead.' ' Isn't it a great risk? ' I asked. ' If it was, I would take it. But even a good rumour is worth something.' "

The Frenchman was right, and he won his victory.

The late Lord Dufferin was another man who was very kind to me about my writings. I suppose that they appealed to him for the same reason that they appealed to Dilke. Both of them were deeply interested in Greater Britain, and in travel generally, and I have written books full of enthusiasm for travel and the Colonies.

Lord Dufferin never forgot any one who had served him. When his new title forced a new signature on him, he sent a new photograph with the Dufferin and Ava signature to all his journalist friends, though some of them had passed out of his sphere for years.

He always did the right thing. I remember the late Lord Derby beginning a speech at a dinner at Winnipeg at which I was present, " As Lord Dufferin, who seems to have left nothing unsaid, observed," etc.

On that same vice-regal progress to the West, I was showing Lord Derby some Kodaks I had taken on various occasions at which he had been present—crowded functions in cities, full-dress rehearsals of Chippeway Indians on the war-path, and the like. One print was from a negative which I had of these Chippewas, with their necklaces of cartridges and their feather head-dresses, taken on the top of the massed choirs of Manitoba, singing " God save the Queen." Lord Derby begged this photograph from me, " That's a photograph of the whole trip," he said.

He remained surprisingly popular, considering the mala-droitness of one of his aide-de-camps—a delightful Guardsman

who is now dead. I have heard this A.D.C., whom Nature
had gifted with the most graceful manners, say appalling
things.

At one provincial capital, the mayor gave a ball in Lord
Derby's honour. I had just been presented to the mayor,
and was standing quite close to him, when Lord Derby came
in. When the official presentation was over, Lord Derby,
who always wished to get on a friendly footing with his hosts,
asked his A.D.C. in a whisper, " What is the mayor, M——? "
The Governor-General wished to know if his host bred cattle,
or ran a timber-mill, or owned a hotel, or what, so that he
might say the appropriate thing. But the A.D.C.'s reply,
which, like Lord Derby's " What is the mayor, M——? ",
was perfectly audible to that functionary, was " Toned-
down Jew." So much for the *entente cordiale* at—we will
call it Medicine Hat.

At a ball given by Lord Derby, I watched that same
A.D.C. taking an important politician, whom he should have
known perfectly well, to introduce him to his own wife, a
young and pretty woman who considered herself one of the
lions of Canadian society. The situation struck me as a
promising one, so I listened to hear what he would say.

" Mrs. Um," he said; " may I introduce Mr. Um-um to
you? " She looked up at him with an amused smile, and
he continued quite blissfully, " He's a stupid old buffer, but
I'll get you away from him as soon as I can."

CHAPTER XXVI

MY TRAVELLER FRIENDS

Considering the number of years which I have devoted to travel, I have not met a great many explorers, certainly nothing like so many as I should have met if I had been a regular attendant at the meetings of the Royal Geographical Society. These interest me extremely, but I have an unfortunate habit of going to sleep at lectures, however interesting I find them, so I shrink from going to them. Otherwise I should have joined the society long ago, and been a regular attendant.

The last time I went there was many years ago, when a great explorer and mighty hunter had just returned from Mashonaland. He read an immensely interesting paper; I quite forgot to go to sleep. Among the speakers who followed was a pompous old gentleman, who scourged the lecturer with the most inane platitudes, winding up with the question, " May I ask the lecturer what he thinks of the climate of Mashonaland ? " and the explorer replied, " There's nothing wrong with the climate of Mashonaland, but it isn't the sort of place where you could get drunk and lie all night in the gutter, without knowing about it the next morning."

The old gentleman gasped, and so, I think, did the audience, but the lecturer seemed quite unconscious that he had done anything beyond giving sound advice.

My friendship with the famous Dr. George Ernest Morrison, of Peking, I have described· in the chapter on Australians. When I was living in Melbourne, I saw a good deal at the Melbourne Club of Augustus Gregory, one of the doyens of Australian exploration, actually the first, I believe, to accomplish the transcontinental journey successfully. He told

ie that when their supplies ran short, the things they missed
iost in the terrific heat were fat and sugar. When their
rater ran short, they more than once refilled their water-
ottles by wringing the dew out of their blankets.

Curiously enough, fat and sugar were the things equally
iost missed by a party of Canadian explorers who were
ngaged one winter in finding the pass by which the Canadian
'acific Railway crossed the Rocky Mountains. Their leader,
rho was running a small steamer up from Golden City to
he source of the Columbia in Lake Windermere, told me
o, when I was a passenger with him. I had just shot a wild
oose on a shoal with my Winchester rifle from the deck of
he steamer, and he had come out of his cabin to see what the
iatter was.

I had a unique experience at that Canadian Lake Winder-
iere. I was lying flat on my back in the reedy shallows at
ts edge, enjoying a bath in water above human temperature,
rhen a deputation of ranchers waited on me to ask if I would
ct as judge in the annual horse-races for Red Indians,
rhich were to be held that afternoon. They had heard that
n author had come up with the steamer from Golden City,
nd wished to pay me this unique compliment. I protested
ay inexperience in the matter, but dressed and accompanied
hem to a sort of pulpit made of fresh lumber, which I occupied
rhile half a dozen races were run on little barebacked horses
I wondered if these were *mustangs*, but did not dare to show
ay ignorance by inquiring) by naked braves and squaws
n trousers with a feather trimming down the seam.
is I escaped uninjured, I suppose that my judgments were
ccepted. Colonel Baker, a brother of Valentine and Sir
amuel, was one of the deputation.

In the time of which I am writing, when people came back
rom the wilds, it was the fashion to fête them at the literary
lubs. In this way I met Captain Lugard, who was fresh
iack from his strenuous efforts in Uganda, and Mr. F. C.
ielous, when he came back from his pioneer expedition to
fashonaland and Matabeleland, which led to their annexa-
ion, and the foundation of Rhodesia. Selous was the
reatest hunter that England ever sent to South Africa.

For twenty years he made his living as an elephant-hunter and collector of rare natural history specimens, and took the chief part in bringing about the annexation of Matabeleland.   In later days he has taken a great part in the measures for preserving the wild animals of Africa by a splendid system of game laws, far stricter than our own.

Of all the author-explorers who came to Addison Mansions, I have known none so well as Arnold Henry Savage Landor, grandson of the poet Walter Savage Landor.   I first met Landor at Louise Chandler Moulton's house in Boston, on one Sunday night in 1888, when he was twenty years old, and I have seen him constantly ever since.   While we were at Washington, as I have said elsewhere, he was my guest for a week.   We were at Montreal together one winter season, and saw each other nearly every day, and when we got to Japan, almost the first person we saw there was Landor. We stayed in the same hotel there for months.

When we first met Landor, he was an artist, who made a considerable income by portrait-painting.   It was not until after we had met in Japan that he went upon his first exploring expedition among the Hairy Ainu in the North Island of Yezo and the Kuriles.

After we left Japan, he went across to China, and went very far afield in it.   But he did not achieve world-wide fame until he made his expedition into the Forbidden Land. Every one has read of the tortures to which he was subjected there, but it is not every one who met him on his way back, as we did, when his spine was so injured that he could not sit down, and his eyes still had a white film over them from being bleared with fire.   I knew of his endurance, because I had seen him go out in Montreal in an ordinary English overcoat and bowler when the thermometer was twenty-five below zero; and I knew of his courage from the fracas he had with the New York police when they were breaking the queue at the Centenary Ball for people who gave them money to get in out of their place, in which he came within an ace of being clubbed.

Landor is always witty.   I heard him say to a man who was bragging to him about the size of everything in his country, "You see, I am so small that I have to come into a room twice before any one can see me."

He is also extremely courageous. I once heard a dispute between him and a man of six feet two, whose portrait he was painting. While he was painting it, he did a small commission for this man's partner, who wanted it in a great hurry as a wedding-present.

"If you work for other people, I won't have the portrait," said the giant.

"You must have it," said Landor.

"Upon my word as a gentleman, nothing can make me have it," said the giant, whose name was B——.

"Mr. B——," said Landor, "*nothing* could make you behave like a gentleman."

And his courage in taking other risks is just as great.

Undismayed by his experiences in Thibet, he was back in the Himalayas two years afterwards, and reached an altitude of 23,490 ft. He was with the Allied troops on their march to Peking, and was the first European to enter the Forbidden City. He visited four hundred islands in the Philippines in a Government steamer, lent him by the United States for the purpose. He crossed Africa in the widest part, marching 8,500 miles to do it, and he crossed South America from Rio di Janeiro in Brazil to Lima in Peru, over the great central plateau, across the swamps of the Amazon and the heights of the Andes, with followers selected from the most desperate criminals in the gaols, because they were the only Brazilians who would undertake the risk. That last journey alone cost him seven thousand pounds. All Mr. Landor's books are illustrated with his own paintings and photographs. It must be remembered that he was an artist before he was an explorer or an author.

Though he is contemptuous of hardships and semi-starvation in his explorations, and travels with a lighter equipment than any other explorer, he likes luxurious surroundings when he is back in civilisation, and lives in a charming flat in one of our most luxurious hotels.

He also has a large estate in Italy, near Empoli and Vinci, where he has carried on the wine-growing business very successfully.   Landor's mother is an Italian, and he himself was born and educated at Florence, where his father, a younger son of the celebrated Walter Savage Landor, has always lived, and amassed a magnificent collection of works of art.

It is not generally known that Landor was one of the first to take up the invention of aeroplanes.   He began long before the Wrights, as long ago as 1893, when he succeeded in flying a hundred yards, and later he built a more perfected machine not unlike the ordinary aeroplanes.   But he was away, making his celebrated journeys across Africa and South America while the invention advanced with such leaps and bounds, and he abandoned aviation.

Landor speaks many languages.   He has lectured in English, Italian, French, and German, before learned societies, and he can speak several other European and Oriental languages and many savage dialects.   For he has travelled all over the world, although the attention of the public has been concentrated on the big journeys of exploration which have formed the subjects of his books.

Sir H. M. Stanley I only knew after he had retired from exploring, and was living at Richmond Terrace, Whitehall. I met him through having been a friend of his wife, who, as Dorothy Tennant, was a leading figure in the most brilliant set in London Society, and in so many altruistic movements. I had met her brother, Charles Combe Tennant, when we were both at Oxford—he at Balliol and I at Trinity.   He either proposed me or seconded me, I forget which, for the Apollo, my other sponsor being J. E. C. Bodley, who was both at Harrow and Balliol with Tennant.   Bodley has since become a very distinguished literary man.   He is perhaps the best writer we have upon French Constitutional questions, and he was selected by the late King Edward VII to write the book on the coronation, which involved a very wide knowledge of the British Constitution.

Lady Stanley wrote a book on London Street Arabs and put together and edited an admirable autobiography of her famous first husband, whose name she retains.   Her sister married Frederick Myers of Psychical fame, the greatest Cambridge scholar of his generation.

But it is not only the books she has written, and the brilliant intellectual people whom she has gathered around her, which constitute her claim to being remembered, for she has taken a leading part in the betterment of London. She has naturally worked hardest in Lambeth, where she became acquainted with the swarming thousands of Surrey when Stanley was member for one of the Lambeth Divisions, and it was from Lambeth that she drew most of her boy-models to make studies for her book illustrations of London ragamuffins.

Isabella Bird—Mrs. Bishop—one of the most famous travellers in the East, I met once near Hakone in Japan. She was a curious-looking old lady, dressed like a native woman, with nothing but rope-sandals, which cost three-halfpence a pair, on her feet. We came upon her very suddenly, because Norma Lorimer and I had gone in to examine the interior of a pretty building made of some light-coloured, unpainted wood, into which people seemed to go as they pleased. As Miss Lorimer was then not long out of her teens, and the building proved to contain naked men and women bathing together, only separated by a bamboo floating on the top of the steaming pool, we came out much quicker than we went in, and almost fell upon Isabella Bird and her attendant.

When we were at Khartum, the Sirdar, Sir Reginald Wingate, introduced me to the famous Father Ohrwalder, the good old Austrian priest who had made the sensational escape from Omdurman twenty years before, and wrote the extraordinarily vivid account of his captivity which is one of our principal sources of knowledge of life in Omdurman. He was then a venerable old man, with a patriarchal beard, very frail, and exhausted by conversing for a few minutes, but the Austrian Bishop, who spoke excellent English, took his place, and we had an interesting conversation. He was not, he informed me, allowed to make converts in the northern part of the Sudan, where the inhabitants are chiefly Mohammedan. I asked him if he made many converts among the pagans in the southern part. He said not as many as he ought, but I elicited from him that he set his face sternly against polygamy, and the Sirdar's Intelligence officer had informed us that one of the favourite forms of investment in those provinces was to buy as many wives as you could and make them work for you.

Wingate himself was most kind to us during our visit to the Sudan. He placed his three steamers or yachts at our disposal, and deputed his Intelligence officer to accompany us, whenever he had no actual need of him.

The late John Ward, F.S.A., I never met on any of his journeys to Egypt or the Sudan or Sicily, though we corresponded for some years. I have found his books most valuable. He had a perfect genius for collecting indispensable illustrations, and his books are encyclopædias of local colour.

The late George Warrington Steevens, the finest correspondent the *Daily Mail* ever had—it is said that they paid him five thousand a year—a small, pale, delicate-looking man, with double eye-glasses, and an alert, rather humorous expression, used to come to us at Addison Mansions with his wife. She was a good deal older than he was, but he always said that she had been the making of his career, which came to an untimely end while he was besieged in Ladysmith.

His conversation was as sparkling as his journalism. I remember when we were discussing Kitchener's conquest of the Sudan at the Authors' Club one night, telling him that Maxwell (now Sir John Maxwell, late commanding the Army of Occupation in Egypt), who was one of Kitchener's most trusted officers, had been at Cheltenham College with me.

"What sort of man is Maxwell now?" I asked; and he answered, "The sort of man you put in charge of a conquered town."

Arthur Weigall, who was Inspector of Monuments in Upper Egypt when we were there, came to see us several times at Addison Mansions. One hardly expected to find a member of the great Kent cricketing family one of the chief experts in deciphering Egyptian inscriptions and judging their antiquities. Weigall was rather superstitious for so great an Egyptologist, though I confess that I should not have liked to outrage the dignity of the tomb of a queen at Thebes, as he and a house-party he had at his fine mansion on the river near Luxor, proposed to do. They got up a sort of comedy to be performed in the tomb, and the performance was blocked by a series of accidents—sudden illness, the breaking of a leg, and so on.

We had a delightful expedition with him to some of the less-known tombs at Thebes. At his house I saw a couple of articles he had published in *Blackwood's Magazine* on Aknaton, the heretic Pharaoh, and I think Queen Ti. I saw at a glance that, like Sir Frederick Treves, he was a born writer, with quite a Pierre Loti feeling for style, and learned, to my surprise, that he had not been able to find a publisher for two books which he had ready. I gave him a letter of introduction to my literary agent, setting forth the circumstances, which resulted in the instant acceptance of both books by leading publishers. One of them was his admirable *Guide to the Antiquities of Upper Egypt*.

Edward Ayrton, a most brilliant young Egyptologist, who discovered the famous gold treasure in the tombs of the Kings at Thebes, and has since been Government Archæologist in Ceylon, we met at his lonely hut among the tombs of the Kings. We came upon him the first time, dressed in immaculate flannels, as if he was just starting off for a tennis match, and playing *diavolo*. He is young enough to have been at St. Paul's with my son. It required a man of strong nerve to live where he lived, surrounded by the spirits of so many Egyptian monarchs and their great officers, and practically at the mercy of any evilly-disposed Arabs. The spirits of bygone Egyptians have, above all others, in the history of psychical science, manifested their sustained interest in human affairs. Ayrton was acting then, not for the Government, but for a rich American.

John Foster Fraser, who was my colleague on *To-day*, though he is so much younger than I am, a remarkably able and energetic man, who once went a bicycle tour of nearly twenty thousand miles round the earth, and would have gone farther if the land had not come to an end, has made many long and adventurous journeys through dangerous countries, and has written notable books. The story I liked best about his wanderings was that he always used the public tooth-brush, provided by a civilised Shah who had been to Europe, in the rest-houses of Persia. He certainly added that no previous visitor to these rest-houses had ever known what the brushes were used for.

Speaking of teeth, I once knew a dentist who visited Persia. Knowing the prestige of the royal family there, he thought that his fortune was made, when the Shah and his mother ordered sets of false teeth—the Shah's made of pearls, I think, and his mother's of diamonds. But next day he was overtaken by a crushing blow. The Shah, to prevent false teeth from becoming too common, confined their use to the royal family, and the poor dentist had to fall back on writing novels—it was C. J. Wills.

This Shah, or another, on his return from a visit to Europe, made his entire harem adopt British ballet-girls' skirts.

This same Shah, when he visited London, asked the Secretary of State for Foreign Affairs to recommend some one to show him round the gilded hells of London. The man, whose accomplishments thus received official recognition, gave great satisfaction, I believe, but as he is still alive, I shall not divulge his name, lest he should be overwhelmed with overtures from publishers. His mother was a famous Society hostess.

I have known some Arctic and Antarctic explorers. I was, as I have mentioned elsewhere, in the chair at the Savage Club on the night that we entertained Nansen. Trevor-Battye, who afterwards conducted an expedition to Kolguev in the Barents Sea, himself, came up to me, asking me to introduce him to Nansen. Of course, I had great pleasure in doing so. Nansen, who was a tall, wiry man, and looked much less at home in his dress-clothes and his Orders than in his Arctic furs, looked my friend up and down. The latter was a remarkably smart-looking man, and was very well dressed. Nansen was not to know that he came of a family famed for their strength and endurance in Indian frontier warfare, so he said with a smile, which showed the wide openings between his teeth in his lower jaw, " If you come with me, remember that you won't be able to wash for

three years "—he meant, of course, after they had got to
the Arctic regions. Battye, who is a most distinguished
naturalist, and a well-known author, was not deterred, but
Nansen's list was already really full. Battye was editor-
in-chief of Natural History in the Victoria History of the
Counties of England. At the Authors' Club, where he was a
habitué in those days, we used to ask him why he had not
gone to the North Pole whenever we wanted to get a rise
out of him. He was a frequent visitor to our house.

Another Arctic explorer who often came to see us after
he had got back from his three years in the Arctic circle, was
Fred Jackson, who conducted the Jackson-Harmsworth
expedition. Jackson was a very adventurous man. He had
made an expedition across the Great Tundra Desert, and
another across Australia, before he went to Franz Josef
Land. With his swarthy face, bright dark eyes, and general
air of *joie de vive*, Fred Jackson looks much more like the
manager of some great English business concern in the
Tropics than an Arctic explorer. Yet he was an Arctic
explorer, and a very hardy one. Everybody remembers
the photograph of the meeting of Nansen and Jackson in
the Arctic circle—Nansen swaddled to the chin in the fur
clothes of his kind, Jackson showing a starched English
collar, a proper tie, and a triangle of shirt-front.

Back from the Arctic circle, Jackson volunteered for
South Africa, distinguished himself, won medals, and became
a captain in the Manchester Regiment—*Hac arte Pollux.*

We often had with us I. N. Ford, whose advent to England
as correspondent of the *New York Tribune* was practically
the beginning of the *entente cordiale* between Great Britain
and the United States. His predecessor, the well-known
G. W. Smalley, had been very much spoiled in English society,
but he never set himself whole-heartedly to produce hearty
relations between the two countries any more than Harold
Frederic did in his corresponding in the *New York Times.*
The *Tribune*, had, in fact, been frequently in open hostility
to England—so open that I heard the following conversation
at a dinner-party in Washington in the year 1889 at Colonel
John Hay's. General Harrison had just been elected President of the United States, and the moderate Republicans

Y

made no secret of the fact that they would have liked to see Colonel John Hay, who had been Abraham Lincoln's private secretary, Harrison's Secretary of State. His character stood as high as any one's in America; no man since George Washington had been so fit to be President of the United States; for he was as clear-headed and able and unwavering as he was honourable, and his immense private wealth set him above temptation. But it was that very wealth which prevented him from being nominated. Americans are determined that wealth shall not command the Presidency as it has the Senate.

Well, that night Savage Landor and I and a number of leading American politicians—the men who were to form Harrison's Cabinet were most of them there—were dining with Hay at his palatial mansion, built in a heavy-browed sort of Spanish-Moresco style by the celebrated Richardson. The new President's private secretary, a commercialish little Englishman, had promised to come, and he kept us waiting so long that finally we went in to dinner without him, half-an-hour late.

At last he made his appearance, breathless, and, upsetting a water-bottle as he took his seat, blurted out, " Whitelaw Reid " (then editor and proprietor of the *Tribune*) " has been moving heaven and earth to get the Court of St. James' " (*i. e.* the post of American Minister to England), " but the President won't give it him. He's afraid that England will refuse to receive him because of the way in which the *Tribune* has behaved."

A good many years later he achieved the goal of his ambition, for I. N. Ford had come to England in the interval, and had made the *Tribune* to America what the London *Times* is to England in the matter of foreign politics. Ford had won distinction earlier as an author writing on travel in Central America.

Another man who did a lot of spade-work in promoting the *entente cordiale* was John Morgan Richards, who has lived in England for many years, and has more than once been President of the American Society of London. American from his backbone to his finger-tips, John Richards had a fine Quaker sense of justice and peace on earth which made the eagle lie down with the lion like a couple of lambs wherever he was present. His brilliant daughter, Mrs. Craigie —better known in literature as John Oliver Hobbes—was a potent link between the two countries.

Both he and his converse, G. R. Parkin, the Canadian, who was the real father of Imperial Federation, and who is now usefully and congenially employed in managing the Rhodes Scholarship Fund, were often at our house. G. R. Parkin and Gilbert Parker, another Canadian, were sometimes confused with each other in those days, by people who did not know them personally.

Canada has sent us a lot of good men. Beckles Willson, who lives in the old mansion in Kent which was the birthplace of General Wolfe, the conqueror of Canada, has poured out a stream of information about Canada in a most attractive form. Who does not remember the elder Pitt asking Wolfe, a boy of thirty-three, to dinner just after he had appointed him to command the military in Canada? Wolfe got very drunk, and for a moment Pitt feared that he had made a mistake. But he remembered how the boy had behaved under fire in that descent on the Breton coast, and let him go to Canada without misgivings.

I have known Seton Watson, the Perthshire Laird who has done so much for the Slav population of Hungary, since he was a small boy. When at New College, Oxford, he showed his future bent by winning the Stanhope—the University Prize for an historical essay. His first work, after he went down, was to translate Gregorovius's *Tombs of the Popes*. But he soon began to give his attention to Hungary, where he has travelled a great deal, and took up the cause of the Slav races who are being oppressed by the Magyars. He held a successful exhibition of their art in London a year or two ago.

Another friend of mine who has done similar good work is Campbell Mackellar. He, however, has chiefly devoted himself to the Balkans, and in Montenegro no Englishman is so well known and beloved. At his hospitable table I have met some of the leading representatives of the Balkan States who came to England during the war.

Connected both by property and family with Australia, his

book-writing has been chiefly about Australia, and it was he who wrote the description of the Adam Lindsay Gordon country in South Australia which appears in the book I wrote with Miss Humphris about *Adam Lindsay Gordon and His Friends in England and Australia*. Mackellar has likewise done a good deal for the recognition of Australian Art in London—a fact commemorated in an album of original sketches presented to him by the Australian artists who are over here.

It was no mere accident which made Miss Humphris and myself collaborate in *Adam Lindsay Gordon and His Friends in England and Australia*. It was true that we were strangers when she wrote to ask me to collaborate, but we brought common traditions to bear on the book. In Cheltenham, where Gordon spent his boyhood, Miss Humphris lives, and I was six years at the College. Gordon was a College boy, and his father was a College master. Miss Humphris could not be at the College, as I was, but her grandfather was the architect who built its principal buildings. Like Gordon, both Miss Humphris and I went to Australia, and we spent years there, though not so many as he did, and as a connection of one of Australia's greatest racing men—the famous Etienne de Mestre—it was natural that she should take an absorbing interest in the steeplechasing exploits of Adam Lindsay Gordon.

Edith Humphris has an extraordinary power of collecting and sifting materials for a book. Off her own bat, she collected all the facts of Gordon's early life at Cheltenham and Prestbury. The grist which I brought to the mill, besides a study of Gordon's life in Australia and his poems, which I had blocked out more than thirty years before, when I tried to get Cassell's to undertake its publication, was the mass of material put at my disposal by people who had known him in the flesh, and treasured remembrances and keepsakes of him. Miss Humphris knew that the letters to Charley Walker existed; I tracked their owner down and got permission to reproduce them. Henry Gyles Turner, who gave me leave to use all the materials in *Turner and Sutherland*, was a friend of mine in Australia. George Riddoch, who gave us all the Riddoch poems and reminiscences, is a friend

SIR GILBERT PARKER
Drawn by Yoshio Markino

of mine, introduced by old friends in Australia. Lambton Mount, Gordon's partner on the West Australian Station (brother of Harry Mount), is a friend of mine, and gave me all his information orally. General Strange, who was Gordon's friend at Woolwich, and wrote about him in *Gunner Jingo's Jubilee*, is an old, old friend of mine. Frederick Vaughan and Sir Frank Madden and Mrs. Lauder wrote their reminiscences for me, as did Campbell Mackellar of the Gordon country in South Australia. And John Bulloch, the editor of the *Graphic*, who wrote the wonderfully interesting pedigrees and chapters about Gordon's family, wrote them for me.

But Miss Humphris wrote all her part of the book, including a great deal about Gordon in Australia, herself, from studies which she had been making since she was a child.

Talking of Australia, at one time I saw a good deal of Basil Thomson, the son of the great Archbishop of York, who in those days was an author, but is now secretary of the Prison Commission, after having been governor of Dartmoor and Wormwood Scrubbs prisons.

Thomson, when I first knew him, had just come back from being Prime Minister of the Tonga Islands. I asked why he gave it up. He said that things were no longer what they had been in Government circles in Tonga; when he was there, even the Government could only raise the wind by having fresh issues of postage stamps manufactured for them by stamp-dealers in England, who paid for the privilege of selling the stamps in England without accounting for them to the Government of Tonga. But in the palmy days of Tonga it was very different. Then, a Prime Minister, who was also a Nonconformist missionary, procured the monopoly of selling trousers from the King of Tonga, before he induced the king to make the whole population turn Christian, and make it illegal to appear without trousers.

You sometimes hear people say, " What would you do if you were on a desert island? " I once came very near seeing life on a desert island—it was in a little settlement of less than a dozen families, on an island adjoining the mainland on a desolate coast of Asia. It had a Consul.

" It seems an awfully dead and alive hole," I said to him.

" It is not so bad as it looks," he replied. " We have a splendid rule here; as there is no kind of amusement in the place, except making love, we passed a resolution that no one should get in a temper over the infidelity of a spouse. We manage our loves like other people manage their friendships—if a woman likes to have an affair with another woman's husband, it is nobody's concern but hers and his. Since we have made this arrangement, this has been the happiest place in the world, though we live on a mud bank, without even a tennis-court. Before this golden age began, the quarrelling was awful. Two men simply could not get out of each other's way, and they felt obliged to resort to violence to maintain their self-respect, though they might not value the affection they were losing so much as an old glove." I forget the profession of the Solon to whom the community owed this up-to-date method of law-giving.

Fred Villiers, the war-correspondent, was making his way across Canada at the same time as we were, on a lecture tour. He had a number of wonderful battle-slides, and he looked highly picturesque in his service kit. He had also a splendid advance agent, whom I will only call by his Christian name, because he was the son of an English bishop, and had very distinguished connections. Henry never forgot his dignity, and even in the wilds of the North-West always wore a tall silk hat, with its fur worn thin by constant brushing, because he was Villiers' agent.

We had run across him at many C.P.R. capitals before he came to our rescue at a woe-begone place called Kamloops in British Columbia. We arrived there after midnight, and proceeded to the hotel, which should have been expecting us, as it was the only train in the day from Montreal. We found the hotel open, but absolutely deserted. We could have helped ourselves to anything we liked in the bar, and taken our choice of the bedrooms. At that moment appeared Henry, who asked us what we would like to drink, and told us the Kamloops charges for it. He then took us round, and gave us our choice of bedrooms, and when we wanted to know why he had suddenly become landlord, told us that the landlord had just died, and the Irish servants were afraid to be in the house with a corpse.

We slept the night there, and paid our bills to Henry in the morning. Norma Lorimer, who was with us, had a room which smelt horribly of disinfectants. Henry said that the dentist, who came up once a week from Seattle, had used that room as his surgery the day before, but the inhabitants said that the corpse was there.

This was nothing to an experience of Lewis Clarke, a son of the celebrated Marcus Clarke, who wrote *For the Term of his Natural Life*, and edited the first complete edition of Adam Lindsay Gordon's poems—a man who has had an extraordinarily adventurous life. This happened to him, I think, in the wilds of New Guinea. He had gone to sleep under a tree. During the night there came on a violent wind, and he was awakened by something cold and heavy, which kept brushing his face. Whatever it was, it only just touched him, and when he brushed it away, yielded lightly to his touch. After pushing it away for a while, he came to the conclusion that it did not matter, and got to sleep again. In the morning he was awakened by an awful stench, and when he opened his eyes to see what it was, found the bare toes of a dead Chinaman, who had hanged himself, knocking against his nose.

When I was at Canton, I went to visit our Consul-General there. I was with him in his office one day when he was trying a case. An Englishman had gone out shooting, and a Chinaman had sent his children after him, with instructions to get into the line of fire and be shot, which duly happened. The affectionate father then brought an action against the Englishman for damages occasioned to him by the injuries to his children. It was perfectly plain that the children had had themselves shot on purpose, but to my utter surprise the Consul made the Englishman pay.

When the parties had left the room, I reproached him with the miscarriage of justice. His only reply was, " I know it, my dear fellow, as well as you do; but I have been Consul here for thirty years (I forget exactly how many he said), and it is impossible for me to conceive any circumstances under which the British Government would support me."

I may add that he was much loved and respected by the British community, whom he was unable to protect.

CHAPTER XXVII

MY ACTOR FRIENDS

SINCE I came back to London a score of years ago, I have known at least a hundred actors and actresses, but they did not all visit us at Addison Mansions—some, whom I knew quite well, never could summon up the energy to go as far west as West Kensington. Actors like to live right in the centre of things, or right out in country air. There is quite a colony of them at Maidenhead; Maxine Elliot lives near Watford, in the Manor House which belonged to my uncle Joseph, and Edward Terry had a house at Barnes, which is now sublimed into Ranelagh Parade.

Among our chief actor-friends were the Grossmiths. Weedon Grossmith, with his pretty wife, came constantly. That diffident manner of his hides brilliant abilities. We are apt to forget that besides being one of the finest comedians of the day, he was once a regular exhibitor at the Royal Academy (which furnished him with the subject for a farce). What has made Weedon so " immense " is his absence of *mauvais honte*. He has dared to play the humiliating parts, of which he is the finest living exponent, with perfect sincerity. He has often said to me, " Why don't you write me a play, Douglas ? If you make me a bally enough little fool, I'll take it; if you make me a big enough coward, I'll take it; if you make me a bad enough cad, I'll take it. It is my art to put this kind of character into the pillory." And so it is; there is no one who can excel him in depicting the ignoble, foreign as it is to his own character.

His brother George, with his wife and daughters and his son Lawrence—George the younger had already flitted from the paternal nest, and was earning forty pounds a week— were also constant visitors. Lawrence was always the mirror of smartness. I think he was very bored with that sort of party, but he adorned it.

328

Geegee, as he loved to call himself, was full of frolic.
He could make light of anything. He made light of the
awful play in which he appeared, which was written for the
mistress of a millionaire. The author was given five thousand
pounds to write a play and put it on the stage. The only
condition was that the millionaire's mistress should be on
the stage the whole time, and have nothing to say.

He was once the cause of my seeing the finest piece of
acting off the stage which I ever saw. One of our greatest
living actors is always chaffed about his *penchant* for duchesses.
Grossmith and I were having supper together by ourselves
at his party at the Grafton Galleries. Presently we saw the
great actor standing beside us, and Grossmith, without
bothering about his being within earshot, said, " We'll ask
—— to sit down and have some supper with us; when he's
been there about two minutes, he'll look at his watch, and say
that he must leave us because he promised to be at the
duchess's in a quarter of an hour."

The great man sat down and attacked a mayonnaise vigor-
ously. Presently he looked at his watch, and made an
elaborate and rather snobbish apology to Grossmith for having
to leave, but he had promised the Duchess of ——d, etc.,
and all the time he was making it, trod on my foot till I
nearly yelled. Then he got up and left us, pausing to speak
to some one a few yards off to have the satisfaction of hearing
Grossmith's " There, didn't I tell you ! "

Fred Terry, the " manliest actor on the stage," and his
beautiful wife, Julia Neilson, used to come and see us sometimes. I met them first at Hayden Coffin's, where she was
filling the room and the garden with her glorious singing
one summer dawn. When she rose from the piano, she made
several vain efforts to get Terry away; he was telling Coffin,
myself, and one or two others, some of his experiences.
When she came back the third time, he said, " My wife always
has a devil of a trouble to make me put on my dress-clothes,
but when I have once got them on, I never want to go home."

That night, a rather shy little man, very alert and intelli-
gent-looking, had given us a recitation of his own which was
so breathlessly witty, that the audience could not seize all
the points. Coffin introduced him as " a very clever friend

of mine, Mr. Huntley Wright," and his name meant nothing to the audience. A year later they would have stood on the mantelpiece to get a better view of the king of musical comedians. Both he and his sister Haidée, that brilliant character-actress, used to come to Addison Mansions in those days. That the Coffins should do so was natural, because I had known Charles Hayden Coffin since he was a boy at school and I was a man at Oxford. He and his sisters and I and my sisters used to skate together at Lillie Bridge. His father was the leading American dentist of London, and Coffin himself was a dentist, or, at all events, in training for it, for several years. But he had such a glorious voice that it was inevitable that he should find his way to the musical stage, and have the longest reign on record as a *jeune premier*. He thrilled London with his " Queen of My Heart To-night." He has deserved his success twice over—both on account of his singing, and for the way in which he has helped others; no one has done more for the beginners in his own profession, and for helping unknown composers of ability to get a hearing. There are many people quite famous now whom I heard before they were known to fame at all, at his charming cottage, that *rus in urbe* on Campden Hill, which has the same initials as himself —C. H. C., Campden Hill Cottage, Charles Hayden Coffin.

With Julia Neilson I should have mentioned her handsome cousin, Lily Hanbury, who was, till her premature death, one of the beauties of the London stage. She came often to us.

It is natural, in connection with her, to think of Constance Collier, now Mrs. Julian L'Estrange, who filled her place, and has gone so much farther, for she has not only personal attraction, but real power. She was, as all the world knows, leading lady at His Majesty's before she went to America, but all the world does not know that she is the most accomplished tango-dancer on the stage.

There is no more attractive figure on the stage than Ben Webster. Young as he is, he found time to be a barrister before he began his long succession of leading parts, and though he is one of the least stagey actors on the stage, he was born in its purple. He is a grandson of Ben Webster I., who had a claim to fame besides his acting which has long since been forgotten, for he was the founder of the great

Queen newspaper, which he sold to Sergeant Cox—strange godfathers for the *Queen, the Lady's Newspaper.* Sergeant Cox was the uncle, not the father, of Horace Cox, who was at the head of the *Field,* the *Queen,* and the *Law Times* for most of the last half century. Webster married an actress, May Whitty, so well known, not only for her acting, but for her activity in woman movements. They were very often at Addison Mansions, and among the strongest supporters of our Argonauts Club.

Lena Ashwell we have known better than any other great actress, because we came to know her family long before she went on the stage, through her sister, Mrs. Keefer, wife of the engineer who built the famous bridge over Niagara. In those days she was studying at the Royal Academy of Music, and she is an F.R.A.M. She has a singularly beautiful voice for singing as well as speaking. Conscious of the burning dramatic temperament which won her her fame in the impersonation of the heroine in *Mrs. Dane's Defence,* she has always cast her eyes on the stage. When she was only fourteen she spoiled a chicken she was cooking by forgetting to remove the insides because she was so enthralled with reading *King John.* In intensity she is unsurpassed by any actress on the stage. She is really as good in tender parts as in grim parts, but she is less known in them, though every one should remember how delightful she was in *The Darling of the Gods.*

Lena Ashwell enjoys the almost unique distinction of having been born on a British man-of-war, the fine old ship which did duty under Nelson, and was the Wellesley training-ship till she was accidentally burnt a few months ago. Her father was a captain in the Navy.

Having been brought up in Canada on the St. Lawrence, she is a wonderful canoeist. Her grace on the water used to be the theme of the frequenters of Cookham Reach.

Her brother, Roger Pocock, has written the best novels of the Canadian North-West. They are descendants of the famous traveller, and had a great-great-uncle, Nicholas Pocock, the sea-painter who painted Nelson's Battle of the Nile and Lord Howe's Glorious First of June. Another ancestor wrote farces in the reign of Queen Elizabeth.

Lena Ashwell owns the Kingsway Theatre, and has produced some notable successes there, in which she showed her determination to give brilliant beginners—whether actors or dramatists—a chance. But since 1908, when she married Dr. Simson of Grosvenor Street, she has chiefly given herself up to feminist and benevolent movements—the chief of which was the founding of the Three Arts' Club for young actresses, musicians, and painters to make their home as well as their club. The Three Arts' Club has an excellent magazine of its own, and confers the various advantages of an Institute on its members. She is also a prominent worker for the Suffrage Movement.

One of the earliest of our actor friends, and one of our most frequent visitors, was James Welch, who first came with his brother-in-law, Le Gallienne. He had given up chartered-accounting for the stage for five or six years before we knew him. But a good many years more had to pass before he came into his own as the genius of farce, though he played with real power and success in several of Ibsen's plays, and Bernard Shaw's first play, *Widowers' Houses*. It was in *Mr. Hopkinson*, in 1905, after he had been on the stage for eighteen years, that he became an idol of the public, and was enabled to go into management.

Ever since then he has been enormously successful, and in spite of it, has remained the same simple, impulsive, unspoiled person as ever. He used often, as I have told in another chapter, to go to the Authors' Club with me.

One night not long since, when I was chatting with him in his dressing-room at the theatre, and was asking him when he could have another game of golf, he said, " I don't know, I'm sure. I have contracts with cinema-film photographers for seven thousand pounds, and I don't see how the devil I am going to get them all in."

I felt quite oppressed with the unfairness of things, for I had known this same man when he was just as brilliant an actor, eating his head off with chagrin at not being able to get an engagement (of which I am sure he was badly in need pecuniarily), and now here were photographers and film-makers tumbling over each other in their anxiety to take him in his inimitable fooling in *When Knights were Bold*, or his misery and stupefaction in his great condemned cell-scene from the Coliseum.

Welch is quite a decent golfer—down to 8, I think, though the time was when I had to give him 8. He is also a remarkably good spinner of golf stories. I tell him that whenever he is hard up for a curtain-raiser, he could easily hold a house for half-an-hour with his golf-stories.

One of his favourites is about his caddie at Aberdeen, to whom he gave two seats to see him in *When Knights were Bold*. Next day on the links, he asked the man how he liked it.

" My wife laughed," said the cautious Scot.

" And what did you think of it ? "

" Oh, I ? Now tell me, mon, do you make a guid thing of it ? "

" I do pretty well."

" Ye do ? " said the caddie. " Then my advice to ye is, to drop golf—ye'll never make a living at that."

Mrs. Welch is a daughter of Lottie Venne, one of the best women comedians we ever had on the English stage—a frequent visitor to us at one time, as was that fine actress, Fanny Brough (Mrs. Boleyn), an eminent member of an eminent family, whom we first met at an Idler tea.

At the Idler, too, we met the Beringers, of whom we saw a good deal at that time—Mrs. Oscar Beringer, the playwright, and her daughters Esme and Vera, who were both on the stage.   Vera, the younger, has followed in her mother's footsteps, and written plays—one with Morley Roberts. Esme, who is very popular both as a woman and an actress, has played in a large number of parts with an unvarying success.

We knew Beatrice (Robbie) Ferrar much better than either of her sisters, though all three came to our at-homes, just as they were all three on the stage.   Though she had been on the stage six years when we met her, she still looked a mere child.   She was for years one of the best *ingénue* actresses (for which her pretty, small features, bright colouring and demure expression, gave her natural advantages) on the stage.   She was one of the most familiar figures at the Idler functions.

Rowena Jerome, who has scored several successes in her

father's plays, was only a little child, playing horses, remarkably clever and precocious, in the days when we were
going to the Idler teas and Jerome's house in the Alpha
Road, St. John's Wood.

Among other actors and actresses we met at the Idler teas
or at Jerome's were Ian (Forbes) Robertson and his wife,
and their daughter, Beatrice Forbes-Robertson, Nina Boucicault, the Henry Arthur Jones's, Kate and Mary Rorke, Olga
Nethersole, George Hawtrey, Lindo and Phyllis Broughton.
I saw Phyllis Broughton the other day, looking absolutely
the same as the very first time she ever came to our flat,
twenty years ago, the gentlest-faced actress I ever met.

Forbes-Robertson's brother, Ian Robertson (who never
used the name of Forbes himself, though his pretty daughter
Beatrice resumed it when she went on the stage), came to
us less frequently than his wife and daughter, who were
habituées.

Mrs. Robertson was a daughter of an old friend of mine,
that remarkable man Joe Knight, who always seemed to
me as if he ought to have been Henty's brother. As dramatic
critic of three leading newspapers, the *Athenæum*, the *Globe*,
and I forget the other, he had almost as much power to make
and unmake as Clement Scott had. He used his influence
most generously. At the same time he was a scholar of
omniscience; he performed the Herculean task of editing
Notes and Queries for the proprietors of the *Athenæum ;* and
he had a daughter so good-looking and charming that I
always thought of her as Romola when I thought of her with
him. I have no doubt that before she married Ian Robertson
she had made herself as useful to the scholar as Romola.

Their daughter, Beatrice, has made a distinguished name
for herself on the American stage.

It was an odd thing that I should not have met (Sir J.)
Forbes-Robertson at Jerome's, considering how much they
have done since to make each other's fortunes in the *Third
Floor Back*, for which Jerome, as he always does when I
am in England, sent me stalls on one of the opening nights.
But, as a matter of fact, I met Forbes-Robertson at Palermo
in the Venetian palace which Joshua Whitaker, the head of
the great Marsala wine-firm, built for himself, adjoining the

old Ingham house in the Via Bara. Forbes-Robertson was staying there, and I am in and out of the Whitakers most days when I am in Palermo. He was convalescing from a severe illness, and we went about, the little which he could manage, together in Sicily, and afterwards for a whole week together in Venice.

He was, I remember, very tickled with one trip which he took in Sicily when he got stronger. A nephew who lives in England, but has very large possessions in Sicily, came out to stay with the Whitakers. They wished him to visit his various properties in the interior when he was there. But the thing did not interest him; he was a subaltern in the Guards, taken up with much more important thoughts. But he was an ardent admirer of Forbes-Robertson on the stage, and he was willing to go wherever his uncle desired if Forbes-Robertson would go with him.

Forbes-Robertson was eager to oblige his hosts, and captivated with the manner of the expedition, for, as they were going into brigandy parts of the island, and the person of a great landowner is the favourite prey of the brigand, they had to have an escort, and sit with loaded revolvers on their knees.

Everything passed off happily, and Forbes-Robertson came back with the knowledge that an orchard in which pistachio trees bear freely is as good as a gold-mine.

In Venice he was quite well again, and spent all day in letting us show him the *artist's bits* of Venice, for there was a time when, like another of our leading actors, he expected to make his living as a painter, not as an actor. He was educated at the Royal Academy till he was twenty-one, after leaving the Charterhouse, where he was four years the senior of Baden-Powell.

He was especially delighted with the gondola expeditions we made to the back canals of Venice. One day it would be along by the lagoon, where the timber-rafts lie floating, and collect weeds and local colour, past the ruining abbey of the Misericordia and Tintoretto's Church, S. Maria del Orto, to Tintoretto's house, now woefully humiliated by being a " tenement," but unrepaired and unaltered since that prince of painters lived and worked in it. It may easily be found, since it is near the Camel sign of a mediæval Moorish merchant. Another day it would be across the Giudecca, where the big Adriatic fishing-boats, with figures of saints and monsters on their scarlet and orange sails lie anchored, generally with their sails flapping against their masts, as if they knew that they were there for ornament to the landscape. Across the Giudecca there was the famous Redentore Church, with its three far-famed Madonnas by the pupils of Bellini, and there was more than one house with that rarity for Venice—a garden.

Over the other side of the Giudecca we all went into the great old garden of some Marchese. Venice has gardens there, but the Venetians are so unused to gardens that they abandon them to dull evergreens, when, having nothing to overshadow them, they might be as full of gay flowers as a sarcophagus in Raphael's pictures of the Resurrection. The only person I know who does make use of his garden chances is Dr. Robertson, the Presbyterian Minister, who wrote that wonderful book, *The Bible of St. Mark's*.

I think Forbes-Robertson enjoyed the visit to Tintoretto's house best of all. The well-head in the court was untouched except by the soft fingers of three centuries; the studio, with its open timber roof and huge fireplace, had nothing about it to distract the eye from memories, for it was a bare tenement of the poor. And it was such a very little way from S. Maria del Orto, a name made classic to the British public by the robbery of one of the most precious Madonnas of John Bellini—Santa Maria del Orto, which contains a frescoed choir by Tintoretto, and his " Presentation in the Temple," and his tomb. When we were looking at the immortal Venetian pictures in the Accademia and the Doge's Palace, or studying the faded marbles which jewel the interior of St. Mark, he was so overcome with reverence that it seemed almost a pain to him. He had not, I think, been in Venice before. At all events, he did not know it as I did—I could take him to any point of interest in the city by a few minutes' walk, and perhaps crossing the Grand Canal by a traghetto. I have written half a book about Venice, and some of my best writing is about it. I do not know why I never finished it.

Henry Arthur Jones's family I have known since they

were children. Mrs. Jones used to come to our parties before
the eldest of her children was out of the schoolroom, and we
spent one summer in the same house at Ostend, so we have
watched the elder girls coming to the front on the stage with
interest. Of the great dramatist himself I have spoken
elsewhere. If he had chosen, he could have been equally
famous as a writer of books. He has a profound mind, and
a popular method of statement.

Olga Nethersole could not come in the evenings to our
at-homes, because she was generally acting, but she came for
long talks in the afternoons. I found her remarkable, not
only as an actress of a singularly emotional type, but from
the interest which she takes in the social problems of the day,
such as criminology and emigration. A year ago, at a party
given by the C. N. Williamsons at the *Savoy*, when we were
comparing notes on the Canadian North-West, from which
she had just returned, and which I knew twenty years ago,
I was much struck by her grasp of the subject.

I cannot remember whether it was at the Idler or at " John
Strange Winter's " that I first met Martin Harvey, who, like
Forbes-Robertson, is a painter in his leisure moments. He
was with Irving in those days, recognised already as the
most capable all-round actor in the company, and for his
wonderful conscientiousness and finish. Harvey had the
good sense to bide his time, and when he did launch on his
own account in *The Only Way*, which Frederick Langbridge, the poet, dramatised in collaboration from Dickens's
Tale of Two Cities, he made an instantaneous and gigantic
success. In the days when he used to come to us, he was
singularly boyish-looking, and delightfully modest about
his powers, though all his friends knew that he was a genius.

It was certainly " John Strange Winter " who introduced
us to Mary Ansell, at that time one of the twin stars of
Barrie's first play, *Walker, London*.

It may have been Mary Ansell, who was noted for her
beauty, who introduced us to the other star of the play,
Irene Vanbrugh, equally noted for her prettiness and her
archness, who continues to this day to interpret the whimsicalities of Barrie with such delightful *espièglerie*. She was a
Miss Barnes, daughter of a Prebendary of Exeter—there were

z

four daughters living with their mother in Earl's Court Road. Violet, the eldest, and Irene, the youngest, then unmarried, were on the stage, Angela was a violinist or violoncellist— I never remember which of these instruments my friends play—and Edith, the fair one of the family, frowned on the stage, and married somebody of importance in India. Angela came to us oftenest. A little later Violet Vanbrugh married Arthur Bourchier, whom I had met long before when he was at Christchurch, Oxford, and the leading light of the Oxford A.D.C., of which Alan MacKinnon, an old friend of mine at Trinity, who introduced us, was another leading light.

Bourchier, the inimitable, is, I fancy, the only professional Shaksperian actor who could have the chance of taking the part of one of his own family in Shakespeare. For Cardinal Bourchier, Archbishop of Canterbury, is a character in Shakespeare's *Richard III*. He was also Henry VI's Chancellor, as Sir Robert de Bourchier was to Edward III in 1340—the first of the lay-Chancellors of England.

The first time I saw Bourchier act was when he was an undergraduate at Oxford—the part was Harry Hotspur, and he was superb in it, because this was a part in which he could use his art and his personality in equal proportions. Since then I have seen him blend his two great qualifications of character-acting and potent personality, in many parts, in Henry VIII pre-eminently, and I have seen him exercise the two qualifications separately in many parts, now as an old seventeenth-century Bishop, overflowing with goodness, now as a bluff, practical joker in boisterous farce with Weedon Grossmith. He is certainly one of the finest actors on the stage, when you consider him from the double stand-point of his tremendous personality, and his power to disguise it in parts entirely foreign to one's idea of Bourchier. I cannot help liking him best as himself on the stage, because to me there is nothing so interesting as personality, and he has such an inexhaustible flow of wit and high spirits.

If Bourchier had had no success on the professional stage, his name would have been immortalised in its annals, for it was he who persuaded Jowett, of Balliol, the then Vice-Chancellor of Oxford, to abolish the statute of the University against Oxford having a theatre, and he actually enlisted Jowett's services into raising the money for building one.

When I first went to Oxford, we had no theatre on account of the famous statute. Our ancestors regarded actors as " rogues and vagabonds," and only a year ago a well-known actor got off serving on a jury on the grounds that he was legally a rogue. But though the town might not have a theatre, it might have as many low music-halls as it liked, because the University did not consider what went on in " the halls " as acting at all. The real point at issue— would the ladies of a caste like Irving's or Tree's be as likely to tempt the St. Anthonys of Oxford out of their hermitages in the deserts of learning—was entirely lost sight of.

With Bourchier one naturally thinks of Aubrey Smith, who had to play Sir Marcus Ordeyne in Bourchier's theatre— Smith, who was the chief light of the Cambridge A.D.C., and the crack Cambridge bowler of his time in the 'Varsity matches.

Smith's beautiful sister, Mrs. Cosmo Hamilton, who latinised her name into *Faber* when she went on the stage— she told me so herself—was only just coming into her own when she died—cut off in her very flower. There was no more genuinely liked and esteemed woman on the stage.

Granville Barker, the typical clever, red-headed boy, though he was not then old enough to have been promoted to dress-clothes, used to come with an extremely intelligent and charming mother, the mother of a large family, I always understood, though she looked far too young. They were brought by Edwin Waud, the artist, as far as I remember, and they were friends of Gleeson White's. Granville was a very bright boy when you spoke to him, but he was never much in evidence; he left his mother, so that she might enjoy herself, instead of having to keep him amused. He may have gone to the sandwiches and lemonade in the dining-room—more probably, he was not allowed to smoke, and went to do that.

I fancy that Acton Bond, who now runs the British Empire Shakespeare Society, must have been a friend of Gleeson White's, because he came into our life so very early. Bond was an institution in Bohemia. He was a singularly handsome and distinguished-looking actor, who took Shakespeare and other " costume " parts. He was one of the most courteous men I ever met, and I knew that I could confer pleasure on anybody by introducing Bond. This was an important consideration to a host who made a point of keeping all his guests introduced and amused for all the evening. Bond knew all the denizens in Bohemia, and had a fund of conversation about them, in addition to being personally very interesting;   and, as a fair golfer, a good man in a boat, a good dancer, and so on, was a " find " for a country house. Even when he was acting most, his heart inclined to the other side of his profession—to training people for the stage and running the Actors' Association—a sort of Union for Actors. He did an immense amount of useful work. He married the charming Eve Tame comparatively lately. A tall man, with a graceful figure, he carried himself extremely well, and, with his fine classical head, perpetuated the tradition of the Kembles.

Ray Rockman was one of our Argonaut friends, and became a very intimate friend indeed. She stayed with us at Salcombe and elsewhere, besides being constantly at our house. With her tall, slight, aristocratic figure, the face of a marquise of Louis XV's court, and her wonderful Oriental eyes, she had the presence of the greatest *tragédiennes* who have adorned our stage. When you see her in a drawing-room, you think instinctively of Sarah Bernhardt's great parts, and rightly, because she was Sarah's understudy in them in Paris before she came to England. If any actor-manager had wanted a leading lady for tragedy, she would have been one of the most famous actresses on our stage to-day, for she had the divine fire. But London does not run to tragedies, except for the glorification of an actor- or actress-manager, so she had to descend to being the villainess of melodramas generally finishing up with suicide in the last act. In the *Great Ruby* she showed her real dramatic power. But she has never had the chance of becoming the leading lady at one of our chief theatres like His Majesty's, where she could have taken London by storm with her magnificent presence and carriage and the passion she can put into her acting with her marvellous Oriental eyes and coal-black hair. These she owes to her being a South Russian. I am not sure whether she was born in Russia or the United States, where her father is a doctor in Montana—a friend of the Copper King. If any one were to make a play out of Sarah Siddons, Ray Rockman would be the ideal actress to cast for the leading part.

It was Ray who introduced me to the wonderful Annie Russell, the most temperamental of American actresses. I say American, though she was born in Liverpool, because practically all her work has been done on the other side, and it was Ray who introduced me to Sarah Bernhardt. Unfortunately, Sarah does not like talking English, and I am not equal to saying anything very interesting in French, though I read it with facility, and know plenty of " kitchen " French for use at hotels and railway-stations. Sarah sent me seats to see her in *Hamlet,* which she pronounced " omelette." I found it rather wearisome, to be quite honest, because I hear French so badly, and when I went down to see Ray and her in her dressing-room at the end of the first act, I gladly accepted her invitation to spend the rest of the evening in her dressing-room, " if I could not follow her easily."

It was extremely interesting to watch her dressing, and she did not take any more notice of my presence than if I had been a fly, while she was actually being got ready for the stage, though she made herself extremely pleasant during the acts when she was off the stage. She could divest herself of the personality of Hamlet, and resume it at a moment's notice. Ray speaks French as well as English, so everything was quite simple, with her there to interpret. During the longest interval a message came down for her that the Prince of Wales (afterwards King Edward VII) was in the house, and Sarah went off to see him for a long time; it seemed like half-an-hour. She invited me to go with Ray to visit her at that wonderful rock island off the Breton coast, but for some reason or other I did not make the effort. I think I had made arrangements to go to St. Andrews.

Elizabeth Robins I met at the Idler. One always thought of her as the actress in those days, and not, as one now thinks of her, as the novelist. Elizabeth Robins is a tall, spare, Western woman, with a very eloquent face. She is the greatest Ibsen actress we have had in England. She had the unusual courage, for the stage, to think that good looks and elegance in dress were of no consequence, when she was presenting Ibsen's characters. Her one desire was to fulfil his conception exactly, and she did it most convincingly.

A few people, like myself, knew that she was the " C. E. Raimond " who wrote *George Mandeville's Husband* for that series of Heinemann's, but we imagined it to be a passing phase with her, instead of the prelude to a series of great novels on burning questions.

I do not know who brought Gertrude Kingston to us first, but she often came. She was the accomplished violinist mentioned in Lord Roberts' dispatch of September 13, 1901, as having rendered special service during the war in South Africa. Mrs. Silver, for this is her real name, is an authoress as well as an artist and a collector, as I discovered when we were going over the old things in Phillimore Lodge together before the sale.

Alice Skipworth was a lovely woman with a gorgeous voice, whose fortunes on the stage were made in an extraordinary way. An actor-manager engaged her without any experience of acting to understudy his wife, who financed his plays, in an American tour. When they got to Philadelphia, I think it was, on the second night his wife took ill, and Mrs. Skipworth duly took her place. Philadelphia went wild over her beauty and her voice, and the actor-manager found himself in the unpleasant predicament of having to decide whether he would close his doors, or persuade his wife to let Mrs. Skipworth go on taking her place. His wife, who was, I believe, very charming herself, was a sensible woman, and thought it would be better to coin money by doing nothing than to bankrupt herself by acting, so the understudy acted and sang throughout the tour, and came back a leading lady in musical comedy. She was a very clever woman; she could have written an excellent novel about Bohemian life; she had the knowledge; and she was both witty and epigrammatic.

I need not explain who Murray Carson is. He was a very great light in those circles, because he was an actor-manager, and as such had the distinction of giving Lena Ashwell one of her first chances in *Gloriana*. In addition to his successes as an actor and a manager, he was joint author with Louis Napoleon Parker in that delightful play *Rosemary*, since which he has written many plays. He is quite a well-known figure at various literary clubs, noted for his remarkable resemblance to the first Napoleon. The collaboration of these two Napoleons was, I imagine, a mere coincidence.

My last meeting with Decima Moore I am never likely to forget. She was very fond of watching polo, and we were sitting together in the pavilion at a club to which I belong, when a man was thrown from his pony, and dragged along the ground for several yards on his face, his nose ploughing a regular furrow till it was broken. I went down to where he was lying. Every one thought he was killed, because he lay insensible for so long. When he did come to, he said, " Is my nose broken, doctor? " The doctor said it was, and then he said, in my hearing, " Then I hope you will make a better job of it than God did," which seemed to me the most extraordinary piece of *sang-froid* for a man who, the moment before, had been almost across the threshold of life and death.

Sir Charles Wyndham, whose real name I cannot for the moment remember, and " Mary Moore," I have seen chiefly on the Riviera at Cimiez. I make it the excuse for my forgetfulness that he forgot what he was forgetting once, when, coming up cordially to shake hands with me, he said, " I remember your name quite well, but I can't recall your face."

Wyndham fought in the war between North and South in the United States, and he was a member of the company of John Wilkes Booth, the actor, at the time that the latter assassinated President Lincoln in the theatre; I have never heard if he was actually on the stage at the time. He was brought up, I understood, as a doctor.

As an instance of Wyndham's lapses of memory, I may quote that one day at Ranelagh he asked me if I was a member of the Club. I said " Yes." " Can I telephone from here ? " " Oh, yes."

When we got to the telephone, he began turning up the name of his man of business, who had a name, which I will not mention, as ordinary as Skinner; there might have been a couple of score of the name in the telephone book. He read down the list. " I can't remember his initials," he said. I looked at him as if to say, " Don't you often see him ? " He caught my eye. His actor's intuition told him my thoughts. " I know what you're thinking," he said. " Yes, I do 'phone to him every day, but I can't for the life of me tell which of all this lot he is."

Irving once told me at lunch a story which he probably told many others. He was touring in the United States, and staying either at St. Louis or Cincinnatti. One morning at breakfast a large rat ran across the room. As he had been up till past five that morning, being entertained by the local Savage Club—I forget its name—he was feeling rather cheap, and gave a little start. " You needn't mind him, Mis' Irving," said the negro waiter; " he's a real one."

The Trees I have known for a long time. It is an undiluted pleasure to meet Tree out at lunch—like all actors, he affects lunches more than dinners. There are few men so witty. When most of the great actors and actresses were exhausting their powers of polished vituperation on the unhappy Clement Scott for his generalisations upon the morals of the stage, Tree's reply as to what he thought of the matter was, that nothing Clement Scott had said made him think any less of him, and Lady Tree's rejoinder to the late W. T. Stead is historical.

Cyril Maude always gives me his smile when we meet at a certain polo club, and often " passes the time of day " to me very pleasantly. But I know that he is another of the people who remember your name, when they meet you, but cannot recall your face. Still, I forgive him for the sake of that Major in *The Second in Command*. His charming wife, Winifred Emery, whose triumph I saw the night she won her place in the first rank as Marguerite in Irving's *Faust*—she was the understudy—always remembers my face as well as my name. There never was an actress on our stage who showed more spirit, unless it is Lena Ashwell turning on a bully, for Lena turns to bay like the lion " on that famed Picard field."

The Maudes' daughter is now rapidly coming to the front. I saw her as one of Portia's ladies in the *Merchant of Venice* looking (intentionally, I suppose) for all the world like the exquisite Tornabuoni heiress in the choir frescoes of Santa Maria Novella at Florence, and could hardly believe that it was the same merry, everyday girl that I meet at the Adrian Ross's.

Edward Terry I first met at the Savage, where he was one

SIR HERBERT BEERBOHM-TREE
From the drawing by Yoshio Markino

of the most influential members, and afterwards at Barnes, where he had a dear old house near the church, which has been improved away to make room for a sweet-shop and a garage and an auctioneer's lair. Though he was so capable in the chair, and such an excellent comedian, I don't remember his ever saying anything worth remembering when we walked or " bussed " down Castelnau together.

Penley I never met in private life; I only met him at the Savage, where he never would do a turn, and where his dignity—not assumed—when he was in the chair was as funny as *Charley's Aunt*, and proceedings were conducted in the voice of the curate in *The Private Secretary*.

I first met Mrs.—and Mr.—Patrick Campbell at a party at Oswald Crawfurd's in the very early 'nineties. She had been enjoying triumphs in the provinces for some years, but London was for the first time being thrilled by that marvellously seductive voice, that languorous grace, and that panther-like personality, which is sleek till it springs. Of all actresses, Mrs. Campbell is most closely connected with Kensington, for she was born in the Forest House, Kensington Gardens, and lives no farther off than Kensington Square, where she occupies one of the old houses on the west side.

The Second Mrs. Tanqueray at one end of her career in London, and *Bella-Donna* at the other, established the fact that for parts in which the infidelity of a wife brings in passion and intrigue of tragic proportions, she has few equals on the stage of any country. It is the Italian side of her nature coming out—her mother was a Miss Romanini. Indeed, one can picture her at her very finest in an Italian mediæval play —such as the scene where his beautiful mother mourns over the body of the terrible young Griffonetto Baglioni.

Like Lena Ashwell and Julia Neilson, Mrs. Campbell (Mrs. George Cornwallis West) might have expected to make her name by music.

She supplies one more illustration of the siren voice of Africa, which never ceases to call to those who have once listened to it. For Patrick Campbell made his work in Africa, and died there in the Boer War, and now their daughter Stella, who had made her mark on the stage with her *Princess Clementina* in Mason's play, has married and gone to live at Nairobi.

CHAPTER XXVIII

MY ARTIST FRIENDS

My first connection with artists came through my cousin, David Wilkie Wynfield, who was the nephew and godson of the great Sir David Wilkie. He was a popular artist in both senses of the word, for engravers used to multiply his pictures like " The New Curate," and there was no more popular figure at the Arts' Club or in the homes of his brother artists. A repartee of his was the origin of the picture in *Punch*, where a painter who wants to know why he does not get into the Royal Academy is told that he should not wear such thick boots. He and some brother artists, of whom I think Marcus Stone and G. A. Storey are the only survivors, took Ann Boleyn's castle of Hever (when, if not abandoned to the owls and bats, it had not yet become the home of the Astors), as a summer sketching-box, and I have a picture of them grouped round the entrance arch, which he painted.

So that he might have a better opportunity of introducing me to all his friends, he put me up for " The Arts," of which I remained a member till his death. In those days it was located in a delightful old house in Hanover Square, which had belonged to and been frescoed by Angelica Kauffmann. There I made the acquaintance of the most famous artists of the day, both painters and sculptors, for your artist, unlike your author, loves to go to the club at night to relieve his mind after his long day's work, by playing pool or demolishing the claims of his rivals to be considered artists in long technical conversations through clouds of smoke. The art of blowing smoke-rings is a speciality of artists. I have heard a famous R.A. recommend a young painter, who was complaining that *he* could never get his pictures into the Royal Academy, to paint small grey pictures. " Why ? " asked the disappointed aspirant. " Because they are the pictures which Leighton

346

needs to show off his own pictures properly, and he always picks them out first."

Another time, at the committee meeting when Herbert Schmaltz was up for election, the chairman asked, " Does anybody know anything about Mr. Schmaltz?" and the most popular landscape painter of the day replied, " Mr. Schmaltz is a man who has taken the illustration of the Bible into his own hands."

It was Wynfield who introduced me to Joe Jopling. There have been few at-homes more popular than Mrs. Jopling-Rowe's. Jopling, who was a great rifle-shot—he won the Queen's Prize at Wimbledon—as well as a regular exhibitor in the Academy, died a few years after I came to know them, and his widow married George Rowe. Mrs. Jopling-Rowe, who is a popular and admirable portrait-painter, and a constant exhibitor at all the principal picture-shows, like the Academy and the Salon, when first I knew her lived at Beaufort Street, Chelsea, but an epidemic of burglars drove her from there to Pembroke Road, Earl's Court, and from thence to an old house in Pembroke Gardens. It made no difference to her at-homes, which have always been crowded with really distinguished people, for she has known all the leading artists, most of the leading authors and actors, and not a few of the leading public men and women of her time. Millais painted her portrait in her youthful prime, and if one sees her standing near it, where it hangs in her house, one notices how little she has altered in those intervening years, which have been so full of painting triumphs and brilliant society.

Many artists used to come to Addison Mansions. West Kensington is not like St. John's Wood or Chelsea; there was no West Kensington Arts' Club, and artists had not many meeting-places except Phil May's studio and our flat. Solomon, already nearing his zenith, used often to come with his brother Albert, and so did Arthur Hacker, though they both lived some way off. We were asked to Solomon's wedding—we and Henry Arthur Jones, I think, were the only Gentiles present at this splendid ceremony, carried out with all the historical rites. Albert Solomon very good-naturedly sat with us to tell us the significance of everything. It was as interesting as an Easter service in a Sicilian cathedral.

It was easier for J. J. Shannon, for he lived quite close, in Holland Park Road, in an old farm-house, which he gradually transformed into a charming mansion, where one used to meet most interesting people.

David Murray, the famous landscape painter, was another frequent visitor among the Academicians, very popular for his wit and camaraderie, very ready to help any one who needed a push in high quarters.

He has altered surprisingly little—only last summer I met him at a ball at Sir St. Clair Thompson's, the eminent throat specialist's, whom I knew as far back as 1886 when he was honorary secretary of the Club at Florence. David was dancing as much as most of the young men, and not looking perceptibly older than when I met him a quarter of a century ago. He is another of the intellectual artists who read deeply, and he is much interested in Japan. He very good-naturedly came to advise me about my pictures when I was selling the contents of Phillimore Lodge, but we had already parted with the celebrated Nattier of Louis XV dressed as Hercules—a Burke heirloom—my father sold that to Colnaghi for £1500.

Alfred Drury, that delightfully poetical sculptor, was another Academician who came often. Drury has a beautiful voice.

It was only in our last days at Addison Mansions, after we had given up those large evening at-homes, that William Nicholson, not an Academician, but one of the greatest artists of them all, came. Nicholson was not only one of the finest painters of the day in inspiration and technique, but was the pioneer of a new movement, being the first painter to have an artificial reproduction of daylight installed in his studio—a costly and highly scientific combination of various lights. By means of this painting is rendered independent of the weather and the time. He has painted all night before now. Mark Barr, a scientific friend of ours, who devised the apparatus for this, the most brilliant man I ever met, brought him.

Another pioneer of art who used to come to Addison Mansions often, when he had a studio in Brook Green, was Francis Bate, the moving spirit of the New English Art Club. His influence on art has been profound. The new English

Art Club may have been identified with a certain extravagant phase by scoffers, but it has embraced men like Sargent and Shannon, as well as apostles of stiff blue cabbages.

The public were quick to appreciate the charm of the soft grey studies, in which so little was indicated and so much implied, of Theodore Roussel and Paul Maitland. Maitland, in spite of his delicate health, was a student as well as a painter. He was a very clear thinker, like the late Sir Alfred East, another Academician who often joined our symposia. I always felt that East could have made his name as easily in literature as in art.

The artist who has played the greatest part in the book life of his time is, of course, Walter Crane, a really profound student and thinker, who has held all sorts of most important directorships in art, and delivered lectures of historical importance. No artist has such a record in *Who's Who*, for Crane is not only an illustrator of books, but a writer, and as eminent a socialist as he is an artist. He describes himself as " mostly self-taught," but he was apprenticed to W. J. Linton, and exhibited in the Royal Academy when he was only sixteen. He lives in ideal surroundings, in a rambling house, more than two centuries old, in Holland Street, Kensington. The thing which always struck me more than the old curios which find such a fitting niche in the house, are the rubbings of the brasses of his ancestors, for Crane has a long line of knightly ancestors, one of whom was Chancellor of England in Stuart times. Of his work I need not speak. for he has founded one of the schools of modern English Art.

When I asked Walter Crane if he had been turned into an artist by any sensational incident, he said—

" My progress—if I may so call it—has been very gradual and quite unsensational, I think—except to myself. I had the great advantage of having an artist for a father, and never remember the time when I did not handle a pencil of some kind, though it was often a *slate* pencil. I had no early struggles to have my wish to be an artist allowed and encouraged, or any strife about the realisation of that ideal with a bourgeois-minded family, as one so often hears about in artists' histories. I never started for anywhere with half-a-crown in my pocket—anything of the sort usually quickly burnt a hole in what little pocket I may have had—and no doubt that is the principal reason why I remain poor.

" My early fondness for drawing animals caused confident and friendly critics to say, ' He will be a second Landseer ! ' and nothing could have had a more glowing prospect for me at the time; but times have a way of changing, and ideals change with them, especially when one is ' growing up.'

" At the age of sixteen I had what might be called my first picture accepted at the Royal Academy—first time of asking —but the subject was ' The Lady of Shalott,' and my source of inspiration was by no means Landseer, but rather the pre-Raphaelites, and I was already deeply read in Ruskin.

" You speak of the ' paradox of my being a socialist ' in spite of my descent. Why should it be a paradox for one who loves beauty and harmony, and strives to realise it in his work, but who sees around him a world scrambling for money, glutted with riches at one end of the social scale, and penniless and destitute at the other, while all the time the bounty of Nature and the invention and labour of man provides abundance—but only for those who can exchange the necessary counters, and for those who hold the keys of the means of the maintenance of life ?

" Socialism does not mean lowering the standard of life, but raising it, and with the abolition of the struggle for mere bread, and the substitution of co-operation for competition, it will be possible to build a society founded upon some better basis than cash, a surplus value. Indeed, it may be said that a true aristocracy might then become possible, since personal qualities and character would then have their real value, purged of the harrowing, selfish burden of private ownership of the means of life, and estimated by service to the community."

My most intimate artist friend is Réné de l'Hôpital, who, in spite of his name and his descent, speaks not a word of French. De l'Hôpital is one of those happy portrait-painters who can get a likeness; but he is more than that; if he had a literary turn, he could write as good a book as any one on " collecting " economically, for he has a wonderful knowledge of old furniture and its West-end and East-end values. I know the extent of his knowledge because he and my brother-in-law, the late Frederick Robert Ellis, were my advisers when I sold the contents of Phillimore Lodge, and the auctioneer said they fetched half as much again as they were worth, because we knew their value and their points were so well brought out. De l'Hôpital owed his knowledge partly to the fact that he was born in a great old house full of treasures. Having known what it was to struggle himself, when he became an artist against the wishes of his family, he does a great deal for the poor.

De l'Hôpital, who is a French count, son of the sixth Duke de Vitry, has had the honour of painting Prince Arthur of Connaught and Pope Leo XIII, and was a Gold Staff officer at the coronation of King George V. He married a daughter of John Francis Bentley, the great architect who built the Westminster Cathedral. Mrs. de l'Hôpital has written a book entitled *The Westminster Cathedral and its Architect*, and collaborated with me in one of my books in which she would not allow her name to appear.

Two painters who used to come to Addison Mansions arise in my mind with East. Both were portrait-painters, recognised as among the soundest executants of their craft—J. H. Lorimer and Hugh de Trafford Glazebrook—for both were interested in literature as well as art—a not common trait among artists—and both of them paint portraits with enduring and outstanding merit. Lorimer, as I have said, was the son of the late Prof. Lorimer of Edinburgh University, the eminent international jurist who made the restoration of Kellie Castle his hobby, and brother of Sir Robert Lorimer, who restored St. Giles' Cathedral at Edinburgh, and a cousin of Norma Lorimer, the novelist. Glazebrook was a brother of Canon Glazebrook, late head master of Clifton, an Oxford friend of mine who never won the high jump, though he could clear five feet eleven, because he happened to have for a contemporary the only man who ever cleared six feet in the 'Varsity sports.

A new school of black-and-white artists was coming rapidly to the fore. Pictorial journalism on an unprecedented scale had invaded England from America, and a number of new illustrated papers and magazines had started, and they relied for their pictorial side on ideas which must have seemed revolutionary to those who had been brought up on the old standard productions of the *Illustrated London News.* The foundation of *The Graphic* a decade or two earlier had been a sign of the times.

The most extraordinary artist of the movement could hardly be called a journalist proper, because most of his work was done for books published by John Lane, and for the *Yellow Book.* Beardsley, who was a mere boy, with his boyishness accentuated by his fair hair and consumptive's pink-and-white complexion, came nearly every week with a very pretty sister who made her name rapidly on the stage. Beardsley, who had a workmanship of spiderish delicacy and an imagination like Edgar Allan Poe, which resulted in the creation of female types of appalling wickedness and snake-like fascination, did not talk much " shop "; he was more occupied with the studies on which these extraordinary creations were founded. He was a very interesting man to talk to, very modest. He always impressed me as a man with a wonderful future if he were not cut off, as he was, by an early death.

Phil May, another genius of the movement, was one of our most constant visitors. He lived, as I have said, in a studio improvised from a stable, almost opposite Shannon, in those days. He did more than most men to revolutionise black and white, because he was one of the first who grasped the value of Japanese effects and introduced them into his work. But his method of producing these Japanese effects was not Japanese. A Japanese artist fills the brush, which he uses as pen and pencil, with Indian ink, and secures his effects with a few dexterous sweeps. Phil May drew his picture in the English way with comparatively few lines, then studied his own work to see what was superfluous, and rubbed out every superfluity. He was not the rapid worker which one imagined from his style. After he left the Australian paper with which he was connected, he remained a free lance for years, drawing whatever came into his head as irresistible, and selling it to one or other journal, and bringing out collections of his drawings of the year in his famous annual. It was, perhaps, not the best way of making money, but it came very naturally to him, for he was as brilliant a wit as he was an artist. He was a man of inspirations; he could be irresistibly funny with such simple materials as the henpecked husband. He was the reverse of henpecked himself. He had a devoted and very pretty wife, who was forgiving to all the faults he committed in his bland and childlike way, and I often used to think that his jokes about henpecked husbands formed his way of crying " peccavi." Who that had ever seen it could forget his picture of the husband coming home at three o'clock in the morning and being asked, " What do you mean by coming home at this time of night? " and pleading that there was nowhere else open? Or his picture of the drunken lion-tamer, who had taken refuge from his wife in the lion's cage, with his wife outside the cage crying " You coward ! "

I do not think he ever made his speech in the rooms of the Piscatorial Society the subject of a picture, but it was worth it. He was the guest of the evening and had dined a little too well—at any rate, as far as drink was concerned. When he rose to respond to the toast of his health, he looked round the room and saw dozens of glass cases stuffed with salmon and pike of monstrous size, the pride of the Society. He took them all in with a wave of his hand, and said, " I suppose you will tell me that there is only one ——y kipper on that wall ! "

On another occasion I was with Phil and Corbould at the Savage Club. We stayed there very late, and when Phil finally made up his mind to go home, he could not remember where he lived. Of course, we knew his own studio quite well, because it was close to our homes, and we had been there scores of times, but he was not residing there; he was staying in lodgings, for he had just come back from the Japan fiasco. He had received a commission from the *Graphic* to go to Japan for a year or more, and do sketches for them. They offered him very liberal terms, and he accepted them. He let his studio for a year, and started off full of good intentions. But he never got to Japan. He stopped somewhere on the way—a very long way from England—and abandoned himself to a lotus life of mild dissipation—we might, perhaps, have called him a lotus-drinker—and the *Graphic* had to bring him home again. It was soon after he got home that this event at the Savage happened.

A A

" Where to ? " asked the cabby.

" I don't know," said Phil. " I have forgotten where I live; it is not my own house."

" Well, how am I to get you there ? " asked the cabby.

" I do not know what the name of the house is," said Phil; " but I think I could draw it."

" There are a good lot of houses in London," said the cabby, " and they are mostly all alike."

" But there is a church near it," said Phil; " and I could draw that."

A menu card and a pencil were procured, and he drew a picture of the ordinary London house and a rather toyshop church. The cabby looked at it and said, " I know where it is; that's Osnaburgh Terrace," so Phil got into the cab, and then the cabby turned round to Corbould and myself and said, " That's Phil May, ain't it ? " We said yes, and he unbuttoned his coat and put the menu card carefully in his pocket, remarking, " It will be worth something some day."

The extraordinary thing was that any one who was so witty and such a consummate artist should have been ignored by *Punch* for so many years, though he became in the end one of its most honoured contributors. The editor approached him in a very curious way when he felt that he could not ignore him any longer. He did it through the firm who at that time reproduced illustrations for *Punch*.

Phil May was one of the best-hearted of men, generous to a fault, alike with his money and in his attitude to his rivals.

Very famous people used to come sometimes to those ultra-Bohemian gatherings in his studio, including some of the Queens of the music-hall stage.

It was Phil May, I believe, who drew the inimitable cartoon in the *St. Stephen's Review* of Mr. Gladstone, with a male-volent eye, gathering primroses on the banks of the Thames on the anniversary of his illustrious rival's death, which had for its title—

> " A primrose by the river's brim,
> A yellow primrose was to him,
> And it was nothing more."

The cartoon was received with universal acclaim, but the general public—*quorum pars fui*—did not bother as to who the artist was. I did not know Phil at the time. He was just back from Australia, where he had been working for the *Sydney Bulletin*.

Phil May had the head of a mediæval jester, and was fond of drawing himself in the cap and bells.

Another black-and-white humorist of a different type who was with us just as much was Dudley Hardy, whose satirical sketches of ballet girls and their admirers filled the periodicals of the day, obscuring Dudley Hardy's claim as an artist. He was a son of the well-known marine painter, T. B. Hardy, and was lured from doing the really admirable work with which his friends are familiar, by the fatal popularity of his theatrical caricatures. It was long before he could make up his mind to break away from that and do himself justice in painting. His sister married a very great friend of ours, a water-colour painter of extraordinary cleverness and charm, Frank Richards. We have many of his pictures, mostly impression-ist water-colours, which prove the heights to which Richards could have risen if he had continued to have the leisure to which he was born. He might have done very well in black-and-white too. He could have come nearer to Phil May than most people, for he too had caught the spirit of Japan in the simplicity and bold curves of his drawing; and he had considerable humour. His limpidity and the charm of his colouring were especially shown in his paintings of Venice.

His portrait of Dudley Hardy is simply admirable, for Dudley, with his whimsical smile and jaunty way of wearing his hat, looks like a Parisian notable.

For some years we saw more of Reginald Cleaver than any other artist. Cleaver was at that time the favourite artist of the *Graphic*, as well as a regular contributor to *Punch*. He was excellent in catching likenesses, and his crisp and beautiful handiwork made his pictures of passing events most attractive. The *Graphic* always sent him to the most impor-tant functions, such as royal weddings. He hated this work, because he was far too gentlemanly and too shy to push, and the people in charge of royal functions seemed to take a pleasure in putting every disadvantage they could in the way of the artists and journalists who had to immortalise the occasion for their fellow-countrymen. The artist was expected to stand behind the organ or anywhere else provided he was sufficiently out of sight; whether he could see or not was of very little consideration. But one day Fate overtook the autocrat who used to browbeat the Press. It was in the days when the late King was Prince of Wales, and his brother, the Duke of Edinburgh, had just become a German reigning prince as Prince of Saxo-Coburg Gotha. Cleaver, who was posted where he could not see the procession as it entered, imagined that the Duchess of Edinburgh as a reigning princess would take precedence of the Princess of Wales, and gave her precedence in his picture in the *Daily Graphic*. Before ten o'clock the next morning a messenger from Marlborough House arrived at the *Graphic* office to know the meaning of this libel, and the editor explained that the artist had been placed in a position where he could not see the Princess. The Princess was furious. She attached no blame to the artist, but she sent for the autocrat and gave him to understand that there must be no more accidents of this kind, and from that day forward there was a great change in the way in which artists were treated at royal functions.

We spent several of our summer holidays together. Cleaver's sketches of famous people at historical functions will have a permanent value. He had no rival in fidelity and charm in this kind of work. In recent years the world has seen too little of his work owing to his being so much abroad. He is the elder brother of Ralph Cleaver, the well-known political caricaturist.

Holland Tringham, a very good-looking and well-bred man, of whom I saw a good deal at that time, had a battle royal with a millionaire duchess over a similar question. He went down to represent one of the chief illustrated papers at a great ball she was giving at her country house. When he got there, he was received with scant ceremony, but began his work. When supper-time came, the housekeeper arrived to tell him that he would find his supper in the still room. He showed her the beginnings of his sketch—and he was a brilliant artist—and said, " Take this to her Grace and tell her that if she does not come and fetch me to supper with her guests, I shall tear it up, and go home."

Her Grace came, took him to supper, and introduced him to her friends galore, and the picture appeared. Of course, Tringham was very sure of his position as an artist with the paper, or he would not have risked the chance of being sacrificed on the altar of the offended duchess. I should like to have heard what the housekeeper told her.

There has not been so much of this snobbery lately among hostesses; the race for publicity having become too acute.

I must have met Sambourne, who succeeded Sir John Tenniel as chief artist of *Punch*, when I was a boy, for he married a Miss Herapath, and when we were children she and her brothers were generally having tea at our house in Upper Phillimore Gardens if we were not having tea at theirs a few yards away. I never lost sight of him, and in the last years of his life saw more rather than less of Sambourne, whose thoroughness was always a marvel to me. No pains were too great for him to be accurate in the details of his cartoons and whimsicalities. I forget how many thousand photographs he told me he had, which he could use like a dictionary. But I remember that his idea of the best day's holiday one could take was to go to Boulogne in the morning on a day when there was a good sea on, lunch there, and come back in the afternoon.

His successor on *Punch*, Bernard Partridge, was very often at Addison Mansions in the old Idler and Vagabond days. He had already achieved fame in two directions—as a black-and-white artist whose handiwork was unexcelled for delicate beauty and romantic charm, and as an actor. But he did not act under his own name; he was Bernard Gould behind the footlights. Partridge's father, the late Prof. Richard Partridge, was a Fellow of the Royal Society and one of the greatest surgeons of his day. Mrs. Partridge, then Miss Harvey, was also often at our at-homes.

Another *Punch* and *Graphic* artist often with us was Alexander Stuart Boyd, whose wife, Mary Stuart Boyd, is a favourite novelist of the great house of Blackwood. Boyd has the dry wit of his race, so it is not surprising that such a fine artist should have found his way to *Punch*. He now gives his time to painting and spends much of his time at a

house he has in the Balearic Islands.   He was a very old
Vagabond.   I met him there or at the Idler teas.

There, too, I met Hal Hurst, my neighbour and constant
associate for years, though we do not often meet now.   I
have various pictures of his in my present house. . Hurst,
who was a very clever artist, and his friend Alyn Williams,
the president of one of the two Miniature Painters' Societies,
not only shared a studio in Mayfair, but married beautiful
young wives about the same time, who were constantly
together, one very dark and the other very fair.   Mrs.
Williams was the picture of health, but suddenly she was struck
down by a mysterious malady, and almost wasted to death,
a terrible shock to all who had seen much of them.   Then,
for no apparently sufficient reason, she suddenly picked up
again, threw off her malady completely, and was restored
to her old radiant health; it was like coming back from
the grave.   The Royal Family have been great patrons of
Williams' miniatures.

Oddly enough, I knew the president of the other society
of miniature painters equally well—Alfred Praga, an Italian
by extraction, a well-known and popular member of the
Savage Club.   Praga lives in a picturesque grey house off
Hornton Street.   His wife is a well-known writer.

With them it is natural to mention the brilliant Robert
Sauber, a German by extraction, who for years was one of
the most popular artists in journalism; whatever paper or
magazine you took up, it was almost sure to have a cover
with a charming female figure designed by Sauber.   I have
a delightful specimen painted for the menu of the Vagabond
Club on some important occasion.   But Sauber was not
only a journalistic artist; he has been painting large decora-
tive panels and ceilings and portraits for the last thirteen
years, and has done no illustrations for the last twelve years.
He is an exhibitor at the principal Salons in London, Paris
and Munich.

While mentioning *Punch* artists, I forgot two who were
constant visitors at Addison Mansions—John Hassall and
Chantrey Corbould.

The man who helped to keep our at-homes going more than

any one else was Chantrey Corbould, the artist, a godson of
the great Sir Francis Chantrey, whose bequest is almost as
famous as his sculpture; he was a nephew also of Charles
Keene, the immortal *Punch* artist and etcher, on the mother's
side. Edward H. Corbould, his father's eldest brother, taught
the Royal Family.

Corbould was a huge man, with a very jovial, high-
coloured, handsome face, and a very horsey appearance,
as becomes one of the best hunting-picture artists who ever
drew for *Punch*. He had a very loud and hearty laugh, which
could be heard all over the house, and told good stories,
and always had a court of the ladies of Bohemia round him
in the inner room. He had one golden quality; whenever
he saw a woman sitting neglected, he went over and fetched
her to join his circle, and the older and uglier she was, the
more particular he was to do it.

I was wrong in saying that we never had an entertainment
at our at-homes—Corbould's stories were an entertainment,
but people had not to keep silent with them; the more noise
they made, the better he liked it. He was very funny sometimes.

When I asked Corbould what first turned his attention to
Art, he said—

"I was always for the Arts. Charles S. Keene, my
mother's brother, took me in hand, saying 'sketch from
Nature,' so I am altogether self-taught. I never went to
any Art school. Keene's idea was that I should eventually
step into a 'staff appointment on *Punch*.' I began under
Shirley Brooks, then Tom Taylor, and later under F. C.
Burnand. Tom Taylor promised me the first vacancy at
'The *Punch* Table,' but he died, and F. C. Burnand took on
Furniss. I began with *Punch* in the early 'seventies; later
I worked for the *Graphic*, the *Illustrated London News*, the
Daily Graphic (1890), etc. I have always loved 'gee-gees.'"

John Hassall is a universally popular man, and certainly one
of the most capable artists of the day. One cannot be sure
to what heights he will rise. He was not much more than a
boy when he first came to our house, and he was not much
more than a boy when he first got into *Punch*. As he is a

brilliant caricaturist, with a strong political sense, he could be the Conservative F.C.G. whenever he chooses. Probably he would dislike the drudgery of producing constant political cartoons—all work done against time. G. R. H., the famous cartoonist of the *Pall Mall Gazette*, found the work too exacting, and Hassall, the most popular poster designer of the day, has many irons in the fire which require attending to. But he is a born caricaturist of the unexaggerating kind which the future will demand.

Joseph Pennell, the artist, and his charming wife, one of the best travel-writers in America, have been friends of ours for many years. They live in an old house in Buckingham Street, Strand, near the gate, which now does nothing on the Thames Embankment but is, I suppose, the last of the water-gates of the Thames. Pennell confered one of the great pleasures of our lives on us by making us go to Le Puy, at the source of the Loire, which he had been drawing for some periodical. The statues of saints and tiny chapels standing up on needle rocks against the sky, which look so fascinating in his sketches, are not a whit less fantastic in real life, and, until quite lately, you could see from the plain High Mass being celebrated in the cathedral, which was at the western end of the rock. The great west doors were flung open for the purpose, until the mortality among the priests became too great. At Le Puy the old market-women wear their hats over their caps, and frogs are as cheap as dirt—real edible frogs.

I went to a banquet given by the town to its most famous son, M. Dupuy, who was then Prime Minister of France, and was, as it happened, a native, though he did spell the Puy in his name with a small p. We paid three francs a head —less than half-a-crown—for the banquet, including wine, and an introduction to the Premier.

INDEX

of the leading people about whom Personal Reminiscences or
New Facts are related.

RICHARD CLAY & SONS, LIMITED,
BRUNSWICK STREET, STAMFORD STREET, S.E.,
AND BUNGAY, SUFFOLK.

Lightning Source UK Ltd.
Milton Keynes UK
UKOW021810190413

209504UK00004B/96/P